What People Are

Zakariya

I've had a number of tarot readings by Zakariya, in fact he is the only person that I allow to read for me. His ability to interpret the cards is intuitive and skilled and he conveys their message in a way that is accessible, direct & honest, but positive & constructive. Whatever is going on in my life and in those cards, I'm always left with food for thought, actions to consider, and a strong sense of hope. Zakariya's readings are uncannily accurate and also uplifting.

DJ Ritu

I love the whole picture approach that Zakariya had to my astrological reading. Compassionate and insightful, the session with him helped give me perspective and courage.

Zoe Simone

Zakariya has an astounding knowledge, ability and talent for both Eastern and Western Astrologies combined. Over the last ten years, his predictions for the year ahead based on both Chinese and Western astrology have been scarily accurate. I was single when I met Zakariya, and would excitedly ask him each Chinese new year if this year would be the year that I met the man of my dreams. For the first few years he would tell me that this year was not a good year for romance for me. The optimistic part of me would dismiss this as 'just astrology', but he was always right. I was single for 5 years. The year of 2008 was the Year of the Rat (my Chinese sign). He told me that this year I would meet the man that I would marry...and I did! I have now been happily married for 5 years. I still hassle him every year to find out what lies in store for me in the new year, and he gets it right, year after year. He is truly an inspiration.

Debbie Hearn

All of my readings with Zak have been consistently correct over the many years I have consulted with him. Much of the information he has given me has allowed me to consider my options and be more consciously aware before making decisions. Zak genuinely has been blessed with a gift that he can share with you as he has with me.

Neena Baid - Professional Coach and Artist

www.neenabaid.com

Zak has a real skill at combining Chinese and Western astrology and making it personal to your signs and understands both very well. His ability of reading tarot and explaining the situation is very clear and really helped to guide me.

Claire Heffron

I first met Zakariya on the set of a Crimewatch reconstruction where he was casually giving readings to all the actors between takes. I sidled up and waited for my reading. It was brief, accurate and so revealing I was a little freaked out. It was his incredible insight and empathy that drew me to him and has done for the last 15 years or so. He has not only successfully combined Eastern and Western astrology, but uses it to show people who they are, and in the process empower themselves, for the better.

Oliver Gatz

When it comes to the complex understanding of how Western astrology meets Eastern astrology, Zakariya interprets this on a most accurate level. With years of experience and with true passion for the craft Zak delivers astounding observations every time.

Alexia Chellun

www.alexiachellun.com

I won't do a reading with anyone but Zakariya. In every instance of Zak doing a reading for me, I had felt it was the perfect timing for it. I would feel his words and predictions linger in the back of my mind while I would see them come into fruition. What I love the most is how Zak has

such a fantastically insightful and honest way of speaking that I am gracefully given a few steps back to see my life with more perspective and direction.
Sara K.

After any of Zak's tarot readings, I am always left feeling positive, hopeful, curious and excited for things to come. I believe his readings for me have been accurate because he is so naturally in tune astrologically. I always look forward to and enjoy a tarot session with Zak. He is the only reader I trust to give me a constructive reading.
Magdalene Coley

I met Zak at a time when I was feeling like my love life had become kind of pointless. My career was the highlight in my life, and any time I did meet a guy I kind of liked, I'd be hesitant to give him too much of my attention – I just didn't feel that these men were worth the effort.

Zak gave me a 12-month reading in around Feb/March 2013. He selected a card for each month and explained in detail what I could expect from each. He also recorded this so I was able to look back and check my forecast for the beginning of each month.

One month, however, stuck in my mind. It was January the following year, for which he selected the Lovers card. He told me that this would be the month I really solidify a lasting relationship. I was dubious, of course...

However, a few months later, as if from out of nowhere, it's no understatement to say I met the man of my dreams. Only problem was, he was living in a different country. To me, it seemed hopeless. But as things developed, my 'perfect guy' decided that he wanted to be with me full-time. And so, he left his native USA and relocated his life to China, where I was living at the time.

He arrived on my doorstep in Beijing on December 30th, 2013. Needless to say, January really was the month we solidified our relationship!

Several months later we were married and are now expecting our first baby together. Zak was absolutely right.

Nikki Aaron-Gilliand

My wonderful interaction happened with Zakariya this past summer in Vancouver Canada. I was intrigued listening to readings he was doing. I quickly realised this man was something special. Upon reading my cards I was taken in by his energy and thoughtful process in delivering the intriguing lessons. I learned about me and situations in my life, past and present. Later in the evening I got to just sit and chat with this electric man. I have kept in touch and hope to have many many more readings. Cheers Lianne C.

Lianne C

I was introduced to Zak a few years ago through a mutual friend. I was not particularly aware of astrology, Eastern or Western, and only read horoscopes occasionally, rather than seeking them out. I still know very little about astrology but I can say that since we met, Zak has made two completely accurate predictions about events in my life neither he nor I could have forseen. It was surreal but somehow reassuring. The process opened my mind to new possibilities and I thank him for that.

Lucy Barrett

Zak, your readings are intuitive and compassionate. You tell it like it is and you offer warmth and that extra level of precision. I love watching you read the cards. You know them like some people know their own children, reading every expression they offer you. It's always a privilege to have a reading with you.

Jude Claybourne

Zak, Thank you for helping me find clarity through your tarot readings. Your guidance and insight is honest first and foremost, but delivered with wisdom and a kind heart. And your knowledge of Chinese Astrology is almost scary!

Chryso Chellun

I have known Zakariya for over 10 years and during that time he has read tarot for me and shared his in depth knowledge of astrology on numerous occasions.

His exceptional ability to combine Western and Chinese astrology gives him an edge over most as well as incredible insight into people's personalities and patterns of behaviors.

He undeniably has a gift when using his cards to read for people and I have witnessed him calling situations and bringing clarity to people over and over again.

He is a genuinely talented and gifted individual.

Celine Boulhaya

Zak's readings are, intuitive, clear and insightful, delivered with honesty and compassion. It's evident in his readings that he has a deep knowledge and understanding of Tarot and Chinese Astrology.

Yinka Williams

Astrology and leaning about my star sign has always been a hobby. I had the pleasure of Zak reading my cards and tell me more about my star. Zak's been a great advocate and demonstrates strong knowledge in the field. I continue to follow my sign yet on year. Thanks a million Zak!! From the Rabbit-Taurus.

Priya Patel

I have had my cards read and I have gotten a Western/Chinese astrological combination summary. His card reading helped me decide to apply for graduate school...which I just finished. His summary was amazing and eerily accurate. His description allowed me to become more confident since I gained a better understanding of myself. I have had it for more than a year and I still read it when I need a pick-me-up. Plus I found out I am a moon child which is pretty badass. :p

Grace Heiderman

Secrets of the Combined Astrology

The Full 144 Combinations of the Chinese & Western Zodiac Signs

Secrets of the Combined Astrology

The Full 144 Combinations of the Chinese & Western Zodiac Signs

Zakariya Adeel

Winchester, UK
Washington, USA

First published by Dodona Books, 2016
Dodona Books is an imprint of John Hunt Publishing Ltd., Laurel House, Station Approach,
Alresford, Hants, SO24 9JH, UK
office1@jhpbooks.net
www.johnhuntpublishing.com
www.dodona-books.com

For distributor details and how to order please visit the 'Ordering' section on our website.

Text copyright: Zakariya Adeel 2015

ISBN: 978 1 78279 468 4
Library of Congress Control Number: 2015950690

A CIP catalogue record for this book is available from the British Library.

Design: Stuart Davies

Printed and bound by CPI Group (UK) Ltd, Croydon, CR0 4YY, UK

We operate a distinctive and ethical publishing philosophy in all
areas of our business, from our global network of authors to
production and worldwide distribution.

CONTENTS

Acknowledgements   xii

Introduction   1

About the Author and his Process   2

Departing from Traditional Chinese Astrology   5

The Point of this Book   8

The Chinese Legend   10

The Chinese Calendar   14

Mind Map Pie Chart   17

Rat   21
Ox   77
Tiger   133
Rabbit   191
Dragon   249
Snake   311
Horse   375
Sheep   437
Monkey   499
Rooster   561
Dog   621
Boar   685

Bibliography   746

Acknowledgements

As it is, it took me nine years to put this book together, longer if I consider how long it was a figment of my imagination. My first acknowledgement are the angels and spirits that have guided me from inception to completion for I would be lying if I said this content came purely from my own experience. Much of it enlightens me as I read it and I feel myself saying, "Oh yeah, that is so true!" Secondly, this book would not have been possible without the love and support of my family and friends. My siblings were also Chinese Astrologers whether they wanted to be or not, partly because of my constant "astro-babble", but also because they too could see the legitimacy of its wisdom. Even if they deny it now, I am grateful that we shared this interest and I will always remember how we learned this art together. My friends...I apologize for imposing my astrology upon you, it was and is never my intention to let my astrology color my every perspective or conversation, but we all know it does. Anyway, I thank you for tolerating it and encouraging me with this project. There are a few very special people who I want to acknowledge for their specific contributions: Sonia Likhari for being my rock, not just in the writing of this book, in general life too. Asif Rashid, for your not so quiet and not so subtle motivations to get off my bum and get this book written and for your not so quiet laughter too. I also want to thank Penny Montague for all of your support, encouragement and technical work, without you, I would never have completed this project. Malti Patel, Celine Boulhaya and Muna Ahmed for your astrological support and for allowing me to test my theories on your respective astro-knowledge.

Introduction

About the Author and His Process

I was always an inquisitive child with unconventional interests: while other boys were playing football or rugby or cricket, I was reading Theodora Lau's Handbook of Chinese Astrology. By the age of nine, I knew the signs of everyone in my class, to be fair, they were either a Sheep or Monkey, but soon I was able to attribute traits to the different signs in the other year classes too. And when our class 6 teacher lead a project on the Chinese New Year, to her annoyance, the Chinese Astrologer in training corrected her many mistakes.

This was the start of my career in the Divination realm. Armed with my understanding of Chinese Astrology, study of psychology and genuine interest in people, I came to understand human nature as it related to each individual sign. Being born in the West, I already had a basic understanding of the Western Zodiac, but it was when I combined the two that the heavens opened for me.

Adding the 12 Zodiac signs to the 12 Chinese archetypes creates 144 detailed and specific profiles. The first time I saw this done was in Theodora Lau's Handbook of Chinese Horoscopes and then later in greater detail in Suzanne White's book, *The New Astrology*. Being the sort who likes to come to my own conclusions, I had avoided reading Suzanne White's book outside of my own combination and that of close friends and family because I did not want to be influenced towards a certain perception. I have my own process as an Astrologer, one that I have developed over the years that is very different to most conventional Eastern Astrologers (which is discussed in detail, please see the chapter on Departing from Traditional Chinese Astrology). I prefer to apply my methods to come to my own conclusions. That being said, I playfully told a friend she had a dictator's combination because people like Saddam Hussein, Napoleon and Machiavelli shared her chart, even Hitler was born on the cusp of this combination, which of course my friend did not like at all, who would? She disagreed with it entirely. In my humble opinion, she was a tad "controlling" but like most crazed dictators intent on world domination she refused to acknowledge this so looked for other Chinese Astrologers to refute my claims. Suzanne White had named this Ox-Taurus combination, The Deliberate Dictator. My friend was not impressed, but Suzanne White had most definitely impressed me. Yes there are overlaps between all good Astrologers and even all divination methods.

Although there are examples of people of all combinations who have found fame within the entertainment world, you will notice specific patterns emerge: combinations or people with similar elemental constitutions tend to go for similar occupations because they share similar needs and talents. For example, most Ox signs are drawn to positions of power, yet they are also pulled towards standup comedy (especially when attached to a Western Zodiac fire sign); Bill Cosby (1937) inspired Eddie Murphy (1961) who inspired Dave Chappelle (1973) who is undoubtedly inspiring the next generation of Ox stand-ups. See the Ox chapter for more details. Tiger musicians are generally drawn to alternative rock/folk genres, especially when attached to an air sign from the Western Zodiac: Alanis Morrisette, Natalie Imbruglia, Sheryl Crow, Robbie Williams, Phil Collins and so forth (see the Tiger chapter for more details).

Certain signs are drawn to certain careers or certain specialisms within a broader generic sector. When I was doing my degree, I worked for a prominent retail bank in the UK. They had many branches and as a part time employee, I was shipped all over the place, only too happily, in order to cover ad-hoc shifts so that I could make some extra money. Of the six branches in that group four of the line managers were Ox-Libra. The other two were Ox-Taurus and Tiger-Virgo. When I shifted to a different bank, the line manager was an Ox-Aries and his second in charge was another Tiger Virgo. There are Astrological patterns in all areas of the world.

www.adeelsastrology.com

Departing from Traditional Chinese Astrology

I started my journey into the Eastern Astrological World knowing a little bit about the Western system including the role of the four elements. What really intrigued me was that each of the Zodiac signs had an Eastern equivalent; there are 12 Zodiac signs and 12 Chinese signs, therefore were easily interchangeable. However, this was not the case with the elements. The West use four (Earth, Air, Fire, Water) whereas the Chinese use five (Earth, Water, Fire, Metal and Wood).

As I read more and more books on the topic, I realized that certain Astrologers did things differently in order to come to a final reading, some included the Western Zodiac sign and some rejected it altogether, some used the traditional elements fixed to each sign as well as the years element, some only used one and rejected the other. Different Astrologers attributed Yin to a sign when others would attribute it Yang. I tried different combinations but found much of it difficult and confusing, especially when the five Eastern elements were not interchangeable with the four Western elements.

As previously mentioned, a number of Oriental Astrologers link the Western Zodiac signs to an Eastern counterpart sign but the way this is done can differ. My entire method is primarily inspired by Theodora Lau's work so the following is how I choose to translate the signs in my process.

Rat	–	Sagittarius
Ox	–	Capricorn
Tiger	–	Aquarius
Rabbit	–	Pisces
Dragon	–	Aries
Snake	–	Taurus

Horse	–	Gemini
Sheep	–	Cancer
Monkey	–	Leo
Rooster	–	Virgo
Dog	–	Libra
Boar	–	Scorpio

It is important to note that although these signs share many attributes, they are not exactly the same, meaning that there will be attributes coming from the Western sign (specifically because of their date and month of birth) that will not be there if you were trying to read someone's year of birth. For example, the Sheep sign = Cancer sign: most Cancerians either have a secret or an overt desire to lead, whereas Sheep signs do not particularly. That being said, they are equally as emotional, sensitive and creative. However, if someone was born in a Sheep year and was also a Cancerian, it would most likely create a personality with a greater desire to lead because of the chemistry created by the dilution of these signs.

Linking on from the Western signs is the matter of elements. As mentioned before, Eastern elements can be very useful for detailed personal profiles created purely in the traditional method but they get confusing when attached to a sign in an East and West combined reading because of the way elements are interpreted by a Western audience. For example, Fire is read to mean proactive, aggressive, forceful, and Yang, whereas in China, Fire is fixed to the year of the gentle Sheep which is characterized as reactive, passive, peaceful and Yin. The elements are interpreted differently by Eastern and Western audiences. It is for this reason that I apply the element attached to each Eastern signs Western counterpart.

Sagittarius	–	Fire	–	Rat
Capricorn	–	Earth	–	Ox

Aquarius	–	Air	–	Tiger
Pisces	–	Water	–	Rabbit
Aries	–	Fire	–	Dragon
Taurus	–	Earth	–	Snake
Gemini	–	Air	–	Horse
Cancer	–	Water	–	Sheep
Leo	–	Fire	–	Monkey
Virgo	–	Earth	–	Rooster
Libra	–	Air	–	Dog
Scorpio	–	Water	–	Boar

In this way the Sheep sign's fixed element becomes Water read by a Western audience as creative, fluid, emotional and Yin as are all of the Water signs:

Eastern: Rabbit, Sheep, Boar.
Western: Pisces, Cancer, Scorpio.

In my experience these Western elements attached to each Eastern sign greatly aid the understanding of the 12 signs and more significantly, a personal combination. But many traditional Astrologers see this as a huge transgression and would slap my wrists for even considering such sacrilege. Doing this messes with traditional practices that have worked for centuries and they will continue to work in the very same way. But this work is not intended for hard core Chinese Astrologers. It is to highlight just how influential the Chinese sign is to anyone's personality chart (so much so, that I place the Chinese sign before the Western one), to expand the understanding of the combined astrological method of divination to as wide a Western audience as possible and to highlight how the use of the Western elements serves as a short cut to the knowledge because of the Western frame of reference.

The Point of this Book

There have been numerous books on Chinese Astrology most of which agree on the basic characteristics of each sign, as do I, but when they are mixed with a Western sign the chemical reactions are often unexpected. For example, when you mix the soft, sweet, non-confrontational Sheep with the dreamy idealistic Pisces, I doubt many people would expect Rupert Murdoch to be the result. Seen separately, he would not fit the Sheep template, nor would he fit the Piscean, but when seen together, both are water signs, as the old proverb goes, "There is nothing stronger than the force of the ocean" and double water combinations are as creative as they are ruthless. Never be fooled by their innocent looks!

This book hopes to shed light on matters such as this encouraging discovery through application as much as possible in order to develop such a breadth of knowledge that they will soon be able to pick out what people's signs are by their clothes, language, body language, energy or even emotional set place.

Having spent many years studying the 144 combinations, the patterns that I found are astoundingly specific and when illustrating these looking at famous people who share the same combination you may be shocked at the similarities. Many even share physical attributes. Ox-Scorpio women such as Vivien Leigh and Aishwarya Rai often have green cat-like eyes and are known for their seductress-type charm.

When Snake-Leo, JK Rowling was looking to cast a Harry Potter who shared many of her own characteristics, after seeing thousands of young actors, isn't it strange that she agreed upon Daniel Radcliffe who also happens to share her own combination of Snake-Leo.

There may be many of you who may be thinking, that's just a coincidence. But this sort of thing happens again and again and I have many examples which you will find in this book.

Another would be when Snake-Pisces, Kevin Williamson, the writer of the Scream films franchise and Dawson's Creek was looking to cast a Dawson for his semi-autobiographical TV series. He eventually decided upon James Van Der Beek, another Snake-Pisces. Snakes are notoriously known for finding the right person for the right job at the right time, but this type of thing is not restricted to Snake signs alone as you will find out.

When reading about someone who shares your combination, you may be surprised to find out, that that person's friends or family share the exact same combinations of people in your life. This is because combinations have certain in-built patterns of behavior that attract other patterns of behavior in the form of specific combinations.

The point of this book is to inform you of such phenomena as it relates to a specific sign or combination, entertain you with my little insights and help you to incorporate Chinese Astrology with your application of Western Astrology so that your understanding can be even more precise.

The Chinese Legend

The traditional Chinese zodiac has enamored people all over the world for centuries and its origins are widely disputed. Some say Buddha laid on a farewell dinner to celebrate leaving earth and sent an invitation to all animals but only twelve turned up. In gratitude, he assigned a year to each animal in the order they arrived. Another version is that Buddha was calling a meeting to reorganize the state of the Chinese nation, and another still purports that it was in celebration of his birthday.

Perhaps the most common legend is that of the Jade Emperor who invited all the animals of the universe to take part in a race to see who could reach him first.

When the Cat was told about the race he became very excited and asked his neighbor, the Rat to awaken him at dawn so that he could start his journey. The Rat agreed to the request.

Of course, at first light, the Rat was away leaving the sleeping Cat behind. He knew he was the smallest animal taking part but he was also the most determined. Being fast and versatile, the forest, the plains and grasslands were no problem and he was the first to reach the river stream. However, now he was at a loss. He knew he couldn't cross the stream by himself.

At that moment, the Ox arrived. He surveyed the river wondering how he was going to get across this muddy stream with his poor eyesight. The Rat offered to navigate if he would let him ride on his back. The Ox felt that was fair and let the Rat onto his back and they both entered the river. That is when the Cat arrived at the riverbank angry at not being woken up. The Rat apologized saying he was so excited himself that it had slipped his mind. Knowing that the Cat also couldn't swim, he asked the Ox whether his friend could also ride on his back. The unassuming Ox was happy to help. The Cat climbed on board somewhat placated by the Rat's actions.

As the Ox slowly made his way through the muddy waters, a dragon flew over them effortlessly taking the lead. She looked down from her superior vantage point and noticed that a tiny Rabbit who had been hopping from one stone to the next had become trapped; the Rabbit had no more stones left to hop onto. Noticing a passing log, she made a leap for it but now found herself being dragged downstream on the log.

Meanwhile, the Ox was halfway across the stream and listening to the Rat sing him directions to get them across. However, the Cat was getting increasingly annoyed at the noise and asked the Rat to be quiet. As he was busy preening himself, the Rat crept up behind him and pushed him overboard, then returned to direct the Ox. By that point, the Dragon had disappeared but there was a mighty roar that came from behind them. The Rat saw the mighty Tiger enter the river. He told the Ox to swim as fast as he could otherwise they would be overtaken. They were nearly there.

Not far behind the Tiger was the noble Horse who leapt into the water with a huge splash. The Rooster, Ram and Monkey reached the river stream at the same time. They agreed to work together to get across. The ever vigilant Rooster noticed a small raft and ordered that the Ram obtain it and set it on the water, which he did. She then told the Monkey to clear off its weeds, which he did. Then all three jumped on board, tugged and pulled and worked together to get through the stream.

The Rat encouraged the Ox to keep going and both could see that they were nearly there. Suddenly, the Dog, being one of the best swimmers passed by and overtook them. She got near the end first but instead of coming out of the stream, she remained in the water to clean off all of the mud and weeds. Just as the Ox reached the riverbank, the Rat climbed onto the Ox's head and made it to Jade Emperor first. The Ox followed thanking the Rat for all of his help. The Tiger came next bemused at the Dog still washing herself.

A huge gust of warm wind blew the tiny Rabbit's log to the riverbank and she made it into fourth place. Seconds later, the Dragon landed on the bank. As the Horse emerged from the water, the Snake uncurled herself from one of the Horses hooves, which gave him a fright. The Snake slithered over the bank and made it into sixth position, the Horse made seventh. At this point, the little raft made it to the other side. The Ram climbed off first helping the Monkey off next, followed by the Rooster. They approached the Emperor together making eighth, ninth and tenth positions respectively.

Eventually, the Dog approached the Emperor looking flawless. The Cat was still splashing in the water but was picked up by the compassionate Boar as he slowly but steadily swum across. By the time the Boar reached the Emperor, the Cat had passed out. The Boar was awarded twelfth position and as the Cat, coming thirteenth was not assigned a year at all.

The Emperor then asked why the Tiger didn't come first being the strongest, he said he had the furthest to travel. The Dragon was asked why she didn't come first considering she could fly, she said she had to stop to create rain to help the creatures of the earth and returned to help the Rabbit reach the shore. The Emperor blessed the Dragon for her good deeds. Then the Emperor asked why the Dog didn't make first position if she reached the bank first, she replied that she was no state to be in the presence of Royalty and needed to clean up.

The Emperor assigned the first year to the Rat and he was celebrated for his ingenuity. When the Cat regained consciousness, he swore revenge on the Rat and it is believed this is why Cats chase rodents even today.

There are many variations on this story. Some say it was Buddha who did summon them to race. This story, in its various guises, has been told since 2637 B.C. during the reign of Emperor Huang Ti when the Chinese Lunar calendar was introduced. The ancient Chinese used to count the years with 10 celestial stems and 12 terrestrial branches but most people were illiterate at this time so an animal was assigned to each terrestrial branch, which symbolized the ethereal influences of that particular year.

The Chinese Calendar

Find your year of birth to see which Chinese sign you were born under. Be sure to double check especially if you are born under the Western zodiac signs of Capricorn or Aquarius as the Chinese use the lunar calendar which is based on movements of the moon meaning the Chinese New Year always takes place at some point during the time of the sun sign Aquarius. So January Capricorns and all Aquarians have to check to see which Chinese Year they belong to.

Alternatively, visit my website: www.adeelsastrology.com and put your date of birth into my Astrology Calculator and you will be given your combined astrological combination.

Year 1924–1983		Element	Associated Animal	Year 1984–2043
1	Feb 05 **1924**–Jan 23 1925	Fire	Rat	Feb 02 **1984**–Feb 19 1985
2	Jan 24 **1925**–Feb 12 1926	Earth	Ox	Jan 22 **1985**–Feb 08 1986
3	Feb 13 **1926**–Feb 01 1927	Air	Tiger	Feb 01 **1986**–Jan 28 1987
4	Feb 02 **1927**–Jan 22 1928	Water	Rabbit	Jan 29 **1987**–Feb 16 1988
5	Jan 23 **1928**–Feb 09 1929	Fire	Dragon	Feb 17 **1988**–Feb 05 1989
6	Feb 10 **1929**–Jan 29 1930	Earth	Snake	Feb 06 **1989**–Jan 26 1990
7	Jan 30 **1930**–Feb 16 1931	Air	Horse	Jan 27 **1990**–Feb 14 1991
8	Feb 17 **1931**–Feb 05 1932	Water	Sheep	Feb 15 **1991**–Feb 03 1992
9	Feb 06 **1932**–Jan 25 1933	Fire	Monkey	Feb 04 **1992**–Jan 22 1993
10	Jan 26 **1933**–Feb 13 1934	Earth	Rooster	Jan 23 **1993**– Feb 09 1994
11	Feb 14 **1934**–Feb 03 1935	Air	Dog	Feb 10 **1994**–Jan 30 1995
12	Feb 04 **1935**–Jan 23 1936	Water	Boar	Jan 31 **1995**–Feb 18 1996
13	Jan 24 **1936**–Feb 10 1937	Fire	Rat	Feb 19 **1996**–Feb 06 1997
14	Feb 11 **1937**–Jan 30 1938	Earth	Ox	Feb 07 **1997**–Jan 27 1998
15	Jan 31 **1938**–Feb 18 1939	Air	Tiger	Jan 28 **1998**–Feb 15 1999
16	Feb 19 **1939**–Feb 07 1940	Water	Rabbit	Feb 16 **1999**–Feb 04 2000
17	Feb 08 **1940**–Jan 26 1941	Fire	Dragon	Feb 05 **2000**–Jan 23 2001

18	Jan 27 **1941**–Feb 14 1942	Earth	Snake	Jan 24 **2001**–Feb 11 2002
19	Feb 15 **1942**–Feb 04 1943	Air	Horse	Feb 12 **2002**–Jan 31 2003
20	Feb 05 **1943**–Jan 24 1944	Water	Sheep	Feb 01 **2003**–Jan 21 2004
21	Jan 25 **1944**–Feb 12 1945	Fire	Monkey	Jan 22 **2004**–Feb 08 2005
22	Feb 13 **1945**–Feb 01 1946	Earth	Rooster	Feb 09 **2005**–Jan 28 2006
23	Feb 02 **1946**–Jan 21 1947	Air	Dog	Jan 29 **2006**–Feb 17 2007
24	Jan 22 **1947**–Feb 09 1948	Water	Boar	Feb 18 **2007**–Feb 06 2008
25	Feb 10 **1948**–Jan 28 1949	Fire	Rat	Feb 07 **2008**–Jan 25 2009
26	Jan 29 **1949**–Feb 16 1950	Earth	Ox	Jan 26 **2009**–Feb 13 2010
27	Feb 17 **1950**–Feb 05 1951	Air	Tiger	Feb 14 **2010**–Feb 02 2011
28	Feb 06 **1951**–Jan 26 1952	Water	Rabbit	Feb 03 **2011**–Jan 22 2012
29	Jan 27 **1952**–Feb 13 1953	Fire	Dragon	Jan 23 **2012**–Feb 09 2013
30	Feb 14 **1953**–Feb 02 1954	Earth	Snake	Feb 10 **2013**–Jan 30 2014
31	Feb 03 **1954**–Jan 23 1955	Air	Horse	Jan 31 **2014**–Feb 18 2015
32	Jan 24 **1955**–Feb 11 1956	Water	Sheep	Feb 19 **2015**–Feb 07 2016
33	Feb 12 **1956**–Jan 30 1957	Fire	Monkey	Feb 08 **2016**–Jan 27 2017
34	Jan 31 **1957**–Feb 17 1958	Earth	Rooster	Jan 28 **2017**–Feb 18 2018
35	Feb 18 **1958**–Feb 07 1959	Air	Dog	Feb 19 **2018**–Feb 04 2019
36	Feb 08 **1959**–Jan 27 1960	Water	Boar	Feb 05 **2019**–Jan 24 2020
37	Jan 28 **1960**–Feb 14 1961	Fire	Rat	Jan 25 **2020**–Feb. 11 2021
38	Feb 15 **1961**–Feb 04 1962	Earth	Ox	Feb 12 **2021**–Jan 31 2022
39	Feb 05 **1962**–Jan 24 1963	Air	Tiger	Feb 01 **2022**–Jan 21 2023
40	Jan 25 **1963**–Feb 12 1964	Water	Rabbit	Jan 22 **2023**–Feb 09 2024
41	Feb 13 **1964**–Feb 01 1965	Fire	Dragon	Feb 10 **2024**–Jan 28 2025
42	Feb 02 **1965**–Jan 20 1966	Earth	Snake	Jan 29 **2025**–Feb 16 2026
43	Jan 21 **1966**–Feb 08 1967	Air	Horse	Feb 17 **2026**–Feb 05 2027
44	Feb 09 **1967**–Jan 29 1968	Water	Sheep	Feb 06 **2027**–Jan 25 2028
45	Jan 30 **1968**–Feb 16 1969	Fire	Monkey	Jan 26 **2028**–Feb 12 2029
46	Feb 17 **1969**–Feb 05 1970	Earth	Rooster	Feb 13 **2029**–Feb 02 2030
47	Feb 06 **1970**–Jan 26 1971	Air	Dog	Feb 03 **2030**–Jan 22 2031
48	Jan 27 **1971**–Feb 14 1972	Water	Boar	Jan 23 **2031**–Feb 10 2032
49	Feb 15 **1972**–Feb 02 1973	Fire	Rat	Feb 11 **2032**–Jan 30 2033
50	Feb 03 **1973**–Jan 22 1974	Earth	Ox	Jan 31 **2033**–Feb 18 2034
51	Jan 23 **1974**–Feb 10 1975	Air	Tiger	Feb 19 **2034**–Feb 07 2035

52	Feb 11 **1975**–Jan 30 1976	**Water**	**Rabbit**	Feb 08 **2035**–Jan 27 2036
53	Jan 31 **1976**–Feb 17 1977	**Fire**	**Dragon**	Jan 28 **2036**–Feb 14 2037
54	Feb 18 **1977**–Feb 06 1978	**Earth**	**Snake**	Feb 15 **2037**–Feb 03 2038
55	Feb 07 **1978**–Jan 27 1979	**Air**	**Horse**	Feb 04 **2038**–Jan 23 2039
56	Jan 28 **1979**–Feb 15 1980	**Water**	**Sheep**	Jan 24 **2039**–Feb 11 2040
57	Feb 16 **1980**–Feb 04 1981	**Fire**	**Monkey**	Feb 12 **2040**–Jan 31 2041
58	Feb 05 **1981**–Jan 24 1982	**Earth**	**Rooster**	Feb 01 **2041**–Jan 21 2042
59	Jan 25 **1982**–Feb 12 1983	**Air**	**Dog**	Jan 22 **2042**–Feb 09 2043
60	Feb 13 **1983**–Feb 01 1984	**Water**	**Boar**	Feb 10 **2043**–Jan 29 2044

Mind Map Pie Chart

In order to get a complete picture of your astrological make-up, you need to complete the Mind Map Pie Chart.

Mind Map Pie Chart

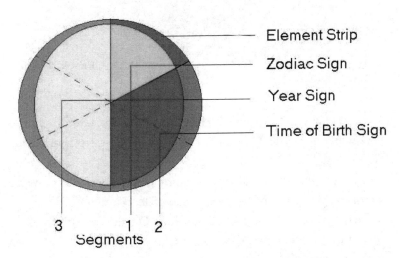

This chart consists of six segments attached to each is a correlating element section. Your year of birth sits in the largest part taking up three segments.

Your time of birth sits in the second largest part taking up two segments.

Your zodiac sign sits in the smallest part taking up one segment.

Once you have all of the signs in place, you add the fixed element from each sign to the element strip.

For an example, see below.

Mind Map Pie Chart

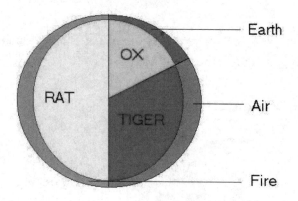

Once all of the details have been complete, it is easy to read the personality as a whole. This person is likely to be entrepreneurial like the Rat and dislike working for other people, however being born in the time of the Tiger and being a Capricorn/Ox sign this person may have a desire to manage or lead a team of his own. Because this person has more Tiger than Ox, they are more likely to be open to other people's opinions and not so ready to act on their own convictions alone. This is likely to be someone who looks at all of the facts, listens to what the majority believe then hands all of the available information to their subconscious and then acts only when the subconscious spurts out an unexpected yet effective solution. They might also be quite charitable. They lead by example and motivate others to work for them using genuine affection and genuine appreciation for their efforts. They do make good team leaders. There is enough Ox to do the hard graft but not too much Ox to become dictatorial, enough Tiger to be open but not too much to make everything personal, but primarily they are Rat enough to keep their ear to the ground for any shifts in people's feelings that may need catering for.

You can see from this chart that this personality combination is made up of the Fire, Earth and Air elements. Therefore this person lacks the water element. This lack is likely to be subconsciously felt by this person and the chances are this person will gravitate towards people who have water in their combination. It's important to note that people containing the water element may not play as significant a role in this person's life if that current year is actually a water year because the lack will be made up by the environment.

The Chinese tend to add any element missing from their child's astrological make-up to their name so that the lack is less felt. Needless to say, this doesn't happen in the Western world. Although it can be astounding to note how many people end up with partners who make up an elemental lack in their own chart, commonly their polar opposite sign, which is traditionally considered to be an inauspicious pairing. There are many ways to determine compatibilities that many astrologers disagree on. The two main methods I employ can be found in the compatibilities section after the main body text of each individual astrological combination.

It's also important to mention that most other astrologers that use both systems place the Western sign before the Chinese one, but I do not. I feel that the Chinese year has the largest impact on the personality as a whole and this is illustrated in the Mind Map Pie Chart that I use, therefore it is only right that the Chinese sign be placed first and the Western one follows, e.g. Rat-Aries. Also, I have found that there is a grading to the personalities as they move along, one to the next. So the Rat-Aries is similar to the Rat-Taurus, then the Rat-Taurus is similar to the next combination, the Rat-Gemini and so it goes on. For example, inventor Thomas Edison was born under the sign of Sheep-Aquarius, which shares traits with the next combination, Sheep-Pisces where Apple genius Steve Jobs is to be found.

THE RAT

THE RAT

I am the instigator, the fire starter, the beginning. I am magic manifested to create an entirely new world, a new order, a new way. Tiny is my body, Vast is my spirit! Feel the power of my energy, see it sparkle in my eyes. Through me you will see colors you have never seen before, experience delights you have never experienced before, I am the one who knows the way to Eden, follow me, I'll take you there. Gracious am I if you value my time, my voice and my contribution; be blind to my gifts and be blind to your own ignorance. I direct you to your own guidance, open you to your own intuition, lead you from the barren lands to the oasis because I know my world intimately: its structure, material and its effective usage. I should know, I was here before all else. I am the oldest sibling. I am the first born of the Chinese Zodiac.

I am the Rat.

Distinctive, with outstanding physical features, you also have strong, sometimes aggressive personalities. You are born entrepreneurs and many Rats like to head their own businesses. From a young age, you know what you want and follow through with your plans. Decisive, active and strong, you like to take the lead and end up in a position of power. Knowing how to apply your charm and sex appeal to propel you up the ladder, you're an expert at making and handling money. Although the Rat is the tiniest of all signs, you can be one of the most aggressive when aroused or when your meticulous plans are being affected.

Career-wise, Rats are primarily drawn to setting up their own entrepreneurial enterprise. This is the sign of the Entrepreneur! Whether they create their own business or set themselves up in their chosen profession as a sole trader, they prefer to work for themselves or as consultants where their expertise is purchased in. Generally speaking, they are not great at taking orders, unless they have chosen the boss themselves in which case they are the first to encourage teamwork. Suitable careers can be established in, finance, medicine, law, science, politics and the arts.

Compatibilities

Best Friends: Dragon & Monkey
Soul Mate: Ox
Good Relations: Snake & Boar
Challenger: Horse

RAT – ARIES

Chinese Name: SHU
Rank: 1st
Hours Ruled: 11pm – 1am
Direction: Directly North
Season: Winter
Month: December
Western Zodiac Equivalent of Rat: Sagittarius
Sagittarius Western Element: Fire
Eastern Zodiac Equivalent of Aries: Dragon
Aries Western Element: Fire
Numerology: 1

The things that come to those who wait may be the things left by those who got there first.
– Steven Tyler

This combination takes the first signs from both the Eastern and Western horoscopes creating the big bang explosion from which everything else proceeds. This combination is the first and it's fitting that Rat fire meets Aries fire. This personality is full of forward motion, someone who is proactive and likes to see tangible results of their labor.

Mandy Moore has said, "I'm a spiritual person and a religious person," while Jill Scott has exclaimed that she is more "spiritual than religious." This conscious desire for spiritual connection makes them highly tuned in to their intuition that guides them towards areas where they are most suited. This is why so many become self-employed in areas that fully fulfil their specific needs. Generally speaking, the Rat is the sign of the Entrepreneur and many examples belong to this combination.

Eli Roth is a good example of a Rat-Aries who, despite initial setbacks such as being fired from film sets, persisted in his preferred work environment and developed a reputation as the filmmaker who has never lost any money on a film. This is quite typical. Rat-Aries' do what they love, complete their work in great detail and do so with traditional values and classical flair. John Madden has said he has just done what he loved most and has managed to secure exceptional financial rewards despite never having "worked a day in my life."

Surprisingly, they are not as money motivated as they initially seem. Jeremy Clarkson has said, "I just don't pay any attention to money, it's rather vulgar." Instead, they do what they love and the money comes. Andrew Lloyd Webber is further proof of this.

Jennifer Garner trained in ballet and performance as a child before deciding upon a career in science (a favorite career sector for Rat signs) but traded it all for her love of performing knowing that it was what would satisfy her most. She has said, "Happiness is your own responsibility."

They have a desire to find honesty in everything they do and in doing so, they are beautiful regardless of what they actually look like. That being said, some of the most beautiful and enchanting personalities of the stage and screen are born under this firecracker combination.

The women of this combination tend to seem vulnerable yet maintain a feminine, not feminist, air of authority, which makes them infinitely intriguing. Dianne Wiest, Jennifer Grey, Kelly Le Brock, America Ferrera, Carmen Electra and Jennifer Taylor are a few examples. Intelligent, funny, but first and foremost, feminine; Carmen Electra has said, "I'm more attracted to a stronger man...someone who would just throw me down take control. I love feeling helpless."

In the Tao Te Ching, it is advised that you "know the masculine, but be like the feminine" in order to maintain a healthy yin-yang balance which is a prerequisite for all round life success. The men of this combination seem to have an innate understanding of this concept despite being a fire (yang) meets fire (yang) combination. Al Gore has said, "I work very hard to get in touch with my feminine side." Even though he may have spoken in jest, there was probably truth to it. The Rat-Aries men tend to seem soft on the surface but rough on the inside, however, this is only revealed once you really get to know them in depth. Peter O'Brien, Linford Christie, Chris Barrie, Hugo Weaving and John Snider are a few examples.

A number of the most influential actors of all time are of this combination. Marlon Brando is said to have overshadowed any actor that came before him apart from Spencer Tracy and Laurence Olivier. It is interesting to note that Spencer Tracy was not only born two days after Brando in the general calendar, but he too was born in the year of the Rat, which means he also was born with this combination. (For more information on Laurence Olivier please see Sheep-Gemini.) The adorable Doris Day who charmed everybody with her beauty, bubbly personality and undeniable natural talent was actually born on the same day as Brando (3rd April 1924).

The Rat-Aries believes in its ability to rule and rule best for the benefit of everyone else. Secretly, they think relatively highly of themselves but their spiritual connection keeps them grounded. Carmen Electra has said, "People are surprised at how down to earth I am. I like to stay home on Friday nights and listen to 'The Art of Happiness' by the Dalai Lama.

Even in the Indian Cinema we find the likes of Jaya Bhachan and Mamta Kulkarni both belonging to this combination. In the conservative Indian film industry, Mamta Kulkarni's outspoken nature had her outcast for being true to who she was. Jaya Bhachan at one point in her career had attempted to play outside of her middle class good girl stereotype but audiences vehemently disliked it, so sensibly, she returned to what she did best playing vulnerable, yet in-control women.

Being the very first combination, there is something exceptionally childlike juxtaposed with something mature beyond their years about them; on the one hand, they are full of desires, dreams and they are completely prepared to chase them down; on the other hand, they speak like they have already completed everything and have learned the lessons beforehand. This is likely down to that spiritual connection again which they consciously or unconsciously cultivate. They are both, the newborn baby and the wise old sage simultaneously.

With such ambition, proactive drive and so much charm that they achieve their goals effortlessly because of their ability to elicit other people's support. In a word, these people are usually described as "adorable" because they never seem to lose their enthusiasm for life.

Soul Mate:	Ox-Virgo
Challenger:	Horse-Libra
Siblings:	Rat-Leo, Rat-Sagittarius
Best Friends:	Dragon-Aries, Dragon-Leo, Dragon-Sagittarius, Monkey-Aries, Monkey-Leo, Monkey-Sagittarius

Abigail Breslin
Leslie Mann
Ron Perlman
Hugo Weaving
Mandy Moore
Jennifer Garner
Marlon Brando
Kelli Garner
Jennifer Grey
Nick Frost
Katharine McPhee
Eli Roth
America Ferrera
Bonnie Bedelia

Carmen Electra
Jennie Garth
Brad Garrett
Dianne Wiest
Jennifer Taylor
Kelly LeBrock
Doris Day
Leigh Allyn Baker
Claire Foy
Sung Kang
John Schneider
Rhea Perlman
Steven Tyler
Spencer Tracy
Jeremy Clarkson
Lisa Ray
Leslie Phillips
Jill Scott
Andrew Lloyd Webber
Chris Barrie

RAT – TAURUS

Chinese Name: SHU
Rank: 1st
Hours Ruled: 11pm – 1am
Direction: Directly North
Season: Winter
Month: December
Western Zodiac Equivalent of Rat: Sagittarius
Sagittarius Western Element: Fire
Eastern Zodiac Equivalent of Taurus: Snake
Taurus Western Element: Earth
Numerology: 2

I'm about empowering people and making their dreams come true.
– Simon Fuller.

When the nobility of the Rat couples with Taurus's strength, it creates a personality that is willing to serve the needs of others as if it were serving itself. This altruism is genuine and they get a real sense of satisfaction from helping people out, sometimes, completely anonymously. Capable of amazing feats, they use their personal clout to break down barriers and support others to live their highest ideals.

Irish singer and activist Bono is the perfect example of the Rat-Taurus; artistically gifted with mass appeal who has a deep understanding of the human condition. Without this, he couldn't possibly be so evocative lyrically, nor could he be so persuasive in his philanthropic endeavors. "Ask big questions, demand big answers." The key to his effectiveness and the power of the Rat-Taurus in general is their ability to communicate. "I'm fully aware of the futility of rock 'n' roll music but I'm also aware of its power. Similarly, Mark Zuckerberg has said about Facebook,

"For me and my colleagues, the most important thing is that we create an open information flow for people."

The Rat-Taurus understands itself and how to add value, that is why they are able to charge so highly for their services. But customers will return time and time again. Simon Fuller has said, "My business is creating fame and celebrity and I'm one of the best in the world; I know it to the finest detail." Being so detail oriented, they thirst for more information that could help them move forwards. Benefitting from the forward thrust of Rat-Aries combination that preceded it, they also approach challenges proactively but with more balance and in a much more under-stated way.

Concerned primarily with their own opinion of themselves and how they can serve, they are sometimes attacked for their success. "People in the UK think I'm too commercial, too this or too that, but who cares? Why waste energy in such a negative way," Simon Fuller has said. Likewise, Mark Zuckerberg seems to be attacked for whatever he does with his Facebook brand.

With such commercial talent, it may be difficult for this combination to switch the business mind off to relax and just be still. Meditation and yoga would offer many benefits and help them return to a freer place. Essentially, they have a knowing of who they are and how they can personally make a difference to the whole. Craig Scheffer said, "Follow your own path, you can't compare an apple to an orange, it will cause a lot of esteem issues." So they follow their own guidance and let the road take them where it will.

Dwayne "The Rock" Johnson is another member of this club who rose to success due to his ability to engage an audience, in addition to being a great wrestler. Once again, communication was the weapon of choice. As previously mentioned, they place a high price tag on their skills so the universe reflects this. He currently (2011) holds the record for the highest salary ($5.5 million) for an actor in his first leading role for The Scorpion

King. He also started the 'Dwayne Johnson Rock Foundation' charity for at-risk and terminally ill children.

The best example of placing a high price for their services is probably Master Zuckerberg. At 27 years of age, his personal fortune amassed $17.5 billion. Among his other philanthropic projects, he has also signed a pledge to donate at least half of his wealth to charity over a period of years.

The men are generally well read, intellectual and with an understated, almost scruffy style that neatens as they age. The females tend to be dainty in frame, vulnerable-looking yet elegant. But when they reveal their intelligence, strong will, ambition and penchant for details, many a male ego has been threatened. And Lady Rat-Taurus remains ignorant of her own power of presence. The situation is exacerbated by the fact, nobody saw her coming; she is not what she seems. This can cause some issues, often in work place environments. It makes sense to allow these women to lead, even if they claim they don't want to. Rat women have a tendency to please people being more sensitive to criticism. It is not unusual for them to make themselves smaller than what they are or live up to people's lesser expectations. It would be a tragedy to let a Rat-Taurus's woman repress her abilities and she must assume responsibility to take charge.

Roy Orbison said, "I must be one of the un-loneliest people in the world." Maybe he said this because loneliness is something they struggle with. Despite being attractive and popular (usually later in life) they find it hard to leave their early rejections behind. However, with their irrepressible desire to serve and will to succeed, all else becomes irrelevant and for any typical Rat-Taurus at any given moment, as Yazz said, "The only way is up!"

Soul Mate: Ox-Leo
Challenger: Horse-Scorpio
Siblings: Rat-Capricorn, Rat-Virgo

Best Friends: Dragon-Capricorn, Dragon-Taurus, Dragon-
                  Virgo, Monkey-Capricorn, Monkey-Taurus,
                  Monkey-Virgo

Charles Aznavour
Bono
Charlotte Bronte
Albert Finney
Tony Hancock
Glenn Campbell
Dennis Hopper
Roy Hudd
Englebert Humperdnick
Roy Orbison
Busta Rhymes
William Shakespeare
Simon Fuller
Mark Zuckerberg
Craig Scheffer
Dwayne "The Rock" Johnson
Yazz

RAT – GEMINI

Chinese Name: SHU
Rank: 1st
Hours Ruled: 11pm – 1am
Direction: Directly North
Season: Winter
Month: December
Western Zodiac Equivalent of Rat: Sagittarius
Sagittarius Western Element: Fire
Eastern Zodiac Equivalent of Gemini: Horse
Gemini Western Element: Air
Numerology: 3

Stay far from timid, only make moves when your heart is in it and live the phrase, 'Sky's the limit.'
– Notorious BIG.

When this lightning hot Rat combines with airy Gemini, it creates an active person who is full of ideas with the motivation to make them happen. They might not make happen themselves directly, but they are quick to pick up on others' talents and know how to utilize them. They believe in living from the heart, the problem there is that these subjects, especially the men, find it difficult to differentiate between the heart and the *id* so they often end up serving their own egos and that can lead them into all sorts of complications. Mick Hucknall has said, "I am one of the best singer songwriters this country has ever produced. Ever. If people don't like me saying that, tough shit. You can't sell 50 million albums without something."

When the Screen Actors Guild were on strike in 1980, Powers Booth won an Emmy for his portrayal of Jim Jones in *Guyana Tragedy: The Story of Jim Jones*; Booth was the only actor to cross picket lines to attend the ceremony and pick up his award. In his speech, he said, "This is either the most courageous moment of my career or the stupidest... I also thought long and hard whether or not I would attend but I came here because this is America and one must do what one believes. I believe in the Academy. I also believe in my fellow Actors in their stand." This tendency to serve their own ego leads them into conflicts and karma draws difficult experiences into their lives asking them to learn from their mistakes. They usually do and start down the road of humility.

The women are similar but are much less egotistical in their behavior. Stevie Nicks said, "As a member of Fleetwood Mac, for two weeks I was still working at the restaurant because I'd given them notice. I didn't just want to walk in there and say, 'I'm going to be a famous rock star so I quit and I never liked your food anyway.'"

Intelligent, articulate and quick learners, they usually end up in positions where a broad skill set is required, as well the ability to think outside of the box. Known for his naturalistic style and socialist views, film director Ken Loach turned down the OBE "because it's not a club you want to join when you look at the villains who've got it. It's all the things I think are despicable: patronage, deferring to the monarchy and the name of the British Empire which is a monument of exploitation and conquest."

Outspoken and brave, they often say what others are thinking but not dare utter. That being said, social acceptance is important to Rat-Geminis, but their convictions are more so. Despite appearances, they are not as strong as they project. They have just developed a thick shell over the years. This is important as they often receive a lot of criticism for being 'too honest' yet conversely, also for hypocrisy.

Both the Men and the women of this combination have the typical prettiness that many Rat signs are blessed with, but even if they are not traditionally attractive, their sex appeal is undeniable. Despite the ups and downs of their self-esteem, they tend to have strong convictions, even if they haven't figured out entirely who they are as people. Gemini lends its chameleon skin to an already slippery Rat sign making them difficult to define. They are also quite private about their life so it could just be that they are choosing to remain on a surface level to the general public opening themselves only to a select few.

Not particularly consistent creatures, they have a tendency to change their minds, sometimes an entire belief around a subject, seemingly on a whim. This inconstancy comes as a result of a lack of personal exploration. They are powerful thinkers, but they thrive in an entirely new way when they take the time to understand their own psychological functioning.

A major lesson for these types is perseverance. Perceived failure hits them hard and can lead to periods of withdrawal. However, life pushes them onwards and upwards and this lesson of continuing despite the pressure, powerfully impacts upon their productivity. Phylicia Rashad said, "The stubbornness I had as a child has been transmitted into perseverance. I can let go but I don't give up. I don't beat myself up about negative things." Wentworth Miller said, "I've had 12 (acting) jobs but I've been to over 450 auditions so I've heard 'no' a lot more than I've heard 'yes.'"

When Rat-Geminis understand the consequences of moving forwards, they can often become very results oriented and over commit themselves. Thomas Hayden Church said, "I am always wondering, 'am I doing as much as I can do?' But then my wife reminds me I run four cattle ranches, a commercial beef operation and I have an acting career." With the Rat's ambition, this person has a lot to achieve, when a lesson is learned and changes are required, the Rat-Gemini sees no point in wasting time and gets straight down to business. Their abundance of energy, motivation and talent ensures that the Rat-Gemini inevitably becomes an active participant in the game of life.

Soul Mate:	Ox-Cancer
Challenger:	Horse-Sagittarius
Siblings:	Rat-Aquarius, Rat-Libra
Best Friends:	Dragon-Aquarius, Dragon-Gemini, Dragon-Libra, Monkey-Aquarius, Monkey-Gemini, Monkey-Libra

Notorious BIG
Mick Huckall
Tony Hadley
Paul Dano
Powers Booth
Stevie Nicks
Ken Loach
Phylicia Rashad
Thomas Hayden Church
Enoch Powell
Leo Sayer
Arthur Askey
Anthea Turner
George Bush Snr

RAT – CANCER

Chinese Name: SHU
Rank: 1st
Hours Ruled: 11pm – 1am
Direction: Directly North
Season: Winter
Month: December
Western Zodiac Equivalent of Rat: Sagittarius
Sagittarius Western Element: Fire
Eastern Zodiac Equivalent of Cancer: Sheep
Cancer Western Element: Water
Numerology: 4

As soon as you learn to never give up, you have to learn the power and wisdom of unconditional surrender, and that one doesn't cancel out the other; they just exist as contradictions. The wisdom of it comes as you get older.
– Kris Kristopherson

When the Fiery depths of the Rat merge with the silent lake water of Cancer, the result is a sleek, subtle and soft surface with an emotionally turbulent creature inside that is seeking clarity at all times. Cancer's sensitivity opens the door to all sorts of influences that is both an asset and a detriment. In the early years of their development, their naïve trust in the good of mankind may have taken them in directions where lessons had to be learned the hard way.

Often these hardships lead to a heightened defensive stance that it takes many years to release. In time they realize that they must and eventually, little by little, they learn to open up again, but this time with fight in their eyes in case anyone dare try to mislead them again. The real reason for this? The naïveté that nature intended still lives at the Rat-Cancer inn and they know it. It's actually one of their most attractive traits and why so many make allowances for their awkward and sometimes difficult ways. Kathy Bates has said, "I am a very private person... Not shy exactly, but it takes me a very long time to make friends. I still have such a hard time navigating the waters out here."

A noted tendency with this combination is their taking on, living with and managing guilt. This combination takes some sort of sadistic pleasure out of reliving the past, wishing that things had been different and feeling remorse for what could have been. Jane Lynch has said, "I also learned how I made things much harder on myself than they needed to be. I have my own deep, dark places, but the message coming out of it is that it's all a choice on whether you suffer through your life." In time they learn that guilt is absolutely futile, that it is a wasted emotion and that their wonderful energy could be better spent. In fact, they often go to the other extreme, learn how to manage their emotions, channel them in a successful way and whether literally or through mentoring, become teachers of effective living. Like its sibling combinations, Rat-Pisces and Rat-Scorpio, this Rat with Western Water sign is also an inspirational leader whose example motivates others to be bigger, bolder and *badass*!

Success for this combination is not a question of if; it's a question of when. Sidney Lumet has said, "I think I'm a talented man. But then there's luck. I think there's a reason luck doesn't always happen to others. They don't know how to prepare the groundwork for luck. I do." Rat signs and preparation go hand in hand anyway, but Cancer's Water takes hurt personally and seeks to avoid it at all costs so preparation is a kind of plan of attack. Yet another reason for their overly meticulousness is they also have a strong sense of duty and would never want to let anyone down.

This combination tends to find greater success, whatever that means to them, later on in life. They need time to live and even more time to contemplate the meaning of what they have lived.

Their receptive senses feed them so much information, there is much to consider. But that is why when they do make their plans and take action, it is ever so well conceived and their arrow hits the red target precisely in the center.

The men of this combination sometimes struggle with their own masculinity, allowing others expectations of them to oblige them in directions they would not choose for themselves leading them to repress their desires. But repressing desires only makes them stronger and the spring uncoils ferociously often leading them to seek the highs they feel they missed out on. Kris Kristopherson has said, "I was a slow starter. I wasn't even laid in high school. Looking back on it, I didn't know anything, which was kind of unfortunate for my first couple of wives. When I found out that girls like sex as much as guys, I was, for many years, feeling like that was my function. I mean, I wasn't as bad as Clinton, but I was led by the pecker." It is common for these men to play catch up in many areas of their lives in which they feel they are lagging behind.

Women of this combination are not particularly concerned with superficialities like many of their peers. They are the way they are and a bit more make-up is not going to change that so what's the point? The truth is, they are more attractive, more intelligent and more worthy than they allow themselves to acknowledge. Selma Blair has said, "I've always felt like a tomboy but especially beside Christina and Cameron. God bless anyone who looks at the three of us in one frame and still finds me sexy." Similarly, discussing how she struggled with looks, Kathy Bates has said, "I was never an ingénue. I've always just been a character actor. When I was younger, it was a real problem, because I was never pretty enough. It was hard, not just for the lack of work, but because you have to face up to how people are looking at you."

This combination just needs time to see through the mist to the truth, which is waiting for them, like a beaming rainbow just beyond it. And when they reach it, much enlightenment lightens their load. As previously mentioned, this combination finds success slightly later than most. Jane Lynch has said, "I'm very excited! It's a great and wonderful thing at the tender age of 49 to have finally found somebody that I want to be with. I'm so lucky."

Soul Mate:	Ox-Gemini
Challenger:	Horse-Capricorn
Siblings:	Rat-Pisces, Rat-Scorpio
Best Friends:	Dragon-Pisces, Dragon-Cancer, Dragon-Scorpio, Monkey-Pisces, Monkey-Cancer, Monkey-Scorpio

Selma Blair

Jane Lynch

Kathy Bates

Erin Brockovich-Ellis

Cat Stevens / Yusaf Islam

Richard Wilson

Katrina Kaif

Fantasia Barrino

Duffy

Sofía Vergara

Claire Forlani

Louis van Amstel

Sangeeta Bijlani

Wayne Sleep

Kris Kristofferson

Khloé Kardashian

Rachael Taylor

RAT – LEO

Chinese Name: SHU
Rank: 1st
Hours Ruled: 11pm – 1am
Direction: Directly North
Season: Winter
Month: December
Western Zodiac Equivalent of Rat: Sagittarius
Sagittarius Western Element: Fire
Eastern Zodiac Equivalent of Leo: Monkey
Leo Western Element: Fire
Numerology: 5

Real artists have the responsibility to break rules.
– Antonio Banderas

When the sparkly fire of the Rat meets the Leo's raging inferno, there is usually an explosion so loud it can be heard in space. Welcome the Rat-Leo. The abundance of fire creates personalities that are seen and heard. And if they are not, they make sure that they are.

Intelligent, calculating and smart, they know how to project themselves in order to be commercially appealing. Once they have decided what they want to do, they will research the market in detail, check out the competition, figure out what has worked in the past and, most importantly, *why* it has worked. Then they will go to work on creating a package that will sell just as well, if not better than the first. Even if that package happens to be themselves, many figure out whom they have to become in order to get a particular job or a partner and relentlessly work at it until they have achieved their goal.

Success oriented, they value themselves according to their achievements until their thirst for achievement, attention and external affirmation is quenched. That is when they begin to really enjoy their lives. Sarah Brightman has said, "It really is strange the way I work for success but when I get there cannot appreciate it. I enjoy the road to success and the struggle – even when it becomes hard. But when I achieve my goal, I feel suddenly and totally stressed. Only in retrospect can I begin to enjoy the moment and admit just how great it was." Many get stuck in the phase of making money, creating business after business, deal after deal because it is what they do best. Their entrepreneurial skills are unbeatable and they can get addicted to the pursuit of making money.

Once they notice their friends growing and changing, along with this, their values and priorities, then Rat-Leos begin to question their own value system. These withdrawals can be a lonely time for them and for their families, but Rat-Leos believe the solitude is required so that they can make personal decisions without external interference. They then return, reconnected to their source energy ready to undertake their next mission, one that will fulfil their true desires.

Rat-Leos have unconventional habits and eccentricities but nobody denies how effective they are. With an indomitable spirit, they put all of their energy into everything they do with the desire to be recognized for it. The men especially struggle to reconcile the world's perception of them with the way they know themselves to be. Robert Redford has said, "All my life I've been dogged by guilt because I feel there is this difference between the way I look and the way I feel inside."

Fairness, living authentically and truth is very important to them. This is why there are so many prominent actors, writers and filmmakers of this combination. Sean Penn has said, "I've always operated under the notion that audiences don't always know when they're being lied to, but that they always know when they're being told the truth... The best way to be honest is to try to emancipate ourselves from the effects of fashion, to try to find what will stay with us forever." Maybe these personal convictions are why his work resonates so powerfully. Isn't it interesting that Sean Penn and Robert Redford have both been seen as the best actors of their generation?

The Leo is a highly sociable beast whereas the Rat likes to stick to a small group of people usually some sort of field-specific elite and if they cannot have this, or it feels insincere, they prefer to go off as the lone warrior. This is why so many Rats start up their own enterprises. So when the Rat meets the Leo there is conflict in the merging of these two brands of fire. What happens is their desire to serve overpowers all else and they try to do so by creating events or situations where people can be social but there is some sort of aspect that will distance them from actually having to take part. The vicarious pleasure of watching others socialize, learn and grow is almost as good as the actual thing. The surprise for most is that they seem like such naturally sociable people.

The men of this combination tend to be tall, very pretty and almost as sensitive as their female counterparts. This previously mentioned internal conflict rears its head again even in the type of work these highly skilled men choose to do. There is usually a political component, especially so for the artists. Robert Redford has said, "Political activism has been a part of my life and part of the films I try to make. But we don't take any ideological stance."

The women of this combination often have lively, frisky, vivacious personalities that can lift the mood of even the most cynical person. They are often mid-height, busty with twinkling eyes. Intelligent, brave and driven, these are the sort of women who start a business without telling anyone whilst continuing to have an active social life, maintain a full-time job and within a year surprise everyone with their startling success. Where do they find the time one wonders. They are also highly sensitive and feeling-led. Geri Halliwell said, "I want everything I do to be special and fun. Everything I have done I have always done passionately, with all my heart and soul." Coming from such a visceral place gives them a perception many lack which leads to interesting insights. Maya Rudolph said, "I've met people who are baffled by children, as though they were never children themselves. I think that people who don't like kids are awful people."

This combination excels at many things, is well read and most significantly is blessed with much vision. It is the internal struggle with their own self-worth to make manifest their daydreams that takes up the majority of their time. They always get a handle on this and it gets easier as time goes on. The higher they can elevate their consciousness, the more goodies they get. And they definitely like their goodies! Antonio Banderas has said, "I don't want anything I don't deserve, [but] if they offer me more money, I'm not stupid."

Soul Mate:	Ox-Taurus
Challenger:	Horse-Aquarius
Siblings:	Rat-Aries, Rat-Sagittarius
Best Friends:	Dragon-Aries, Dragon-Leo, Dragon-Sagittarius, Monkey-Aries, Monkey-Leo, Monkey-Sagittarius

Antonio Banderas
Sarah Brightman
Jean Reno
Robert Redford
Vyjayanthimala
Geri Halliwell
Sean Penn
Ben Affleck

Maya Rudolph
Marlon Wayans
David Duchovny
Yves St Lauren
Elizabeth Berkley
Wil Wheaton
Simon Bird
Quinton Aaron
Jay Manuel
Timothy Hutton
Gene Kelly

RAT – VIRGO

Chinese Name: SHU
Rank: 1st
Hours Ruled: 11pm – 1am
Direction: Directly North
Season: Winter
Month: December
Western Zodiac Equivalent of Rat: Sagittarius
Sagittarius Western Element: Fire
Eastern Zodiac Equivalent of Virgo: Rooster
Virgo Western Element: Earth
Numerology: 6

Imagination is the highest kite that can fly.
– Lauren Bacall

When the Rat's aggressive fire merges with Virgo's fertile earth, it creates a personality that is as sensitive as it is forceful, as tranquil as it is uneasy, as clued up while feeling utterly clueless... but you'd never know it. Setting their own strange boundaries as they choose, it is difficult to entirely grasp the reasons why they take certain actions. The contradiction is that they are the most logical, practical, reasonable people of all, yet their heightened emotions blind them to everything and encourage them to take socially risqué routes to fulfil latent desires that could otherwise have been given a healthier expression.

They would rather live now and worry about the consequences later. Cameron Diaz has said, "Your regrets aren't what you did, but what you didn't do. So I take every opportunity." As do many Rat-Virgos and they often end up apologizing afterwards. After dressing as a Nazi as a joke for a fancy dress party, Prince Harry Windsor said, "Looking back on it now and at the time as well, it was a very stupid thing to do and I've learnt my lesson, simple as that really,"

Despite the attempt to present themselves as conservative and proper, the twinkle in their eyes suggests a barrelful of naughty intentions. They effortlessly exude sex appeal. And it's all natural; they don't even have to try. Colin Firth has said, "Forget 'trying' to be sexy. That's just gruesome." They just have it. With that suggestion of roughness or rebelliousness that adds to their magnetism, the men of this combination appeal that much more. Make no mistake they are very sought after. It is not surprising that many performers born under this combination are from the UK with a somewhat regal quality, stars such as Jeremy Irons, Idris Elba, and both *Bridget Jones's* lover's Colin Firth and Hugh Grant are Rat–Virgos. From American cinema, Gene Kelly, Kevin Zegers, Damon Wayans, Chris Tucker, John Ritter and Scott Baio all are members of this elite club.

Talking about his notions of love, Hugh Grant has said, "I just don't believe in love at first sight any more, even though I've based my whole career on the concept. In my experience, power, money and influence always attract the opposite sex. It's something that I've always exploited – with good results." Joking or otherwise, there is truth to this statement when discussing this combination in particular because they usually strive for and get money power and influence in that order. With that trilogy in your pocket, along with looks and good humor, is it any wonder they are eternally popular. Talking about his older fan base, Colin Firth said, "I find I'm increasingly lusted after by people beyond pensionable age. I was told of a woman in hospital, diagnosed with high blood pressure, who was told not to watch any more *Pride and Prejudice*. She was 103."

There is a lot of masculine yang energy in this combination, which comes from the Rat but is left for the feminine yin side coming from the Virgo to manage. It is easier for men to expend this excess energy than it is for the women; those who do so successfully tend to come across as quite tomboyish, but once again, not without their charm. Cameron Diaz has said, "I grew up with a lot of boys. I probably have a lot of testosterone for a woman... Growing up, I was the plain one. I had no style. I was the tough kid with the comb in the back pocket and the feathered hair." Similarly, Lauren Bacall talked about her boyish figure: "I was this flat-chested, big-footed, lanky thing." This aspect of the Rat-Virgo personality leads them not to place so much emphasis on their looks and more on their personalities. Humor is exceptionally important. Nicol Williamson has said, "If you can make a woman laugh you can do anything with her."

One thing that afflicts all Rat-Virgos alike is the constant struggle with their insecurities. They are rarely as strong as they project. Most of them have had to consciously create personas or use some sort of psychological technique to keep them moving onwards and upwards. Lauren Bacall has said, "I was always a little unsteady in my self-belief." Often times there is a tendency to pigeonhole them by their perceived skillset, but the truth s, they are surprisingly multitalented. Gene Kelly has said, "I never wanted to be a dancer. It's true! I wanted to be a shortstop for the Pittsburgh Pirates."

Although not all Virgo combinations are likely to be perfectionists, this combination is likely to be one of them. Meticulous and detail oriented, they like to be sure that they have checked everything twice, considered everything from various perspectives and covered their back from potentially negative consequences. Jeremy Irons has aid, "Anyway, I'm never satisfied. I think were I ever satisfied with my work, I'd be in trouble." They always strive to be better and that is why they are so good at everything they attempt. Liam Gallagher has said, "People are always going on about 'Oh, you've failed in America.' I've never failed at anything in my entire life. I got out of the bedroom when I was a young f**king lad, and I'm in a great f**king band. And now we're playing at Madison Square Garden."

They take their work very seriously and expect others to do the same. Kevin Zegers has said, "I don't take crap from anyone who compromises the success of my movies." Many Rat-Virgos go into scientific or medical research fields, anywhere the faculties of their powerful minds can be used to benefit others. Philanthropic and spiritual occupations also appeal to these types as long as their practical minds are satisfied that a decent profit is obtainable. Regardless what direction they choose, they may prefer to take mini retirements throughout their lives rather than actually ever retire. They love life and they love to serve which they do through their work. Lauren Bacall has said, "I am still working, I've never stopped and, while my health holds out, I won't stop."

Soul Mate:	Ox-Aries
Challenger:	Horse-Pisces
Siblings:	Rat-Taurus, Rat-Capricorn
Best Friends:	Dragon-Capricorn, Dragon-Taurus, Dragon-Virgo, Monkey-Capricorn, Monkey-Taurus, Monkey-Virgo

Gene Kelly
Lauren Bacall
Buddy Holly
Nicol Williamson
Jeremy Irons
John Ritter
Hugh Grant
Collin Firth
Damon Wayans
Garrett Hedlund
Kevin Zegers
Liam Gallagher
Prince Harry Windsor

Cameron Diaz
Idris Elba
Jane Greer
John McCain
Hugh Hudson
Scott Baio
Aimee Mann
Laura Vandervoort
Katie Melua
Chris Tucker
Jimmy Car
Sonam

RAT – LIBRA

Chinese Name: SHU
Rank: 1st
Hours Ruled: 11pm – 1am
Direction: Directly North
Season: Winter
Month: December
Western Zodiac Equivalent of Rat: Sagittarius
Sagittarius Western Element: Fire
Eastern Zodiac Equivalent of Libra: Dog
Libra Western Element: Air
Numerology: 7

When I was young, my ambition was to be one of the people who made a difference in this world. My hope still is to leave the world a little bit better for my having been here. It's a wonderful life and I love it.

– Jim Henson

When the Rat's ferocious fire meets with Libra's serene air, it is a perfect blend of ability and discernment, power and focus, talent and execution. The desire to rule and the desire for spiritual wholeness reside side by side, even though at times there is an internal fight where one necessarily overcomes the other. It's interesting that there are many powerful political people belonging to this combination, yet, equally, as many spiritually leaders of influence.

Primarily, they choose to meet the needs of that inner child that never really grows up. Jim Henson said, "The most sophisticated people I've ever known had just one thing in common: they were all in touch with their inner children... Life is meant to be fun, and joyous, and fulfilling. May each of yours be that... It's a good life, enjoy it." Of course, some members of this particular group may take it a little far; infamous Italian PM Silvio Berlusconi has said, "According to a survey, when Italian women were asked if they would like to have sex with me, 30 percent said yes, while the other 70 percent said, "What, again?" Similarly, when asked if he was going to attend President Obama's inauguration, Silvio Berlusconi responded, "No. I'm not an extra. I'm a lead."

Although it is easy to frown on this sort of behavior, one begs the question, would they have risen to their position without this heightened notion of themselves? At the end of the day, it is nothing more than self-belief. Talking about the performance world, Freida Pinto has said, "This industry is for fighters and those who do not give up! It is very important to believe in yourself. Even when a hundred people rejected me, I did not lose hope and, finally, one of the biggest directors of all times [Danny Boyle] believed in me!"

Whether they place themselves on a pedestal or whether they just have a healthy self-regard, they understand the value in turning inwards and listening to the guidance from within. For that is where they receive these messages of their true greatness. Similar messages reside there for all to receive, but not everybody tunes to them in quite as powerful a way. Although in some regards, members of this combination can be seen as quite controversial, they are also powerfully authentic and refuse to change themselves to please anybody else. Avril Lavigne has said, "Why should I care what others think of me?" Similarly, talking about why he did not attend the Oscar ceremony where he won the *Best Song* Oscar for the film 8 Mile, Eminem said, "I'm thankful for it, I'm not ungrateful. I'm very grateful. I just don't choose to rub elbows with the whole Hollywood scene. It's not me."

Like them or loathe them, their ability to remain true to their beliefs regardless of any outside influence is respect-worthy. Discussing not going to war with Iran over the hostages, Jimmy

Carter said, "... it would probably have resulted in the death of maybe tens of thousands of Iranians who were innocent, and in the deaths of the hostages as well. In retrospect I don't have any doubt that I did the right thing. But it was not a popular thing among the public, and it was not even popular among my own advisers inside the White House. Including my wife." It would be easy to say that the men of this combination are just ego-maniacal and think they know best because they cannot see beyond themselves but that is clearly not true. Yes, they believe in the validity of their opinions and are prepared to do what it takes to be heard, but does not mean that they do not struggle with their decisions.

The women are as strong as their male counterparts but struggle more with the Rat's innate desire to please. That being said, they do manage to assert themselves at the same time. They are every woman, but with added flair. Dita Von Teese has said, "I advocate glamour. Every day. Every minute." Similarly, Gwyneth Paltrow has said, "Beauty, to me, is about being comfortable in your own skin. That, or a kick-ass red lipstick." They are somewhat unconventional and ahead of their time. Many prefer not to have children or may be the primary bread-winner of the family.

An interesting point to note about this combination is that both singers Bernie Nolan and Olivia Newton John overcame breast cancer and chose to use their stories to spread awareness and raise the profile of this issue. When the going gets tough, the Rat-Libra reconnects with the power within and it is not long before they realign with their higher selves and are in major manifestation mode. Jim Henson said, "I believe that we form our own lives, that we create our own reality, and that everything works out for the best... I spend a few minutes in meditation and prayer each morning. I thank whoever is helping me – I'm sure that somebody or something is – I express gratitude for all my blessings and try to forgive the people that I'm feeling negative toward. I try hard not to judge anyone, and I try to bless everyone who is part of my life, particularly anyone with whom I am having any problems."

After all is said and done, they want the best for themselves and for everyone else too. Living from their gut, they are not ashamed of serving their own needs but not without encouraging others to do the same. They take their responsibilities seriously and lead by example as often as they can. Occasionally, the ego does go too far and the defense mechanisms come into play. As previously mentioned, they do not like to reveal the extent of their sensitivity. If they regret an action they have taken, they will be their own biggest critics. As Olivia Newton-John has said, "I do have high standards, but I don't expect anything from anyone that I don't expect from myself."

Soul Mate:	Ox-Pisces
Challenger:	Horse-Aries
Siblings:	Rat-Aquarius, Rat-Gemini
Best Friends:	Dragon-Aquarius, Dragon-Gemini, Dragon-Libra, Monkey-Aquarius, Monkey-Gemini, Monkey-Libra

Jean-Claude Van Damme
Nusrat Fateh Ali Khan
Jackson Browne
Brian Blessed
Jim Henson
Philip Kaufman
Marcello Mastroianni
Steve Forrest
Silvio Berlusconi
Phil Hartman
Donna Karan
Michele Dotrice

Mimi Kennedy
Bernie Nolan
Jennifer Rush
Jennifer Holliday
Rob Marshall
Daniel Baldwin
Chiaki Kuriyama
Jermaine Dupri

RAT – SCORPIO

Chinese Name: SHU
Rank: 1st
Hours Ruled: 11pm – 1am
Direction: Directly North
Season: Winter
Month: December
Western Zodiac Equivalent of Rat: Sagittarius
Sagittarius Western Element: Fire
Eastern Zodiac Equivalent of Scorpio: Boar
Scorpio Western Element: Water
Numerology: 8

When the going gets tough, the tough reinvent.
– Rupaul

When the Rat's rocket fire meets Scorpio's lake of mystery two primary traits emerge; professional drive and sexual confidence. The members of this group are highly sensual and seek out as many experiences as the hot meals they eat. The best way to describe this personality would be the sensual adventurer.

Overflowing with energy and a zest for life, this Rat may well have been the one from the Jade Emperor story. Like the preceding and following Rat combination, this type is highly sexed. They bore very easily and like the taste of new experiences. After much play and much experimentation, they settle down, willing and ready to behave. If courting a Rat-Scorpio, it is probably wise to make yourself a little unavailable so that they are always left with the feeling that there is more to unravel.

Thriving on experiences, they are multi-faceted and their perception is broadened in a unique way. Excellent communicators, they do well in just about any working environment but they really flourish in sales. Intuiting other people's values they get them on side effortlessly. It is for this reason so many Rat-Scorpios enjoy working in middle management because ultimately, everybody falls in love with them and then the Rat-Scorpio can really have some fun.

They learn to see people and situations with a sort of-objectivity; they will see intentions, strategies, abilities and latent potential. That is why they do so well in middle management; they know how to get the best out of people if they choose to. They can also manipulate the hell out of situations if they really want their way badly enough, but they usually refrain from such methods unless absolutely necessary. Because of their special powers of observation, they have a knack for breaking down situations for people to understand. That is why Jonathon Ross is the biggest film reviewer in the UK and why Kathy Griffin is a prima celebrity piss taker, she has said, "A lot of celebrities, especially when you're talking about the really big ones, live in what I call the fame bubble. Nobody ever says no to them or challenges them or even teases them."

Toni Collette has said, "The better you know yourself, the better your relationship with the rest of the world," which is very pertinent as Rat-Scorpios do tend to know their inner selves meticulously. Stanley Tucci has said, "I'm a control freak. Totally." Similarly Scarlett Johansen has said, "I have an obsessive character. I manicure my nails at three in the morning because nobody else can do it the right way. Maybe that's the secret to my success." Maybe it is. When they want something, they will take responsibility for every single aspect not only so that it gets done but to ensure that it gets done to their exceptional high standards. That being said, because their superpower is seeing what other people's superpowers are, they will delegate the right jobs to the right people so that things get done even better than they could do themselves.

Humor also plays an integral part of people born with this combination, especially humor bordering on the camp. This is especially noticeable with the ladies here as Jenny McCarthy, Rebecca Romaijn, Kathy Griffin, Katy Perry and of course RuPaul who explained the Rat-Scorpio legacy best when she said, "My goal is to always come from a place of love...but sometimes you just have to break it down for a motherfucker!"

In many ways, their sex appeal and humor is intrinsically linked. Rebecca Romaijn has said, "I'm not for gratuitous nudity, but if there's humor, I don't have a problem... Sexy at the millennium means having a solid sense of self but never taking yourself too seriously." Similarly, Jenny McCarthy has said, "I'm not a sex symbol. I'm the comedic girl next door and a lot of fun. People don't come up to me and say, 'Love your butt.' They say, 'You're funny!'"

This aspect of humor and sex appeal extends to the men also. Josh Duhamel has said, "I feel sexiest when I can make you laugh." Humble, talented and quick learners, they essentially do understand their own worth yet in observing their behavior closely it is not hard to pick up on their insecure need for regular affirmation. Know that you really are all that you secretly think you and more to the point, it is not arrogant to think that way. Do as your sister RuPaul do: "With hair, heels, and attitude, honey, I am through the roof."

An interesting side note about this combination is that Katie Perry wrote "I kissed a Girl" about Scarlett Johansen, both are sexy sensual and colorful Rat-Scorpios.

Focused, ambitious and real, one lifetime would never be enough for them to undertake all the journeys they would like to take, maybe that is why Michael Landon said, "Whatever you want to do, do it now. There are only so many tomorrows." With that adventurer spirit they manage any feelings of doubt and go forth knowing that they will be more than able to handle anything that they comes their way. Tilda Swinton has said, "I don't work the future – I don't want to know what's coming. I don't feel I need any guarantees."

Spiritually speaking, they feel their way as they go along. It is somewhat of a contradiction, they set rules for themselves inwardly yet set forth in the world with such abandon. Or maybe it isn't. Maybe it is because they have set their internal boundaries that they are freed to fly so high externally. Leading by their own free flowing example they are always in close proximity to their liberal moral center. And because they mean it, their words are that much more potent. Like the colorful, flamboyant and downright fabulous RuPaul has said, "You are not your religion. You are not your skin color. You are not your gender, your politics, your career, or your marital status. You are none of the superficial things that this world deems important. The real you is the energy force that created the entire universe!"

Soul Mate:	Ox-Aquarius
Challenger:	Horse-Taurus
Siblings:	Rat-Pisces, Rat-Cancer
Best Friends:	Dragon-Pisces, Dragon-Cancer, Dragon-Scorpio, Monkey-Pisces, Monkey-Cancer, Monkey-Scorpio

Vincent Schiavelli
Mala Sinha
Lulu
Prince Charles
Kate Jackson
Kim Wilde
Jonathan Ross
RuPaul
Kathy Griffin
Elizabeth Perkins
Michael Nyqvist
Tilda Swinton
Jeremy London

Jason London
Eric Dane
Gemma Atkinson
Jena Malone
Delta Goodrem
Kelly Osbourne

RAT – SAGITTARIUS

Chinese Name: SHU
Rank: 1st
Hours Ruled: 11pm – 1am
Direction: Directly North
Season: Winter
Month: December
Western Zodiac Equivalent of Rat: Sagittarius
Sagittarius Western Element: Fire
Eastern Zodiac Equivalent of Sagittarius: Monkey
Sagittarius Western Element: Fire
Numerology: 9

If you cannot be a poet, be the poem.
– David Caradine

When the Rat's fire meets with the Centaur's, they realize that it is of the same texture and consistency as Sagittarius is the Rat's Western equivalent sign. That means that this is the double Rat or the pure Sagittarius combination, thus amplifying the Rat or Sagittarius traits more so than any other Rat combination.

Born entrepreneurs, they have a desire to go it alone so that they can see how far they can push their own limits and prove their worth to themselves. This combination may actually possess the greatest desire for success out of all 144 combinations. They do not appreciate being told what to do and always have their eyes on the throne.

Naturally introspective, they think through things in depth and plan obsessively. They figure out what their end goal is and have faith that they will get there if they carry on taking small steps towards it. As David Carradine has said, "One foot, in-front of the other, things happened, as I try to make them happen, so it wasn't exactly, no real surprises." They think big and understand their own worth. What some perceive as arrogance is merely powerful confidence. And they prove this time and time again.

Many start businesses at a young age because they like to learn through experience. They do not make good followers so would rather deal with the pitfalls of getting it wrong than subserviently doing as they're told. That does not mean however, that they are not good team players, they are. In fact they thrive in working environments that are social at the same time. They doubly thrive if they are in charge in some way.

This concentration of Rat here creates a personality that seems available to all but really knows who its core group of friends, staff and family are. They have enough charm and allure to disarm anyone they choose but do not think that you have made it to any sort of "friend" level with them. They are just a little bit exclusive; it's how they make themselves feel special. It's only if they respect you for your knowledge, ability or talent that you could possibly hope to break down the barrier into their world and even then, it takes time for them to trust you.

The men of this combination are typical pretty boys. There are more male models at this part of the 144-combination cycle than anywhere else. Often blessed with alpha male bodies with pretty faces and undeniable sex appeal. Even the smaller, not as pretty men of this combination tend to have no problem attracting mates as there is just an effortless sexuality here that emanates from within. They may be pretty and soft on the outside, but make no mistake excessive yang energy always creates the potential for machismo attitudes. Poke them a little and it surfaces quickly.

The women of this combination are also pretty, often dainty but unlike Rat-Sagittarius men, they look as intelligent as they are. That is how the excessive yang manifests here. They do not always find it easy to communicate how they feel and can sometimes come across as harsh. But they are equally as comfortable with their sexuality and it gives them a powerful tool. They love life and need to be where the action is. Alyssa Milano has said, "I've always believed in experiencing everything in life. When you walk out with blinders on, you cut yourself off from the angels and the fairies."

The way they perceive themselves and the way the world perceives them does not always match; Samuel L. Jackson has said, "I was a square for so long and it totally amazes me that people think I am cool." Similarly, Julianne Moore has said, "In grade school I was a complete geek. You know, there's always the kid who's too short, the one who wears glasses, the kid who's not athletic. Well, I was all three."

Ultimately, the Rat-Sagittarius is a sorted type who knows where he is going and why. They do not let obstacles hold them back and face them readily knowing that a minor setback will never derail them from achieving their long-term goal. As David Carradine has said, "There's an alternative. There's always a third way, and it's not a combination of the other two ways. It's a different way." Whatever happens, they will find a way to get what they want because their desire for success is all consuming. And what is success to a Rat-Sagittarius? Kenneth Branagh has said, "My definition of success is control." With such powerful inner direction, drive and ambition, it does not take them long to assume a position of authority. Secretly, they have always known that this Rat was born to Lead.

Soul Mate:	Ox-Capricorn
Challenger:	Horse-Gemini
Siblings:	Rat-Aries, Rat-Leo
Best Friends:	Dragon-Aries, Dragon-Leo, Dragon-

Sagittarius, Monkey-Aries, Monkey-Leo,
Monkey-Sagittarius

Samuel L. Jackson
Sammy Davis Sr.
Raj Kapoor
David Carradine
Hector Elizondo
Tom Wilkinson
JoBeth Williams
Dee Wallace
James Avery
Ozzy Osbourne
Noel Edmonds
Thierry Mugler
Julianne Moore
Kenneth Branagh
Daryl Hannah
Amy Grant
Rati Agnihotri
Gary Lineker
Alyssa Milano
Stuart Townsend
Rusty Joiner
Vanessa Paradis
John Abraham
Arjun Rampal
Miranda Hart
Mary Elizabeth Winstead
Basshunter

RAT – CAPRICORN

Chinese Name: SHU
Rank: 1ˢᵗ
Hours Ruled: 11pm – 1am
Direction: Directly North
Season: Winter
Month: December
Western Zodiac Equivalent of Rat: Sagittarius
Sagittarius Western Element: Fire
Eastern Zodiac Equivalent of Capricorn: Ox
Capricorn Western Element: Earth
Numerology: 10 = 1

My only obligation is to keep myself and other people guessing.
– Jude Law

When the Rat's sparkles meet Capricorn's dense earth, a truly enigmatic persona emerges. These people are never what they seem, whether that be deemed "good, "bad" or "other." Early on in their lives, they want to be seen as intriguing, lively, unique, but they soon figure out that the more they seek to present such, the further they will actually be from it, because in the most traditional sense, it is the commonest method of conforming. The only way of being unique is to let go of any pretense in order to allow a true individual voice to come through. It is only when they do this that ironically they manage to achieve their goal. Andy Kaufman said, "What's real? What's not? That's what I do in my act, test how other people deal with reality."

People of this combination can be quite controversial as they live life on the edge, take risks and open themselves to questionable influences. Many have been loved, despised and then loved again on a grand scale. Often times it seems their ego gets the better of them to the detriment of themselves and their family. Jude Law's marital indiscretions and Richard Nixon's Watergate incident are examples. Yet despite everything, they always maintain that their family remains the most important thing in their lives and it truly is. They just struggle balancing their need for risky thrills and fitting into a stable familial structure. They want it all, even if what they want are on opposing sides of the spectrum.

Essentially the problems arise from a fluctuating esteem paradigm; there is a dramatic disconnect between who they really are and the image they feel that others expect of them. It is very important for this combination to let this go otherwise they will be forever chained to and living up to an image they may end up disliking. That will further exacerbate the esteem challenge. It is not hard to get it under control and most do, but only once they humble themselves, let go of the meaningless, regardless how much mileage they could potentially get from it and consciously enjoy the present moment with those they truly value in simplicity.

In their most naked form, they are introverted and intro-spective with very fast minds. They are constantly thinking and rethinking the smallest of details to develop a greater under-standing of things...and also to sadistically drive themselves a little nuts. Their confidence levels can be surprisingly different in different areas of their lives, but that doesn't stop them from throwing themselves into things whole heartedly despite not having the appropriate qualifications or experience. They are sharp enough to pick up things quickly and usually end up with greater functional understanding than those who have taken more conventional routes.

The men of this combination are, like most Rat men, conven-tionally attractive, with an almost feminine prettiness. They are sexually charged and like to be active. They function on an intellectual level very well and although they tend to have a good level of emotional intelligence, they do not necessarily apply it. Despite how well they do professionally, the playful child is always hiding just behind their eyes. Maybe that is what makes them so attractive. It is when they follow their big hearts that they flourish. Jude Law has said, "I don't want to do anything that I'm not passionate about." Nor should they.

The women are feminine, upbeat and verging on sickly sweet. They have a greater desire to please than most. Although this brings them many admirers, they tend to be conditional admirers who will adore as long as the Rat-Capricorn serves that admirers need. But when the Rat-Capricorn reaches her tipping point and speaks up about the imbalance or injustice of the situation, the admirer is gone! Mary Tyler Moore said, "There is a dark side. I tend not to be as optimistic as Mary Richards. I have an anger in me that I carry from my childhood experiences – I expect a lot of myself and I'm not too kind to myself." Interestingly, Mary Tyler Moore married Grant Tinker who is also a Rat-Capricorn.

Savvy trend predictors, good money makers and excellent savers, they are financially handy to have around. They are never without funds and can be relied upon to have a healthy rainy day stash. In addition to this, they cannot help but continue to up-skill to ensure that their money-making abilities are constantly improving. Sometimes it looks like they have been given everything on a silver plate, but they do not feel inclined to show or express just how hard they work. They earn every-thing they get…the good and the bad. As much as they wish they did not focus on their competitors, their need to present themselves well and be esteemed tends to get the better of them. Richard Nixon said, "Always remember, others may hate you. But those who hate you don't win unless you hate them, and then you destroy yourself." The more integrity they have, the more internal strength they have, the less they care what people think and the more people value them. When they make that their life's focus, they get everything and more.

Soul Mate:	Ox-Sagittarius
Challenger:	Horse-Cancer
Siblings:	Rat-Taurus, Rat-Virgo
Best Friends:	Dragon-Capricorn, Dragon-Taurus, Dragon-Virgo, Monkey-Capricorn, Monkey-Taurus, Monkey-Virgo

Jude Law
Julia Louis-Dreyfus
Katrina Law
Dylan Minnette
Mary Tyler Moore
Grant Tinker
Dyan Cannon
Andy Kaufman
Uday Chopra
Donna Summer
Richard Nixon
Mohammad Rafi
Lloyd Bridges
Danny Kaye
Loretta Young
Shirley Bassey
George Foreman
Haruki Murakami
Sean Paul

RAT – AQUARIUS

Chinese Name: SHU
Rank: 1st
Hours Ruled: 11pm – 1am
Direction: Directly North
Season: Winter
Month: December
Western Zodiac Equivalent of Rat: Sagittarius
Sagittarius Western Element: Fire
Eastern Zodiac Equivalent of Aquarius: Tiger
Aquarius Western Element: Air
Numerology: 11 = 2

Of course, I am misrepresented very often, but so is everybody who has got something to say.
– Vanessa Redgrave

The Rat's mini inferno is amplified by the Aquarian's cyclone, expanding everything, presence, intelligence and courage. Humanitarian Aquarius lends a great deal of compassion, albeit detached compassion and there is a great desire to serve mankind in any way they can best. With the Rat's intellect, foresight and ability to make things happen and Aquarius's compassion, eternal search for truth and service orientation, this is the sort of combination that aims to change the world and often does. This rodent demands respect!

People belonging to this combination are often multi-talented and have many doors open to them at most times in their professional lives. Like many Rats they tend to know what area of work they want to pursue from a young age and set out a plan early on. With exceptionally acute minds, they often go into jobs where detailed analysis or specialized knowledge is required. They undertake their duties without complaint and take full responsibility for all aspects of their work.

There is still a desire to please that comes at this part of the 144-combination cycle, but it is tempered by Aquarius's self-imposed service manifesto. By working for the betterment of society, there is an automatic feeling of fulfilment, as if the world were already satisfied by the service they had provided and continue to do so. This is very helpful for this astrological combination as this lessens internal conflicts and makes them more self-assured. Clark Gable said, "The things a man has to have are hope and confidence in himself against odds... He's got to have some inner standards worth fighting for or there won't be any way to bring him into conflict. And he must be ready to choose death before dishonor without making too much song and dance about it."

They are as intelligent as they are beautiful, as loving as they are assertive, as charitable as they are shrewd. A noted tendency is to just get on with their life without seeming to really get emotionally involved. They do when they remember to do so. Otherwise, they are like a practical architect whose next house is always an improvement on the last and who spends his entire life laying brick after brick until they have made homes all over the town but didn't spend any time living in any of them.

The men of this combination are jovial, warm and friendly. Although at first they seem introverted, they can be surprisingly chatty when their interest is roused, then it might be difficult to shut them up. And like most Rat men, their virility is a given. Burt Reynolds said, "Women are my drugs and alcohol. When I'm involved with one woman, I'm involved with one woman. Period. But between romances, I am carnivorous."

There is something universally fun about Rat-Aquarian men and being a close friend is a real privilege. They will share every-thing...including the details you didn't ask for, but which make a story a thriller. If you have taken care of their emotions, they will be grateful and want to reciprocate but might not know how to respond in like. The Aquarian detachment might overpower them here, but if you need someone to defend you in a fight, they would be happy to knock someone out for you.

The women of this combination use their heightened intellect and emotional understanding to live their lives in a way that is sensible and worthwhile. They often have high-powered professional positions, a prominent role in the community/church and so forth and a family. They also tend be politically active and are prepared to fight for their beliefs publically. Vanessa Redgrave has said, "I've opened my mouth on a lot of subjects. And I thought the more prestige you get, I'd have the power to do what I like. It's not true." If one approach fails, they will try another and another.

Whatever they set their minds on, they achieve. The reason for this is that they spend their entire lives working towards it so it is inevitable that they will eventually reach their desired destination. Like Burt Reynolds said, "You get to a certain age where you know you can't go over the wall, but I'll never get to the age where I can't go through it."

People born with this combination know that they are useful and plan to make the most use of themselves as they can. They see opportunities everywhere and if they come up against any resistance, they find a way past it. They might mope occasionally, but not for long. Their energy is so used to be active and productive that the universe supports them to find solutions even to very complicated issues. This spurs them to continue going and growing. They are successful in every area of their life because they make life work and their example shines like a beacon. Clark Gable said, "The only reason they come to see me is that I know that life is great – and they know I know it."

Soul Mate:	Ox-Scorpio
Challenger:	Horse-Leo
Siblings:	Rat-Gemini, Rat-Libra
Best Friends:	Dragon-Aquarius, Dragon-Gemini, Dragon-Libra, Monkey-Aquarius, Monkey-Gemini, Monkey-Libra

Clark Gable
Sarah Clarke
Billie Joe Armstrong
Portia de Rossi
James Spader
Jonathan Larson
Prince Andrew
David Strathairn
John Belushi
Burt Reynolds
Alan Alda
Vanessa Redgrave
Victor Mature
Rosa Parks

RAT – PISCES

Chinese Name: SHU
Rank: 1ˢᵗ
Hours Ruled: 11pm – 1am
Direction: Directly North
Season: Winter
Month: December
Western Zodiac Equivalent of Rat: Sagittarius
Sagittarius Western Element: Fire
Eastern Zodiac Equivalent of Pisces: Rabbit
Pisces Western Element: Water
Numerology: 12 = 3

Live life fully while you're here. Experience everything.
– Anthony Robbins

When the fresh fire of the Rat meets the deep waters of the innocent Pisces, we get a personality that is a mish mash of great traits merged together. Driven and focused (in lots of short periods) along with a strong desire to serve, they live their entire lives creating magic whilst feeling like they should be doing more.

This stems from an eternal desire to self-improve by doing something new, developing proficiency in the subject then dropping it for another one when the realization that the problem lies within. Interestingly, this combination can become easily charged magnetically to attract money, but find emotional attachments difficult to navigate. Despite the fact that they have exceptionally intuitive guidance systems, many of them fail to listen to the messages they receive. Many may even have healing abilities or the capacity to be a channel, but due to their insecurities and challenge from their scientific minds, they tend to defer its development until they can no longer ignore their voice.

Esther Hicks, channeler of the group of entities known as Abraham belongs to this combination as does Anthony Robbins, two exceptionally powerful forces for positive living. Although their practices are different, their message is almost identical. Channeling Abraham, Esther Hicks has said, "When you find a way to stop resisting who you've become and to allow yourself to become a vibrational match to who you have become, you are in the vortex and you are in a state of thriving. Everything we teach really is about helping you move in the direction of what feels better." This is the essence of how to access the powerful law of attraction. The Rat-Pisces seems to be highly connected to their source and information comes to them readily. Whether they accept it is another thing altogether.

This personality makes lots of unexpected U-turns in their lives. They start by following conventional wisdom, even though they tend to learn early the value of listening to and following their inner voice. They put effort into a career that they usually do not follow although their skills are always transferable. Instead, they will chase down a creative career. They like to be of service, either on a one-to-one basis or on a larger scale. That's why so many become life coaches or counsellors. Within the creative realm they might surge forwards becoming an actor for a few years then decide to shift into the director mode or maybe as a writer.

Shaquille O'Neal studied Business initially, became a basketball player, then a rapper, actor and he even became a reserve officer with LA Port Police. "My secret? See it and stay focused on it." All Rat-Pisceans listen and learn!

There is also an unusual spiritual connection to this combination and they may be drawn to unconventional sciences. The occult, esotericism, dreams and the unknown also appeal. They have difficulty balancing life in the "real" world whilst understanding the limitlessness of the non-physical universe. This is why there are so many high achievers born under this combination. In fact, many Rat-Pisceans remain completely unaware that in the broader context, they achieve more than most. Instead, they have an innate feeling that they have just not lived up to their potential or been able to access the power that is truly available to them.

As long as they manage their tendency to change their mind every few seconds and decide on a priority, they have an amazing ability to learn quickly and become highly proficient at something in a short space of time. They have an ability to see what is useful and what is not so they turn on their focus in that useful place and sharpen their skills where it is required. When they do decide to do something, they get it done. Shaquille O'Neal has said, "I don't believe in if."

The Yin Pisces side enhances the Rat's charm especially in Men and allows them to get away with arrogant remarks in a way others simply could not. Conversely, it makes the women second-guess their intuition even if it has a long proven record of trustworthiness. The women need to fix in their minds that they can trust and rely on their intuition and let themselves be guided by it. Often times, their intellectual and practical minds get in their way countering their intuitive hunches.

Generally speaking, they have an ability to see the gaps left by other people and can capitalize on them. Many entrepreneurs or self-employed people also belong to this group. Although they do not attempt to be different or out of the ordinary, their charm, effervescence and unique skill set makes them stick out from the crowd. Bernadette Peter's said, "You've gotta be original because if you're like someone else, what do they need you for?"

Soul Mate:	Ox-Libra
Challenger:	Horse-Virgo
Siblings:	Rat-Cancer, Rat-Scorpio
Best Friends:	Dragon-Pisces, Dragon-Cancer, Dragon-Scorpio, Monkey-Pisces, Monkey-Cancer, Monkey-Scorpio

Olivia Wilde
Sophie Turner
Jaimie Alexander
Madeline Carroll
Dane Cook
Billy Crystal
Christy Carlson Romano
Richard Ruccolo
Rory Cochrane
Brandon T. Jackson
Kerr Smith
Noureen DeWulf
Jean Louisa Kelly
Karolina Kurkova
Bernadette Peters
Common
John de Lancie
Wilson Bethel
Richard Coyle
Liesel Matthews
Dean Stockwell
Vicki Lewis
Luis Buñuel
Courtney B. Vance
Antonio Sabato Jr.
Shaquille O'Neal
Anthony Robbins

THE OX

THE OX

I am the sturdy rock of the cycle, the immovable object, the monolith! The world is my charge and I alone am responsible for its improvement. Waking before dawn I graft until after sunset without uttering a word. My diligence is noticed and I am given increasingly greater responsibility as well as greater resources; now I set the rules; do as I say, but only do as I do when you stand in my shoes; you'll need unending resolve, military discipline and seductive charisma. My presence and humor cast an enchanting spell that makes me irresistible. The masses want to follow me, do what I ask and enjoy my dominance! I control my external world because I am but an alien in my emotional one, pretending that feelings don't exist doesn't work, so the emotional arena seems to be my steepest learning curve, but I'm already halfway up the hill and as everyone knows I keep going until I reach my finish line: I either win, or I end. There is no alternative option.

I am the Ox.

Hardworking, introverted and humble, it is said that you dislike the limelight, but you are usually thrust into it because of your immense talent. Being blessed with self-confidence, you are known as a slow and steady achiever even when all others have given up. Being difficult to influence or dissuade, you stick to your beliefs or opinions firmly and are labelled as the most stubborn sign of the Chinese zodiac. However, with your strong sense of duty, work ethic and forcefulness, you are relied upon by people in positions of power to carry out jobs that most others are incapable of completing. It is in your nature to be a bit authoritarian, which does not always go down well, but you don't really care that much. Although many Oxen are stand-up comedians, politicians or actors, they can be surprisingly shy in one-to-one situations. They are also known for their special eyes.

Career-wise, Oxen are known to be the leaders or the managers of any professional environment. They are drawn to politics, comedy (especially stand-up comedy and sports; the harder the better. They are also attracted to working with gardens, land and property. Other occupations include: carpenters, mechanics, sculptors and teachers. It is interesting that many nuns and criminals are also born under this sign; nuns because the Ox seems to think that they must make their lives hard in order for it to be worthwhile and criminals because Oxen will not be told anything by anyone. The Ox makes the rules for others to follow. It is a do as I say, not as I do deal.

Compatibilities

Soul Mate:	Rat
Challenger:	Sheep
Best Friends:	Snake & Rooster
Good Relations:	Rabbit & Monkey

OX – ARIES

Chinese Name: NIU
Rank: 2nd
Hours Ruled: 1am – 3am
Direction: North
Season: Winter
Month: January
Western Zodiac Equivalent of Ox: Capricorn
Capricorn Western Element: Earth
Eastern Zodiac Equivalent of Aries: Dragon
Aries Western Element: Fire
Numerology: 13 = 4

Life is a tragedy when seen in close-up, but a comedy in long shot.
– Charlie Chaplin.

When formidable Ox earth meets the forceful fire of Aries, it is inevitable that the result is a powerful creature with many contradictory traits. The Ox sign is a cerebral one, Aries is less so, together, they prioritize following their feelings over more traditional methods. Both of these signs are connected to the tarot card The Emperor, so it is quite appropriate to see this personality as a leader. With the Ox's desire to control and Aries's ability to connect with people, this is a combination that has mass appeal. They do not seek affirmation from others and have an innate self-approval system; they tend to rely solely on their own resources (and perhaps on a select few who have proven their loyalty) to get them by which is likely the reason Eddie Murphy said, "The advice I would give to someone is to not take anyone's advice."

Aries imbues the Ox with a zest for life and the ability to relax in their chosen company. Yet, that Ox always feels a tad clumsy in social environments (because it can't control them) so often chooses to avoid them altogether. Keira Knightly has said, "I don't like parties very much. I'm not a very sociable being." Most important to them is their family and domestic lives, which they strive to prioritize because this is the sort of combination that runs organisations (especially financial institutions or those involved with property or agriculture). They also tend to be given charge of groups of people. In the arts, they tend to be multi-talented but tend to specialize in comedy.

Where this combination arrives in the 144 cycle is where many controversial personalities are to be found. Infamous dictators belong to this and some of the following combinations, but that does not mean that these signs have a predisposition towards "evil." It's more that the self-confidence found here, along with the ability to justify one's choices easily can be pushed to an extreme. But these same traits also work to support creation. Charlie Chaplin was an advocate of de-arming altogether having said, "I hope we shall abolish war and settle all differences at the conference table... I hope we shall abolish all hydrogen and atom bombs before they abolish us first." It is common that people who share similar signs are a source of inspiration to younger genera-tions. Eddie Murphy has always said that Charlie Chaplin was a huge inspiration to him. They are both Ox-Aries. A slightly more sinister connection is that Adolf Hitler was also a fan of Charlie Chaplin and was also an Ox-Aries.

The men of this combination can be unashamedly sexual and often have a dirty, crude sense of humor. But they do it with a glint in their eyes and a cheeky grin so it's hard not to be taken in by their charm. They look for people who make them feel comfortable and don't judge them, because they often make faux pas which embarrass them and make them shy away. Because Aries craves connection, when it is attached to the Ox, this personality is easier to pry open than any other Ox combination. Although they can be arrogant, they are also humble. Discussing women, Warren Beatty has said, "Just because you need a quart of milk doesn't mean you have to go out and buy a whole cow." Yet he has also said, "For me, the highest level of sexual excitement is in a monogamous relationship." They can be shockingly judgmental but equally charitable. A bucketful of contradictions!

The women of this combination are not naturally fashionable, it is something they have to learn, usually through their Snake or Rat friends. Keira Knightly said, "Producers usually hire a stylist for me when I go to premieres because they think I'm so pathetic." They are often ill at ease as they never really feel like they fit in. They are given to mini bouts of defensiveness that seemingly come out of nowhere. Jessica Lange has said, "All through life I've harbored anger rather than expressed it at the moment." These women often choose socially aware men with a soft center to complement their own overt strengths. Keira Knightly said, "The most manly thing ever is a guy who can cry, who's in touch with himself."

Ox-Aries' are known to put off prioritizing what is truly meaningful to themselves until the sheer mass of mental energy that they have put into over-thinking their dreams builds up behind them spurring them into action. Interestingly, both Leona Lewis and Susan Boyle, two of the most successful contestants on UK talent shows ever, belong to this combination.

Ultimately, with their mental acuity, self-belief and ability to connect humbly with people, they are constantly given opportunities to take charge of their lives. The decisions they make usually affect many more people than just themselves so with this power comes a huge responsibility. The universe demands more from them than others because they can offer more. They are given the persistence and tenacity for long haul journeys because it is what is expected of them. As Charlie Chaplin said in his movie parodying Hitler, The Great Dictator, "We think too much and feel too little. More than machinery, we need humanity.

More than cleverness, we need kindness and gentleness. Without these qualities, life will be violent and all will be lost."

Soul Mate:	Rat-Virgo
Challenger:	Sheep-Libra
Siblings:	Ox-Leo, Ox-Sagittarius
Best Friends:	Snake-Aries, Snake-Leo, Snake-Sagittarius, Rooster-Aries, Rooster-Leo, Rooster-Sagittarius

Jim Parsons
Keira Knightley
Asa Butterfield
Eddie Murphy
Jessica Lange
Adam Scott
Robert Carlyle
Emma Caulfield
Maisie Williams
Jessica Szohr
Jennifer Esposito
Roselyn Sanchez
Leona Lewis
Christopher Meloni
Charles Chaplin
Amy Sedaris
Jane Leeves
Warren Beatty
Guillaume Canet
Kris Marshall
Jamie Bamber
Rod Steiger
Nicholas Lyndhurst
Adolf Hitler

OX – TAURUS

Chinese Name: NIU
Rank: 2nd
Hours Ruled: 1am – 3am
Direction: North
Season: Winter
Month: January
Western Zodiac Equivalent of Ox: Capricorn
Capricorn Western Element: Earth
Eastern Zodiac Equivalent of Taurus: Snake
Taurus Western Element: Earth
Numerology: 14 = 5

I'd rather laugh with the sinners, than cry with the saints.
– Billy Joel

When the obstinate Ox's earth mixes with the Taurean's stubborn soil, the creation is a powerful personality with a lot of presence, influence and authority. This is where the bull meets the bull; not only can they annihilate their opponents, sometimes they subconsciously turn against themselves indulging in self-destructive behavior. With people like Saddam Hussein, Napoleon, his nemesis Wellington, the man dubbed "the teacher of evil" Nicolo Machiavelli and even Adolf Hitler being born on the cusp of this combination (although technically an Ox-Aries), this one combination is perhaps the most controversial of all. Speaking about funding a spy satellite that would monitor Omar Al-Bashir, the President of Sudan, Actor George Clooney said, "I want the war criminal to have the same amount of attention that I get."

Firstly, this is not an evil, bad or a negative combination; no such thing exists with any combination. The intricacies of the Ox-Taurus personality are such that they are blessed with authority, presence and strong convictions. With such rare leadership traits in natural abundance, it does not take long for them to find themselves in a leadership role, sometimes against their own personal choice. But once there, their Ox sense of obligation will make them take the responsibility very seriously. However, they find it difficult to open up to new ideas because they have defined themselves and their world so narrowly. Also, their belief that their way is the right way and any opposition is easily justified away. The more firmly fixed one's boundaries are, the greater the strength of character they are able to project even if the validity of those beliefs are questionable. This part of the 144-combination cycle is where people are the most cerebral, where they take facts, figures and other empirical results into consideration in order to make their decisions, relegating emotional impulses that cannot be conventionally measured.

Despite this, they often have the highest of moral codes, are the most sensitive, loving and noble of people. It is the mind games that they play with themselves that is the cause of their own frustrations, which they sometimes take out on others. It is interesting to note where powerful political leaders are born, it is common to have many prominent comedians, especially standup comics, the reason for this is because the skill set is the same; the ability to penetrate the mind, body and spirit of the masses. George Carlin said, "I think it's the duty of the comedian to find out where the line is drawn and cross it deliberately."

Time moves slower to this combination than any other; a favorite saying or mantra is, "I will not be rushed." Not only do they take their time, they take everybody else's too. Jack Nicolson said, "Every director implored me, 'Jack, can't you talk a little bit faster?' It was like a hot button for me and I would become hateful."

The men of this combination are inescapably politically oriented. Powerful, opinionated and respected, they can be found peppered along the entire political spectrum. George Clooney has said, "It's not a bad thing to hold a mirror up and look at some of the things we're doing [politically]. Everybody makes moral choices that better themselves and hurt someone else." Machiavellian sentiment or universal truth? It's debatable. With an overpowering sex appeal that completes the bad boy package, they are irresistible. As Jack Nicolson said, "Happily, when it comes to girls hitting on me, I'm not undernourished." Making lasting emotional connections is difficult because they struggle to surrender their will in relationships.

The women are equally as tough as their male counterparts. Not only are they as strong, they tolerate even less bull shit. They live their lives on their wits and never apologize for who they are. Lily Allen has said, "People in this day and age are still under the illusion that every woman who is successful must be being controlled by a man... I'm the boss." Even Enya has said, "I don't need a man in my life." Blessed with a great sense of humor, they love children, animals and make exceptionally giving friends. As long as they feel your loyalty, you will be cherished in a way that will make you feel special, but if she feels that you have been disloyal in some way, the double bull will be out for blood.

Ultimately, Ox-Taureans are politically intellectual creatures who choose to function within that realm so that they feel that they can take a hands on approach to influence the world. They tend to end up spending much of their energy trying to hide how emotionally vulnerable they feel because it is one thing that they cannot control externally, so are often defensive, use their humor as a deflection device and project their own issues on those they actually hold dear. They have a bad habit of pushing away the ones who really love them because they will not acquiesce and become a cog in the machine that enables the Ox-Taurean's own downfall. Self-awareness and letting go of the need to control helps them strike a healthy balance but almost like an addict would, they need daily self-patience. George Carlin said, "Don't confuse my point of view with cynicism. The real cynics are the ones who tell you that everything's gonna be all right."

Soul Mate:	Rat-Leo
Challenger:	Sheep-Scorpio
Siblings:	Ox-Virgo, Ox-Capricorn
Best Friends:	Snake-Taurus, Snake-Virgo, Snake-Capricorn, Rooster-Taurus, Rooster-Virgo, Rooster-Capricorn

George Clooney
Jack Nicholson
George Carlin
John Neville
Tim Roth
Zoë Wanamaker
Billy Joel
John Corbett
Janet McTeer
Stephen Daldry
George Lopez
Lily Allen
Jorge Garcia
Tori Spelling
Damon Lindelof
Akon
Sachin Tendulkar
Dennis Rodman
Enya
Chris Packham
Alan Titchmarsh
Anita Dobson

Saddam Hussein
George Cole
Malcolm X
Sid James
Stewart Granger
Gary Cooper

OX – GEMINI

Chinese Name: NIU
Rank: 2nd
Hours Ruled: 1am – 3am
Direction: North
Season: Winter
Month: January
Western Zodiac Equivalent of Ox: Capricorn
Capricorn Western Element: Earth
Eastern Zodiac Equivalent of Gemini: Horse
Gemini Western Element: Air
Numerology: 15 = 6

I'm not intimidated by lead roles. I'm better in them. I don't feel pressure. I feel released at times like that. That's what I'm born to do."

– Morgan Freeman

When the Ox's deep earth meets with Gemini's inconsistent whirlwind, each extends a hand to the other and they agree to use their respective abilities to reach for the stars. These are two very different beings with different ways of handling their business; the Ox is firm, fixed and likes to have everything prepared in advance, whereas the Gemini is free flowing, open and likes to play everything by ear. So what happens when these two come together? The Gemini lends the partnership ease and a relaxed approach while the Ox brings the discipline and the desire for achievement. Crazy creativity meets crazy work ethic. Gemini's speed also impacts Ox powerfully, making it faster to make decisions. Tony Curtis said, "At 17, I dreamed of seeing the world. At 19, I had been around the world and back."

The personality of this combination is not straight forward as the two signs are very different so they are selfish, forceful and flighty, yet they are also, caring, compassionate and domestic. They are often both traits on separate ends of the spectrum, e.g. selfish and selfless and it would be hard to say which was more prominent. Where they do meet the other Ox combinations is their tendency to dwell on the past over what has gone wrong. Tony Cutis has said, "I used to be good friends with my depression, saying, oh I'm so depressed, or life is terrible." Remembering how they have pulled themselves out of worse helps immensely. Let the soldier out to remind themselves of their own inspirational ways. Juliette Lewis has said, "The bravest thing I ever did was continuing my life when I wanted to die."

The men of this combination usually have the tough, gruff looks of the Ox, yet also have the temperament and sensitivity of an artist, so they may be more open to gentler pursuits than their stereotype might suggest. Painting and dancing are common natural talents. They do not feel alive unless they are engaged in some sort of work, whether it is paid or otherwise, they need to keep busy to feel worthwhile. Although they do not need to, they feel like they constantly have to earn the love of their family. Michael J. Fox has said, "Family is not an important thing, it's everything." That being said, they are still the butcher than butch Ox men and like to be surrounded by butch greatness. As Morgan Freeman has said, "I gravitate towards gravitas."

The women of this combination have that grounded, earthy Ox beauty with the sparkling Gemini wit that makes them universally attractive. They have quiet class and it is not hard for them to attract suitors. These women are seductresses fuelled by the Ox's audacity and Gemini's naughtiness. Their conflict comes from being naturally quite conservative which they get from the Ox, versus the wild-child Gemini's desire to experience everything. Once again, it is hard to say which will win out. In time they recognize the importance of being choosy about where they expend their energy and how important self-preservation is. Heidi Klum has said, "I think it's important to get your surroundings as well as yourself into a positive state – meaning surround yourself with positive people." This is when they appreciate just how powerful the effect of lightness and levity has on the quality of their lives.

An interesting said note about this combination is that both Lea Thompson and Michael J. Fox are Ox-Geminis and they were cast as mother and son in *Back to the Future* together; the Bollywood movie *Action Replayy* (based on *Back to the Future*), cast Aishwarya Rai and Aditiya Roy Kapoor as mother and son, both are Ox-Scorpio. It's a coincidence that all the roles required an Ox presence but that in both movies, both of the roles required them to be the exact same combination.

Ultimately, this combination is an unusual Ox sign in that it does not follow the established conventions, nor does it feel any pressure to, even though it still retains the Ox, *victory at all costs* attitude. Morgan Freeman said, "The best way to guarantee a loss is to quit." What sets them apart is that they are open enough to see that there are always alternative options available and that there is such beauty in diversity. Melissa Etheridge and Neil Patrick Harris have been bravely open about their sexuality, Melissa Etheridge has said, "Don't let anyone tell you that you have to be a certain way. Be unique. Be what you feel." The Ox spirit here is so strong that it just refuses to give in, even if it is one against the world, the Ox has the self-assurance to believe that it has a chance so will go for it. Victory at all costs remember? This combination is totally on board with this aspect of the Ox's way of life. Even though it has caused the downfall of many, it has also been what has brought them glory. Michael J. Fox described this refusal to give in to subduing influences to life when he spoke about his struggle with Parkinson's disease, "One's dignity may be assaulted, vandalized and cruelly mocked, but cannot be taken away unless it is surrendered."

Soul Mate:	Rat-Cancer
Challenger:	Sheep-Sagittarius
Siblings:	Ox-Libra, Ox-Aquarius
Best Friends:	Snake-Gemini, Snake-Libra, Snake-Aquarius, Rooster-Gemini, Rooster-Libra, Rooster-Aquarius

Peter Cushing
Tony Curtis
Morgan Freeman
Sally Kellerman
Jim Broadbent
Tom Berenger
Pam Grier
Lionel Richie
Hank Williams Jr.
Michael J. Fox
Lea Thompson
Aaron Sorkin
Harry Enfield
Boy George
Melissa Etheridge
Neil Patrick Harris
Juliette Lewis
Adam Garcia
Heidi Klum
Faith Evans
Dermot O'Leary
Maxwell
Carey Mulligan
Sonam Kapoor
Colbie Caillat

OX – CANCER

Chinese Name: NIU
Rank: 2nd
Hours Ruled: 1am – 3am
Direction: North
Season: Winter
Month: January
Western Zodiac Equivalent of Ox: Capricorn
Capricorn Western Element: Earth
Eastern Zodiac Equivalent of Cancer: Sheep
Cancer Western Element: Water
Numerology: 16 = 7

I don't go by the rule book... I lead from the heart, not the head.
– Princess Diana

When the Ox's fertile earth meets with Cancer's sweet waters, it combines steadfastness with creativity, intellectual endeavor with social conscience, fearlessness with heart. Looking at the two signs in their purely Chinese or Western form, you will notice that they are polar opposites (Ox and Sheep or Capricorn and Cancer) which does cause some internal friction, therefore indecision and second guessing themselves can be rife although they would not like that to be visible. They have enough nerve and confidence to put themselves on the line for their beliefs as human rights advocate and youngest ever Nobel Peace Prize laureate (17 years old) Malala Yousafzai said, "When the whole world is silent, even one voice becomes powerful." She was shot by the Taliban for her work encouraging education for women in Pakistan.

Ox signs perceive themselves as leaders and have a huge sense of duty, which they will apply to anything they undertake.

Talking about why staying in her marriage to Prince Charles, Princess Diana said, "Any sane person would have left long ago. But I cannot. I have my sons." They do not strictly adhere to established conventions even though they may like everyone else to. Cancer also perceives itself as a bit of a leader, although, with more reticence, so when these two signs converge, a powerful leader is born who wants to make a difference in the lives of the masses and will do so sometimes at great personal risk or sacrifice. Discussing the criticism he received for his comments whilst hosting the Golden Globes, Ricky Gervais said, "Recently I have been accused of being a shock comic, and cruel and cynical... But nothing could be further from the truth. I never actively try to offend. That's churlish, pointless and frankly too easy. But I believe you should say what you mean. Be honest. No one should ever be offended by truth."

Their ego is one that does not take bruising lightly and if slighted, could go to extreme lengths to obtain the justice they feel they deserve. The Ox-Cancer is one major grudge holder. But as with most Ox signs, they also have a fantastic sense of humor and many become comedians by default. Bill Cosby and Ricky Gervais are two examples. Meryl Streep has also spoken of her disappointment that she does not get offered more comic roles.

Naturally intelligent, they often excel academically and find that they have a presence people take seriously. This leads to an early self-confidence that both attracts admirers and causes jealousy from an early age. So they get used to handling both types of attention. People learn quickly though that one must not be too vocal in their disapproval as these are not live-and-let-live types, they will come after you to challenge you and hold you accountable for your words or beliefs.

The men of this combination tend to be softly spoken, with an effortless intelligence that they do not need to try to project, it is clear. In fact, they often go the other way and try to dumb down their intelligence so that they are more accessible. Bill Cosby has said, "A word to the wise ain't necessary – it's the stupid ones who need the advice." Insatiably curious and sometimes judgmental, they can be disdainful of people they do not identify with, sending hot and cold signals confusing the vibrational message they emit and confusing themselves as to where they stand. Yes, they can be smarter, more talented and more physically gifted than most, but they must avoid the tendency to believe that that makes them "better." But it is their confidence that typifies them as these two signs merge to create a creative powerhouse. Chaceford has said, "Doubt your doubts before you doubt your beliefs."

When Western water signs are attached to the Ox (Ox-Pisces, Ox-Cancer and Ox-Scorpio), the women have a noted tendency to be seductresses of the highest standard. One look into this seductress's eyes is all it takes to be taken in. They are experts at wrapping men around their fingers. The problem tends to be that this often remains at a surface level; it is only when they learn to open emotionally making themselves accessible, not needy (an important distinction required for this combination), that they get to experience fulfilling romantic relationships. This is so important for this combination because they value family above all else. Meryl Streep has said, "I think I was wired for family. You know how they say people are wired for religion, or wired for this or that? I always knew I would like to, if I could find the right person, have a family. I can't imagine living single."

Controversy might as well be the Ox's middle name because like it or not, they always find themselves in the thick of it. This is because the Ox does not feel the need to please other people. Bill Cosby has said, "I don't know the key to success, but the key to failure is to try to please everyone." The Ox-Cancer derives self-esteem from within and much of what the masses choose to do is more than just a tad puzzling to the Ox sensibility. Malala Yousafzai has said, "I don't want revenge on the Taliban, I want education for the sons and daughters of the Taliban." Whatever one thinks of them, one cannot deny that they are exceptionally smart, savvy and genuinely want to be of service. At the same time, they usually have a personal agenda too. The more they genuinely want to use their intelligence, wisdom and position to elevate other people to a higher plain, the more karmic rewards return to them. Princess Diana said, "I knew what my job was; it was to go out and meet the people and love them."

Soul Mate: Rat-Gemini
Challenger: Sheep-Capricorn
Siblings: Ox-Scorpio, Ox-Pisces
Best Friends: Snake-Cancer, Snake-Scorpio, Snake-Pisces,
                Rooster-Cancer, Rooster-Scorpio, Rooster-
                Pisces

Guru Dutt
June Lockhart
Farley Granger
Ned Beatty
Bill Cosby
Richard Jordan
Tom Stoppard
Anita Desai
Meryl Streep
Shelley Duvall
Nigel Lythgoe
Iain Glen
Jackie Earle Haley
Elizabeth McGovern
Forest Whitaker
Ricky Gervais

Princess Diana
Toby Keith
Meera Syal
Robin Antin
Patrick Wilson
Brian Austin Green
Carson Daly
Rufus Wainwright
Peter Kay
Chace Crawford
Léa Seydoux
Ashley Tisdale
Paloma Faith
Ranveer Singh
Malala Yousafzai

OX – LEO

Chinese Name: NIU
Rank: 2nd
Hours Ruled: 1am – 3am
Direction: North
Season: Winter
Month: January
Western Zodiac Equivalent of Ox: Capricorn
Capricorn Western Element: Earth
Eastern Zodiac Equivalent of Leo: Monkey
Leo Western Element: Fire
Numerology: 17 = 8

We need to internalize this idea of excellence. Not many folks spend a lot of time trying to be excellent.
– Barrack Obama

When Ox's deep dense earth meets Leo's *extreme* fire, it creates a personality with major presence. The Ox perceives itself as the supreme leader, as does the Leo; when these two signs combine, the result is a magnificent character with intelligence, charisma and serious backbone. There is also a powerful connection to nature; it is interesting to note how many people of this combination are avid gardeners, animal lovers and vegetarians. Super self-assured, self-defined and valiant, they set out to prove the impossible possible. It is absolutely no surprise whatsoever to people of an astrological persuasion that Barack Obama was the first black President of the United States.

With such strength of character they are the types of people who make decisions for themselves and even if they seek external counsel, they have much confidence in their own mental faculties. Sometimes that comes at a cost; Woody Harrelson has said, "I've found that every time you stand up for something and open your mouth, you alienate someone." Maybe this is that much harder to do when working in a creative capacity, but perhaps even more necessary. Kristen Wiig has also said, "If you're creating anything at all, it's really dangerous to care about what people think." So they autonomously carry out their goals and see them through to completion, often through pure perseverance. As Barrack Obama has said, "If you're walking down the right path and you're willing to keep walking, eventually you'll make progress." The Ox is the most persistent sign of all and Leo has a winner's mentality; when the two mix, this personality refuses to accept anything less than the best.

Firmly rooted in the physical world, they aim to make tangible, practical changes in their environment, changes in people and changes in established ways of the world. Again, as is the Ox stereotype, they often neglect the emotional in lieu of visible, measurable progress. Even though they attempt to come at everything with a light attitude and their contagious levity, there is often a contradictory heaviness of energy trailing along with them. This is a consequence of not exploring their own internal depths; you cannot tend to the issue if you ignore the symptoms and never even attempt to diagnose the problem in the first place. Exploring their subconscious, highlighting their true emotional needs and setting out to serve them is the hardest thing for them to have to do, but it is the most necessary. When they do, their energy shifts in powerful ways.

The men of this combination tend to be tall, intelligent, powerful looking with an appeal that seems to increase as they get older. Exceptionally well read, despite the level of education they have received, they are the sorts that know something about everything. They have a mental library that stores details which they use to clarify, back up and hammer home any point they feel requires to be made. Being in a position of influence is very important to the ego of the Ox-Leo because without this, they can become jaded, self-destructive and end up wasting their incomparable abilities. Talking about how he struggled with his self-esteem, Dustin Hoffman said, "It's very painful for us to feel we deserve a life. That's the toughest thing. That we deserve to have a life. That can take a lifetime."

The female of the Ox-Leo species are not always easy to navigate as they don't give much away. They respect strength, emotional, psychological and physical, in that order. Owning every inch of themselves they expect their friends and family to hold themselves to similar standard. That being said, they like to be in control and have a tendency to be the dominant one within any group dynamic. Kate Beckinsale has said, "No one is more enslaved than a slave who doesn't think they're enslaved." Being so independent themselves, they do not always seek a partner as strong, this woman will wear the trousers in the relationship. Often the primary breadwinner, she may seek to set up home with a househusband. Striving for authenticity in everything they do and are far more likely to set out on that journey to explore their subconscious depths earlier than their male counterparts. Kristen Wiig said, "Don't become something just because someone else wants you to, or because it's easy; you won't be happy. You have to do what you really, really, really, really want to do, even if it scares the shit out of you."

What they present on the surface is often a calm, quiet, in-control personality who leads with a quiet voice but with a loud authority; what happens on the inside is somewhat different. Woody Harrelson said, "Chaos and creativity go together. If you lose one percent of your chaos, you lose your creativity." This is a good description of the Ox-Leo's internal functioning. The truth is nobody is 100 percent certain or sure of themselves, but the Ox-Leo strives to present that, forcefully muffling the voice of its inner critic for better and for worse. As a result, this inner voice will scream out in the subconscious. They often learn the "letting go" lesson the hard way, but once they have, their entire universe transforms in seemingly miraculous ways. Barack Obama has said, "The future rewards those who press on. I don't have time to feel sorry for myself. I don't have time to complain. I'm going to press on."

Soul Mate:	Rat-Taurus
Challenger:	Sheep-Aquarius
Siblings:	Ox-Aries, Ox-Sagittarius
Best Friends:	Snake-Aries, Snake-Leo, Snake-Sagittarius, Rooster-Aries, Rooster-Leo, Rooster-Sagittarius

Kate Beckinsale

Anna Kendrick

Michael Ealy

Kristen Wiig

Woody Harrelson

Dustin Hoffman

Vera Farmiga

Kevin McKidd

Laurence Fishburne

Stephen Dorff

James Lafferty

Steven Berkoff

Loretta Devine

Maggie Wheeler

Barack Obama

Barbara Windsor

OX – VIRGO

Chinese Name: NIU
Rank: 2ⁿᵈ
Hours Ruled: 1am – 3am
Direction: North
Season: Winter
Month: January
Western Zodiac Equivalent of Ox: Capricorn
Capricorn Western Element: Earth
Eastern Zodiac Equivalent of Virgo: Rooster
Virgo Western Element: Earth
Numerology: 18 = 9

In a way, one gets stability from being able to order the rational mind.
– Richard Gere

When the Ox's tough terrain meets with Virgo's fertile soil, both blend to create a new type of earth, one that is firm, moist and perfect for most seeds to flourish. That is why the members of this club are solid, approachable and humble, but they are also as stubborn as an Ox sign is expected to be. Externally secure, highly creative and quite particular, these two signs merge to create one who requires expression, so it's important to find an appropriate outlet early on. Dave Chappelle has said, "Whether it means having a show, or a movie, or just being on a stage, I need an avenue to say what I have to say." Even though they may be quiet types on the surface, this double earth combination is another standup comic. More than anything, they love to have an impact on other people. James Gandolfini has said, "I love hearing people laugh. Especially in New York, and especially now. To hear somebody out there just belly-laughing."

Their hyper-intelligence comes across despite their laid back façade they present and one senses power, presence and strength. They can actually come across as intimidating and those Ox-Virgos who are true to their principles frustrate a lot of people because no argument or rational debate seems to have any impact. This bodes well as long as you are in the camp with them, but woe to you if you have done something to upset them, or worse, upset one of their loved ones. Andrew Lincoln has said, "I like to think that I've got determination, and I'm fiercely protective of the people I love."

The men of this combination tend to have had the ugly duckling syndrome but eventually blossom into beautiful swans. James Marsden said, "I grew up in an area where girls liked athletic football players and I was never that kind of guy... it was not until fairly recently that I became reasonably happy with my appearance and the way I am." This does not hold them back as these men have a deep inner knowing that they are worthy and valuable, yet at the same time have a multitude of hang-ups that would surprise anyone who does not know them well.

Dave Chappelle has said, "I'm an introspective dude," as many Ox-Virgo men are. They have often had many emotional hiccups in their past that they find difficult to overcome so they require many positive influences that help them stay uplifted when they have too much time to think. In fact, too much time spent in contemplation for the Ox-Virgo man can be dangerous. They get into enough trouble when they are impulsive, but when they have had time to create an elaborate plan, they are can be just devilish. Developing a spiritual practice, whatever form that may take, is always helpful. Richard Gere has said, "Meditation is such a more substantial reality than what we normally take to be reality." It also helps if they continuously set new goals and get working on achieving them whilst shifting the focus to simpler things. Comic Dave Chappelle has said, "I don't want the money. I don't want the drama. I just want to do my show. I want to have fun again."

The women of this combination have two main types of looks, the dainty beauty or the big-boned Boudicca battle-axe. But both are kind of prickly. Jennifer Coolidge has said, "I'm kind of harsher than most people." Maybe that is because they do not feel a need to subscribe to the airs and graces that others do and instead reveal their thoughts directly. Even Rose Mcgowan has said, "Why should I downplay myself to make someone else more comfortable?" These women love to be ladies, playing coy, flirting, but don't take anything that they say in flirt mode seriously, the fun for them is to get the fish to bite, when it has, the fisher-lady will gut the fish and eat it for dinner...unless it hooks a shark. This combination needs a shark! Rose Mcgowan has said, "I've always admitted it: I'm a man with really nice breasts – I'm so guilty of doing every single male thing."

Ultimately, the journey for this Ox, as it often is for many Ox signs, is to learn to accept their own vulnerability. Nobody asked them to be invincible and they are placing that expectation on themselves. They must try to curb their desire to control all of the external circumstances of their life and trust that the universe, God or the powers that be will provide for them; this surrender of will has a powerful impact upon them. Richard Gere has said, "I don't think that bravery is about skin. Bravery is about a willingness to show emotional need." It most definitely is for this Ox! With all of the confidence, grit and determination that they have, external success can come easily to them. It would be wiser to stick to the rules at least 75 percent of the time and for them to open their hearts early, even if it means that they get hurt; it's the best way that these types learn. It makes them bold and coura-geous. Journalist Lisa Ling has said, "Try to accomplish things you have always dreamt of while you can. I know it sounds cliché, but the biggest lesson I have learned is that life is precious;

enjoy it while it lasts."

Soul Mate:	Rat-Aries
Challenger:	Sheep-Pisces
Siblings:	Ox-Taurus, Ox-Capricorn
Best Friends:	Snake-Taurus, Snake-Virgo, Snake-Capricorn, Rooster-Taurus, Rooster-Virgo, Rooster-Capricorn

Paul Walker
James Marsden
Shannon Elizabeth
Rose McGowan
Andrew Lincoln
Dave Chappelle
Ben Falcone
Nas
Mahima Chaudhry
Lisa Ling
Jennifer Coolidge
Virginia Madsen
James Gandolfini
Bonnie Hunt
Billy Ray Cyrus
Richard Gere
Shelley Long
Peter Sellers
B.B. King

OX – LIBRA

Chinese Name: NIU
Rank: 2nd
Hours Ruled: 1am – 3am
Direction: North
Season: Winter
Month: January
Western Zodiac Equivalent of Ox: Capricorn
Capricorn Western Element: Earth
Eastern Zodiac Equivalent of Libra: Dog
Libra Western Element: Air
Numerology: 19 = 1

I do not know anyone who has got to the top without hard work. That is the recipe. It will not always get you to the top, but should get you pretty near.
– Margaret Thatcher

When the Ox's impenetrable earth combines with Libra's light breeze, it creates a personality that who places such great importance on living a life of authenticity or nobility and their ultimate goal is to inspire others to live in a similar fashion. But alas, not everybody is as disciplined as an Ox-Libra and not everybody wants to be. This causes some friction as the Ox-Libras tend to be convinced of their superior opinion, whether they say so or not. Johnny Carson said, "Whatever you do, you're going to be criticized. I feel the one sensible thing you can do is try to live in a way that pleases you. If you don't hurt anybody else, what you do is your own business."

An interesting contradiction of this personality type is how openly vulnerable they seem yet live their lives with such definite boundaries and sometimes, prickly defensiveness that prevents loved ones from being able to help or protect them from their own psychological prison. The ability to open to alternative perspectives helps greatly, to see the many shades of grey and when they do this, their entire lives begin to sparkle. Bruce Springsteen said, "Adult life is dealing with an enormous amount of questions that don't have answers. So I let the mystery settle into my music. I don't deny anything, I don't advocate anything, I just live with it."

They know who they are and what they stand for so they put ever more energy into magnifying their personality and expanding their productivity. Margaret Thatcher said, "I think sometimes the prime minister should be intimidating. There's not much point in being a weak, floppy thing in the chair." Although they can be masters of justifications, they are well aware of their internal functioning. Johnny Carson said, "Find me any performer anywhere who isn't egocentric. You'd better believe you're good, or you've got no business being out there." With the ability to delay gratification, focus on the job at hand, no matter how difficult and no matter how confrontational they have to be, eventually, they rise to the top of their respective fields. They are not scared of saying what needs to be said or doing what needs to be done.

The men of this combination are often a delight on the eyes. Dealing with them personally is not always an easy task though as some have inflated egos as a result of their looks, exceptional skills and work ethic that tends to be better than their peers. Some Ox-Libra men tend to think they are just that little bit better. Ed Sullivan said, "I am the best damned showman in television." With such self-importance it is difficult to make yourself heard and even when they do make out they are listening, there is a sense that they are just waiting for you to shut up so that they can be heard. Of course, the more spiritually evolved Ox-Libra male is more aware of the oneness of the universe and has a more genuinely humble perspective. They also tend to have buckets full of humor too.

The women of this combination can be exceptionally audacious powerhouses. They often have to consciously learn about the prevalent established conventions because they are so reliant upon their own ideas and self-constructed world. What other's do or don't do is fine for them, but the Ox-Libra lady will do what she pleases. Once she has made up her mind about something, she will not back down. As Margaret Thatcher said, "To those waiting with bated breath for that favorite media catchphrase, the U- turn, I have only one thing to say: You turn if you want to. The lady's not for turning." Their self-assurance can be intimidating, especially to men who are unable to apply their preferred stereotypes of subservient women here so instead, their stereotypes leap to the other end of the spectrum. Sigourney Weaver has said, "In Hollywood, if you are a man and speak your mind openly, you're considered a man in full. But, if you are a woman and do the same, you're nothing but an annoying bitch."

Ultimately, it is easy to come to a decision regarding them because they have defined themselves so sharply. But the truth is, nobody is easily definable, least of all the Ox-Libra. Actually, they are sweet-hearted beings who just want the best of the simple things in life. They want to push themselves as far as they can to prove the super-elasticity of the human spirit and are not afraid of falling on their face to do it. Neve Campbell said, "When I look back on it now, I am so glad that the one thing that I had in my life was my belief that everything in life is a learning experience, whether it be positive or negative. If you can see it as a learning experience, you can turn any negative into a positive." Being so self-confident they often attract yes-men which sometimes affects their objectivity. The upside of their confidence is that they boldly go where no man has gone before, or few have been at least. They do not always succeed right away but they learn a lot from the experience that supports their future success. Ioan Gruffudd said, "They say the most successful people are the ones who have failed more than they have succeeded." Succeed they will or die trying…and they out rightly refuse to die, so that leaves only one outcome.

Soul Mate:	Rat-Pisces
Challenger:	Sheep-Aries
Siblings:	Ox-Gemini, Ox-Aquarius
Best Friends:	Snake-Gemini, Snake-Libra, Snake-Aquarius, Rooster-Gemini, Rooster-Libra, Rooster-Aquarius

Ed Sullivan
Johnny Carson
Angela Lansbury
Margaret Thatcher
Jackie Collins
Wanda Jackson
Sigourney Weaver
Pedro Almodóvar
Bruce Springsteen
Eric Stoltz
Heather Locklear
Martin Kemp
Michelle Trachtenberg
Lena Headey
Neve Campbell
Ioan Gruffudd
Mario López

OX – SCORPIO

Chinese Name: NIU
Rank: 2nd
Hours Ruled: 1am – 3am
Direction: North
Season: Winter
Month: January
Western Zodiac Equivalent of Ox: Capricorn
Capricorn Western Element: Earth
Eastern Zodiac Equivalent of Scorpio: Boar
Scorpio Western Element: Water
Numerology: 20 = 2

God put me on this earth to raise sheer hell.
– Richard Burton

When the Ox's tough terrain is met by Scorpio's acid rainstorm, some interesting mutations occur. Immense beauty is one of them; the men and the women are often gifted with either, physical beauty, charisma, talent, pure unbridled confidence or all of the above. Of course, all combinations contain their contradictions, but this one would take the gold. Their thought process is intriguing; they play mind games with themselves so create a set of rules or a manifesto that seems illogical or shockingly self-serving. That's not to say that they are selfish, because they are not, they are humble and generous people, but, this authoritarian Ox will make their own rules as they go along, so if they benefit you, great, if they don't, just give them way and let them pass, otherwise they will quietly trail you forever waiting for an opportunity to kick your butt! International Superstar, Aishwarya Rai has said, "I'm like the Terminator. I won't stop till I win. Just everything must be perfect."

This hardly comes as a surprise as the Ox sign's work ethic is legendary to those who are astrologically inclined; songwriter David Foster has said, "Every single day I wake up, I try to do my very best. I give 100 percent, and absolutely 100 percent love what I do every day." KD Lang has said, "We never let myself just sing. We were always trying to get the perfect vocal." Because nothing less than perfect will do. But what about those lazy Ox-Scorpios? They prefer to live on their power of their persuasion, which often comes from some sort of mutant confidence and abilities to influence. Beware! Know which Ox-Scorpio type you're dealing with.

The men of this combination give off a presence of laid-back ease; they like to be seen as in charge, a rough, tough and gruff ladies' man. Their calm surface belies their numerous insecurities and often, state of panic. Here's a little secret; in a crisis, the calmer they get, the more lost they actually are; they just think that presenting a calm face will ease everyone else sending off the message that they know what they are doing, when they do not have a clue. But still, this combination is often given great responsibility, often at a young age and why? Rock Hudson has said, "I can't play a loser – I don't look like one." That would be why. They look like winners; they look like leaders. They have a presence, a confidence and a charm that people want to trust, even though deep down, they might know that that trust is misguided. Richard Burton has said, "I've a fundamental and basic loyalty. Next year I'll be fifty and I've only been married twice. Yes, I betrayed them both a couple of times, but not mentally, only physically. You see, I may fall in love and it may last six months, but then the affair breaks up." There's that bizarre egocentric contradictory illogic again.

The women of this combination are some of the world's most exquisite; women such as Aishwarya Rai, Vivien Leigh and Meg Ryan, have all been described as the most beautiful women in the world in their own heyday. Incidentally, their cat like, green blue eyes are also telltale Ox-Scorpio (mutant) traits. Vivien Leigh has said, "Scorpios burn themselves out and eat themselves up and they are careless about themselves – like me. I swing between happiness and misery and I cry easily... I am part prude and part non-conformist and I say what I think and don't dissemble." Vivien Leigh was more accurately describing the Ox-Scorpio, rather than the generic Scorpio sign, but here is another interesting contradiction. They can be careless about themselves when they have committed their time to someone, then they will get to the finish post even if it means utter self-destruction in all too typical Ox fashion, but they also, can't ever care more about anyone else than themselves. They are selfish and selfless in equal measure at the same time. Get your head around that one. Nobody can, especially not the Ox-Scorpio! Meg Ryan has said, "I think there's an ongoing effort involved in trying to get a bigger perspective, trying to let go of things that limit your capacity to love and be loved or your capacity to hear and to really speak."

Ultimately, it comes down to that saying, you can only give to someone else, what you give to yourself, so those that provide a healthy self-love expect to be loved, those who believe in their abilities and develop them expect their efforts to be rewarded. Maybe that is why Aishwarya Rai has said, "I always knew I would be successful. So there was no element of surprise." This combination is not one for the faint hearted; they are quietly ambitious and are driven beyond anyone's comprehension. They have a strong will and are not easily intimidated, which unfortunately tends to draw negative comments from those who envy their success. Because, they tend to stick out for all the right and sometimes wrong reasons. Richard Burton said, "You may be as vicious about me as you please; you will only do me justice." And Aishwarya Rai said, "I'm amazed how many people feel good hitting out at me. They're welcome to do it." It only makes them reach for the next star.

Soul Mate:	Rat-Aquarius
Challenger:	Sheep-Taurus
Siblings:	Ox-Cancer, Ox-Pisces
Best Friends:	Snake-Cancer, Snake-Scorpio, Snake-Pisces, Rooster-Cancer, Rooster-Scorpio, Rooster-Pisces

Lee Strasberg
Vivien Leigh
Burt Lancaster
Hedy Lamarr
Albert Camus
Richard Burton
Rock Hudson
Robert Hardy
June Whitfield
Kader Khan
Nigel Havers
David Foster
Bonnie Raitt
Meg Ryan
Peter Jackson
Ralph Macchio
Dylan McDermott
k.d. lang
Randy Jackson
Aishwarya Rai Bachchan
Seth MacFarlane
Yunjin Kim
Nick Lachey
Asin

Ciara
Jack Osbourne
Wayne Rooney

OX – SAGITTARIUS

Chinese Name: NIU
Rank: 2ⁿᵈ
Hours Ruled: 1am – 3am
Direction: North
Season: Winter
Month: January
Western Zodiac Equivalent of Ox: Capricorn
Capricorn Western Element: Earth
Eastern Zodiac Equivalent of Sagittarius: Rat
Sagittarius Western Element: Fire
Numerology: 21 = 3

It's kind of fun to do the impossible.
– Walt Disney

When the Ox's tough terrain is charred from below by the magma belonging to Sagittarius, creating a finer substance, darker, more delicate and infinitely more fertile; however, the fruit that this soil which eventually nurture tend to take longer to grow. The Ox sign requires more time than most anyway, with this union, the cerebral mind and subconscious mind are given equal airplay, even though this creature might choose not to present such. Talking about his process as an actor, Jeff Bridges said, "When you start to engage with your creative processes, it shakes up all your impulses, and they all kind of inform one another." They do not like to be seen as "foolish" or have their reputation affected by any labels that they may deem detrimental, so they present whatever face is necessary in order to fit the environment, even though they may be so much more spiritually inclined than many may ever know. Jane Fonda has said, "When I start down a path that I know is the right path, I go with all of me."

Work is a big deal to the Ox-Sagittarius because it is how they prove to themselves and to the rest of the world of their value and therefore, their worthiness. Multi-talented Dick Van Dyke said, "I've retired so many times now it's getting to be a habit." Also, this combination is quite alpha, so they put everything they have into everything they do so that they do not feel inferior to anyone. Inevitably, the perfectionist syndrome arises here as it does so often with the earth heavy signs. Supermodel, performer and producer, Tyra Banks has said, "I'm a perfectionist. Sometimes I have to remind myself that it's OK if there are flaws here and there." Sometimes this seemingly endless pursuit of perfection can give them a reputation of being overly fussy or difficult. Director Ridley Scott has said, "Because I'm so experienced I need the very best people around me... I want the Earth. And I want the Earth in 10 minutes."

The men of this combination are typical Ox traditionalists. They are quite conservative in their outlook, belief system and in the way that they thing things should be carried out. A good example is when Walt Disney discussed how he ran his organization. Walt Disney said, "You know, every once in a while I just fire everybody, then I hire them back in a couple of weeks. That way they don't get too complacent. It keeps them on their toes." The Ox has a need to be seen as strong, in charge and in control, the centaur is easily influenced into taking the easy way out when it comes to handling other people, even if they are excruciatingly hard on themselves. This means that this combination will to and fro between these two modes driving themselves crazy while presenting an unpredictable and unstable personality even though that is precisely what they want to avoid. It is when they accept that they are who they are that they leave this unhelpful process behind. Dick Van Dyke said, "I've made peace with insecurity...because there is no security of any kind."

The women of this combination are constantly juggling their roles and struggle to define whom they actually are. Actually, it serves them exceptionally well to aspire to be like someone inspirational and model themselves upon that person. Through their journey to emulate that person, they soon find who they are whilst setting out to make a difference all of their own. Albeit with the same battle with insecurity throughout. Talking about her childhood, Amanda Seyfried said, "I felt so extremely ugly. When I look back, I was not ugly – I was cute, and had a gap in my teeth. But I wish I could have enjoyed that part of my life and be more confident." Although most Ox women have egos to rival the men of the same species, the women of this particular combination are more open and like to learn which bodes well, as they overcome bad habits that would otherwise hold them back quickly. Tyra Banks has said, "Self-love has very little to do with how you feel about your outer self. It's about accepting all of yourself. You've got to learn to accept the fool in you as well as the part that's got it goin' on." It is when they start down that road that the world begins to offer them the rewards that really bring joy into their lives.

Ultimately, the Ox-Sagittarius pushes boundaries and creates change. Walt Disney said, "I happen to be an inquisitive guy and when I see things I don't like, I start thinking why do they have to be like this and how can I improve them." Similarly, Tyra Banks said, "I have made it one of the missions of my life to redefine and to open up the small box of what beautiful is." Despite their shortcomings, how harsh they can be on themselves and through all of the ego-serving behavior, they are actually striving to do the best that they can. Opening themselves to positive influences, to new ideas and adopting a meditative pursuit helps them immensely to reconnect to their inner child. Whatever they can do to foster that connection is exactly when they need to succeed and enjoy life. This Ox usually does find its way to happiness. As Jane Fonda has said, "It's never too late – never too late to start over, never too late to be happy."

Soul Mate:	Rat-Capricorn
Challenger:	Sheep-Gemini
Siblings:	Ox-Aries, Ox-Leo
Best Friends:	Snake-Aries, Snake-Leo, Snake-Sagittarius, Rooster-Aries, Rooster-Leo, Rooster-Sagittarius

Walt Disney
Dick Van Dyke
Sammy Davis Jr.
Ridley Scott
Jane Fonda
Robin Gibb
Maurice Gibb
Bill Nighy
Jeff Bridges
Don Johnson
Rajnikanth
Shane Black
Angie Stone
Tadanobu Asano
Peter Facinelli
Tyra Banks
Kaley Cuoco
Amanda Seyfried
Frankie Muniz
Raven-Symoné

OX – CAPRICORN

Chinese Name: NIU
Rank: 2nd
Hours Ruled: 1am – 3am
Direction: North
Season: Winter
Month: January
Western Zodiac Equivalent of Ox: Capricorn
Capricorn Western Element: Earth
Eastern Zodiac Equivalent of Capricorn: Ox
Capricorn Western Element: Earth
Numerology: 22 = 4

Once you accept the fact that there's nothing to fear, you drill into the primal oil well. I believe when we do things without fear, we can do anything. As long as you don't worry about the consequences.

– Anthony Hopkins

As the Ox's fertile earth is the same as Capricorn's, its strength, power and force is magnified. The obvious assumption would be that the double Ox combination would become even more rigid, but no. This combination manages to keep the Ox's powerful presence but loses some of its need to control its external world. The Ox-Capricorn has a more pronounced spiritual dimension than other Ox combinations and knows how to surrender its will to the universe. This is why so many Ox-Capricorns work in spiritual, new age metaphysics or avant-garde environments rather than the traditional services that most Oxen are to be found in. Jim Carrey has said, "With the power of the sub-conscious mind I can learn how to do anything...I could...learn how to dance, or, yodel like an Austrian."

Wearing the face of a clown, they absorb criticisms or knocks straight into their blood stream, rather than point the finger at someone else, they will point it at themselves, bypassing half of the usual Ox sign process of blaming, shaming and justifying, instead, they head straight for the masochistic self-attack. That is why this Ox occasionally finds itself with the rest of the Ox's in the depressive club. Jim Carrey has said, "I'm charming, but I dip into the Prozac now and then."

If there's one thing that annoys the Ox-Capricorn more than anything else is when people absolve themselves of responsibility for their lot in life; whining, whimpering and wallowing is enough to make them run away in despair. Ironically, they have a noted tendency for similar such behavior themselves, maybe that is why they do it in private or with very close friends where they will not be judged. Anthony Hopkins has said, "Beware the tyranny of the weak. They just suck you dry. They're always complaining. I go, "How are you doing?" They say "Ahh…" and they moan and try to take from you. I know a number of people like that, but I can't waste my time on them." Similarly, Marlene Dietrich has said, "The weak are more likely to make the strong weak than the strong are likely to make the weak strong."

The men of this combination tend to arrive into this world with some sort of visible Achilles heel which they feel an overwhelming compulsion to overcompensate for. Their external softness belies their determination. Being unable to run from the unconventional label for whatever reason, they may develop complicated personalities fighting their desire to fit in whilst knowing they never will. This is why they look for answers in places most Ox men do not. So without becoming "people pleasers" as such, they find creative ways to get the affirmation or adulation whilst being able to maintain the distance their fragile sensibilities need to feel comfortable. Jim Carrey has said, "I tend to stay up late, not because I'm partying but because it's the only time of day when I'm alone and I don't have to be on, performing." Similarly, Anthony Hopkins has said, "I don't have many friends; I'm very much a loner. As a child I was very isolated and I've never been really close to anyone. Ask nothing, expect nothing. That's my creed. We're all just a bunch of sinners crashing around in the darkness."

The Ox-Capricorn women, like most Ox combinations are tough, no nonsense types that set high standards for themselves to live up to. This combination is much like the Empress card of the Tarot; the fertile and creative earth mother that is full of love, understanding and compassion for all of humanity. But her love is not submissive, it is forcefully potent that demands that you throw yourself into the deep end to explore your depths. This is what she facilitates. Ox-Capricorn women expect you to be self-sufficient and support that without being enablers. Victoria Principal has said, "Maybe my greatest fear in life is not to be challenged, is to grow weary of life, and not to be passionate about it."

There is something hyper-rational about the way Ox-Capricorn women conduct their business; they make initial logical choices then let their intuition guide them through the ensuing maze until they reach their goal. Kate Moss has said, "People think your success is just a matter of having a pretty face. But it's easy to be chewed up and spat out. You've got to stay ahead of the game to be able to stay in it."

Overflowing with passion, they have an eagerness to get started with life so many do not have the patience for conventional education. Kate Moss has said, "I kind of lost interest in school. I was never academic." Similarly, Anthony Hopkins said, "I was lousy in school. Real screwed-up. A moron. I was antisocial and didn't bother with the other kids." This does not mean they do not have the capacity for academia; the Ox excels in most environments. But because of the spiritual guidance that this combination receives early on, they have an overpowering desire to chase down their dream in the most practical way. After the initial second-guessing and worthiness debate has passed, they are off. And although most Oxen are slow-paced, this Ox is part cheetah. In fact sometimes their speed is the cause of some considerable issues. When asked what his life motto was, Jim Carrey said, "Always turn your wheel in the direction of the skid." Despite their hang-ups, emotional instability and perceived loner-dom, they are well rounded, inspirational and full of heart.

Soul Mate:	Rat-Sagittarius
Challenger:	Sheep-Cancer
Siblings:	Ox-Taurus, Ox-Virgo
Best Friends:	Snake-Taurus, Snake-Virgo, Snake-Capricorn, Rooster-Taurus, Rooster-Virgo, Rooster-Capricorn

Jim Carrey
Anthony Hopkins
Gemma Arterton
Beth Behrs
Kevin Durand
Charlyne Yi
Sissy Spacek
Natassia Malthe
Hrithik Roshan
Jason Behr
Marlene Dietrich
Victoria Principal
Barbara Steele
Kate Moss
Deepika Padukone
Debbie Allen

Wilson Cruz
Devon Odessa
Stephenie Meyer
Deepa Mehta
Johnny Lever

OX – AQUARIUS

Chinese Name: NIU
Rank: 2nd
Hours Ruled: 1am – 3am
Direction: North
Season: Winter
Month: January
Western Zodiac Equivalent of Ox: Capricorn
Capricorn Western Element: Earth
Eastern Zodiac Equivalent of Aquarius: Tiger
Aquarius Western Element: Air
Numerology: 23 = 5

A man can only be judged by his actions, and not by his good intentions or his beliefs.
– Paul **Newman**

When the Ox's tough terrain meets with Aquarius's quiet hurricane, many interesting things happen; the Ox's strong will is channeled by Aquarius's noble intentions; the Ox's work ethic is directed by Aquarius's supernatural wisdom and most importantly, the Ox learns how to observe its emotions in a detached way without taking everything personally. This means that we get an Ox without so much of the self-importance, but rather one that wants to use its presence and power to influence positive change in all of the areas where this person is involved. Democracy and freedom for all is more important to this Ox than just getting compliance form the "little people." As with most Aquarian combinations, learning, development and leading by example are the way this noble creature rules. That being said, it is important to remember that this is still an Ox sign, with an Ox ego.

The childhood pattern for this combination is one of excelling beyond that of their peers and them being somewhat ostracized for it. Although, no one thing comes to them as second nature, their gift is their mental flexibility and capacity for hard work. Paul Newman said, "I had no natural gift to be anything – not an athlete, not an actor, not a writer, not a director, a painter of garden porches – not anything. So I've worked really hard, because nothing ever came easily to me." Similarly, Peter Gabriel said, "I'm not a good keyboard player, and I'm even worse on the guitar. In fact, I'm a terrible musician! But I do think that I can find disparate elements and put them together in a way that's different to other people." Of course, there is a little bit of that endearing Ox humility there also, but astrologically speaking, this combination's gift is the learning, the absorbing of information and effective consolidation of it beyond anything else.

The men of this combination have that quiet yet powerful presence that most Ox men come with, but with a more approachable nature. One might feel more able to question this Ox male's decisions to his face and he is likely to consider the comments because being right is not as important as doing good. This Ox man just thinks differently to his other Ox brothers. He is open enough not to make his career all consuming and consider other options. As Peter Gabriel has said, "I've not been bored but then I've also made decisions to have an interesting life rather than trying to maintain a successful career. And they are slightly different paths." This man is in tune with his spirit and his inner child and that is why he is so fun and alive. His sensitivity is clearly visible even though he tries to hide it and he feels a huge responsibility to make sure everybody around him is uplifted. Jack Lemmon has said, "The worst part about being me is when people want me to make them laugh."

The women of this combination know how to make use of the Ox-Aquarius energy to its maximum. It suits the female form; all of the spark, pizazz and emotional intelligence just makes more sense coming from a woman. Unfortunately, for these gifts, the Ox-Aquarius lady is often the victim of jealousy from those less open and not as capable. They often have a hard shell to protect themselves when they need to or they will just cut off from everyone and everything until they are strong enough to come back out again. They are not being rude even if it seems like they are: it is self-protection. Like their male counterparts, they have a huge sense of responsibility to be who they are expected to be to fulfil their perceived set of duties, whatever form that may take. Morgan Fairchild has said, "They're not paying me to play a chairwoman. They're paying me to show up looking glam and, damn it, I'm gonna show up looking glam!" However, because these women are more likely to be in sync with their higher selves, they tend not to make sacrifices that they regret later too often as they learn their lessons well.

Ultimately, members of this combination strive to remain open to all things so that they can stay on the edge of the new waves or trends that hit, not because they are interested in fashion or being "hip", it is more so that they can gain an insight into the next generation, because in doing so, they can extend the childhood of their own inner child. This is how they maintain their childlike zest for life, which often extends even into their elderly years. This is perhaps the most open and forward-looking Ox combination of all 12. With Aquarius in the mix, it is also the most idealistic. As Peter Gabriel has said, "I think that anyone who doesn't have some sense of idealism when they're young is really missing out a bit of their humanity, because you have the chance to go into the world and feel, quite rightly, that it is soon going to be yours and you can change it." Giving back is hugely important to them and as they find their way to contribute, the universe rewards them. The Ox-Aquarius comes in many forms and some of them can be prickly, but if you judge them by their actions and most importantly, their results, you will see that this is an inspirational breed: Paul Newman said, "I'm not running for sainthood. I just happen to think that in life we need to be a little like the farmer, who puts back into the soil what he takes out."

Soul Mate: Rat-Scorpio
Challenger: Sheep-Leo
Siblings: Ox-Gemini, Ox-Libra
Best Friends: Snake-Gemini, Snake-Libra, Snake-Aquarius, Rooster-Gemini, Rooster-Libra, Rooster-Aquarius

Chloë Grace Moretz
Dane Dehaan
Victor Webster
Roberta Flack
Paul Newman
Jack Lemmon
Mischa Barton
Clint Black
Richard Dean Anderson
Morgan Fairchild
Linda Bassett
Peter Gabriel
Natalie Cole
Michael Attenborough
Billy Ocean
Derek Acorah
Peter Beard
Etta James
Patricia Neal
Leslie Nielsen

OX – PISCES

Chinese Name: NIU
Rank: 2nd
Hours Ruled: 1am – 3am
Direction: North
Season: Winter
Month: January
Western Zodiac Equivalent of Ox: Capricorn
Capricorn Western Element: Earth
Eastern Zodiac Equivalent of Pisces: Rabbit
Pisces Western Element: Water
Numerology: 24 = 6

Good luck happens to people who work hard for it.
– Patrick Duffy

When the Ox's tough terrain meets the potency of Pisces's water, we get a lively character endowed with exceptional creative abilities. But there is an interesting disconnect within here that causes friction and problems for this native. Pisces wants to listen to its creative intuition and head down more ethereal paths whereas the Ox absolutely forbids that sort of wishy-washiness and wants them to apply their innate discipline to something that will reap tangible results. It's a right brain versus left brain fight for dominance. Kellan Lutz said, "I worked my butt off in high school and received a lot of scholarships for college and to throw all that away for acting was tough for my family…" The Ox's military nature steps up here and eventually takes the lead collecting Pisces's creative elements, assembling them together and forcing them to work out every day to get even better as they age. Robert Altman said, "Retirement? You're talking about death, right?" They may end up in creative environments, but if they, the Ox will ensure that they will work harder than anyone else in order to have broader skillset, better machine and greater impact so that success will be forthcoming and any competition intimidated from the start. Patrick Duffy said, "I miss regular television. I miss the work ethic of those 5 day a week things."

Once the defining vision has been set, the execution is easy. Work is paint by numbers and there is nothing that intimidates them because under the banner of professional activity, any action can be justified. They are great at networking, attracting attention and causing a commotion. Not just because of their physical attributes but because of their lively personalities and sense of fun. Kellan Lutz said, "I love life way too much and find fun in almost anything. I'm a chameleon." This changeability stems from requiring affirmation from without. They may claim that they do not need anybody's approval, but their moods fluctuate depending on where their reputation sits along the popularity scale. Emile Hirsch said, "I think I've always been half out of my shell and half in. Sometimes I can be extremely wild and sometimes I can be extremely shy. It just depends on the day."

The men of this combination have a need to project themselves in a very masculine way, even though they may not be in particularly macho in personality, they often build their body's muscular structure to look like they are. This need to project strength comes from an internal insecurity about their own self-worth. They often think that by channeling all their time into such projections or by working all of the hours available, that their value might increase in the eyes of others, then hopefully in themselves. Kellan Lutz has said, "With my feelings, I hold a lot in, because I didn't always have boundaries and people would take advantage of situations because I'm a nice guy." Of course, it would be better for them to express who they really are without projecting layers of protective defense. In time, they get there, but the Ox needs to believe in its own constructed greatness. But sometimes does so neglecting its actual greatness. Ox-Piscean men are better at the game of finding love than actually being in a relationship. They often perceive heightened emotions as weakness and try to convince themselves of their own invincibility. Love is a real block in the road to that, so they don't really know how to navigate such terrain. The truth of the matter is, they are absolute suckers when it comes to love. Robert Altman has said, "Wisdom and love have nothing to do with one another. Wisdom is staying alive, survival. You're wise if you don't stick your finger in the light plug. Love – you'll stick your finger in anything."

There are many dainty beauties of this combination who are tough and seemingly born with a sense of entitlement. They know how to use their special talents to get what they want and they often do. However, they have a tendency to squeeze their associates to bursting point and often times, the good will runs out. As Ivana Trump said, "Don't get mad, get everything!" Although they are primarily self-focused, they have a humility that has them extend a hand to all that might need their help. As long as it is not financial help, their purses belong to themselves. Like most Ox signs, they have a mind for facts and figures and could astound people with their mental acuity. Dawn Rae Chong said, "I have a good mind but I don't like to bore anyone with it." They are experts in that which interests them, but their deep well of knowledge allows them to speak with confidence about subjects that influential others are interested in. Ivana Trump said, "For example, if I make money, I put it in real estate. I always did very well. Location, location, location... I'll take real estate rather than go to Wall Street and get 2.8 percent. Forget about it."

Ultimately, the Ox-Pisces journey is one of accepting the frailties of the human species and recognizing that they too belong to that race. With expectations that would bring anyone else to their knees, they continue to demand greater and greater results from an increasingly aging body and they do not know when to quit. Learning to be kinder and more compassionate with themselves is a good starting point and allows them to genuinely relax rather than presenting a chilled out persona for effect. When they access their inner power and find true self-acceptance, their life seems to change overnight. Camryn Manheim has said, "You can either destroy your spirit or you can accept and love yourself just the way you are." They often go through periods where they shed entire groups of people and find entire new groups. At the end of the day, the overpowering Ox condition wins out choosing to go it alone and rely on the left-brain activity the majority of the time even though they are so creatively gifted. Independence is paramount to the detriment of all else. Robert Altman said, "I'll give you the same advice I give my children: Never take advice from anybody."

Soul Mate:	Rat-Libra
Challenger:	Sheep-Virgo
Siblings:	Ox-Cancer, Ox-Scorpio
Best Friends:	Snake-Cancer, Snake-Scorpio, Snake-Pisces, Rooster-Cancer, Rooster-Scorpio, Rooster-Pisces

Nikki Lauder
Ivana Trump
Victor Garber
Levi Strauss
George Frederic Handel
Kellan Lutz
Emile Hirsch
Isabelle Fuhrman
Shiloh Fernandez

Elias Koteas
Len Wiseman
Eva Amurri
Victor Garber
Jack Davenport
Titus Welliver
Scott Michael Foster
Rae Dawn Chong
Bingbing Li
Zach Roerig
Nathalie Kelley
Boris Kodjoe
Penny Johnson
Tim Kang
Jane March
Uriah Shelton
Steven Weber
Sam Peckinpah
Robert Altman
Gates McFadden
Christopher Atkins
Patrick Duffy
Matthew Marsden
Camryn Manheim

THE TIGER

THE TIGER

I am passion personified with more confidence than I can keep up with. Curiosity has nearly killed me a million times, but I'm quick on my paws and love the thrill of the game. Calm on the surface, a storm on the inside; nobody understands the enigma that I am. I feel so much, I care so much, but I need my freedom even more! Wealth, status or fame, rarely impress me as these cat-eyes see bullshit for bullshit. Earn my respect, give me the truth and I'll infuse you with my energy, a rush of a trillion stars that flow from my veins into yours. I can fuel you when you're depleted, I can excite you when drabness threatens: my aliveness revives even the dead. As a feral cat, expect the unexpected, but also know that what I really want is to be tamed... actually, I'll never be tamed but I'll let you think I am. I'm the impulsive, independent, improviser; the lone warrior, I trust myself and myself alone, even if I love you, I'll always be alone in my Tiger-ness, you wouldn't understand.

I am the Tiger.

Highly attractive and highly sexed with a massive need for attention. You strut about wearing the face of an all powerful predator yet in private, you suffer with extreme insecurity. Extroverted and captivating, you know how to allure your prey. Moving from one self-induced drama to the next, you spend your time in the midst of activity. You never stop, even when you should, but lucky for you, you have an abundance of energy to call upon. You also hold strong social and political beliefs for which you're not afraid to fight. Tigers have big, bold audacious personalities, even the quieter ones and like adrenaline pumping activities. Interestingly, many tigers have a severe fear of growing old and of death.

Careerwise, Tigers prefer to be independent of hierarchies and seek autonomy in their work life. They usually try to fit into corporate environments until that first sacrifice of their integrity, which shocks their stripes right off them. Then when the politics and backstabbing start, the Tiger ducks and dives for a bit until their intentions are misconstrued, work is ignored and honesty is taken advantage of. Then they're off. And they often choose to commit to their creative occupations, they commonly work as/in; musicians (often rock and folk), singer-songwriters, lawyers, sports, teachers, journalists, PR workers, military positions, and jobs within science and technology.

Compatibilities

Soul Mate:	Boar
Challenger:	Monkey
Best Friends:	Horse & Dog
Good Relations:	Rabbit & Sheep

TIGER – ARIES

Chinese Name: HU
Rank: 3rd
Hours Ruled: 3am – 5am
Direction: East – Northeast
Season: Winter
Month: February
Western Zodiac Equivalent of Tiger: Aquarius
Aquarius Western Element: Air
Eastern Zodiac Equivalent of Aries: Dragon
Aries Western Element: Fire
Numerology: 25 = 7

Failure has a thousand explanations. Success doesn't need one.

– Alec Guiness

The Tiger's whirlwind meets Aries's raging fire to create a dramatic personality wearing its heart on its sleeve but locking the rest of the world in a cage to keep this precious heart protected somehow. Even though this is not possible, the Tiger-Aries simply cannot imagine locking themselves in a cage to keep themselves guarded, no, they have far too much life to live, but they are aware of their own vulnerable sensitivities so they'll attempt to claw the world into submission instead. But with the Tiger-Aries personality, the world enjoys every second of it. Jann Arden has said, "To not think of dying, is to not think of living."

First and foremost, this is a very honest combination. Yet, despite a strong desire to remain grounded, they allow the events of the external world to whip them up into a variety of frenzies that their friends and loved one's hear about. They often need to be calmed down and helped to return to a place of balance. They know what is happening, they can explain the psychological workings of the people involved along with their intentions, yet still their emotional reaction remains heightened. Some may suspect that this is typical Tiger attention seeking, but it is not. They just feel so intensely that their emotional-irrational adrenaline releasing functions cannot be over-ridden by their mental processes.

There is also a strange relationship with what they perceive as "flamboyancy." Whether they like it or not, there is something a little flamboyant about them; some accept it openly, Lady Gaga and Hugh Hefner, whereas others try to distance themselves. Alec Guiness said, "Flamboyance doesn't suit me. I enjoy being elusive." One does not necessarily negate the other. When they accept their naturally colourful nature, they tend to find authentic connection with their true inner diva.

Like many of the Tiger combinations, they can be obsessive perfectionists but do not want this to be known, instead they like to present that everything they do comes easily and naturally. In all actuality, they have organized, plotted and planned every aspect of their act. But the world doesn't mind; it's a great show.

Tiger-Aries people have a fantastic ability to create worlds and draw people into them. Lady Gaga and Hugh Hefner are two examples of people who have this talent. Many are drawn to jobs where they are in charge of setting the parameters of the working environment. Being so emotionally led, they understand how to tug at other's heart strings also.

The men of this combination are driven, hardworking yet ostentatious. Hugh Hefner has said, "If there was going to be a sexual revolution, I would be its pamphleteer." Usually, the men feel like stolid dorks on the inside, so they spend much of their time pursuing more exciting activities in the external world. Spending more time looking at who they actually are and how well this matches up to the image they actually would like to be, tends to be helpful. Being as honest as they are, they are not afraid of sharing their opinions, even if they may be deemed as controversial.

The women of this combination may be innocent looking yet hugely audacious. They might not have felt like the prettiest girl during childhood so they are determined to make up for it. Victoria Beckham and Lady Gaga both have said they struggled with their weight when they were younger. Maybe this is why they strive to support everyone to find their true beauty, to do whatever they have to in order to feel beautiful in every way. Lady Gaga has said, "Be yourself and love who you are and be proud. Because you were born this way, baby." She has also advised, "First thing in the morning, try to think compassionate thoughts about yourself for five minutes. I don't always do it, but I try to." Natural performers, these women know how to captivate their prey. It was Victoria Beckham who chased down her hubby-to-be David Beckham (Rabbit-Taurus) in a very calculated way; she attended the soccer (football) match with the sole goal to attract his attention and asked him out.

Sexual liberation is an interesting concept for them also. Hugh Hefner has said, "The major civilizing force in the world is not religion, it's sex... The part of the women's movement that was anti-sexual was ill-conceived." Lady Gaga has said, "In my opinion, the last thing a young woman needs is another picture of a sexy pop star writhing in sand, covered in grease, touching herself." Yet, Jenna Jameson is also a Tiger Aries born on the same day as Hugh Hefner, 9th April 1974, she has said, "I try my hardest to push the point that I am a feminist. I really think it's important that people know that the women in this industry are empowered. They run it, man. It's awesome." Three different views of sex, yet all three of them claim sexual empowerment. It's very Tiger-Aries!

This particular brand of Tiger is especially emotion-led and loves to be this way despite what they say. Alyson Hannigan has said, "You need to suffer to be interesting." The Tiger Aries artist lives for these experiences so that they can draw from them honestly and with detailed precision. Being of the brave variety, they would rather make the mistake than regret anything. They push boundaries and dare more than most, yet still they feel like they haven't done enough. Alec Guiness said, "I have only one great regret – that I never dared enough. If at all." If they do not get the support they require from the powers that be, they will just go out there and create their dreams by themselves. Lady Gaga has said, "If I have any advice to anybody, it's to just do it yourself, and don't waste time trying to get a favor."

Soul Mate:	Boar-Virgo
Challenger:	Monkey-Libra
Siblings:	Tiger-Leo, Tiger-Sagittarius
Best Friends:	Horse-Aries, Horse-Leo, Horse-Sagittarius, Dog-Aries, Dog-Leo, Dog-Sagittarius

Jann Arden
Elle Fanning
Alyson Hannigan
Amanda Bynes
Leighton Meester
Matthew Broderick
Tricia Helfer
Marley Shelton
Peyton List
Alec Guinness
Jenna Jameson
Lady Gaga
Martin Short
Clark Gregg
Claudia Cardinale

William Sadler
Edgar Wright
Marcia Cross
Rosie O'Donnell
Hugh M. Hefner
Victoria Beckham
David Cassidy
Agnetha Fältskog

TIGER – TAURUS

Chinese Name: HU
Rank: 3ʳᵈ
Hours Ruled: 3am – 5am
Direction: East – Northeast
Season: Winter
Month: February
Western Zodiac Equivalent of Tiger: Aquarius
Aquarius Western Element: Air
Eastern Zodiac Equivalent of Taurus: Snake
Taurus Western Element: Earth
Numerology: 26 = 8

Just because a man lacks the use of his eyes doesn't mean he lacks vision.

– Stevie Wonder

When the Tiger's tornado meets the Taurean's tough earth, it creates a personality that is unapologetic in being who it is. The Taurus allows the Tiger to run wild and do so with abandon so people with this combination are naturally uninhibited and it is a beautiful thing to observe. However, it can also be quite threatening to family structures, organized religions or such similar groups where too much freedom or sexual expression requires reining in. A Tiger's nature can never be contained for long and when it breaks free, guilt, shame and all manner of unhelpful emotions can cause them to jump back and forth from wildness to over-civilized-mildness until they recognize the socialized conditioning for what it is and eventually strike a healthier balance. Then they can run wild with control – it sounds like a paradox but Tiger people will understand. Queen Elizabeth II has said, "It's all to do with the training: you can do a lot if you're properly trained."

The life path that this Tiger seems to be on is one of moderation, finding the mid-point, striking a healthy balance and making the most of itself responsibly. That may mean tempering the extremes of this personality at times, but it most definitely does not mean destroying any trace of the wildness altogether. Firstly, that is not possible and secondly, it is this wildness that makes them so magnetically attractive in the first place. What the moderation does is slows them down so that they can see more than before which expands their understanding, opening them up to a broader perspective which is then reflected in their world view. Emilio Estevez said, "Spiritually, we're all on a path. I haven't declared or defined myself because as soon as you declare yourself you're identifying with a certain dogma." This is an important lesson for this combination: remain open-minded so that you can access everyone and avoid letting your current opinions cloud your future opinions. Just listen without judgment to see how your gut responds to the stimulus. When these Tigers do just this, their potential becomes limitless. As Stevie Wonder said, "Ability may get you to the top, but it takes character to keep you there."

The wild beast requires expression of course, in fact, the Tiger-Taurus is here to share its wildness that makes everyone go weak in the groin. They are effortlessly attractive and as sexual beings are in their element. Megan Fox has said, "I'm just really confident sexually, and I think that sort of oozes out of my pores. It's just there. It's something I don't have to turn on." Most Tigers have this. But when Taurus lends its earthy confidence to this marriage, its power is multiplied. There is no denying, the Tiger-Taurus is HOT! That being said, their hygienic habits often leave a lot to be desired. Robert Pattinson said, "I have so much residue crap in my hair from years and years of not washing it and not having any sense of personal hygiene whatsoever." Interestingly, some head in the opposite direction of the spectrum; OCD is also common with this combination.

The men of this combination seem somewhat tamer than the ladies. Their manner and language is often quite suggestive and they rarely attempt to conceal their naughty intentions. They are known for using their humor to get themselves out of holes that they have behaved themselves into. As Jay Leno said, "You can't stay mad at somebody who makes you laugh." They do need to be cautious that they do not push people too far too often because the Tiger-Taurus mope when all is lost and gone, can go on for a long time. They like to live life on the edge so that they can experience all of the highs and lows as viscerally as possible because, like all Tigers, it is the only way they feel alive. Emilio Estevez has said, "We need to risk, we need to dare to risk and fail greatly because that's the only way we grow."

The women of this combination are sexy, flirty and are not afraid to say what they think. They can be both the playful kitty cat and the wild tigress depending on her mood but it is wise to get her in the right mode for the appropriate setting. Despite their strength and naturally feral side, they have a strong need for family and comfort. Traditions, ceremonies and fairy tales are not as important as real emotional connection. Penelope Cruz said, "I don't know if I believe in marriage. I believe in family, love and children." Much of their strength, power and firmness comes from a place of defense as the Tiger-Taurus needs more time to think things over. You may find that she might change her mind altogether about something once she has had some time to really get her head around a proposition but press her immediately and you'll get a "NO!" As Megan Fox has said, "I'm self-loathing, introverted, and neurotic." This feline requires space, non-judgment and genuine affection so that she feels free to reveal her inner most secrets, which she really wants to do.

Ultimately, this combination seeks creative expression without judgment. They want to use their artistic sensibilities to capture moments of beauty and share them. They also want to share themselves as much as they can. With the over-developed custodian sense of justice that they have, they also want to serve and protect, open eyes to injustices and open minds. They must go through their own transformations before they influence others so they set off on their journeys early. As mentioned previously, their journey is one of moderation, learning to strike a healthy balance and not caring what other people think. Stevie Wonder has said, "You can't base your life on other people's expectations."

Soul Mate:	Boar-Leo
Challenger:	Monkey-Scorpio
Siblings:	Tiger-Virgo, Tiger-Capricorn
Best Friends:	Horse-Taurus, Horse-Virgo, Horse-Capricorn,
	Dog-Taurus, Dog-Virgo, Dog-Capricorn

Queen Elizabeth II
Emilio Estevez
Penélope Cruz
Stevie Wonder
Robert Pattinson
Megan Fox
Breckin Meyer
Sendhil Ramamurthy
Derek Luke
Gabriel Byrne
Jay Leno
John Hannah
Dianna Agron
Danny Huston
Lynden David Hall
Andrea Corr
Craig Ferguson

Jeremy Paxman
Buck Taylor
Eric Morecambe
David Attenborough
Don Rickles
Cloris Leachman
B.R. Chopra
Tyrone Power
Robert J. Wilke
Amber Heard

TIGER – GEMINI

Chinese Name: HU
Rank: 3rd
Hours Ruled: 3am – 5am
Direction: East – Northeast
Season: Winter
Month: February
Western Zodiac Equivalent of Tiger: Aquarius
Aquarius Western Element: Air
Eastern Zodiac Equivalent of Gemini: Horse
Gemini Western Element: Air
Numerology: 27 = 9

Everyone's a star and deserves the right to twinkle.
– Marilyn Monroe

When the Tiger's tempest meets Gemini's inconstant cyclone it creates a personality that tends to live in the clouds. They have high expectations of themselves and of others even though they are unlikely directly to impose their views. They are too polite. But that does not mean that they do not think it. They have a winner's mentality and are happy to go out and make their dreams a reality regardless of how seemingly impossible. In fact, on some level they get a real kick out of it: the more difficult the better. Bring it on! Paula Abdul has said, "When you wish upon a star, you just might become one."

With so much air in this combination, they are hugely impacted by their inner urges and lead with their instincts. Through their absorption of the life around them they are powerfully drawn to certain environments or activities and without much thought, they will find themselves getting involved. They think on a subject, obsess about it, let their subconscious receive their ultimate goal and then they watch it manifest in tangible reality. This combination does this quite naturally when they are not in self-doubt mode. Talking about lacking worthiness Shia LaBeouf has said, "I have no idea where this insecurity comes from, but it's a God-sized hole. If I knew, I'd fill it, and I'd be on my way." That being said, they do have a good grasp of their functioning and as has been said, the first step towards change is self-awareness. Alanis Morrisette has said, "I was motivated by just thinking that if you had all this external success that everyone would love you and everything would be peaceful and wonderful."

Letting the instinct lead, their internal observer kind of tags along after them, like a kite on a string taking everything in from a higher vantage point. Their need to please and feel special may have them temper the full force of their personalities until someone takes their good humor for granted; that is when the Tiger fangs really come out. Yes the Gemini is a social creature and the Tiger also flourishes amidst groups of people but there is also this aspect of the Tiger that always wants what it doesn't have. Even with all of their self-awareness, staying in the moment to experience the happiness that they have managed to manifest is not an easy thing for them to do. They mistakenly think that physical achievement will improve their sense of self-esteem and although it may do so temporarily, the effects are rarely permanent. Marilyn Monroe said, "To put it bluntly, I seem to have a whole superstructure with no foundation. But I'm working on the foundation."

The men of this combination are unconventional in many respects, they may not be typically attractive but their winning spirit is exceptionally so. Their inner power is palpable and they are often recipients of special awards or honors at a considerably young age. That may be enough for some, but not for the Tiger-Gemini. They might not even be satisfied if they toppled Zeus. Wanting to feel like they are constantly pushing the boundaries, constantly improving, forever growing, they will not settle for mediocrity in anyway. Miles Davis said, "I know what I've done for music, but don't call me a legend... A legend is an old man with a cane known for what he used to do. I'm still doing it." Maybe Miles knew there was more juice in him?

The women of this combination tend to be delicate and delicious on the outside and a tad feral on the inside. They are always hungry for sensual feasts and want to taste everything that is out there. This balance tends to make them very attractive sexually, but can leave them sour that they are not as respected for their other qualities. So they may go to an extreme to project them. Marilyn Monroe said, "I'm selfish, impatient, and a little insecure. I make mistakes, I'm out of control, and at times hard to handle. But if you can't handle me at my worst, then you sure as hell don't deserve me at my best." Similarly, Alanis Morissette said, "When I was producing on my own, I was doing it in order to – in a very patriarchal entertainment industry, let alone planet – very much hell-bent on trying to prove to myself, if nothing else, that I could do it as a woman."

The Tiger-Gemini is perhaps the biggest dreamer of all. Marilyn Monroe has said, "I used to think as I looked at the Hollywood night, '"There must be thousands of girls sitting alone like me, dreaming of becoming a movie star. But I'm not going to worry about them. I'm dreaming the hardest." It is a very apt quote actually as they have very vivid visions of what they want to create because of what they might describe as deprivation. This is not deprivation in the common sense, but more of a relative deprivation; they weren't perceived or loved as much as their friends or siblings, or got the same amount of love or attention or whatever it is. Yet they have bucket loads of ambitions and desires that they feel will get them the adulation their ego craves but because the only person they can rely on is themselves, they will set out as an army of one to get them met. Shia LeBeouf said, "I like to think of myself as an ordinary man with extra ordinary determination. That's it."

Soul Mate:	Boar-Cancer
Challenger:	Monkey-Sagittarius
Siblings:	Tiger-Libra, Tiger-Aquarius
Best Friends:	Horse-Gemini, Horse-Libra, Horse-Aquarius, Dog-Gemini, Dog-Libra, Dog-Aquarius

Marilyn Monroe
Andy Griffith
Miles Davis
Tommy Chong
Raymond Carver
Kathy Baker
Ally Sheedy
Gina Gershon
Arnold Vosloo
Paula Abdul
Fairuza Balk
Steve-O
Bear Grylls
Alanis Morissette
Denise Van Outen
Kat Dennings
Shia LaBeouf
Mary-Kate Olsen
Ashley Olsen
Rafael Nadal

TIGER – CANCER

Chinese Name: HU
Rank: 3rd
Hours Ruled: 3am – 5am
Direction: East – Northeast
Season: Winter
Month: February
Western Zodiac Equivalent of Tiger: Aquarius
Aquarius Western Element: Air
Eastern Zodiac Equivalent of Cancer: Sheep
Cancer Western Element: Water
Numerology: 28 = 1

I don't really keep counsel with others. I'm the kind of person who will think about something, and if I know it's right I'm not going to ask anybody... I've made every decision for myself – in my career, in my life.
– Tom Cruise

When the Tiger's tempest meets Cancer's deep water, the result is a driven, humble and self-sufficient creature. With enough self-assurance to go it alone, they take risks and work ridiculously hard to ensure that their risks work out. And they usually do. Business is first on their minds, sex is second. Of course family is very important but with an ego that needs constant feeding, self-preservation, elevation and freedom are prerequisites required to provide them with enough comfort before they set off to start a family that they can serve. On the surface, it may look selfish but it is anything but; if you do not give to yourself first, what will you have to give? In fact they are highly likely to be philanthropists. Their moral code is well developed much like all Tigers but with Cancer blended in, they are also leaders, albeit of the shy variety. Embarrassed by their desire to want to lead and often questioning their validity, they procrastinate making decisions that they will ultimately make anyway. Let's save everybody some time. Yes, you are a leader, Yes, you will lead for the betterment of all you serve and making that unconventional choice may make you seem strange, but you know it is the right road for you to take so take it! Tom Cruise said, "I always tell young actors to take charge. It's not that hard. Sign your own checks, be responsible."

Quiet on the surface with an overpowering protective energy. As a loved one of a Tiger-Cancer, there is a sense that they would fight tooth and nail for you and for what is right. As the first of the three humanitarian signs of the Chinese horoscope (Tiger, Horse, and Dog) their sense of justice is well-developed and many are drawn towards jobs within law and law enforcement. Attorney General, Janet Reno said, "Until the day I die, or until the day I can't think anymore, I want to be involved in the issues that I care about." Many Tiger-Cancerians receive inner promptings to direct them towards jobs that will really fulfill them and serve the rest of the world too, but they have trouble accepting that such big things were meant for them so they remain in menial jobs, living a half-life on the surface, whilst living fully in the realm of their powerful imagination. Once they get their excuses out of the way and build up their self-esteem enough, taking the plunge pays off in so many ways. As Lindsay Lohan said, "Life is full of risks anyway; why not take them?"

The men of this combination are very straightforward and have a low tolerance of bullshit. They have a raw sexuality and the more they use it, the more potent it becomes. It is their adventurous, daring spirit that is the most appealing thing about them. When in alignment, they make a decision and act on it knowing they can handle whatever consequences arise. They also feel a deep responsibility to those who depend or look up to them in some way. They hate letting people down and sometimes set impossible expectations for themselves. Joel Edgerton said, "I just want to be satisfied all the time, and I want to be proud. I don't want to sit here and talk to you and know that in your mind you're going, 'I fucking hated this movie and this guy is a sell out and I hate him.'"

The women are much like their male counterparts, how many times did Lindsay Lohan apologize for letting down all the young girls who looked up to her because of her "wildness." Most Tiger women need that period of untamed expression and it does them a lot of good later on in their lives. On the day she was to start her prison sentence for lying under oath in an attempt to protect friends, Li'l Kim said, "Today begins a new saga in my life which I expect to strengthen me and allow me time for reflection... I plan to write music while in prison, read and pray regularly and will come out a stronger, more confident woman." These sensuous creatures do need to focus mostly on what is best for them and not let themselves be too influenced by what other people want them to do. When they do that, they take charge of their own power and are able to be who they really are without interruption. That is when the cute kitten turns into the Tigress she really is. Janet Reno has said, "I'm not fancy. I'm what I appear to be."

Being of the self-improvement ilk, they get a real kick out of cracking a new skill. That is why conventional employment does not suit this combination as it is far too restrictive. They have minds eager to learn, to grow, to expand and being stuck in an office carrying out mundane routine tasks is more than a little soul destroying. It is so important to commit to a work life that gives you the freedom to direct your own path. Tom Cruise said, "I've always been changing and evolving and growing. There's no pinnacle of power where you can sit back and rest." Get yourself higher up the ladder quickly or start up your own business, make mistakes if necessary, but provide yourself the freedom you crave otherwise you will do your talent, creativity and heart a disservice. Joel Edgerton said, "The sum total of all my stop-starts have made me less concerned about the future. I'm just aware now that I'll always land on my feet somehow."

Soul Mate:	Boar-Gemini
Challenger:	Monkey-Capricorn
Siblings:	Tiger-Scorpio, Tiger-Pisces
Best Friends:	Horse-Cancer, Horse-Scorpio, Horse-Pisces, Dog-Cancer, Dog-Scorpio, Dog-Pisces

Tom Cruise
Joel Edgerton
Donald Faison
David Mitchell
Steve Byrne
Karisma Kapoor
Kimberly 'Lil' Kim' Jones
Deborah Cox
Sam Claflin
Lindsay Lohan
Solange Knowles
Tom Kenny
Thomas Gibson
Anthony Edwards
Stephen Chow
Neil Morrissey
Peter Hedges
Michael Ball
Pam Shriver
Geraldine James
Bruce McGill
Naseeruddin Shah

Huey Lewis
Leonard Whiting
Richard Branson
Natalie Wood
Terence Stamp
Diana Rigg
Brian Dennehy
Paul Verhoeven
Sanjeev Kumar
Bill Withers
Janet Reno
Harry Dean Stanton
Mel Brooks
Fred Gwynne
William Wyler

TIGER – LEO

Chinese Name: HU
Rank: 3rd
Hours Ruled: 3am – 5am
Direction: East – Northeast
Season: Winter
Month: February
Western Zodiac Equivalent of Tiger: Aquarius
Aquarius Western Element: Air
Eastern Zodiac Equivalent of Leo: Monkey
Leo Western Element: Fire
Numerology: 29 = 2

You can change your fate. You can sit back, or you can go after your life and all that you want it to be.
– Hilary Swank

When the Tiger's tornado mixes with Leo's blazing fire, the sparks fly so far and so high, they can be seen in outer space. This is the only double feline combination of all 144 combinations; the Tiger is like a smooth warrior and the Leo is the royal ruler so when they merge, one may expect to see a somewhat alpha personality. This is sort of accurate, but not in an in-your-face way. Subtlety is the Tiger's specialism and with the additional Leo power here, this creature knows how to get their way without directly asking for it. But that doesn't mean that they will manipulate, just because they can. It's enough for them to know that they have that weapon as part of their arsenal; for the most part they are led by an inner core of genuine integrity…with a little ego thrown in. Usain Bolt has said, "If I get to be a legend, I've achieved my goal."

Being highly sexed and magnetically attractive are typical Tiger traits and they are plentiful here. But their biggest asset and most cherished personal trait is their tenacity. Fuelled by two jungle cats, there is such an abundance of energy that keeps them going when all other competitors have fallen away. There is the need to win, to succeed, to be the last one standing, even if they keep this manifesto secret their entire lives. Maybe that's why one-on-one sports really appeal to their sensibilities. Talking about Boxing, Wesley Snipes has said, "I love the idea of the man-to-man, against one another. I like that. I don't know why." Taking the Boxing theme further, Whilst preparing for he role as a boxer in the movie, *Million-Dollar-Baby*, Hilary Swank said, "And the second you think, 'I have this person,' and get cocky, you can lose and you usually do. It's a great analogy to life. You have to remain humble and have respect for the other person."

When they feel they fall short of their personal best the self-destructive inner voice starts up. Ferocious as this jungle cat can be to its opposition, it can be equally as tough on itself, which is definitely a development issue. It is far more helpful to natives of this combination to tell themselves grandiose stories of who they are even if they are fibbing on a minor scale. As per the law of attraction, they soon become the image that they uphold. Recognizing that that the Jungle Cat is a leader and that it must lead by example is re-energizing and they are soon back out there doing their thing. It is quite typical for Tigers generally to live lives in a staccato pace. They need extended periods of rest after their intense periods of work.

The men of this combination are kings of comedy and of unconventional sex appeal. Steve Carrell typifies this combination, "You can't seem to have any sort of inhibition. Or shame. Or absolute horror at your own physical presence. I know I'm not a woman's fantasy man; I don't have to uphold this image of male beauty, so that's kind of a relief in a way." That does not prevent him from being highly appealing in many ways. If asked why they think they are so popular, they would put it down to their sense of humor; yes, that's an important part, but more to the fact, it is their frisky charm. When people see a weird looking guy in the street with a drop dead gorgeous girl in laughing hysterics, take a wild guess that the guy is a Tiger-Leo. Kenny Rogers said, "I have this theory about performers who last for a long time, and that is, if you break it down, music is not as big a part of it as personality and who you are."

The women of this combination do everything with heart, compassion and determination. They often tread into what may be deemed as man's territory but with the wily charms of the Lioness-Tigress. Although they are not naïve, when they take something on, their commitment is absolute which sometimes causes problems. They find it difficult to change course if the new direction does not make sense to their logistical minds. Being so fearless, independent and honest is not without its problems; if you look at these qualities they are not entirely conducive to working with dictatorial influences. This woman will courageously say what she thinks in order to improve the situation for all involved, even if it looks like she is being difficult. Amy Adams has said, "I have worked with some of the meanest people in the world. You can't do anything to intimidate me." Often their acts of bravery are rewarded with punishment. But this is nature's law to encourage them to find greener pastures.

However they decide to make their living, they undertake every one of their duties seriously. They take pride in a job well done and often hide just how much work they have put into even the smallest task. Kenny Rogers said, "It's never been important that everyone leaves their seat thinking 'he's the best singer I've ever heard,' but it is important everyone leaves saying, 'I really enjoyed that.' That's my goal when I perform." Whether they know it or not, they are highly valued by the people around them. One wonders whether they even know or whether they are able to take this affection on board or whether this amount of affection is ever going to be enough. They love to be loved loads, but wish they didn't. Oh the weaknesses of this human skin for a royal jungle cat! They attract affection from all quarters, mostly because of their humorous observations, vivacity and self-adoring/self-exploring/self-effacing humility. Hilary Swank said, "Every day when I look at my pets, I know they're thankful I've adopted them. I'm just as thankful they've adopted me."

Soul Mate:	Boar-Taurus
Challenger:	Monkey-Aquarius
Siblings:	Tiger-Aries, Tiger-Sagittarius
Best Friends:	Horse-Aries, Horse-Leo, Horse-Sagittarius, Dog-Aries, Dog-Leo, Dog-Sagittarius

Amy Adams
Steve Carell
Josh Radnor
Hilary Swank
Michael Shannon
Kathryn Hahn
Wesley Snipes
Natasha Henstridge
John Slattery
James Marsters
Michelle Yeoh
Kajol
Suzanne Collins
Kenny Rogers
Usain Bolt
Jeremy Castle
Felipe Calderón
Patrick Ewing

Roger Clemens
Gary Larson
Steve Wozniak
John Landis
Judge Lance Ito
Connie Stevens
Peter Jennings
Jiang Zemin
Fidel Castro
Beatrix Potter
Emily Bronte

TIGER – VIRGO

Chinese Name: HU
Rank: 3rd
Hours Ruled: 3am – 5am
Direction: East – Northeast
Season: Winter
Month: February
Western Zodiac Equivalent of Tiger: Aquarius
Aquarius Western Element: Air
Eastern Zodiac Equivalent of Virgo: Rooster
Virgo Western Element: Earth
Numerology: 30 = 3

If you want more, you have to require more from yourself.
– Dr Phil McGraw

When the Tiger's tempest merges with Virgo's fertile earth, this personality is gifted with focus and clarity at the same time. Virgo's earthiness lends the ability to channel the force of the Tiger's storm in productive directions so that they are always working towards achieving some goal. To the outside, people with this combination seem very lucky with money. To call it luck is to denigrate and undermine the work of this creature. As Dr Phil has said, "The most you get is what you ask for." And they have no qualms about asking for more. They are good moneymakers because they like the feeling of financial security. They go with their hunches, research to expand their understanding and then work around the clock until they have achieved their objective. That's why they are always "lucky" with money. They make it happen.

Attractive, energetic and compassionate, they make an impression everywhere they go and tend to be considered fondly even by acquaintances. With an ability to bring excitement to every endeavor, they are coveted in working environments. Just being around them makes one feel more alive. They bring a sense of play to all things yet are trusted to get any job done to the highest professional standard. People fight to access their time because of the way they make other people feel. Bill Murray has said, "I think if you can take care of yourself, and then maybe try to take care of someone else, that's sort of how you're supposed to live."

In their youth, they have superficial tendencies but they become less and less important as the clock ticks on. On some level they have always known what their true priorities were, but in seeking external validation they may have let their ego take them on trips they might later regret. They also feel less inclined to live up to an image that other people have created. Although they strive for personal authenticity, it is not always easy for them to stave off the ego's need for attention. Not all Tiger-Virgos are as evolved as their pin up Dr Phil, but they all have the ability to get there and go beyond. As Dr Phil said, "Awareness without action is worthless." When they know better they must do better and this could almost be their mantra. Application in all areas of their life would also be helpful as they have a tendency to focus on their professional lives because there is a greater level of control. When they open and allow themselves to be honestly, painfully, shamelessly vulnerable, they are on the right track.

The men of this combination are sexy, intelligent and sharp. They are also known to have long eyelashes. Being such precious pretty beings, they are often made the center of attention so they get used to it and expect to play Prince Charming in every fairy tale. Through their interactions, they begin to realize that they have picked up a few false premises along their life journey and they often reach a pivotal point in their lives when they need to set the story straight. This usually happens around their third visit to the Rat year, so when they are roughly 34 years old. Then their lives are set on a different trajectory altogether. Ryan

Philippe has said, "To be more involved and more aware is appealing to me." Like most Tigers they are chivalrous to the end and believe in old fashioned decorum when it comes to romance. Armie Hammer has said, "I think a primal role of a man in a relationship is to protect his woman." Family is the most important thing and they have no qualms about working around the clock if necessary to ensure that their family's financial health is stable.

The women of this combination have a sort of siren like presence. They draw men, especially gay men, towards them like rivers rushing to join the sea. Often they are top heavy, with hypnotizing eyes and a permanent smile on their face. Their carefree attitude belies the pressure they constantly place on themselves to meet everybody's demands. Although they are not perfectionists in the typical Virgo sense, they do have a need to look like they can cope with everything that life throws at them with effortless ease. Highly skilled, talented and joyful, life looks like it is easy for them, but if you understand just how much they expect of themselves, their constant push for self-improvement begins to make sense. Talking about how her strong personality was perceived in Hollywood, Lea Michele said, "When I first heard those references used towards me, I found it incredibly hurtful. I'm a girl who knows what she wants. I am outspoken. I am strong... If a man is strong and opinionated, he's considered powerful, but if you're a woman, it's regarded negatively." As has been said, mediocrity always attacks excellence, take it as a compliment and keep going.

Tiger-Virgos are well aware of their superpowers and choose to lift the mood of all that enter their life, even if it is for a short period of time. By being a spiritual catalyst for other people, they must be careful not to take on emotions that do not belong to them. This is not an easy task. In order to overcompensate for emotional depletion, many eat to excess and this may cause other issues so is important to bear in mind. On the whole, however, they are positive, focused and driven to succeed. They do not depend on others for much and the more they open their hearts, the more admirers fall at their feet. As Lea Michele said, "I've always felt good about myself, that is to say, I've always felt beautiful, but I didn't necessarily think other people thought I was beautiful." It doesn't matter what their shape or size, there is just something about the Tiger-Virgo, they are simply HOT!

Soul Mate: Boar-Aries
Challenger: Monkey-Pisces
Siblings: Tiger-Taurus, Tiger-Capricorn
Best Friends: Horse-Taurus, Horse-Virgo, Horse-Capricorn,
                Dog-Taurus, Dog-Virgo, Dog-Capricorn

Ryan Phillippe
Paddy Considine
Clare Kramer
Xzibit
Armie Hammer
Lea Michele
Mario
David Fincher
Baz Luhrmann.
Bill Murray
Julie Kavner
Phil McGraw
Shabana Azmi
Elliott Gould
Caryl Churchill
James Lipton
Noor Jehan
Jimmy Fallon

TIGER – LIBRA

Chinese Name: HU
Rank: 3rd
Hours Ruled: 3am – 5am
Direction: East – Northeast
Season: Winter
Month: February
Western Zodiac Equivalent of Tiger: Aquarius
Aquarius Western Element: Air
Eastern Zodiac Equivalent of Libra: Dog
Libra Western Element: Air
Numerology: 31 = 4

Love is always the answer to healing of any sort.
– Louise Hay

When the Tiger's tempest meets Libra's cool calm breeze, the result is an unconventional, vibrant creature that lives off its wits and is guided strongly by its instincts. Not that the Tiger-Libra always listens, but they do kick themselves afterwards; when they know better, they want to do better, but don't always have the confidence to see this through; at least until the universe demands it of them which they often learn the hard way. Unlike the snake sign that needs to project an image to the outside world while knowing who they actually are within, the Tiger will justify the existence of any chosen image regardless of whether the external world sees this image or not. That does not mean that they don't care what others think, they do, in fact they lose a lot of sleep over what people are going to think or say about them, but they need to be seen as "good people" to themselves, whatever that means. This aspect of the airy Tiger is magnified when joined with airy Libra. Louise Hay has said, "As my mind can conceive of more good, the barriers and blocks dissolve. My life becomes full of little miracles popping up out of the blue."

With this excess of air, there is a restlessness present that makes them run and often keep running from situations but primarily themselves. It is part of the Tiger's nature to keep moving without necessarily deciding upon a destination, this combination especially so, but the powerful connection to their source, guides them even without conscious awareness and they end up exactly where they are most useful. That is when they begin to step onto the spiritual plain and their life develops a momentum they could not have dreamed of. Metaphysical Teacher, author and publisher, Louise Hay said, "Your mind is a tool you can choose to use any way you wish." Louise Hay was instrumental in spreading the message that that thoughts and emotions create one's experience so if one is going through difficulties, it is because they are choosing negative thoughts which lead to negative vibrational emotions which communicate with the universe; then the law of attraction brings you that physical experience. Therefore, success or failure is imminent depending upon the thought you choose to think. Louise Hay said, "You are not a helpless victim of your own thoughts, but rather a master of your own mind."

Libra's ability to see through facades and maintain mental equilibrium supports the Tiger here in a potent way by amplifying their practical objectivity which, when combined with Tiger's abundance of energy, helps to contain and focus it. This makes them highly creative and bestows upon them the wherewithal to take their ideas further and make them a reality. Like all Tigers they will have their ups and downs, living in one end of the spectrum before sliding to the other, then back again. Randy Quaid said, "When I was a kid and the carnival would come to the shopping center, I'd go down and talk to all the people running the rides. I like that whole lifestyle, moving from town to town in a nomadic existence."

The men of this combination tend to have an overtly raw sexual energy inherent to both the Tiger and Libra. Both signs are Yang, so of the masculine, but that seems to be an exterior construct. Tiger-Libra men are made of marshmallow inside. Despite outer appearances, there is an inner loveliness, tenderness and open armed acceptance that emanates from them even if they never say it or try to deny it. They cannot help but exude a loving energy even when they are upset, annoyed or plain right pissed off. Being the type that has to be in the midst of the action, live on the edge, experience the knocks, get the bruises and occasionally scrape with death, they know they have earned their wisdom. Chuck Berry said, "It's amazing how much you can learn if your intentions are truly earnest."

The women of this combination tend to be tall, attractive with a sort of aerodynamic build, almost like a jet plane. Like their male counterparts are also well aware of their sexuality, but might not know how to focus so much energy. Where some use it clumsily until they learn how to channel it with grace, others repress it, scared of their own power. Whatever they do, it is there, these are radiantly beautiful women that sparkle into their old age. Much of this has to do with their inner spirit that is Tigress tough and moral nature, which keeps them in spiritual alignment with their source. Kelly Preston said, "Once I was at an audition and they told me, 'You must show your breasts!' and I was like, get outta town. I just laughed and slammed the door on my way out."

Eternally youthful, exuberant and fun, they never lose their sense of humor and they have the ability to lift the mood of an entire room with their presence. There is also something very social worker about them in that they want to support, love and protect everyone that comes into their experience, even though they know they cannot and more to the point that they should not. Because of the way they live life, they grow in spurts throughout their life and they want their experiences to help other people do the same. When they figure out that their example is the best way to inspire others, they can finally relax and just be. That is when their *joie de vivre* returns with a punch. This is one combination that seems to have stumbled upon the elixir of life, because they just seem to be young forever. Louise Hay said, "You are the power in your world!"

Soul Mate:	Boar-Pisces
Challenger:	Monkey-Aries
Siblings:	Tiger-Gemini, Tiger -Aquarius
Best Friends:	Horse-Gemini, Horse-Libra, Horse-Aquarius, Dog-Gemini, Dog-Libra, Dog-Aquarius

Chuck Berry
Raaj Kumar
Christopher Lloyd
Eddie Cochran
Evel Knievel
Ben E. King
Waheed Murad
Randy Quaid
Om Puri
Tom Petty
Kelly Preston
Joan Cusack
Evander Holyfield
Chunky Pandey
Jack Dee
Matthew Macfadyen
Martin Henderson
Gok Wan
Louise Hay
Michel Foucault

TIGER – SCORPIO

Chinese Name: HU
Rank: 3rd
Hours Ruled: 3am – 5am
Direction: East – Northeast
Season: Winter
Month: February
Western Zodiac Equivalent of Tiger: Aquarius
Aquarius Western Element: Air
Eastern Zodiac Equivalent of Scorpio: Boar
Scorpio Western Element: Water
Numerology: 32 = 5

When I was young, I used to have this thing where I wanted to see everything. I used to think, 'How can I die without seeing every inch of this world?'
– Leonardo DiCaprio

When the Tiger's tempest meets with Scorpio's dark murky waters, the result is an exuberant life-loving beast that gluttonously feasts on all manner of worldly delights before wearing itself out requiring solitude to recuperate its energies so that it can get out there and devour life all over again. Determined, intelligent and highly attractive, these felines know how to make things happen and function best in a sort of contained chaos that they know how to create and manage, even if nobody else does. There is a noted tendency towards a sort of hibernation every now and then because they need solace and time to get their heads right about the drama that ensues around them. Jodie Foster has said, "It's an interesting combination: Having a great fear of being alone, and having a desperate need for solitude and the solitary experience. That's always been a tug of war for me."

Ambitious and focused, they know what their ultimate

outcome is so develop a sort of antennae for what will support them to reach their aims and when something is within their reach, the feline will pounce. Like all Tigers, they learn best on the job, in the field, and when they have scars to prove they have been in the war. That being said, there is an academic side to them, which is as developed as their instinctual wits. Despite the overriding Tiger's need to experience life viscerally, a few of the Tiger combinations lean towards risk calculation and perfectionism; Tiger-Scorpio is one of them. They want everything to look effortless, as if they are naturally good at everything. Yes, they are hugely talented in ways that others just are not, but more importantly, they are exceptionally hard workers, despite what they would have you believe. Joaquin Phoenix said, "I never think that I'm good at anything I do. I can always do it better, I know my weakness. I've never been perfect." Maybe this is because they set their own standards too high. Leonardo DiCaprio said, "There was always an element of me that needed to prove something to myself. It's something I don't want to get rid of, because it's what drives me. I'm never settled and I'm never satisfied." Similarly, Demi Moore said, "We have to continue to be willing to take a risk so that we don't get too safe."

The Tiger-Scorpio's journey is an interesting one; as children they are stand out as old beyond their years in much the way Jodie Foster and Leonardo DiCaprio did as child performers. This does two things to their psychology, gives them an adult work ethic but deprives them access to childlike freedom, which they chase for the rest of their life. Maybe that is why so many of them choose to work in creative environments where they can set the parameters of how they work. Working in an office environment does not suit their temperament unless there is a sense of freedom, open space and the ability to chill out or play in some way. Inevitably though, they are essentially non-conformist and do not ever fit into anyone's categorization box (except the Tiger-Scorpio one!). Jodie Foster said, "Normal is not something to aspire to, it's something to get away from." Similarly, Leonardo DiCaprio has said, "I'm the rebel type in the sense that I don't think I'm like everyone else. I try to be an individual."

The men of this combination are typically Tiger-gorgeous with sexy slit eyes and pouted lips at the ready. They seem at home everywhere they go and their casual nature puts everyone at ease. They have a strong sense of what they can do and even if their self-confidence fluctuates, they always get a handle on it when they need to. They are also at one with nature. Joaquin Phoenix has said, "I like to spend a lot of time on my own in the woods. I don't exactly sneak off in the middle of the night, but I like to be in a place where no one can reach me by phone or e-mail." Similarly, Leonardo DiCaprio said, "When I'm acting and I take a break, the first thing on my list is spending time by the sea."

The women of this combination are vulnerable in a feminine way but their appeal is their strength and determination to overcome any obstacles. They also understand how self-destructive it is to seek approval from external sources so they try as much as they can to keep themselves to themselves as less exposure means more esteem-protection. Although this may make them seem even more unusual or somewhat eccentric, to them it is preferable to opening themselves to parasitical influences. Jodie Foster said, "Being understood is not the most essential thing in life." Beautiful, intelligent and complicated, their desires are pretty uncomplicated in that they just want to be admired, loved and seen as special; in fact they expect it, demand it and get it! They are that little bit ahead of their time. Demi Moore has said, "There's still a negative attitude in our society towards women who use a strength that's inherent – their femininity – in any way that might be considered seductive." Maybe that is because their particular brand of feline-feminine seduction is dangerous.

Ultimately, Tiger-Scorpios are visionaries, achievers and hard grafters. Their main areas of improvement are that they should learn to ask for help when they need it and stop playing such childish mind-games with themselves. The truth is that they know this already and they do have a good level of emotional intelligence, the reason they behave in this sort of way is because they find the drama of it entertaining. Joaquin Phoenix said, "My significant other right now is myself, which is what happens when you suffer from multiple personality disorder and self-obsession." You crazy cat!

Soul Mate:	Boar-Aquarius
Challenger:	Monkey-Taurus
Siblings:	Tiger-Cancer, Tiger-Pisces
Best Friends:	Horse-Cancer, Horse-Scorpio, Horse-Pisces, Dog-Cancer, Dog-Scorpio, Dog-Pisces

Johnny Walker
Prem Nath
Jimmy Savile
John Candy
Dennis Haskins
Jodie Foster
Demi Moore
Cary Elwes
Anthony Kiedis
Leonardo DiCaprio
Joaquin Phoenix
Chloë Sevigny
Nelly
Chad Kroeger
Sonali Kulkarni
Penn Badgley
Leslie Bibb

TIGER – SAGITTARIUS

Chinese Name: HU
Rank: 3rd
Hours Ruled: 3am – 5am
Direction: East – Northeast
Season: Winter
Month: February
Western Zodiac Equivalent of Tiger: Aquarius
Aquarius Western Element: Air
Eastern Zodiac Equivalent of Sagittarius: Rat
Sagittarius Western Element: Fire
Numerology: 33 = 6

What you are, you are by accident of birth; what I am, I am by myself. There are and will be a thousand princes; there is only one Beethoven.
– Beethoven

When the Tiger's tempest meets the Centaurs frisky fires, wildness meets cultivated civility, restlessness meets drive, subconscious merges with conscious with effortless ease. These people are constantly in communication with their inner selves and take intuitive, inspired action most of the time without their even being aware of it. That is why things work out for them even in the midst of chaos in fact, oftentimes, that is when they will function at their best. It is a good thing, for although they have an amazing ability to focus, as all Tigers do, this combination may prefer physical exercise or dance or movement based yoga as well as traditional meditation forms as a spiritual practice. This beast knows it needs to self-tame but must find a method it enjoys. Ralph Fiennes said, "I'm not very good at being domesticated. I've tried. The domestic life I find claustrophobic – the rituals and habits and patterns."

Even the adults exhibit an eternally "eager child" disposition; their enthusiasm for life never falters and they enter each experience with excitement fuelling their endeavors. That does not mean that they are naïve, not at all; their eyes are fully open, but so is their heart which is why they do everything with such passion and they overflow with optimism. When they find something they love, they cannot help but allow this love to completely consume them. Their gift and their curse is their focus; they cannot turn it off, but instead have to constantly shift it. Jon Stewart has said, "The real challenge is when I'm at work, I'm at work. I'm locked in, I'm ready to go, I'm focused. When I'm at home, I'm locked in and I'm ready to go and I'm focused on home. We don't watch the show. We don't watch the news. We don't do any of that stuff. I sit down, I play Barbies. And sometimes the kids will come home and play with me."

This combination often produces potent artists who have refined their skills and continue to do so throughout their lives. As Beethoven said, "Don't only practice your art, but force your way into its secrets; art deserves that, for it and knowledge can raise man to the Divine." Maybe that is why these artists stand out from the rest in a pronounced way. They believe in their talent, artistry and ability to become legendary; to expect anything less would be self-denigrating. As Giovanni Ribisi has said, "Every artist should consider himself Picasso. Otherwise, you're doing yourself an injustice."

Learning the lessons of life quickly and comprehensively, they know there is no substitute for experience and actually, there is nothing more fulfilling. Ralph Fiennes has said, "You have to just dive over the edge. You haven't got time to mess." One of the most difficult lessons for the Tiger-Sagittarius to learn is that of facing their own weaknesses. Beethoven said, "Nothing is more intolerable than to have to admit to yourself your own errors." But once they start, it gets easier and their development sky-rockets. Even though they can acknowledge that they may have made mistakes, that they might not be good at everything, they do not accept limitations. Beethoven also said, "The barriers are not erected which can say to aspiring talents and industry, 'Thus far and no farther'...I will seize fate by the throat; it shall certainly never wholly overcome me."

The men of this combination tend to be tall with sharp features and a hardness that belies the actual child that lives in this mind. There is something very satisfying when little children are able to get this adult child to come out of his shell. He feels free and alive and grateful and alive and supremely creative and alive! As Afemo Omilami said, "Never be too big to do the little things."

The women of this combination are typical Tigresses in that they are drawn to all that glitters while knowing that it is not necessarily gold. Like their male counterparts, they see the world as a huge playground that they can't wait to revel in. Margaret Hamilton has said, "My only mistake was wanting to do everything." They come at everything with their common sense and seeming grounded-ness but then allow themselves to be taken over by whatever is sexy in the moment. The great news is that they do learn their lessons in the end. As Felicity Huffman said, "The pressure on women to be thin is like a plague. I have gone through my life, like a lot of women, rating my experiences on the basis of, 'Was I thin at that time or fat?' And it doesn't seem to let up... Beauty can make you powerful in a way that isn't good for you." Tiger-Sagittarius women become less competitive with other women when they start accepting themselves and instead become the biggest champions of women.

Two of the most famous children's movie villains belong to this combination; Margaret Hamilton who played the Wicked Witch of the West in "The Wizard of Oz" and Ralph Fiennes who played Voldemort in the "Harry Potter" movie series. Both characters were over the top, visually deformed, evil creatures requiring actors with an understanding of how to play *sinister* for children. Actually, Margaret Hamilton was also a kindergarten teacher before she became an actress. Yes, this combination knows how to connect to children because their own inner child is very much alive within them. That could be why they have a simple yet effective approach to life: Ralph Fiennes has said, "Success...is all about being able to extend love to people... Little by little, task by task, gesture by gesture, word by word."

Soul Mate:	Boar-Capricorn
Challenger:	Monkey-Gemini
Siblings:	Tiger-Aries, Tiger-Leo
Best Friends:	Horse-Aries, Horse-Leo, Horse-Sagittarius, Dog-Aries, Dog-Leo, Dog-Sagittarius

Margaret Hamilton
Joe DiMaggio
Ed Harris
Wendie Malick
Afemo Omilami
Ralph Fiennes
Andrew McCarthy
Felicity Huffman
Jon Stewart
Giovanni Ribisi
Marissa Ribisi
Stephen Merchant
Katie Cassidy
Johnny Simmons
Prateik
Amir Khan (Boxer)
Joseph Stalin

TIGER – CAPRICORN

Chinese Name: HU
Rank: 3rd
Hours Ruled: 3am – 5am
Direction: East – Northeast
Season: Winter
Month: February
Western Zodiac Equivalent of Tiger: Aquarius
Aquarius Western Element: Air
Eastern Zodiac Equivalent of Capricorn: Ox
Capricorn Western Element: Earth
Numerology: 34 = 7

When I play ball, I play hardball.
– Kirstie Alley

When the Tiger's tempest meets with Capricorn's fertile earth, the storm pulls this creature to the skies while the earth pulls it down which causes some internal friction in the early years for people of this combination. This starts them on their ever-intensifying search for personal authenticity. When they choose to take charge and consciously decide to pick the particulars of their life, their natural power returns and lots of little things begin to happen which serve as symbols that they are heading in the right direction. As Eartha Kitt said, "The river is constantly turning and bending and you never know where it's going to go and where you'll wind up."

Some Tiger-Capricorns struggle with an intense feeling of not belonging, of not being enough and they are very tough on themselves. They bury their issues deep within the Capricorn's earth and it is hard for the Tiger side to dig it back up again so they worry, are fearful and try to control whatever they can to improve the perception the world has. As Eartha Kitt said, "I punish myself more than anybody else does if I am stupid about my actions, and I suffer, really suffer."

However, this is not a fixed state; in fact, this is only a Tiger-Capricorn functioning at the lower levels, usually when experiencing a crisis. They learn to free themselves either by removing the emotions and making a cerebral decision, or the wait for the crap to hit the fan. Talking about his struggle with addiction, Bradley Cooper said, "I don't drink or do drugs anymore. Being sober helps a great deal... I remember looking at my life, my apartment, my dogs and I thought, 'What's happening?' I was so concerned what people thought of me, how I was coming across, how I would survive the day. I always felt like an outsider. I just lived in my head. I realized I wasn't going to live up to my potential, and that scared the hell out of me. I thought, 'Wow, I'm actually gonna ruin my life.'" The universe often uses this combination to experience this massive extreme because they have the capacity to go to that edge yet return to function at exceptionally high levels, thereby serving as supreme inspirations.

The men of this combination tend to know that they are geeks, even the ones that look like models (of which there are many) are probably more academically inclined than they would like anyone to know. Masi Oka has said, "Being a geek is a great thing. I think we're all geeks. Being a geek means you're passionate about something and that defines your uniqueness. I would rather be passionate about something than be apathetic about everything." All Tiger men are passionate creatures, although what they are passionate about tends to differ. Ryan Seacrest has said, "I could lie and pretend that I hunt and camp, but that wouldn't be me. Clothes? Shopping? That's stuff I like!" They love to get inside of the details and pick things apart and figure out how things work and why they work in that way. The men are like scientist-artists; they undertake their work in the most established yet effective ways yet they are constantly experimenting, trying to find new ways to make things even more effective. As Steven Soderbergh has said, "I'm purposefully going after things and doing things that I'm not sure if it's going to come off or not."

The women tend to be exceptionally beautiful, but, because they are so beautiful, they feel obligated always to remain so which comes with its own inherent problems. They are also more open than most, probably because of the lessons that they have learned along their life journey. But ultimately it has the effect that these women are charming, funny and full of love. Naya Rivera has said, "My heart is a Slushee full of love and I want to toss it all over you." They are equally as passionate as the men but express it much more openly. Kirstie Alley has said, "I sort of feel sorry for the next man who gets me. I may just kill him with passion." Tiger-Capricorns are ardent pet lovers. They have a lot of empathy for their pets and tend spoil them rotten. Eartha Kitt has said, "Having my animals or my children with me exorcises that feeling of not being wanted." Bradley Cooper has said, "I have two beautiful dogs that I cherish... They're my kids."

Their personal search for authenticity is an important journey for the Tiger-Capricorn. It starts with them and extends to inspire others to do the same. Ryan Seacrest took it one step further, he has said, "I use every opportunity, whether on my radio show or on television, to break stereotypes." Having fans of all races, religions, cultures and being somewhat of a gay icon, Eartha Kitt was exposed to many walks of life and realized that what bonded everyone was the universal similarities; perhaps that is why she said, "I'm not black and I'm not white and I'm not pink and I'm not green. Eartha Kitt has no color, and that is how barriers are broken." At the end of the day, who you are speaks louder than what you say, so that is why the Tiger-Capricorn strives to always be better tomorrow than they were today and some have figured out the best way to stand out from the crowd; Kirstie Alley has said, "The only thing you can ever be in life is yourself because that's the only thing someone else can't be."

Soul Mate: Boar-Sagittarius
Challenger: Monkey-Cancer
Siblings: Tiger-Taurus, Tiger-Virgo
Best Friends: Horse-Taurus, Horse-Virgo, Horse-Capricorn,
               Dog-Taurus, Dog-Virgo, Dog-Capricorn

Bradley Cooper
Lyndsy Fonseca
Steven Soderbergh
Naya Rivera
Shelley Hennig
Jon Voight
Dax Shepard
Kirstie Alley
Ryan Seacrest
Masi Oka
Eartha Kitt
Twinkle Khanna
Nana PatekarCharo
Crystal Gayle
Maury Povich

TIGER – AQUARIUS

Chinese Name: HU
Rank: 3rd
Hours Ruled: 3am – 5am
Direction: East – Northeast
Season: Winter
Month: February
Western Zodiac Equivalent of Tiger: Aquarius
Aquarius Western Element: Air
Eastern Zodiac Equivalent of Aquarius: Tiger
Aquarius Western Element: Air
Numerology: 35 = 8

Developing the muscles of the soul demands no competitive
spirit, no killer instinct, although it may erect pain barriers
that the spiritual athlete must crash through.
– Germaine Greer

When the Tiger's tempest meets Aquarius's cyclone, the resulting
hurricane is mammoth. The Tiger and Aquarius are each other's
east-west equivalent so in effect we have the pure Tiger or double
Aquarius combination here. This means that the traits of the
Tiger and of Aquarius are amplified, which is really interesting
considering what those traits are. Tigers are fearless fighters of
freedom, Aquarians are humanitarians with an eccentric bent led
by their heart anywhere they please regardless how alternative. It
is very easy to say that they are likely to be unusual in many
regards, compassionate and ahead of their time by a century or
two. The first image that crops up is the alternative rock/folk
artist, casually strumming away with a few simple words of
poetry that speaks millions. Talking about being a responsible
artist, Sheryl Crow said, "If we can't turn to our artists, who can
we turn to?" Tiger-Aquarians are masters of communication and

many have no idea just how influential they are; it comes as no surprise that this combination is jam-packed with singer-songwriters, writers and artists of all varieties.

Staunch defenders of freedom, Germaine Greer has said, "Freedom is fragile and must be protected. To sacrifice it, even as a temporary measure, is to betray it." They need to feel like all doors are open and all people are available to them at all times. One might think that this tendency lessens as they age but it does not. The combination of these two signs creates something of an eternal teenager, their youthfulness, faith in mankind and infectious energy never diminishes. They become more and more attractive as they age because of this. At the same time there is a fear of growing old and leaving the free abandon of the adolescent phase behind. Garth Brooks jokingly said, "I'm much too young to feel this damn old."

The upside to this equation is that they never forget what it is like to be young and those feelings live on in them as fresh as the day they happened. Talking about the ability just to *be* without pretention, John Hughes said, "It's like being at the kids' table at Thanksgiving – you can put your elbows on it, you don't have to talk politics…no matter how old I get, there's always a part of me that's sitting there."

Appealing in that typical Tiger way, the men of this combination are open to life, they say yes to every experience that comes their way and they like to expand the boundaries of where men have not yet gone. They seemingly have no limits and enjoy life most when they do not feel tied down. It is so interesting that these are the type of men that women desperately try to cage. The best way to handle them is to give them as much space as they need and act as if you really do not need them – then they'll come running. Talking about his complicated sexuality, Eddie Izzard said, "If I had to describe how I feel in my head, I'd say I'm a complete boy plus half a girl." Men of this combination tend to be more sexually ambivalent than most because of their no boundary manifesto and desire to live life to the fullest. The pure Tiger combination has a huge sexual appetite. Robbie Williams said, "When it comes down to it, I just like taking my pants down."

The women of this combination are premier feminists while being highly feminine at the same time. Tough, intelligent and forceful, they find it difficult taking a back seat in anything and will always take the decision where they have most hands on influence. Talking about the role of women, Cybil Sheperd said, "I never wanted to be Jane. I always wanted to be Tarzan. I didn't want to vacuum the tree house. I wanted to swing from the vines." Whether on a macro level or micro, it is clear that women of this combination have been instrumental in pushing forward the women's movement, especially with patrons such as Germaine Greer who has said, "All societies on the verge of death are masculine. A society can survive with only one man; no society will survive a shortage of women."

Unafraid of their sexuality either, they are likely to be early developers and have a greater understanding of how to use their feminine wiles. Cybil Sheperd said, "I had to lie so much about sex, first when I was 15 because I wasn't supposed to be having it. And when I got older, I lied to everybody I was having sex with, so I could have sex with other people." Not that they would encourage promiscuity, sexual freedom of expression is and always has been high on their manifesto.

Playful, youthful and life-full, they absorb everything that happens, relate it to themselves, find the universal human connection and share it with the world to enlighten and uplift. Is it any wonder they are so highly sought after? They know who they are and what impact they have because the surplus of Aquarius here analyses everything as it happens providing immediate feedback of every single nuance. That is why they are artists that know how to connect with people in a personal way. Christian Bale said, "It's the actors who are prepared to make fools of themselves who are usually the ones who come to mean something to the audience." Similarly, Elizabeth Banks said, "Every once in a while I play a true idiot, and they're really fun to play." But they are anything but idiots. To quote Germaine Greer one last time, the Tiger-Aquarius is in all respects a "Spiritual Athlete."

Soul Mate:	Boar-Scorpio
Challenger:	Monkey-Leo
Siblings:	Tiger-Gemini, Tiger-Libra
Best Friends:	Horse-Gemini, Horse-Libra, Horse-Aquarius, Dog-Gemini, Dog-Libra, Dog-Aquarius

Christian Bale
Elizabeth Banks
Seth Green
Tiffani Thiessen
Robbie Williams
Urmila Matondkar
Amber Riley
Jennifer Jason Leigh
Eddie Izzard
W. Axl Rose
Sheryl Crow
Garth Brooks
Cybill Shepherd
John Hughes
Sherman Hemsley
Oliver Reed
John Guare
Sara Gilbert

Mia Kirshner
Preity Zinta
Natalie Imbruglia
Mark Wright
David Patrick Kelly
Phil Collins
Russell Grant
Mike Farrell
Germaine Greer

TIGER – PISCES

Chinese Name: HU
Rank: 3rd
Hours Ruled: 3am – 5am
Direction: East – Northeast
Season: Winter
Month: February
Western Zodiac Equivalent of Tiger: Aquarius
Aquarius Western Element: Air
Eastern Zodiac Equivalent of Pisces: Rabbit
Pisces Western Element: Water
Numerology: 36 = 9

Success is falling nine times and getting up ten.
– Jon Bon Jovi

When the Tiger's tempest meets the potency of Pisces's water, the result is raw sex appeal and a commitment to make manifest the art that lives in their soul. Many have exceptionally special looks. They stick out even from the good-looking crowd because they are more than just attractive, they are powerfully sexually appealing. Perhaps it is because they blessed thus, that they value relationships more than merely chasing sensual highs. Pisces's water opens the airy Tiger's mind so that psychology becomes much more important. These types seem to know what they want from a young age, why they want it and how they are going to get it. In order to be work focused, they often have to fight their Tiger tendency to want to indulge in ego-serving play and ending up in complicated emotional situations. Eva Mendes said, "The celebrity world can be so ugly. Everyone seems to have slept with everyone else and it's some sort of strange weird cycle. I don't want to get into that." Similarly, talking about the Hollywood celebrity club, Jamie Bell said, "That community is really small, so everybody knows each other. I kind of don't like that. It's not really a community I feel very welcome in."

The Pisces energy serves to temper the vivacious Tiger personality encouraging introversion but the Tiger's extreme nature never goes down without a fight. Describing himself, Jon Bon Jovi has said, "Introverted maybe, but incredibly focused to do whatever it is that I want to do. If it's to go running this morning or to drink tonight, it's gonna be the whole bottle. I don't sip." This muted cover for the creature that resides within draws the Tiger's perfectionist streak to the surface. Karen Carpenter said, "We spent an awful lot of time trying to achieve perfection as close as we can come." They do not like to do less than what they are capable of and they work very hard to develop their abilities. Jamie Bell said, "Learning my skill was more important than getting a big pay check or running away from big robots."

There is a kind of inward push that keeps them going and they select their work projects carefully. They do not like to sell out and any such experiences sting them for years to come so they eventually get to a place where they find work that they believe in or on their own terms. Jon Bon Jovi has said, "My real friends and my family know that if I'm not working I'm miserable. It's not for monetary reasons. I already have fame and fortune. Now I want to find the greatness in things – which is why I was attracted to the arts in the first place."

The men of this combination are often shorter than their peers but their sensual looks, buoyant spirit and sex appeal are undeniable. The glint in their eyes and their pouty kissable lips drive people crazy. Jon Bon Jovi has said, "Trying to seduce an audience is the basis of rock 'n' roll, and if I may say so, I'm pretty good at it." They know their sexual power and they know how to "work it." What is most appealing about Tiger Pisceans is their quiet self-assurance. This is not something they are born with, it's something they develop over time and they feel that they have earned. Jerry Lewis said, "I'm a multi-faceted, talented, wealthy, internationally famous genius. I have an IQ of 190 – that's supposed to be a genius. People don't like that. My answer to all my critics is simple: I like me. I like what I've become. I'm proud of what I've achieved, and I don't really believe I've scratched the surface yet."

The women of this combination have vitality, passion and are easy to relate to. They come across as very real and approachable, even though most of them look like goddesses from naughty magazines. Like their male counterparts, there is something special about the way they are, they just exude an appeal that is hard to explain and hard to ignore. Although they are not money motivated, they need to live well so learn to attract money to them. They think it is because of their ever-increasing skillset, but it is because they believe they are becoming more valuable, not necessarily because they can do more. Eva Mendes said, "I wanted to be a nun when I was very little. Well, that was until my sister told me that they don't get paid. Then I went off that idea quickly." Much like their male counterparts, they discipline themselves to practice and work until they become hugely proficient and this impacts the way that they perceive themselves. That is when miracles start occurring for them. Julie Walters said, "Self-worth is everything. Without it life is a misery."

A side note is Julie Walters played teacher to Jamie Bell in Billy Elliot and mother to twins James and Oliver Phelps in the Harry Potter series: all are Tiger-Pisces.

Ultimately, the Tiger-Pisces masters itself in time and earns its own respect, the respect of the world then follows. It's as if they set out to do this relatively young and when they reach this point in their mind, a button gets pushed and the rewards they believe they deserve are forthcoming. After allowing their ego a little anarchic fun in their early days, they settle down and commit to their own future. They discipline themselves to deny little luxuries that may serve short-term desires but cause long-term problems. The key to understanding a Tiger-Pisces is this: they know exactly how they are presenting themselves, what impact they are having and what they can get as a result. Eva Mendes has said, "I know I walk a fine line between being a respected actor and being what they call a sex symbol. It's a hard one to walk if you want to be known as a real, credible actor. But I've never felt objectified. Nothing you see me do is an accident. I might act like it's an accident, but the opposite is true. I'm incredibly calculated when it comes to my career."

Soul Mate:	Boar-Libra
Challenger:	Monkey-Virgo
Siblings:	Tiger-Cancer, Tiger-Scorpio
Best Friends:	Horse-Cancer, Horse-Scorpio, Horse-Pisces, Dog-Cancer, Dog-Scorpio, Dog-Pisces

Teresa Palmer
Eva Mendes
Jamie Bell
Alexandra Daddario
Jenna Fischer
Adam Baldwin
Kevin Connolly
Brad Dourif
Brittany Snow
Mark-Paul Gosselaar
William H. Macy
William Hurt
Grace Park
Matt Lucas

Paula Garcés
Dean Geyer
Julie Walters
David Faustino
Justin Berfield
Jon Bon Jovi
Ethan Peck
Lesley Ann Machado
Miko Hughes
Jerry Lewis
James Phelps
Oliver Phelps
Margo Harshman
Richard Beymer
Bonnie Somerville
Peter Graves

THE RABBIT

THE RABBIT

I am the sensual Casanova, the seductive siren and the political artist. With aristocratic manners and cultured flair I waltz through my world wanting to inspire greatness in others through my own amazing talents, yet hoping that nobody embarrasses me by highlighting my genius. It separates me from the mere mortals but I am one too and I see the greatness of being regular. But for some reason, this bunny is placed on a pedestal even though I am not the sort that likes to be paraded for the sakes of entertainment, well, not for too long anyway...I have real work to do. My art is my life and I do it to elevate consciousness to an unearthly plane, for some divine interruption, occasionally intervention for I bridge the real and surreal worlds. I am the psychic channel that communicates with spirit that is why the future flows from me. I just know that which is beyond psychology, beyond philosophy and beyond regular comprehension – I am of this world but my mind is beyond. Because I'm noble, responsible and divinely beautiful, don't mistake me for an angel – I choose not to live up to anyone's expectations and will hop away in the blink of an eye.

I am the Rabbit.

Refined and beautiful, a rabbit's physical appearance can be so beautiful it hurts. Graceful, quick with a good level of emotional intelligence, you are blessed with a highly tuned intuition and many have psychic abilities. Sensitive and emotional you are naturally empathic so have an advanced understanding of the human condition which you use to make money, whether that be in positions where understanding people is required, or more prominently, in the arts.

Career-wise, they are led by their heightened emotions so the arts and theatre appeals in particular. There are many actor turned writer or director of this sign. They start wanting to the canvass but they soon realize they were born to be the paint. In a similar way, many Rabbits are open psychic channels for spirits to share their wisdom. Teaching and being on the creative edge also appeals. They also flourish in engineering, business, health care, medicine, specialists in niche products, florists and anything to do with colors and design.

Compatibilities

Soul Mate: Dog
Challenger: Rooster
Best Friends: Sheep & Boar
Good Relations: Ox & Horse

RABBIT – ARIES

Chinese Name: TU
Rank: 4th
Hours Ruled: 5am – 7am
Direction: Directly East
Season: Spring
Month: March
Western Zodiac Equivalent of Rabbit: Pisces
Pisces Western Element: Water
Eastern Zodiac Equivalent of Aries: Dragon
Aries Western Element: Fire
Numerology: 37 = 1

If you don't bet, you don't have a chance to win.
– Francis Ford Coppola

When the deep waters of the refined Rabbit meet with the raw fire of Aries, it creates a creative personality that is imbued with drive. They are highly passionate people effortlessly guided by internal powers towards that which will be most fulfilling for them. They are often drawn into artistic vocations where they have something resembling an X-ray for what works and what doesn't. They eat, sleep and breathe their passion until it fully consumes them. Their enthusiasm for their special vocation is akin to lovemaking. Quentin Tarrantino has said, "Movies are my religion and God is my patron... When I make a movie, I want it to be everything to me; like I would die for it."

Discipline is not necessary, pure biological chemistry is enough to keep them engaged. Tarrantino has also said, "If you want to make a movie, make it. Don't wait for a grant, don't wait for the perfect circumstances, just make it... If you just love movies enough, you can make a good one." Whether it is a movie, a novel or a painting, the universe provides everything that is required when action is taken with faith. Guidance is forthcoming to these intuitively connected creatures and proceeding necessary steps tend to be revealed in surprising ways exactly when required. There is also something sexy about everything they do. They just cannot escape from this little label. Although their physical looks are sexy, even the ones that are not exude this energy making them powerfully attractive. It is their power but can also be their curse, as potential partners stereotype them as the *sexy fun*, without providing them the same opportunity to be more than that. In time, they learn to wield their sexual energy in such a way that they project both, sex appeal and a persona that lends itself to a long term relationship.

Discussing big studio heads in relation to his first feature film *The Garden State* that he wrote, directed and starred in, Zach Braff has said, "They put all this money into these huge movies, and then no one goes to see them... That sort of shows that they're out of touch. Then, everyone in town passes on my little movie, and it does really well." More important than money is heart and Rabbit-Aries' have heart by the bucket load. One is tempted to say they are also extremely talented however, some Rabbit-Aries people may disagree; Francis Ford Coppola said, "I probably have genius. But no talent." Genius or talent, they infuse every one of their endeavors with so much of themselves that their work just reeks of their idiosyncrasies. The outcomes may be artistic and usually profitable, but the process to get there was probably anarchy. Coppola said, "I bring to my life a certain amount of mess...anything you build on a large scale or with intense passion invites chaos."

The men of this combination approach everything through the eyes of a child, the dirtiest pebble is a gem just waiting to be cleaned up and sold as gold. They have an unending interest in the human condition. While some explore it through acting or directing, other's will interrogate their subjects before a live studio audience. Graham Norton has said, "To be a good chat show host you have to want to be a chat show host." At the finale of his show, Harvard graduate Conan O'Brien said, "All I ask is one thing and this is...I'm asking this particularly of young people that watch. Please do not be cynical. I hate cynicism; for the record, it's my least favorite quality, it doesn't lead anywhere. Nobody in life gets exactly what they thought they were going to get. But if you work really hard and you're kind, amazing things will happen. I'm telling you, amazing things will happen. I'm telling you, it's just true."

The women of this combination are gutsy types with the inner strength to allow their individual personalities to shine through. Olivia Hussey has said, "Have the confidence to be your own person." Often blessed with minds suited to academia, sparkling wit and grounded common sense, they are also highly attractive. In fact, the more attractive they are, the less it really matters to them. Although they understand the value of their beauty, they do not buy into the superficial nonsense that sometimes accompanies it. The elemental mix of water (yin) and fire (yang) here creates this; a burning gets put out by the water, then reignites then gets put out again and again. Yin and yang in perfect harmony. Rosie Huntington-Whitely has said, "I'm not here to win a popularity contest. I'm here to work and have a career. Let the haters hate. I'm ready for the criticism... I want to pay my bills and make my family proud. I've got no other criteria apart from that."

Ultimately, Rabbit-Aries is a combination drawn into serving the universe through its powers of perception and strength of character to allow the full force of their punch to be felt. Francis Ford Coppola said, "Not taking risks in art is like not having sex and then expecting there to be children." Similarly, Quentin

Tarrantino has said, "I'm never going to be shy about anything, what I write about is what I know; it's more about my version of the truth as I know it." They have a real desire to share their version of the world with others so they arrive with the capacity to do just that, plus artistic integrity.

Soul Mate: Dog-Virgo
Challenger: Rooster-Libra
Siblings: Rabbit-Leo, Rabbit-Sagittarius
Best Friends: Sheep-Aries, Sheep-Leo, Sheep-Sagittarius,
                   Boar-Aries, Boar-Leo, Boar-Sagittarius

Quentin Tarantino
Rosie Huntington-Whiteley
Brooklyn Decker
Jesse McCartney
Zach Braff
Francis Ford Coppola
Jacqueline MacInnes Wood
Stacy Ferguson
Steven Strait
Shay Mitchell
Olivia Hussey
Sean Maher
Eric McCormack
Conan O'Brien
Joss Stone
Graham Norton

RABBIT – TAURUS

Chinese Name: TU
Rank: 4th
Hours Ruled: 5am – 7am
Direction: Directly East
Season: Spring
Month: March
Western Zodiac Equivalent of Rabbit: Pisces
Pisces Western Element: Water
Eastern Zodiac Equivalent of Taurus: Snake
Taurus Western Element: Earth
Numerology: 38 = 2

When people are very original, sometimes they are original as a way to resist the mainstream.
– Michel Gondry

When the rich Rabbit waters trickle down through Taurus's tough terrain, the earth moistens and softens imbuing the tender artistic tendencies of the fluffy bunny with the bull's confidence and power. This is a strong personality that presents as quiet and malleable. Do not be fooled. These Rabbits know who they are, where they are going and what they want to achieve. They like to get their way while keeping everyone happy at the same time, but if that is not possible, that soft earth dries becoming hard and jagged like a rock. They like to get their way and often do. Tennis superstar Andy Murray has said, "I don't play any tournaments to come second best."

There is a socio-political slant to all Rabbit signs' creative endeavors so this artistic creature will weave a thread of its views in all of the work it carries out but usually in an unobtrusive way. Orson Welles, Michel Gondry and Russell T Davies belong to this combination: three highly inventive minds drawn to creating alternative worlds and having a controlling hand in how they are brought to life. People of this combination are highly original, possibly to resist the mainstream as Gondry said in the opening quote, but one cannot be truly original purely to fit a purpose; they actually have to be original to be capable of being original. And these people are. Orson Welles said, "A film is never really good unless the camera is an eye in the head of a poet." The Rabbit-Taurus as the visual poet is quite fitting actually, even if they might not be entirely comfortable with the label. Talking about his stylistic choices when directing, Michel Gondry said, "It's very hard to say I'm surrealist. It's like saying I'm poetic. It's not something you want necessarily to be aware of."

David Beckham is yet another original albeit in a different way; for the so-called "noughties" decade, he was the most searched person on a prominent internet search site and seems to be popular with every possible demographic. His looks, quiet charm and unknown views on everything except football allow him to be universally adored by all demographics. Tennis player Andy Murray, another British international sport star also belongs to this combination. They like to be liked if they can help it, but are not afraid to be controversial if necessary.

Sharp, clever and disciplined, the Rabbit-Taurus is a master at getting anything completed to a high level usually before any set deadline, even though they may not hand in the work until the date it was requested, just in case any last minute touch ups might be required. Like Harvey Keitel has said, "Make a choice and do it like Hercules." Although, they often live in their own little world, they are not blind to the real one. For that reason, they have a strange habit of behaving "pretentiously" because they find it fun, but get annoyed at others when they do the same thing.

The men of this combination are ambitious and driven. They take what they have and work their fluffy bom-boms off to magnify their strengths as best as they can, then use this as leverage to climb the ladder. External affirmation is important to them as they have an internal hole that they are looking to fill with something, anything and they do not mind working hard to meet their needs and those of their loved ones. There is a somber side to these men, a surprising pessimism from which emerge some of the dystopian worlds these creative cult icons have created. Orson Welles said, "We're born alone, we live alone, we die alone. Only through our love and friendship can we create the illusion for the moment that we're not alone." Even when surrounded by family, friends and loving energy, Welles perceives this construct as illusory. This is a common kind of belief held by men of this combination but it is not one that serves them particularly well and can be replaced for a healthier one. When in rest mode, they are overly contemplative and find themselves heading towards all that is wrong with the world rather than the light. This is when being present is helpful – relaxed play helps a lot.

The women of this combination are highly feminine but also have a need to express a side of the personality many prefer to keep hidden. Natasha Richardson said, "I've played comedy before but not that much. I mostly do get drawn to darker material." Like their male counterparts, these women are multifaceted and like to explore the nooks and crannies of themselves. They may go through many different looks before they decide on one to settle with. Christina Hendricks said, "I was a Goth girl in high school. Perhaps the powdered white face and the black lipstick were not the most attractive."

Women of this combination are psychologically clever and have a deep interest in people. Discussing human behavior, Christina Hendricks said, "To watch it and be able to express it through your version has always been really exciting to me."

Primary to people of this combination is their home and love life which they protect over all else. Despite their ambition and drive, their motivation is always their loved ones and they will serve them with everything they have. It is not difficult for them to turn down a lucrative contract if their partner is sick. They have their priorities right and that is why they are often very successful in their work life. If the motivation is right, the results follow. And how do they feel about their all around successes? Even if they present themselves as the epitome of humility, they may have a higher idea of themselves than they would like to be known; like Orson Welles said, "Nobody who takes on anything big and tough can afford to be modest."

Soul Mate:	Dog-Leo
Challenger:	Rooster-Scorpio
Siblings:	Rabbit-Virgo, Rabbit-Capricorn
Best Friends:	Sheep-Taurus, Sheep-Virgo, Sheep-Capricorn, Boar-Taurus, Boar-Virgo, Boar-Capricorn

Bing Crosby
Orson Welles
Anthony Quinn
Harvey Keitel
Lee Majors
Robert Zemeckis
Tony Danza
Jet Li
Natasha Richardson
Michel Gondry
Russell T. Davies
Johnny Galecki
Christina Hendricks
Enrique Iglesias
David Beckham

RABBIT – GEMINI

Chinese Name: TU
Rank: 4th
Hours Ruled: 5am – 7am
Direction: Directly East
Season: Spring
Month: March
Western Zodiac Equivalent of Rabbit: Pisces
Pisces Western Element: Water
Eastern Zodiac Equivalent of Gemini: Horse
Gemini Western Element: Air
Numerology: 39 = 3

*If you don't get out of the box you've been raised in, you won't
understand how much bigger the world is.*
– Angelina Jolie

When the clear streams of the Rabbit meet the inconsistent
cyclone of the Gemini, the Rabbit's innocence is corrupted time
and time again by the turbulence and excitement the naughty
twins generate. This is where intuition guides freedom, culture
merges with political ideals and gentleness meets careless
abandon to create a kind of natural hippy who has to consciously
learn how to live in this world saturated with rules and expectations that never seem to make sense to them. So they do what
everyone does to a certain degree, they try to fit in and because it
feels so alien to them they stop trying pretty early on and make
peace with the odd creature that they are so that they can be
themselves with confidence. As Johnny Depp has said, "I don't
pretend to be captain weird. I just do what I do."

Authenticity, passion and good intentions are what turns
these rampant rabbits on so they often find work in areas that
bring light to dark places. If they find themselves in arenas where

their value system is not aligned with those of the powers that be, they are usually miserable which creates a miserable environment for everyone around them, especially since their powerful energy has much social influence. It is better for them and everyone else that they slot themselves into a hole that is Rabbit-Gemini shaped. Talking about his poorly fitting job role as a sales man, Johnny Depp said, "The last couple of times I did it, I just said, 'Listen, you don't want this stuff, man.'"

Rabbit-Geminis like to be surrounded by beauty or things that mean something. Often times, there is a side of them that likes to dwell on what went wrong or fixate on the past wondering what should have been, even when they know it is unhelpful. They need to work at changing this pattern and remain present to the joys that are available in the now. This combination knows how to make a mountain out of a molehill, but also, lemonade out of a single lemon.

The men of this combination are highly sensitive with a need to social work the universe. Feeling social injustices powerfully, they want to help, whether on a grass roots level or higher up the ladder. They are likely to be interested in social reform and may even go so far as to get involved in politics to ensure that their cause gets attention. Jamie Oliver is a good example of a Rabbit-Gemini, whose desire to improve the health of the world's children by improving the nutritional content of the food they consume has made him an international name. That and his culinary talent of course. In fact, many of these men are quite adept in the kitchen; David Burtka is another Rabbit-Gemini chef of some repute. Whatever road they choose, they do not leave success to chance, they make it a certainty. Bob Hope said, "I've always been in the right place and time. Of course, I steered myself there." When they have down time, they seek out a project because this Rabbit thrives on activity. That combined with their determination to succeed, these men are unlikely champions but their success rate is impressive. Comic Mike Myers said, "If I went by all the rejection I've had in my career, I should have given up a long time ago."

The women of this combination are intuitive, independent and open. With love absolutely pouring out of them, they have to develop techniques to protect themselves. So in a strange sort of way, they put things in place to make themselves less open, to force themselves to be more private because it is what they need in order to feel secure. Helen Hunt has said, "I don't like people to think they know me. It makes me queasy." Already, they fret about the small stuff but this Rabbit's need for self-preservation adds tension to their tender nerves. This is why they try to bypass the Gemini's desire to be super-sociable, choosing the company of only those they are sure want nothing from them. Angelina Jolie has said, "Well, I have a few girlfriends, I just...I stay at home a lot. I'm just not very social. I don't do a lot with them, and I'm very homebound. I'll talk to my family... But I don't know, I don't have a lot of friends I talk to."

Despite the unnecessary fretting and concealed emotional angst, these creatures know how to love, more importantly love to love and overflow with love unlike any other combination. Sometimes their love is unconventional where they might even be ashamed of how much they love because some people might see it as a weakness or controversial, but darn it, they just cannot help themselves. Ian Mckellan has said, "Be honest with each other. Admit there are limitless possibilities in relationships, and love as many people as you can in whatever way you want, and get rid of your inhibitions, and we'll all be happy." With a natural ability to intuit what human needs one may require, they will try to provide it without thinking twice. Maybe that's why so many of them preach about the healing power of laughter, which to them is sex for the belly. Bob Hope said, "I have seen what a laugh can do. It can transform almost unbearable tears into something bearable, even hopeful." The Rabbit-Gemini lives with every part of themselves viscerally, with every single fiber of their being, so that when they serve the universe, it is done with such intensity the universe rewards their service handsomely.

Soul Mate:	Dog-Cancer
Challenger:	Rooster-Sagittarius
Siblings:	Rabbit-Libra, Rabbit-Aquarius
Best Friends:	Sheep-Gemini, Sheep-Libra, Sheep-Aquarius, Boar-Gemini, Boar-Libra, Boar-Aquarius

Bob Hope
John Randolph
Jerry Stiller
Ian McKellen
Stellan Skarsgård
Richard Thomas
Suze Orman
Johnny Depp
Jason Isaacs
Mike Myers
Helen Hunt
Greg Kinnear
Angelina Jolie
Russell Brand
Hugh Dancy
André Benjamin
Lauryn Hill
Cee-Lo
Melanie Brown
Shilpa Shetty
Ameesha Patel

Jamie Oliver
Ekta Kapoor
Novak Djokovic
Sonakshi Sinha
David Burtka

RABBIT – CANCER

Chinese Name: TU
Rank: 4th
Hours Ruled: 5am – 7am
Direction: Directly East
Season: Spring
Month: March
Western Zodiac Equivalent of Rabbit: Pisces
Pisces Western Element: Water
Eastern Zodiac Equivalent of Cancer: Sheep
Cancer Western Element: Water
Numerology: 40 = 4

I do expose my body but only because I think people should have something nice to look at.
– Brigitte Nielsen

Witty, creative and sexy, Rabbit-Cancers can be extremely attractive although in a somewhat unusual or unconventional way. Physically, they tend to stick out in a crowd because of their special or exotic features. People are drawn to their warmth and spiciness but the interesting thing about Rabbit-Cancers is that what you see is not what you get. As Brigitte Nielsen said, "People think I'm strong, as hard as I look but I've a very sensitive side and need to be loved by everyone." This is very typical of a Rabbit-Cancer. They have a strong desire to be liked and to be accepted as part of a group gaining the approval of their peers. They are not weak by any means but do spend much of their time managing their own insecurities, constantly striving to convince themselves of their own worth. George Michael has said, "I'm surprised that I've survived my own dysfunction, really."

When the Western zodiac signs of the water element (Cancer,

Scorpio and Pisces) are attached to the Eastern Rabbit sign, a concentration of the water element occurs creating the three Moon-Children, the Rabbit-Cancer being the first born. In Chinese Folklore, the image of the Rabbit is believed to be marked on the moon by Sakra, the ruler of the Trayastrimsa Heavens because the Rabbit sacrificed himself for the deity believing he had nothing to offer but himself as food. Because of this the Rabbit has always been seen as a self-sacrificial, humble and loving sign. Furthermore, as Cancer is the only Western zodiac sign ruled by the Moon, the Rabbit-Cancer tends to have an inexplicable connection to our sleeping satellite. Their physiology actually tends to be affected when the moon is full.

Although nobody would doubt how tough rapper 50 Cent is, he has publically said, "I don't display emotions. I have every feeling that everyone else has but I've developed ways to suppress them." Although offering a surface level of protection, the repercussions of this repression can at times be all-consuming and the internal chaos becomes manifest in the external world. Rabbit-Cancers learn to manage this side of themselves later on in life replacing this device with other, more productive methods of self-protection and personal expression.

Endowed with many endearing qualities, one finds it hard to dislike these celestial creatures with their abundance of talent, self-deprecation and comic perceptions. There is something innately child-like about them with an openness to explore any facet of a personality they are confronted by. George Orwell once said, "One can love a child more deeply than one can love an adult, but it is rash to assume that the child feels any love in return." In a similar way, it is quite easy to love a Rabbit-Cancer because of their physical attributes and sparkling personalities, yet it is rash to assume that that love will be returned. Rabbit-Cancers like to be loved, whether they respond in like is totally at their discretion.

With a good psychological understanding, they rarely seem to apply it to themselves. One wonders if they see themselves in the context of the bigger picture because oftentimes their actions seem inconsistent. For example, they may claim you are one of their closest friends and you see them on a weekly basis, then they could leave the country for a year and not think to tell you. When it comes to personal matters, they can be unpredictable, occasionally volatile, but do not always assume that because they have opened the door to discuss matters at one time, that door will always be open. All Rabbits are private creatures whether they say so or not.

They question life, reality and the value of truth in this context. George Michael said, "There's no comfort in the truth. Pain is all you'll find." George Orwell said, "Ignorance is strength." Tracy Emin said, "Truth is such a transient thing." Does that mean that they prefer to live in a world of their own creation? It could explain some of the addictions faced by members of this combination.

At their core, Rabbit-Cancers spend their entire lives trying to convince themselves and the world around them that they are worthy and that they do matter, which is strange, because nobody ever doubted it to begin with. Terence Stamp once said that "As a boy, I believed I could make myself invisible... I certainly had the ability to pass unnoticed," and this notion is shared by many Rabbit-Cancers which is where their professional drive comes from. They have a desire to prove that they do exist, that they do matter and that they are just as good as everyone else, if not better. Huey Lewis said, "I am deluded enough to think I can bring something to the table." Sometimes this notion is misconstrued as arrogance; occasionally it comes disguised in their humor, Tracy Emin once said, "I'm out of here, I'm better than all of you."

Their warmth is inviting, their tenderness addictive and their humor explosive, they would be endlessly popular but for their own insecurities which cause a minor hindrance. Nevertheless, their ambition pushes them forwards and they make great strides despite working against themselves. When they find friends who give them their space yet love them unconditionally, they flourish and reveal surprising talents. Many have beautiful singing voices. Their introspective ways become less pronounced as they age and their defenses lessen. One wonders whether this inner tension is their Achilles heal or their greatest gift? Without it, they might lack their understanding, their sympathy and their intrinsic radiance.

Soul Mate:	Dog-Gemini
Challenger:	Rooster-Capricorn
Siblings:	Rabbit-Scorpio, Rabbit-Pisces
Best Friends:	Sheep-Cancer, Sheep-Scorpio, Sheep-Pisces, Boar-Cancer, Boar-Scorpio, Boar-Pisces

Lorraine Chase
Tracy Emin
Huey Lewis
George Michael
Kate Nash
Brigitte Nielsen
George Orwell
Ken Russell
Terence Stamp
Jack White
Vonda Shepard
Fatboy Slim
Yann Martel
Rupert Graves
Rakesh Omprakash Mehra
Tobey Maguire
50 Cent
Cheyenne Jackson

RABBIT – LEO

Chinese Name: TU
Rank: 4th
Hours Ruled: 5am – 7am
Direction: Directly East
Season: Spring
Month: March
Western Zodiac Equivalent of Rabbit: Pisces
Pisces Western Element: Water
Eastern Zodiac Equivalent of Leo: Monkey
Leo Western Element: Fire
Numerology: 41 = 5

I'm either my best friend or my worst enemy.
– Whitney Houston

When the Rabbit's rolling river meets with the Lion's fierce fire, the elements crash into each other; fighting, loving, merging, conflicting and most of all enjoying the internal interaction. Rabbit signs like complexity, it interests them and keeps their intellect occupied, they find themselves quite fascinating, but not in a pretentious, egotistical way. They like to learn about themselves as objectively as possible so that they can understand their unusual-ness; they never fit *society's mold*, so they do not apply common notions of acceptability upon themselves. That being said, they know that most people will not understand this so they seek out friends who are non-judgmental, empathic and openhearted to provide space, an umbrella of unconditional affection under which they can just be. John Stamos has said, "People look at me and go, 'You must have it made. You have girls. You have a great life.' It's not true. I mean you pull the curtain away, and you see I'm just as insecure and neurotic and scared and vulnerable as anybody, you know."

Although some have a tendency to sacrifice their time or energy in jobs where they feel wasted, they will do so if it means that they can spend their leisure time with as much freedom as possible. And when they are at work, they will find a way to enjoy it. The Rabbit brings empathy to the union and Leo brings joy, light and friskiness; it also brings the capacity to channel pure sunshine through them onto everyone within their general vicinity; wherever they are, they bring the sun with them so they have fun all of the time. George Hamilton said, "While I put forth the suntan and the teeth and the cavalier attitude, I've survived under the worst of eras and times, and I've always had a good time doing it, because I never really took myself seriously, nor did I take life seriously because it is already terribly serious."

The men of this combination like to look good, because looking good makes them feel good and if they feel good, they open the doors to fun in all its incarnations. The feeling of freedom and ability to have a variety of choices in their private lives is very important as is playful intimate connection. Maybe that is why George Hamilton has said, "I will not date a depressed woman. I want to have fun." Most Rabbit men are comfortable with the yin side of their nature so they tend to be intuitive and allow themselves to explore interests that other men may ridicule. John Stamos said, "I started Pilates. I'm the only guy in there." They know what is good for them and what their inner child is asking for. When they allow that child to play, they find success in all areas of their life, but if they do not – it is as if they are locked in a dark room. Rodrigo Santoro has said, "I need to surf – surf and yoga. Whenever I'm in L.A., I go down to San Diego to surf for the weekend, and I always come back perfect." To get to the core of this man, you have to know that he is both a massive wave of feminine energy and a volcano of masculine energy simultaneously.

The women of this combination tend to have heart-shaped faces with big eyes and present themselves with an innocent sweetness with a threat of sharpness if you mess with her. She does not bind herself to any label that might diminish her or lessen her power, instead, she prefers to remain a mystery to people because she does not feel the need to explain herself. Being highly intuitive, she knows how to utilize universal laws, like the law of attraction to draw the experiences she wants towards her. Talking about how she drew her partner into her life, Lisa Kudrow said, "I wanted to be the kind of woman who would attract a certain kind of man that I could respect. That was my thinking. It had to do with the kind of couple I would be a part of." Essentially, these women are comfortable enough in their femininity that they are happy to explore their yang side too. Whitney Houston said, "I like being a woman, even in a man's world. After all, men can't wear dresses, but we can wear the pants." It would be productive for Rabbit-Leos to identify how their creative skills would be best put to use and forge a career in that field early, because they make huge creative contributions as an army of one! They are Game-Changers! Look at how Whitney Houston changed the music scene forever or the impact Sridevi had on "Bollywood", the Indian film industry?

With their innocence, lightness and unusual specialness, they are effortlessly attractive creatures that feel more open than they are, closer than they are and more attainable than they are. They are aware of what they bring to the table so it better be appreciated; otherwise they will pull back and leave you in the shadows. They know what they want, but they do not always share it so it is important for this to be clarified with them otherwise you may realize that this rabbit will have jumped into a hole in the blink of an eye. As Whitney Houston has said, "No one makes me do anything I don't want to do." Work collaboratively with them in all things and they are in heaven, but try to impose your way and you will realize that the Rabbit-Leo is nobody's minion. When in their shadow mode, they need to experience the harsh lessons of life, molly coddling does not serve them, let them fall. More often, they will rise like a phoenix. As Charlize Theron has said, "I think that tragedy is part of the lesson you learn to lift yourself up, to pick yourself up and to move on."

Soul Mate: Dog-Taurus
Challenger: Rooster-Aquarius
Siblings: Rabbit-Aries, Rabbit-Sagittarius
Best Friends: Sheep-Aries, Sheep-Leo, Sheep-Sagittarius, Boar-Aries, Boar-Leo, Boar-Sagittarius

Charlize Theron
Sridevi
Lisa Kudrow
Rodrigo Santoro
John Stamos
George Hamilton
Wes Craven
Whitney Houston
Mara Wilson
Genesis Rodriguez
George Stults
Casey Affleck
Donnie Yen
Alicia Witt
Harold Perrineau
Robert Shaw
Alejandro González Iñárritu
Giuliana Rancic

RABBIT – VIRGO

Chinese Name: TU
Rank: 4ᵗʰ
Hours Ruled: 5am – 7am
Direction: Directly East
Season: Spring
Month: March
Western Zodiac Equivalent of Rabbit: Pisces
Pisces Western Element: Water
Eastern Zodiac Equivalent of Virgo: Rooster
Virgo Western Element: Earth
Numerology: 42 = 6

I was the shyest human ever invented, but I had a lion inside me that wouldn't shut up.
– Ingrid Bergman

When the Rabbit's ocean of creativity meets Virgo's fertile earth, it creates a talented grafter with an intriguing personality. Empathic, caring and self-assured yet they are one of the biggest worriers. The thing is, they have exceptionally high standards and they feel like they are letting the entire universe down if they do not live up to them so they drive themselves crazy whilst working harder and harder on the details to get everything precisely as they want them; only when they have that done can they allow their sensitive nerves some rest. That is until the next project begins. Speaking about her school life, Blake Lively said, "I was class president, on the cheerleading squad, in a competitive show choir, and in, like, six different clubs."

They have social x-ray vision and articulate what they say with finesse even though they may perceive themselves as verbally clumsy. Rabbit brings creativity in abundance; Virgo brings the attention to detail, critical faculties and capacity for hard work.

With these ingredients, talent is expected but so is a dodgy self-esteem. Michael Buble has said, "I have a tendency to sabotage relationships; I have a tendency to sabotage everything. Fear of success, fear of failure, fear of being afraid. Useless, good-for-nothing thoughts." But they also are naturally open, too open and easily susceptible to the parasitical influences of less authentic people. Ever resourceful as they are, they find techniques, mental processes and self-preservation methods that manage these issues in one great big hoppity-hop, even though this may make them look "odd" in general society. Better "odd" than tortured by their own mind or taken advantage of. Ingrid Bergman said, "You must train your intuition – you must trust the small voice inside you which tells you exactly what to say, what to decide.

There is something very socialist about them and they have such a sense of responsibility to the rest of humanity, these people are found setting up creative or social enterprises as the primary instigators because it usually is their idea. Like many Rabbit combinations, the Rabbit-Virgos are serious about their privacy and personal space. Although, they have a tender, soft nature, cross one of their well-defined boundaries and this bunny will bare its teeth and show you its sharp claws; cross a second boundary and you will fully awaken the beast that resides inside this cute package. They actually have an ability to freeze people with one look. It's a great thing to witness but not such a great thing to be at the end of. You have been warned. Rabbit-Virgos in their shadow phase are often given to pretentious behavior in order to fit in or to control their social group in some way. This pushes people away and the Rabbit-Virgo is likely to reject before it is rejected and flee the scene.

The men of this combination usually have pretty features, full lips and big baby eyes. Their appeal seems to come from every aspect of their personage: their intellect, political activism, creativity and passion. On the surface, they are not usually the most masculine of all men, they are on the short to medium height build with an almost feminine beauty, but this only belies the champion's mentality that they have. Just like the energizer bunny, when all else have fallen away, the Rabbit-Virgo will just keep going until they have achieved their goal. Michael Keaton said, "I played a lot of sports when I was a kid so I get in that ballgame mindset of being really, really respectful, but at same time saying to yourself, 'Don't back down a single inch, hang with these guys if you can.' If they throw it high and tight you have to stand in there, you can't take yourself out of that moment."

The women of this combination give freely of themselves and serve unselfishly. Naturally shy, reserved, beautiful, humble, talented hard working and full of heart, the women of this combination are often put on a pedestal by their many admirers. Blake Lively said, "It's like nature versus nurture: I'm naturally very shy, but I was brought up in a way where I had to get up and get out of that." They also work exceptionally hard in whatever field they are in because it gives them a sense of their own worth. Ingrid Bergman said, "The best way to keep young is to keep going in whatever it is that keeps you going. With me that's work, and a lot of it. And when a job is finished, relax and have fun." Being so open, they are susceptible to other people's energies and without realizing it they find themselves morphing into those they are spending a lot of time with, so it is important for them to keep the company of those they aspire to be like rather than those who they are trying to help; even with the best of intentions, sometimes when they give the less fortunate a helping hand up, they end up being pulled down instead.

Ultimately, they spend so much of their time ingrained in their art, it is like they become a work of art themselves. They are also absolutely adored by the few people that they let into their odd little lives. Maybe they consider themselves too neurotic, or strange or too individualistic to be able to be understood by most. Lily Tomlinson has said, "Just remember. We're all in this alone." If they are alone, it is by choice; Rabbit-Virgos are always in demand and always have options. It is more a question of priorities. And the priority for the Rabbit-Virgo is to improve their own skills, grow as a person and emotionally express what is in their hearts. Ingrid Bergman said, "I've never sought success in order to get fame and money; it's the talent and the passion that count in success."

Soul Mate:	Dog-Aries
Challenger:	Rooster-Pisces
Siblings:	Rabbit-Taurus, Rabbit-Capricorn
Best Friends:	Sheep-Taurus, Sheep-Virgo, Sheep-Capricorn, Boar-Taurus, Boar-Virgo, Boar-Capricorn

Ingrid Bergman
Peter Falk
Rosemary Harris
Richard Kiel
Joel Schumacher
Lily Tomlin
Michael Keaton
Mark Harmon
Richard Marx
Jarvis Cocker
Mark Strong
Scott Speedman
Michael Bublé
Mark Ronson
Blake Lively
Evan Rachel Wood
Tom Felton

RABBIT – LIBRA

Chinese Name: TU
Rank: 4th
Hours Ruled: 5am – 7am
Direction: Directly East
Season: Spring
Month: March
Western Zodiac Equivalent of Rabbit: Pisces
Pisces Western Element: Water
Eastern Zodiac Equivalent of Libra: Dog
Libra Western Element: Air
Numerology: 43 = 7

I think that when you don't see the boundaries, you cross them without even knowing they exist in the first place.
– Marion Cotilard

When the Rabbit's refined waters meet with Libra's serene air, a sophisticated creature is born who is intelligent, creative and politically motivated. Much like many of the Rabbit signs, this combination likes to effect political change without necessarily being directly involved with politics themselves. The Rabbit brings genuine concern for people and the Libra brings the humanitarian desire for fairness, so when these two signs merge, it creates a personality that gets a lot out of helping other people from overcoming their own personal demons, whatever they may be. With a gentle, quiet surface, the Rabbit-Libra lives in an unassuming way, going about its business achieving much with very little fuss. They do not like the idea that they might be imposing or affecting another person negatively so they go out of their way to ensure that they remain behind certain set boundary lines. In return, they expect these boundaries to be respected.

In their earlier years, they struggle with their own self-perception, many find it difficult to leave these struggles behind even though they are aware that it is no more than self-created fiction. Kate Winslet has said, "You know, once a fat kid, always a fat kid. Because you always think that you just look a little bit wrong or a little bit different from everyone else. And I still sort of have that." In a similar way, Marion Cotilard has said, "At school I was that black thing in the corner. I was not popular at all. I think I was very boring... I thought everybody was so cool, and I was not." Even Zac Efron has said, "Personally, I was never the cool kid. I was always sort of a bookworm." Whether these perceptions were true or otherwise, they are very true for the Rabbit-Libra. It is difficult for them to leave these fictions behind because they are so bound to them. When they realize that these stories no longer serve them and they choose to believe a new truth that does, they experience a relief and lightness that frees them from their past.

The men of this combination tend to be tall, well built, and pretty. As Roger Moore put it, "I was pretty – so pretty that actresses didn't want to work with me." Just have a look at some of the other males on the Rabbit-Libra list, yes, they are pretty. They are also very connected to their emotions and because of this, their sense of responsibility to all. Talking about his role as a Writer, Arthur Miller said, "The job is to ask questions – it always was – and to ask them as inexorably as I can. And to face the absence of precise answers with a certain humility." These men are also exceptionally talented, usually multitalented. Zac Efron has said, "I can draw really well. And I like to paint. I'm a bit of an artist." Not only do they pick things up easily, they also work so hard at it that they pick up the subtleties that make their artistic works really evocative and moving. Part of it comes naturally to them and part of it is developed through their love of what they do. Sting has said, "I'm so glad I have this way of expressing, in a veiled and artistic way, my most intimate feelings... I'm proud of my being able to make it into artifacts that some people find beautiful or engaging."

The women of this combination are more than just pretty, they are sultry beauties. They emanate a charm and dignity that is attractive and classy. Although, they may not think it about themselves, they are effortlessly popular. They have a huge need to protect themselves from scrutiny, yet ironically, have a huge need to be seen at the same time. This is why they put themselves out there, yet hold back in so many ways, which ends up creating a mystique about them, keeping their stock expensive; however, this is purely a consequence of their insecurities rather than from any thought-out plan. In any case, this woman is a lady and her trust needs to be earned which requires time and patience. Marion Cotilard has said, "I'm not somebody who opens up to people very easily. With this form of expression, I think I've found a way to speak to a lot of people and share something of myself, while still keeping my distance." Similarly, Hilary Duff has said, "I can't really act the way I want to act, or say what I want to say all the time. And a lot of times, I cover that up with a smile."

With a powerful desire to make themselves manifest, they feel compelled to take actions that sometimes confound their friends and family. Sting has said, "My parents didn't really understand what my dreams were. They just thought I was crazy because I had just given up a job with a pension and the security, in their eyes. My dad didn't understand until the end of his days what the hell I was doing. He thought I should have had a proper job. Maybe he was right. I wanted to take a risk and be a star." Remember, Rabbits feel more than most people, so when their heart points them in a certain direction, they will listen. With their Rabbit hearts and their Libra minds, these creatures are destined to live lives of artistic achievement; even if they do not work in creative industries initially, many will change to creative careers later in their lives or spend much of their time indulging in their creative hobbies. One way or another, they will find a way to let the beauty that is in their heart find expression, because the art in their heart is far too beautiful to remain hidden. Kate Winslet has said, "I was a wayward child, very passionate and very determined. If I made up my mind to do something, there was no stopping me."

Soul Mate:	Dog-Pisces
Challenger:	Rooster-Aries
Siblings:	Rabbit-Gemini, Rabbit-Aquarius
Best Friends:	Sheep-Gemini, Sheep-Libra, Sheep-Aquarius, Boar-Gemini, Boar-Libra, Boar-Aquarius

Arthur Miller

Roger Moore

Zac Efron

Sting

Bob Geldof

Hilary Duff

Marion Cotillard

Kate Winslet

India Arie

Elisabeth Shue

Tom Bosley

George C. Scott

Paul Hogan

Ralph Lauren

Feroz Khan

Melvyn Bragg

Clive James

John Mellencamp

Terry McMillan

Parminder Nagra
Declan Donnelly
Kunal Kapoor
Lori Petty
Tate Donovan

RABBIT – SCORPIO

Chinese Name: TU
Rank: 4th
Hours Ruled: 5am – 7am
Direction: Directly East
Season: Spring
Month: March
Western Zodiac Equivalent of Rabbit: Pisces
Pisces Western Element: Water
Eastern Zodiac Equivalent of Scorpio: Boar
Scorpio Western Element: Water
Numerology: 44 = 8

He who laughs most learns best.
– John Cleese

When the Rabbit's rolling river meets with Scorpio's deep murky waters, innocence, grace and intelligence meet a darker, edgier and complicated character. Remember that the symbolic mascots for the Scorpio are both, the regal golden eagle, as well as the stinging scorpion; when this influence joins the Rabbit, a bolder, braver and bigger presence is its universal blessing. Both the Western and Chinese signs here are secretive and concerned with self-preservation too so although that Rabbit warmth abounds, they can be snappier and more firm about maintaining their personal boundaries. However, it does not hold them back from getting out there and living life fully. They are not wallflowers or party animals they are simply led by their passions, political convictions and powerfully compassionate hearts. In fact, a good way to describe the members of this club, is perhaps, the peaceful hero. John Keats said, "There is an electric fire in human nature tending to purify – so that among these human creatures there is continually some birth of new heroism. The pity is that we must wonder at it, as we should at finding a pearl in rubbish."

Rabbit hearts urge them into action over injustices that they see, but not in the same way that the three activist signs of the Tiger, Horse or Dog would, remember, the Rabbit is the political artist, so they bury their messages in their art; in fact, many of them find out what they believe because they unearth them through their own creative work. With the influence of the Scorpio, they are less afraid to be more overt about their feelings in a public forum. The common message is one of uniting through understanding, not fragmenting out of fear and through this, providing a fair system for everybody. Zadie Smith has said, "My feeling is, having lived in different classes, that people want equality of opportunity..." If they could, they would try to change the entire system themselves but they are aware of their own human limitations, but their spirit subconsciously encourages the collective human race towards this goal in their own way. John Cleese has said, "A wonderful thing about true laughter is that it just destroys any kind of system of dividing people."

The men of this combination are often pretty boys who tend to their looks rather narcissistically although they would never let that be known. Self-disciplined and humorous, men of this combination can be serious and seriously funny. Paul McKenna, John Cleese and Rob Schneider are also Rabbit-Scorpios. But most prominently in this combination are literary men such as Leon Trotsky and John Keats, who said, "My imagination is a monastery and I am its monk." Words come easily to them and when they apply that discipline, they are able to become literary heavyweights. But actually, because of their ability to focus and be disciplined, they can succeed in most occupations. Despite being creatively gifted, many opt for professional jobs because they want the security and also, they want to keep their creative life to themselves. These men are unusual in the regard that they can be so honest that sometimes it is uncomfortable to hear the truths they vocalize. Even John Cleese has said, "I just think that sometimes we hang onto people or relationships long after they've ceased to be of any use to either of you. I'm always meeting new people, and my list of friends seems to change quite a bit."

The women of this combination are equally as honest but are more likely to pull their punches with their hyper-honesty. Author Zadie Smith said, "I think I know a thing or two about the way people love, but I don't know anything about hatred, psychosis, cruelty. Or maybe I don't have the guts to admit that I do." There is a strong yin influence here. The feminine anima side of this personality is quite prominent. Fashionable and exceptionally particular about their physical appearance the females of this combination are also maternal and nurturing. That being said, practicality is also of paramount importance. Scientist and first female Nobel prize winner said, "I have no dress except the one I wear every day. If you are going to be kind enough to give me one, please let it be practical and dark so that I can put it on afterwards to go to the laboratory."

Being a double water combination and one of the three moon-children (the others being Rabbit-Cancer and Rabbit-Pisces), they are greatly affected by the moon's phases. Also, as the water element is concerned with beauty and aesthetics so it comes as no surprise that many Rabbit-Scorpio ladies can be found in the various beauty pageants of the world. Both Bollywood actresses Sushmita Sen and Zeenat Aman won international beauty contests for India in their respective generations; and both won in the Rabbit's soul-mate sign, the year of the Dog (Aman in 1970 and Sen in 1994).

Ultimately, with its pioneering spirit, humane perspective and creative gifts, the Rabbit-Scorpio is one combination that cannot be ignored, despite its quiet nature. They make waves because it seems like they are being braver than most by putting themselves out there; they do not see it that way, they are just being themselves and doing what comes naturally to them, following their inner call. But perhaps that is why they end up where they are. John Keats has said, "He ne'er is crowned with immortality who fears to follow where airy voices lead." They are not afraid to take action with conviction, because they know the truth, that there is nothing to be afraid of, that nothing can is or goes wrong and that all roads eventually lead everyone to exactly where they need to be. The problem is not any particular issue of the day, it is the fear itself! Madam Marie Curie said, "Nothing in life is to be feared, it is only to be understood. Now is the time to understand more, so that we may fear less."

Soul Mate:	Dog-Aquarius
Challenger:	Rooster-Taurus
Siblings:	Rabbit-Cancer, Rabbit-Pisces
Best Friends:	Sheep-Cancer, Sheep-Scorpio, Sheep-Pisces, Boar-Cancer, Boar-Scorpio, Boar-Pisces

John Cleese
Paul McKenna
Dermot Mulroney
Nicolette Sheridan
Zadie Smith
Rob Schneider
Tara Reid
Ant McPartlin
Natalie Merchant
Ian Wright
John Barnes
Tatum O'Neal

Sushmita Sen
Zeenat Aman
Trudie Goodwin
Kevin Jonas
Marc Summers
Leon Trotsky
Madame Curie
John Keats

RABBIT – SAGITTARIUS

Chinese Name: TU
Rank: 4ᵗʰ
Hours Ruled: 5am – 7am
Direction: Directly East
Season: Spring
Month: March
Western Zodiac Equivalent of Rabbit: Pisces
Pisces Western Element: Water
Eastern Zodiac Equivalent of Sagittarius: Rat
Sagittarius Western Element: Fire
Numerology: 45 = 9

I believe that if you'll just stand up and go, life will open up for you.
– Tina Turner

When the Rabbit's gentle stream meets the centaurs flickering flame, a subtle, sensual and slick personality is created. With Sagittarius being a mutable sign and Rabbit signs being so open to the energies of other people, this combination is a bit of a chameleon in that they are powerfully influenced by those who surround them and noticeably pick up on others mannerisms and vocal habits. Their values however, are their own. Rabbit signs look after themselves, their family and a very few close friends; they do not need or cultivate acquaintances, even though they tend to have many. They like people to be kind, gentle and classy because it mirrors their own intrinsic nature. As Frank Sinatra said, "I detest bad manners. If people are polite, I am. They shouldn't try to get away with not being polite to me." Of course, they will raise their children with impeccably good manners also; Mayim Bialik has said, "I'm big on my kids being conventionally polite, and it works really well for them."

Born Jewish, Mayim Bialik is also a neuroscientist; some may consider it difficult to reconcile one with the other; what is common with this combination is that they allow their experiences to impact their belief structure, taking what works and dumping what doesn't. Brad Pitt has said, "I grew up very religious, and I don't have a great relationship with religion. I oscillate between agnosticism and atheism." At the same time, they respect all religions and everyone's right to their own choices. As Tina Turner has said, "I believe all religion is about touching something inside of yourself."

These early religious convictions usually morph over time into something very personal and functional, even though many tend to leave conventional religion behind. As Frank Sinatra said, "To me religion is a deeply personal thing in which man and God go it alone together, without the witch doctor in the middle."

The men of this combination tend to be conventionally attractive, with that additional glint in their eyes and a subtle swagger to boot; with men like Brad Pitt and Frank Sinatra belonging to this combination that much is evident. Besides their obvious charms, they have very warm, receptive and inviting personalities that put you at ease. Although they are gentle and sociable, they have learned how to turn on their assertiveness. Self-preservation is key for all Rabbits so take the time to learn where their boundaries lay otherwise risk receiving the cold shoulder if you transgress. Respect them, mirror their receptivity and express your generosity and you will be in their good books. Discussing what he values most, Brad Pitt said, "To me, it's about the value of your time and your day and the value of the people you spend it with. It's about me being a strong father and guide and a good match for my significant other. Then, if I'm going to go to work, it must be something of value to me."

In a similar way, the women also prioritize their parental role.

Tina Turner said, "I regret not having had more time with my kids when they were growing up." Of course, any working mother would, however, the Rabbit-Sagittarius mother takes parenting so seriously that they often integrate their working lives with that of raising their children. Mayim Bialik said, "I have a neuroscience background – that's what my doctorate is in – and I was trained to study hormones of attachment, so I definitely feel my parenting is informed by that." At the same time, this woman is more than capable of juggling a number of roles with relative ease; when she is a mother, she is present, nurturing and playful, when she is at work, she is focused, organized and quietly persuasive. She is also highly creative which feeds her intellect and vice versa. Talking about choosing controversial issues to base movies on, Director Kathryn Bigelow has said, "Once you've opened the window on topical material, it's very hard to close it. Holding up a contemporary mirror is more attractive to me now than ever." This Rabbit lady is a tough creature even though she tends to wear her sensitivity and vulnerability on her sleeve. Talking about love, life and sexuality, Jennifer Beals said, "You have to realize how precious human life is...love is truly one of the most extraordinary things you can experience in your life. To begrudge someone else their love of another person because of gender seems to be absolutely absurd."

Excelling in most professional environments, they are drawn to jobs where they can be sociable, creative and undertake work that requires great detail or precision simultaneously. They are also drawn to IT, Finance and the Sciences. They seek to be challenged by everything that they do. Brad Pitt has said, "I believe I'm quite capable and we, as people, can learn to do anything, and that's proof of it! And my education is on film, on record! Now I can take on anything that comes my way and find truth in it and do a pretty good job." Being an example for their own children primarily and also because they genuinely enjoy the process of growth, they look for things that scare them and push them onwards. Possibly because this combination finds it difficult to figure out where they start and their significant other ends, their primary insecurity is that of never quite knowing who they are. When they start observing their actions objectively, without judgment, they are able to allay their own fears and be content that they are enough. The truth is, the reason they do not know who they are is because they are constantly growing and cannot keep up with themselves. Their values make them who they are; and without question, they are a class act. Tina Turner has said, "I'm self-made. I always wanted to make myself a better person, because I was not educated. But that was my dream – to have class."

Soul Mate: Dog-Capricorn
Challenger: Rooster-Gemini
Siblings: Rabbit-Aries, Rabbit-Leo
Best Friends: Sheep-Aries, Sheep-Leo, Sheep-Sagittarius,
                 Boar-Aries, Boar-Leo, Boar-Sagittarius

Frank Sinatra
Jennifer Beals
Brad Pitt
Tina Turner
Kathryn Bigelow
Eli Wallach
Mayim Bialik
Bill Bryson
Honor Blackman
Édith Piaf
Robert Guillaume
Lalita Ahmed
Til Schweiger

Brendan Coyle
Benjamin Bratt
Helen Slater
Govinda
Paula Patton
Milla Jovovich
James Kyson
Mindy McCready
Michael Angarano
Karen Gillan
Aaron Carter

RABBIT – CAPRICORN

Chinese Name: TU
Rank: 4th
Hours Ruled: 5am – 7am
Direction: Directly East
Season: Spring
Month: March
Western Zodiac Equivalent of Rabbit: Pisces
Pisces Western Element: Water
Eastern Zodiac Equivalent of Capricorn: Ox
Capricorn Western Element: Earth
Numerology: 46 = 1

*Whether you come from a council estate or a country estate,
your success will be determined by your own confidence and
fortitude.*
– Michelle Obama

When the Rabbit's river water meets the Capricorn's dense earth,
refinement meets clumsiness, intelligence meets solidity, heart
meets mind. Both signs are dignified, but only the Rabbit
presents it; the Capricorn tends to project an image somewhat
akin to a caveman as it only knows how to place its value on
substance; whereas, the Rabbit effortlessly projects substance in
style! What the Capricorn lends powerfully to this union is hard
work, modesty and a tough spirit. This person tends to be driven
by passion and details; they see the value in doing things
properly as well as the repercussions of a job done quickly but
with insufficient attention. As novelist Henry Miller has said, "In
this age, which believes that there is a shortcut to everything, the
greatest lesson to be learned is that the most difficult way is, in
the long run, the easiest."

With the Rabbit's common sense and the Capricorn's

pragmatism this personality is expected to be productive, but it has a mystic, spiritual side that seems unusual for this grounded being. Surprisingly, this Rabbit and the Combination following it (Rabbit-Aquarius) are the ones on the spiritual leading edge. Perhaps that is why they achieve a level of success that seems unfitting somehow. What the Rabbit-Capricorn learns early on is whatever they believe they can achieve, they achieve! Henry Miller said, "Back of every creation, supporting it like an arch, is faith. Enthusiasm is nothing: it comes and goes. But if one believes, then miracles occur." Rabbits like to test their assumptions, so they do the inner work and when they get to that point of belief, they throw themselves into the ring. Tiger Woods said, "There's no sense in going to a tournament if you don't believe that you can win it. And that is the belief I have always had. And that is not going to change."

This spiritual connection also guides them to arenas where they will be able to make themselves manifest in the most prolific way; perhaps that is why Tiger Woods found his way to the golf pitch before the age of two. They naturally utilize the law of attraction by following their bliss and pursuing what they enjoy most and manage to turn it into a lucrative business somehow. Discussing parenting, Tiger Woods has said, "To this day, my dad has never asked me to go play golf. I ask him. It's the child's desire to play that matters, not the parent's desire to have the child play. Fun. Keep it fun." Similarly, speaking about his writing process, Henry Miller said, "Whatever I do is done out of sheer joy; I drop my fruits like a ripe tree."

The men of this combination tend to be introverted lone dreamers with a voracious appetite for all things sensual. That is what happens when the water element meets earth. There tends to be something naturally quite feminine about them, in that their neutral set point tends to be sensitive, passive and creative. This does not sit well with many of these men who want to *fit in* or be perceived with greater masculine appeal so many of them choose to be someone else. Cary Grant said, "I pretended to be somebody I wanted to be, and, finally, I became that person. Or he became me." In a similar vein, Nicolas Cage has said, "I had developed an image of being a little bit unusual, different and wild." What is interesting is that they still manage to remain connected to their intuition and their authentic core. But how is that possible one might ask? There is never only one answer, one way or one truth. Not with a Rabbit-Capricorn anyway. Henry Miller explains this paradox in the following way, "One can be absolutely truthful and sincere even though admittedly the most outrageous liar. Fiction and invention are of the very fabric of life."

The women also have an eccentric side but find it easier to navigate when and where to let that part of them find expression. They have greater self-awareness and a heightened self-restraint. In fact, they can often come across as Miss Goody Two-shoes if you didn't know that they could kick your ass too. Discussing her time at school, Michelle Obama said, "I never cut class. I loved getting As, I liked being smart. I liked being on time. I thought being smart is cooler than anything in the world." Like most Rabbit women, they know their worth. They know what they can bring to the party and what impact they can make, so they move with poise and calm reassuring all those around them as they do. This woman is also well aware of energetic transactions that take place, so she tends to nurture those trees that are likely to bear fruit. Michelle Obama has said, "Choose people who lift you up. Find people who will make you better... Of course I've made my husband better!" This lady is no fool and nobody would accuse her of being one either.

Ultimately, the Rabbit-Capricorn is an unusual but active creature who understands that the one who wins is the one who has the psychological upper hand, so they spend much of their time developing their psyche. That is why they manage to self-actualize in such prominent ways. The seed of their success is always visible and can even be spotted in their youth. This is probably due to their unending curiosity and internal spur for continuous growth. They learn from their own experience and their observations of other people's lives, which they seem to be able to inhabit, even without knowing them particularly well. Henry Miller has said, "Develop an interest in life as you see it; the people, things, literature, music – the world is so rich, simply throbbing with rich treasures, beautiful souls and interesting people. Forget yourself... One's destination is never a place but rather a new way of looking at things."

Soul Mate:	Dog-Sagittarius
Challenger:	Rooster-Cancer
Siblings:	Rabbit-Taurus, Rabbit-Virgo
Best Friends:	Sheep-Taurus, Sheep-Virgo, Sheep-Capricorn, Boar-Taurus, Boar-Virgo, Boar-Capricorn

Henry Miller
Haley Bennett
Heather O'Rourke
Lars Ulrich
Nicolas Cage
Cary Grant
Jane Horrocks
Tiger Woods
Michelle Obama
J.R.R. Tolkien
Danica McKellar
Mark Addy
Michael Peña
Thomas Dekker

Robert Sheehan
Paz Vega
Jason Marsden
Vidal Sassoon
J.R.R. Tolkien
Stalin
Anne Bronte

RABBIT – AQUARIUS

Chinese Name: TU
Rank: 4ᵗʰ
Hours Ruled: 5am – 7am
Direction: Directly East
Season: Spring
Month: March
Western Zodiac Equivalent of Rabbit: Pisces
Pisces Western Element: Water
Eastern Zodiac Equivalent of Aquarius: Tiger
Aquarius Western Element: Air
Numerology: 47 = 2

I've missed more than 9000 shots in my career. I've lost almost 300 games. 26 times, I've been trusted to take the game winning shot and missed. I've failed over and over and over again in my life. And that is why I succeed.
– Michael Jordan

When the Rabbit's rich river meets Aquarius's humanitarian hurricane, intelligence meets originality; grace meets wisdom; the political artist merges with the non-judgmental altruist. This creates a highly compassionate personality gifted with many creative skills. They tend to be drawn to physical performance such as dance or physical theatre, as well as music as well as art. They do not necessarily stick to complementary arts, rather they will go wherever their heart takes them and that is usually all over the artistic map. But that's what happens when the Rabbit's need for order attempts to organize the Aquarian's overflow of unfocused energy; this person is likely to be a jack of many artistic genres and a master of at least one. Jane Seymour for example was a classically trained dancer, singer, actress and she also worked professionally as a painting artist. Talking about getting to play a dancer in her later years, she said, "I just did a film in which I had to be a dancer and I was able to do all kinds of extraordinary things. A lot of people turn 50 and talk about what they're not going to do anymore. I embarked on something that I'd wanted to do when I was five."

Quietly, they make their loving presence known through lots of little kind acts, even if many of those acts are done anonymously. They can change the atmosphere of a room when they enter because of their lightness, humility and purity of heart; when people are filled with universal affection for all, they tend to be recipients of affection from all universally. They learn early that in order to achieve their goals, they must use that Rabbit focus on themselves, on their own development and if that means to the exclusion of all else, so be it. Ultimately, it will benefit everyone. Basketball legend Michael Jordan has said, "To be successful you have to be selfish, or else you never achieve. And once you get to your highest level, then you have to be unselfish. Stay reachable. Stay in touch. Don't isolate."

Rabbit-Aquarians have open hearts, and do not entirely understand "adult" ways especially those pertaining to control, force and 9-5 work days. These ethereal creatures just want to play. David Jason has said, "I've never ever 'felt my age,' whatever that means." Although they may be accused of it, they do not have rose tinted glasses; they are well aware of the realties of life, it's just that they refuse to be bound or inhibited by them. Instead, the Aquarius side of their nature has them focus on those things are right with the world, thereby drawing more goodness towards them. Seal has said, "The world is still a fantastic and wondrous place to live." Without even attempting any spiritual practices, Rabbit-Aquarians tend to be more aligned with the higher forces than most. In fact, traditional Chinese Astrologers believe this to be the most naturally psychic combination of all!

The men of this combination tend to be physically very gifted. Rabbit lends the beauty, Aquarius lends edgy individuality, so these men tend to live on that spectrum between beautiful and edgy without alienating anyone and projecting an air that says they belong to all. Again this comes from their being full of pure intentions; people can just feel their goodness. Seal has said, "I like to think that I'm trying to choose love over most things, but that's my choice." That does not mean that they are perfect, nobody is, but they are more likely to be in alignment with their higher self than in their shadow mode, when they are able to activate a big emotional freeze. Keep them warm and fluffy and warm, they are made to be that way! Darren Criss has said, "There's nothing more badass than being yourself."

The women of this combination are more traditional beauties with an innocence juxtaposed with a hint of sauciness. You just get a feeling that thing women can handle herself despite being the epitome of feminine gracefulness. She is gentle, nurturing, caring, softly affectionate, light and an absolute joy to be around. She knows she is beautiful, yet does not place so much emphasis on it; instead she cultivates the being inside. Jane Seymour has said, "Beauty is a radiance that originates from within and comes from inner security and strong character." The Rabbit-Aquarius lady is alluring without needing to conform. However, like all Rabbit women, they struggle with their esteem. They have a need to be "perfect", not project perfect, but *be* perfect which means if they fail to live up to their highest standards then they have failed as human beings. Bridget Fonda has said, "I'm as close to totally neurotic as you can get without being totally neurotic."

Ultimately, this is a combination that is full heart, soul and humor. They set difficult goals to achieve and with their athlete-like mentality, work towards making artistic dreams a reality.

The Aquarian's detachment really serves the Rabbit here in that they are able to go about their business without letting reality or other people's interference get in the way. Michael Jordan has said, "If you accept the expectations of others, especially negative ones, then you never will change the outcome... You have to expect things of yourself before you can do them." As previously mentioned, they are naturally aligned with the spiritual laws and make use of them to get straight to their dreams like an arrow to its target. The Rabbit complements the Aquarian and vice versa allowing the members of this group to live a variety of lives in one lifetime. They get a lot out of what they give and they enjoy every second of the giving. As Seal has said, "The harder you work...and visualize something, the luckier you get."

Soul Mate:	Dog-Scorpio
Challenger:	Rooster-Leo
Siblings:	Rabbit-Gemini, Rabbit-Libra
Best Friends:	Sheep-Gemini, Sheep-Libra, Sheep-Aquarius, Boar-Gemini, Boar-Libra, Boar-Aquarius

Michael Jordan
Seal
Jane Seymour
Laura Linney
Bridget Fonda
David Jason
Darren Criss
Heather Morris
Emma Bunton
Jimmy Tarbuck
Rose Leslie
Harvey Korman
Mariska Hargitay
Sarah Palin

John Hurt
James Cromwell
Glenn Beck

RABBIT – PISCES

Chinese Name: TU
Rank: 4th
Hours Ruled: 5am – 7am
Direction: Directly East
Season: Spring
Month: March
Western Zodiac Equivalent of Rabbit: Pisces
Pisces Western Element: Water
Eastern Zodiac Equivalent of Pisces: Rabbit
Pisces Western Element: Water
Numerology: 48 = 3

Great spirits have always encountered violent opposition from mediocre minds.
– Albert Einstein

When the Rabbit's rich river meets Pisces's creative waters, there is a concentration of the same water energy which seems to multiply its yin power. So these types may come across as soft and meek on the surface but they contain a real punch. This is the last of the three Moon-Children siblings (Rabbit-Cancer and Rabbit-Scorpio being the earlier two) and Rabbit meeting Pisces is especially potent as they are of the same brand (Rabbit equates to Pisces and vice versa in each respective astrological system). This double water combination is highly creative, practical and powerful with an unassuming and unobvious power. They wander the world in a cute little hippy package and seem like the most charming, warm, docile creatures one has ever laid their eyes upon, but when one tries to subvert them from their goals or their personal opinions, one awakens the sweet Rabbit beast. They know who they are and what they stand for, even if they are a minority of one, they will admirably stand their ground.

Actress Ellen Page has said, "When I feel strongly about something, I'm not so quiet."

Wearing the face of a bohemian hippy, they seem more accessible than they are which is a very Rabbit trait. They take this Bohemian hippy-ness into their work life but with a lot of discipline added to the mix, they are likeable and very much respected because they achieve a lot through a laid-back attitude and allow themselves the time to dream whilst figuring out how to make those dreams a reality. Will-i-am has said, "If I didn't mold my reality then I'd still be in the ghetto where people like me are supposed to stay. You have to dream your way out of the nightmare." They decide where they are going, despite Pisces's current of indecision then they work and work and work to create some momentum. Law of attraction takes over after that. Albert Einstein said, "Imagination is everything. It is the preview of life's coming attractions."

Rabbit men always seem so balanced, Rabbit-Pisces especially so. They are more in touch with their intuition and are open to discussing complicated issues that other men choose to avoid. That does not mean that they are not masculine, they are, it's just that their male ego isn't as brittle as other men. They are intellectually and artistically inclined. Forget not, that the Rabbit sign is the *Political Artist*, so they think on a number of different levels, mix it all together and squeeze out something special from it. This goes for creating something new and also to resolve existing issues that have everyone stumped. This is why many give them the "Genius" label. As Albert Einstein has said, "Intellectuals solve problems, geniuses prevent them." Aware that time doesn't stands still, nor does it wait for anyone, they want to enjoy their lives while serving as many people as they can, so they gravitate towards a medium that suits their skillset most. Speaking about encouraging the net generation of artists, will-i-amhas said, "I'm good at thinking outside the box, so much that you realize it's not a box to begin with."

The women of the moon know how to use their sexuality. Eva Longoria has said, "I love being a woman. I love the sexiness we get to exude. But the best thing about being a woman is the power we have over men." Many women of this combination are dark petite beauties such as Eva Longoria, Josie Loren, Ellen Page and Vanessa Williams. The ladies of the moon (including Rabbit-Cancer and Rabbit-Scorpio) are some of the most feminine of all. Beauty, tradition and discipline appeal to them. They may dress conservatively and are easily put off by what they perceive as vulgarity but that does not stop them from enjoying their lady-ness in every way they can. There is something really girly about them yet something a bit tom-boy about them also. Their feminine wiles are hard to resist, as is their bubbly, hippy, charm. Do not be deceived by their innocent looks, these ladies are beautiful monsters! Singer Kesha has said, "I do destroy men on a weekly basis. It's like a hobby. I'm like a preying mantis." Preying Rabbit-Pisces!

An interesting side note is that the Rabbit-Pisces's unconventional nature has them drawn to obscure musical instruments, Kesha played the saxophone and trumpet, Vanessa Williams has said she loves the French Horn and Albert Einstein was an avid violin player.

Ultimately, the Rabbit-Pisces is a wise personality that is prepared to take the long way round. They have a mind that can handle the details and make sense of them for the layman. Their biggest asset is its connection to nature, the elements and most notably, the moon. Perhaps that is why Albert Einstein has said, "Look deep into nature, and then you will understand everything better." His revelations may not have been so forthcoming had he not been so in-tune. This connection is innate within them and being a double water sign, they feel it powerfully. Drew Barrymore has said, "I pray to be like the ocean, with soft currents, maybe waves at times. More and more, I want the consistency rather than the highs and the lows." In time, that is exactly what they develop with the wisdom of handling the highs and the lows behind them. They are sweet natured people, encyclopedias of experience. Yet, despite their ups and downs, they manage to keep their childlike enthusiasm into their older years and they shine in a way that only moon-children do, leaving a mark on every heart they come across. Kesha might not have known how accurate her comment was when she said, "When you're around me, you're going to get glitter on you." Moon-Glitter, that is.

Soul Mate:	Dog-Libra
Challenger:	Rooster-Virgo
Siblings:	Rabbit-Cancer, Rabbit-Scorpio
Best Friends:	Sheep-Cancer, Sheep-Scorpio, Sheep-Pisces, Boar-Cancer, Boar-Scorpio, Boar-Pisces

Ellen Page
Ashley Greene
Drew Barrymore
Kurt Russell
Sienna Guillory
David Thewlis
Alex Kingston
Eva Longoria
Patricia Richardson
Jolene Blalock
Bow Wow
Will-i-am
Tamzin Merchant
Vanessa Williams
William Baldwin
Debra Jo Rupp

Natalie Zea
T.J. Thyne
Miles Teller
Josie Loren
Chelsea Handler
Bryan Batt
Ke$ha
Kangana Ranaut
Neil LaBute
Albert Einstein
Sidney Poitier

THE DRAGON

THE DRAGON

I am the spiritual messenger, the motivator, the mythical monster that channels the sun from within. All know I breathe fire, but what they know not, is that fire comes from a sun that burns in my belly, connects to the suns of the universe and amplifies my charge a million-fold. It is the source of my infinite power and functions on every plain, physical, mental, spiritual. I am a gift to mankind. I came to serve man's mind: to enthuse, to enliven and enlighten for I tread where no others can reach. I run, I climb and I fly. That is why I am beyond comprehension, sometimes even my own, but my inner sunshine god guides me to my next odyssey. Adventure to adventure I expand my experience, then I mirror it back to the world in shades they can see, in shapes they recognize, for I am the everyman in a beautiful beasts shell. I do not need to speak to impassion, my presence is enough, I do not need to touch, my presence is powerfully experienced, I do not need to take any action, my presence is everything. I am nature's purest secret.

I am the Dragon.

You are the self-proclaimed ruler of all you behold. To say you have a big personality is an understatement, you find yourself in a leadership role even in social situations. The dragon's presence is legendary. When you're around, it's like someone put the color back into the black and white world. Magnetic, inspirational and powerful people, you're a workaholic with unrivalled efficiency you tend to define yourself by your profession. Psychologically astute, you have a strong grasp of human behavior and cognitive function.

Career-wise, Dragons can handle the workload of three people and often carry a team with their energy, enthusiasm and example. It is a real loss to any team when the Dragon person leaves. Morale seems to drop like an anchor and pretty soon the team disperses. They are usually in a management or higher position and if they are not, they will have a lot to say about the way the current management unless they are entrusted with special projects that gives them some attention. Politically, they like to be heard, but not seen and those Dragons that are in the political realm are either loved or abhorred. Dragons work in psychological environments and communications. In the entertainment world, they are drawn to comedy, choreography and speaking.

Compatibilities

Soul Mate:	Rooster
Challenger:	Dog
Best Friends:	Rat & Monkey
Good Relations:	Sheep & Tiger

DRAGON – ARIES

Chinese Name: LONG
Rank: 5th
Hours Ruled: 7am – 9am
Direction: Southeast
Season: Spring
Month: April
Western Zodiac Equivalent of Dragon: Aries
Aries Western Element: Fire
Eastern Zodiac Equivalent of Aries: Dragon
Aries Western Element: Fire
Numerology: 49 = 4

It's always the right time when it happens. You make it the right time.
– Reese Witherspoon.

This is a double fire combination and seeing as Aries is also the Western equivalent of the Dragon sign; this is in effect the double Dragon combination. With such concentration of fire, this is a highly energized combination that likes to get stuff done, done well and done quickly. Dragons have a tendency to take on the workload of three mere mortals as it is, but when Aries is added to the mix, this number could be doubled. They do not stop to consider their limitations so they keep going way beyond everybody else's expectations. Discussing his Oscar win, Russell Crowe said, "If you grow up in the suburbs of anywhere, a dream like this seems kind of vaguely ludicrous and completely unattainable. But this moment is directly connected to those imaginings."

The purity of heart that Dragons are known for is also doubled here which can sometimes manifest as naiveté or gullibility. Sometimes they give too much and other times they take too much. It is common for them to give tangibly but take energetically without being aware of it. Continuing to get into the same quandaries, asking for the same advice and then never taking it eventually wears their friends down. But when they realize, they do what they can to deal with it. Maya Angelou has said, "If you don't like something, change it. If you can't change it, change your attitude. Don't complain."

Dragon-Aries people have a bubbly optimistic outlook that barely holds in all of the difficulties that they faced in their lives. They choose to present their happy face and can tell you their most painful back-story seemingly with a smile on their face. It's important for them to find a cause to get behind because the more contribution-based they are, the healthier they seem to be. It keeps them on track, a good track. Without a channel for all of their energy, they meander dangerously all over the place. With their powerful instinctual connection to their source, they tend to have opinionated views. Speaking about the increasing outrageous celebrity culture, James Caan has said, "But the point is that they have the bodyguard so that they can say, "Leave me alone!" It's this revolving door thing. If somebody didn't recognize them, they'd have a heart attack, the bastards."

The men tend to present themselves in an overly macho way, but this is just the thin shell of protection, which is relatively easy to crack through to reveal their unconventional inner child with a huge heart of gold. With so much yang fire, the men are sure to have a volatile side to their character, which takes them to extreme places. While getting divorced, James Caan went to live in the Playboy Mansion for what he called "medicinal purposes." Russell Crowe was caught cheating on his wife and Haley Joel Osment was taken to court for drink driving as a teenager. However, they all take responsibility for their actions. Russell Crowe said, "One thing that I don't want to do is imply that I'm trying to make out it's somebody else's fault, it's not." This self-correcting mental mechanism supports their growth and pushes them onwards with greater wisdom. Steven Seagal has said, "Try to find the path of least resistance and use it without harming others. Live with integrity and morality, not only with people but with all beings." By pursuing a spiritual path, they often go against conventional advice and do what they feel they must.

The women of this combination are in charge of themselves, even when they are unaware of it. They are powerfully led by their inner-selves. They are tenacious, gregarious and could make you laugh until you cry. Reese Witherspoon has said, "There's something timeless and important about making people laugh, about being the right spot in their day." They are gracious, giving and charming with a youthful vigor that is highly attractive. They are also open-minded and open-hearted beings. Melissa Joan Hart has said, "I'm a pretty open person. Like, if I have good sex, then the next day I'm going to tell everyone I know about it." Similarly, Elle Macpherson has said, "Nudity has never been an issue for me." That does not mean in any way that they are promiscuous or undignified, they are anything but. Maria Scheider famously said, "I am an actress, not a prostitute!" when she felt objectified in a movie.

With such a strong desire to live a full life, they push against boundaries that might otherwise cage them in. Maria Schneider said, "I cried because I could not study. I had quite a violent conflict with my mother, so I left home at fifteen and a half. I earned my living by selling drawings and illustrations for restaurant menus. I have also been a young model for jeans." They are feminist influenced, without being fanatical about it, but they do like to move forwards rather than backwards in every regard. Speaking about feminism, Reese Witherspoon has said, "My grandma did not fight for what she fought for, and my mother did not fight for what she fought for, so you can start telling women it's fun to be stupid…" They live life "big" and as the legendary double dragon, they usually inspire the masses with their example. Maya Angelou said, "A wise woman wishes to be no one's enemy; a wise woman refuses to be anyone's victim."

Ultimately, the Dragon-Aries has an indefinable adorability and they also have their priorities right. Constantly pushing to reach the next milestone, people watch in wonder as their endless energy keeps them moving. It's as if their entire life is one massive power-walk session. Many have a hard time controlling all of the energy that they are gifted with. Yet, at the same time, it is this energy that is responsible for their amazing capacity for work. This brand of fire will keep them growing and flourishing while they support the development of those around them also. As Maya Angelou said, "Be a rainbow in someone's cloud."

Soul Mate:	Rooster-Virgo
Challenger:	Dog-Libra
Siblings:	Dragon-Leo, Dragon-Sagittarius
Best Friends:	Rat-Aries, Rat-Leo, Rat-Sagittarius, Monkey-Aries, Monkey-Leo, Monkey-Sagittarius

Michelle Monaghan
Andy Serkis
Russell Crowe
Reese Witherspoon
David Cross
Yorick van Wageningen
Amy Smart
James Caan
Haley Joel Osment
Keri Russell
Steven Seagal

James Garner
Robbie Coltrane
Pedro Armendáriz Jr.
Melissa Joan Hart
Crispin Glover
Gregory Peck
Lukas Haas
Brenda Song
Ed Speleers
Joseph Lawrence
James Roday
Deborah Kara Unger
Candace Cameron Bure
Morgan Lily
Annette O'Toole
Maria Schneider
Elle Macpherson
David Oyelowo
John Gielgud
Ian Ziering
Jessie J
Maya Angelou
Joseph Campbell

DRAGON – TAURUS

Chinese Name: LONG
Rank: 5th
Hours Ruled: 7am – 9am
Direction: Southeast
Season: Spring
Month: April
Western Zodiac Equivalent of Dragon: Aries
Aries Western Element: Fire
Eastern Zodiac Equivalent of Taurus: Snake
Taurus Western Element: Earth
Numerology: 50 = 5

Love and work are the cornerstones of our humanness.
– Sigmund Freud

When the Dragon's soul fire meets the bull's deep dry earth, this complimentary blend produces a personality that doesn't get in its own way much, refuses to take no for an answer and becomes an inspirational beacon guiding others into the light. Often they are completely unaware of the fact that others have put them on a pedestal until it is made blatantly obvious, then surprise washes over them, "why?" they wonder. Wayne Dyer said, "What comes out of you when you are squeezed is what is inside of you," when you squeeze a Dragon-Taurus, expect a loud roar, steam, followed by loving understanding and innovative solutions to any undertaking. An interesting contradiction is that the Taurus's earth makes them quite shy which pulls them back from seeking the limelight, but the Dragon's fire imbues every-thing about them with personality, presence and humor so they cannot help but sparkle everywhere they go. Actually, there is something about them that just screams *Clown!* Al Pacino has said, "My first language was shy. It's only by having been thrust into the limelight that I have learned to cope with my shyness."

Being so non-judgmental, open and ready to serve humanity makes them exceptionally popular. Also, the Dragon's self-assurance makes them seek their esteem from within and as Wayne Dyer has said, "People who want the most approval get the least and people who need approval the least get the most." Their many friends tend to differ in beliefs, backgrounds and general demographics. Oftentimes, they are able to unite differing factions. Without denying their liberal views, these creatures often have a prudish side, which comes a s surprise somehow. While they do like to push themselves outside of their comfort zone in many areas of their life in order to keep growing, they have an aversion to things they secretly believe to be vulgar or improper. As Singer-Songwriter Adele said, "I make music to be a musician not to be on the cover of *Playboy*."

Usually as a result of a childhood where there is little security, materially or emotionally or both, they develop a heightened sense of awareness and a nose for the truth. Burt Bacharach said, "I've always had a problem with people who couldn't tell the truth or admit a mistake and say they're wrong." Having to rely on themselves from a younger age than most, they understand the value of making mistakes and learning from them. Talking about the craft of Acting, Al Pacino said, "The actor becomes an emotional athlete. The process is painful – my personal life suffers." Although he is talking about his work, the term Emotional Athlete captures the Dragon-Taurus well. Probably the most famous Dragon-Taurus is creator of psychoanalysis Sigmund Freud, discussing the basis of it he said, "Being entirely honest with oneself is a good exercise." Understanding their psychological functioning and knowing their emotions well, is a by-product of their self-honesty.

The men of this combination tend to have an excess of energy that they consciously learn to manage in time. They are often small in stature but more than make up for it in energy and sensual appetite. They are most often defined by their humor and humanity. Al Pacino said, "Did you know I started out as a stand-up comic? People don't believe me when I tell them." They have a knack for seeing truths that others miss and are able to bring them to light in a clever, jovial way that encourages people to open their eyes and take charge of their lives more actively. Wayne Dyer has said, "Freedom means you are unobstructed in living your life as you choose. Anything less is a form of slavery."

The women of this combination are almost pure heart. People fall in love with them on first sight. They are who they are, cannot possibly be anything other than who they are, nor would they ever want to be. Sally Hawkins has said, "I'm quite an optimist, quite happy in life, quite smiley." That being said, in their minds, they probably see themselves as quite clumsy, especially verbally, even though the world only sees their grace. Yet they are not deluded or unreasonably insecure, in fact, they have an intrinsic understanding of their own worth, but being as open as they are, parasitical people sometimes try to leach off their good nature. That Emotional Athlete mentality has them prioritize matters of the heart whilst maintaining an overly healthy sense of perspective. Talking about settling down, Martine McCutcheon said, "I'm romantic to a point, but I'm a realistic romantic. I've got to believe in it enough to marry and have children." Whether the Dragon-Taurus is physically attractive or not is irrelevant, she is absolutely beautiful because she projects it. Martine McCutcheon also said, "Real sexiness and real beauty comes from within, which is why so many super-skinny girls aren't as sexy as they could be – because they don't look happy with themselves." Dragon-Taurus women are women's women. Rather than compete, they support other women to be strong, independent and self-sufficient. As Adele said, "I don't really need to stand out, there's room for everyone." Yet stand out they do.

The Dragon is a total workaholic; the Taurus sets a target and builds momentum until it reaches its goal or annihilates its competition; so it is pretty easy to believe that this creature has one heck of a work ethic. Shirley Temple said, "I work a seventeen hour day, and I'm personally responsible for 108 staff members in the embassy." Taking their responsibilities seriously, they feel sick inside if they feel like they have let anyone down. They hate letting themselves down even more. It is for these reasons that they make excellent sports men or women. These people tend to have the Midas touch as well as complicated, dramatic lives; one comes with the other. With their psychological powers, natural charm and big bold hearts this Emotional Athlete is bound to win gold every time.

Soul Mate:	Rooster-Leo
Challenger:	Dog-Scorpio
Siblings:	Dragon-Virgo, Dragon-Capricorn
Best Friends:	Rat-Taurus, Rat-Virgo, Rat-Capricorn, Monkey-Taurus, Monkey-Virgo, Monkey-Capricorn

Wayne Dyer
Salvador Dalí
Glenn Ford
Shirley Temple
Burt Bacharach
Al Pacino
Lance Henriksen
Lainie Kazan
James L. Brooks
Hank Azaria
Christine Baranski

Amy Heckerling
Aruna Irani
Jean-Paul Gaultier
Michael Barrymore
Djimon Hounsou
Stephen Colbert
Martine McCutcheon
Sally Hawkins
Violante Placido
Adele
Lily Cole
Anushka Sharma
Brooke Hogan
Sigmund Freud

DRAGON – GEMINI

Chinese Name: LONG
Rank: 5th
Hours Ruled: 7am – 9am
Direction: Southeast
Season: Spring
Month: April
Western Zodiac Equivalent of Dragon: Aries
Aries Western Element: Fire
Eastern Zodiac Equivalent of Gemini: Horse
Gemini Western Element: Air
Numerology: 51 = 6

The first time you hold your baby in your arms, I mean, a sense of strength and love washes over you. It washed over me and I never thought that possible.
– Colin Farrell

When the Dragon's soul fire meets Gemini's gale, a sparkling personality with a firm moral center is born. Often times they have a strong desire to speak and it can be quite hard to quiet them down when their natter is inappropriate...then are there are those Dragon-Geminis who hardly say a word and let their actions speak for them. In any case, you can't hold a good Dragon down and this one refuses to stay down for long. Resilient, opinionated and stubborn, this Dragon wants to do right by themselves, their family, then, the rest of the world. They usually take responsibility for all three in that order. As Lenny Kravitz has said, "We weren't put here to be miserable. We were put here to do the best we can, and we should take our energy and improve our state of being."

Like all Dragon combinations, this one has a desire to get out there and live life to the fullest; they like to have extreme experiences and push themselves hard whenever they can to see how far they bend and how far their scaly wings can take them. That is why it is wise for them to make plans and not simply play their lives by ear, which is what Gemini's influence might encourage. If they have a plan, they will be less susceptible to life's little hiccups and they will manage to avoid too much responsibility too early. This is a hard thing for this little creature to get its head around, as one of the experiences it wants most is that of its own family. Family is everything. Echoing Colin Farrell's quote above, Liam Neeson has said, "It's extraordinary to look into a baby's face and see a piece of your flesh and your spirit. It makes you realize you are a part of the human race."

Still, this combination ought to play the field before settling down because once they do, they find it hard not to give their all to their family which on some level stifles their true internal desires to taste every flavor the world has to offer. Although this preplanning goes against their natural inclination to free-fall through life, it is wise for them to consider it. Colin Farrell said, "But I dare not think too far into the future on the risk that I'll miss the present." Planning beforehand gives one the freedom to not worry about the future as a track has been set.

The men of this combination ooze sex appeal. Knowing how to project a Mr. Cool image, they are not fooled by their own creation and still manage to have their feet on the ground when they need to. Remember that the Dragon is a close relation of the chameleon and they have an ability to change according to the prevalent energies; adding Gemini amplifies this changeability and the sexiness. Tom Jones has said, "You can't be a sexy person unless you have something sexy to offer. With me, it's my voice: the way that I sing, the way I express myself when I sing." Tom Jones is actually a good example of an older Dragon-Gemini who still retains his appeal, because it is not just about their physicality, it is the Dragon spirit imbued by the Gemini twins vivacity. That is why they are still as sexy as ever even when the get older. Questioning his sexy image, Liam Neeson said, "A sex symbol? A symbol of sex? I don't think that I am a sex symbol, although it's very flattering. I'm 59, now, so I think I'm possibly past my sell-by date. I think I am."

The women of his combination are feisty, tough and like to have things happen their way. They like to set the rules and parameters for other people to follow. That is why they make better leaders than they do followers. As a follower, they question methods, actions and even the manifesto, which is why it is better if they are aware of the values of the working environment before coming on board. As a leader however, these women are in their element; they are organized, productive whilst being fun and inspirational, even if they reject such prestigious labels in order to avoid the pressure of living up to an ideal. Isabella Rossellini said, "But I don't really see myself as a role model. I'm not a dictator, or someone who wants to be adored!"

Ultimately, Dragon-Geminis are highly attractive, clever creatures that know how to project the right image at the right time to the right people without being bamboozled by their own ingenuity. As Lenny Kravitz has said, "The image is an image." And they are well aware of that. As a Dragon sign, their heart is always on their sleeves and they are natural givers. Considering the Gemini always makes the sign it is attached to more sociable, this Dragon is likely to know a lot of people from many different walks of life and therefore, has the opportunity to serve these many people with their big Dragon energy, kindness and love. Even the hardest looking Dragon-Gemini has a mushy heart but they may do everything in their power to prevent this being known, even resorting to immature acts that suggest coldness. But more often than not, they accept that they are loving people albeit with many foibles, that put their family and loved ones on a pedestal and will go all out, including acts of self-sacrifice to ensure that their needs are met. Though the Dragon's generosity is known to extend to anyone who needs it, maybe that is why Liam Neeson said, "I'm a big believer in acts of kindness, no matter how small."

Soul Mate:	Rooster-Cancer
Challenger:	Dog-Sagittarius
Siblings:	Dragon-Libra, Dragon-Aquarius
Best Friends:	Rat-Gemini, Rat-Libra, Rat-Aquarius, Monkey-Gemini, Monkey-Libra, Monkey-Aquarius

Joan of Arc
Colin Farrell
Tom Jones
Liam Neeson
Lenny Kravitz
Isabella Rossellini
Courteney Cox
John Goodman
Johnny Weissmuller
Martin Landau
James Ivory
Bob Monkhouse
John Mahoney
Nancy Sinatra
Carol Kane
Mr. T
Kathy Burke
Wynonna Judd
Cillian Murphy
Alan Carr
Lindsay Davenport

Kevin McHale
Michael Cera

DRAGON – CANCER

Chinese Name: LONG
Rank: 5th
Hours Ruled: 7am – 9am
Direction: Southeast
Season: Spring
Month: April
Western Zodiac Equivalent of Dragon: Aries
Aries Western Element: Fire
Eastern Zodiac Equivalent of Cancer: Sheep
Cancer Western Element: Water
Numerology: 52 = 7

You always have to challenge yourself or else you get soft.
Right?
– Diane Kruger

When the pure soulful fires of the Dragon meet with the Cancer's serene stream of secrets, a complex, compassionate and complete leader is created. Being primarily empathic, they put themselves in other people's shoes and try their best to treat as they would like to be treated, which garners them respect and followers. The Dragon is a born go-getter and likes nothing better than to get busy, remain active and feel productive; when Cancer's sensitivity, perspective and creative bent are added to the mix, this creature is one that knows how to work its art like a business. So they can be highly artistic and financially successful at the same time, which is no mean feat. On top of this, striving for authenticity in all things and bringing their trunk load of witty observations with them, they are pretty much welcome everywhere they go. Their presence is like a gift, their ideas, valuable and their affections, priceless.

This particular Dragon loses its attention if it is not engaged in activities that turn it on in some way. Although, naturally detail-oriented types, if it is on a topic that bores them rigid, they will want to spread their scaly wings and fly away to where there is adventure...or at least hide themselves in their bedroom and dream of it instead. Artists of every type are born under this combination, people who want to dig as deeply as possible into their chosen world. And they cannot help but take it darn seriously; model and actress Diane Kruger has said, "I'm on time even when I try not to be." Similarly, comic David Spade has said, "No one wants to know I set my alarm and get up eight, but I think it's too weird to sleep in too late." Their natural passion for life has them up, ready and revved up for the day not because they *have to*, but because they *love to*!

The men of this combination blend imagination, intelligence and artistry together effortlessly, tending to be naturally talented with the perfect work ethic that builds upon their gifts creating quiet little masters roaming the earth. Maybe that is why Patrick Stewart has said, "I never had teenage years. I guess because I was seen to be more adult than anybody around me." There is something in their make-up that is consoling, it's like they understand the rules of life in a visceral way, like they just know the way the world works so they are calm about everything that happens. David Hasslehoff has said, "When you realize that life isn't fair, you don't act out, you don't get overly wasted, you don't get self-indulgent. You just move forward." They do not like to acknowledge obstacles, because doing so makes the obstacle harder to overcome; they would rather empower themselves, so place their focus on potential solutions. Writer and producer Joss Whedon has said, "With everything that I do, I hope that they see people struggling to live decent, moral lives in a completely chaotic world. They see how hard it is, how often they fail, and how they get up and keep trying. That, to me, is the most important message I'm ever going to tell."

The women of this combination are confident and spunky. They know their minds and they know their hearts. Diane Kruger said, "You should be smart enough to know that you don't know everything. But you have to believe in yourself. I certainly do." They have a quiet faith in themselves and enough belief in universal forces that they set out on their life journey expecting success to be a stone in the road that they will meet. It's a big deal and it is also just a stone, if they feel like it, maybe they will seek out a few different stones of success, but when it bores them, they'll fly off again to find a new world to explore. Discussing her choice to quit acting and go to drama school, Diane Kruger said, "I thought 'f**k everyone' and moved back to Paris, called my agent and said I didn't want to model any more, which they couldn't believe because I was 22 and doing very well. But I left it and went to drama school, and I'm so happy I did."

Gender is not a determinant for them, these women will do what they want, when they want and with whomever they choose, whether it is seen as appropriate or otherwise. Their femininity is obvious in the way that they look, dress and present, for all Dragon women sure love being ladies, but their attitude is such that they refuse to let others gender expectations prevent them from following their chosen goals. Rather than fighting them, they choose not to even acknowledge them at all, bypassing all of the unnecessary stressing of needing to overcome the imagined obstacle; for this Dragoness, there simply is no obstacle. Courtney Love has said, "I like there to be some testosterone in rock, and it's like I'm the one in the dress who has to provide it... I'm not a woman. I'm a force of nature."

Although most Dragons have a need to go big with everything they do, the Dragon-Cancer doesn't seem to but yet does seem to; they do go big with everything, but on an energy level. Their actions are powerfully taken and powerfully received even though on the surface it looks like a casual thing that they did while they were busy doing something else at the same time. What is success to them? To simultaneously be able to live a number of different lives full of excitement and adventure. Benedict Cumberbatch has said, "I've seen and swam and climbed and lived and driven and filmed. Should it all end tomorrow, I can definitely say there would be no regrets. I am very lucky, and I know it. I really have lived 5,000 times over."

Soul Mate:	Rooster-Gemini
Challenger:	Dog-Capricorn
Siblings:	Dragon-Scorpio, Dragon-Pisces
Best Friends:	Rat-Cancer, Rat-Scorpio, Rat-Pisces, Monkey-Cancer, Monkey-Scorpio, Monkey-Pisces

Diane Kruger

Benedict Cumberbatch

Anna Friel

Patrick Stewart

John Leguizamo

Joss Whedon

David Spade

Yeardley Smith

Courtney Love

David Hasslehoff

James Brolin

Ringo Starr

Fred Savage

Tulisa Contostavlos

Jack Whitehall

Stacey Tookey

Amy Breneman

Ross Kemp

Julianne Hough

Dan Brown
Wendy Williams
Sanjeev Bhaskar
Dan Aykroyd
Terry O'Quinn
Celia Imrie
Joel Silver
Raj Babbar
Mary Beth Peil
Ralph Waite
Olivia de Havilland
Naseem Banu

DRAGON – LEO

Chinese Name: LONG
Rank: 5th
Hours Ruled: 7am – 9am
Direction: Southeast
Season: Spring
Month: April
Western Zodiac Equivalent of Dragon: Aries
Aries Western Element: Fire
Eastern Zodiac Equivalent of Leo: Monkey
Leo Western Element: Fire
Numerology: 53 = 8

I have a great deal of faith in faith; if you believe something strongly enough, it becomes true for you.
– Patrick Swayze

When the Dragon's soul sunshine meets the Leo's lava river, this is the hottest zone of the entire 144-combination cycle. Most Chinese Astrologers tend to agree that this combination shines a little brighter than most; the Western zodiac attributes regal qualities to the lion and the Chinese zodiac attributes regal qualities to the Dragon, when these two cross paths, royalty is only to be expected. Members of this elite club are blessed with presence, power and a huge sense of responsibility. They are also exceptionally compassionate people who seem to have a natural understanding of their elite birth right along with the duties that come with it; they understand that their elevated status only exists because of the people they serve, so they put everything they have into serving to the best of their ability. They also define themselves by their occupation, which is why they are worka-holics. When Patrick Swayze was diagnosed with pancreatic cancer, he returned to work before he was advised to because, as he said, "How do you nurture a positive attitude when all the statistics say you're a dead man? You go to work."

Their biggest headaches come from opening themselves to parasitical influences that seek to take advantage of their good nature whilst convincing them of their inadequacy. This is their secret Achilles heal. They aspire towards perfection, nothing less will do, their search is life-long because the better they get, the further they can see themselves going. Discussing the people she keeps around her, Sandra Bullock said, "Always choose people that challenge you and are smarter than you. Always be the student. Once you find yourself to be the teacher, you've lost it." So when they meet someone who highlights their errors or mistakes or *wrongness*, they want to rectify it for themselves and to continue to be a role model. If they can, they will, if they can't, they will let the issue drop away from their consciousness and move on. But when someone holds it up to their face like a smelly sock, they want to actively do something about it, they do not always know that the most effective strategy is to throw the stink-creator out of the most immediate window.

Being a Dragon sign, drama is only to be expected. Combining with Leo, a double dose of drama is inevitable. These types thrive on it, even when they know it is not good for them. The unlived life is not for them. They have to have the experience, be in the moment and obtain the battle scars to prove they were there. It's how they feel alive. Patrick Swayze said, "My big regret is the physical damage I've done to my body. I can do almost anything physically and I used to believe I was invincible, breaking bones over and over, playing football, doing gymnastics, diving, ballet, doing my own stunts, kick boxing, staging fights... It all seems a little stupid to me now."

The men of this combination tend to be alpha male types, regardless of their size or shape, their spirit is larger, more compelling and ultimately pushes other men into effortless submission. What is interesting is how sensitive and accessible they are, considering their alpha label; they have a genuine interest in other people, spirituality and find it easy to tune into the ethereal energies. They are open about their beliefs despite any potential backlash because openness, honesty and truth is their priority. Patrick Swayze said, "I believe in a higher power. I've studied Eastern philosophies, and I've studied the Koran. We've devalued everything worth believing in. Now we're tearing into religion. A line should be drawn." Being openly critical of political figureheads in America, getting involved in activism and even getting arrested may color one with a certain stigma, but it didn't stop Martin Sheen from expressing his beliefs, he said, "I love my country enough to suffer its wrath."

The women of this combination tend to have Amazonian figures, usually dark-haired women such as Sandra Bullock, Mary-Louise Parker and Audrey Tautou who rejoice in their femininity, yet they have the privilege of accessing the man's playing field and being taken seriously as a player. These are the sort of women whose energy can be felt when they enter a room; they are sunshine and happily bestow their light on all of their subjects lucky enough to be in close proximity. Because of their professional and more importantly, social prominence, they are in positions that create changes that benefit all whom they serve. Discussing the changing face of cinema relating to women, Sandra Bullock said, "Why do you need one? I don't understand why there needs to be a love interest to make women go see a film. I think society sort of makes us feel that way – that if you don't have a guy, you're worthless." Yes these women are strong, but just because they can do everything for themselves, it doesn't mean they have to. Discussing her natural self-reliance, Mary-Louise Parker said, "I like to pretend that I'm a tough guy. It's kind of an admission of defeat if I have to ask for help – or even kindness. But if it doesn't come, at some point I snap and demand it."

Ultimately, it is their generosity of spirit that people adore them for. They are open, non-judgmental and have a way of making you feel extra special when you are with them. It is as if they are channeling a form of divine sunshine energy through themselves directly onto whomever they are with, like some sort of life-force regenerators. They are admirable creatures that live life to fullest, strive never to let anyone down and be a shining example to everyone, regardless how adverse their own circumstances. The Dragon-Leo is a champion. They are champions themselves and they champion everyone else. Discussing his life and what the doctors said was his imminent death, Patrick Swayze said, "I've had more lifetimes than any 10 people put together, and it's been an amazing ride... So this is Okay."

Soul Mate:	Rooster-Taurus
Challenger:	Dog-Aquarius
Siblings:	Dragon-Aries, Dragon-Sagittarius
Best Friends:	Rat-Aries, Rat-Leo, Rat-Sagittarius, Monkey-Aries, Monkey-Leo, Monkey-Sagittarius

Sam Worthington
Sandra Bullock
Patrick Swayze
Mary-Louise Parker
Rhona Mitra
Stanley Kubrick
Martin Sheen
Audrey Tautou
Adam Yauch
Will Friedle
Vivica A. Fox
Gus Van Sant

Andy Warhol
J.C. Chasez
Maria McKee
Joe Strummer
Ralph Bunche
Mae West
Joe E. Brown
George Bernard Shaw

DRAGON – VIRGO

Chinese Name: LONG
Rank: 5th
Hours Ruled: 7am – 9am
Direction: East – Southeast
Season: Spring
Month: April
Western Zodiac Equivalent of Dragon: Aries
Aries Western Element: Fire
Eastern Zodiac Equivalent of Virgo: Rooster
Virgo Western Element: Earth
Numerology: 54 = 9

Watch with glittering eyes the whole world around you because the greatest secrets are always hidden in the most unlikely places. Those who don't believe in magic will never find it."
– Roald Dahl

When the Dragon's soul fire meets Virgo's fertile earth, two very passionate, disciplined and ethical creatures merge. Where the Dragon likes to lead with its inner child, the Virgo lives from a place of worry that hat they do will fall below the mark, so when these two signs come together, the Dragon brings its lightness and the Virgo adds an urgency to the Dragon's endeavors. Disarmingly seductive, real and driven, they can wrap people around their little finger with one glance. With Virgo here, this Dragon is likely to be a student for life, learning and sharing its lessons. Being that the Dragon is a karmic sign and the Virgo here is prone to neurotic behavior, it is not unusual for this combination to be born into complicated circumstances where parental supervision is severely restricted so that they have to find their own way exceptionally young in life. But this is often the source of their creativity and hugely expanded vision. Angela Cartwright said, "My shadow in my art is one way I trace who I was and where I have been. My shadow and I have been on a journey for quite a while now!"

When a zodiac sign of the Earth element is attached to the Dragon, you normally find someone with innate psychological astuteness. They are not intimidated to explore the darker recesses of their inner selves. This increases their self-knowledge and depth. Alexander Skarsgard has said, "I have to be careful because there is something destructive within me, I think, and I can have a tendency to just search for the kicks. I can't really get too close to someone who's too destructive, or too dark, because then I might go down the rabbit hole myself." Dragon-Virgos have a huge capacity for goodness and with their big open hearts they like to serve others, sometimes, before they have served themselves. In time, they learn that they must cater to their own needs first. Raquel Welch said, "Once you get rid of the idea that you must please other people before you please yourself, and you begin to follow your own instincts, only then can you be successful. You become more satisfied, and when you are, other people will tend to be satisfied by what you do."

The men of this combination are rugged, yet pretty and have a noted tendency towards nomadism. They do not accept the status quo as it is and seek to find or create circumstances that suit them. Despite this, they are often misunderstood and under-mined because of the way that they look. Knowing that they can utilize this to their advantage, sometimes, they might even cultivate this image. Keanu Reeves has said, "I'm a meathead. I can't help it, man. You've got smart people and you've got dumb people. I just happen to be dumb." Visceral creatures that lead with their intuition rather than with the intellect, it is the source of their innovative creativity. Speaking about the characters in his books, Roald Dahl said, "I find that the only way to make my characters really interesting to children is to exaggerate all their good or bad qualities, and so if a person is nasty or bad or cruel, you make them very nasty, very bad, very cruel."

The women of this combination are energized, feisty yet warm, despite seeming icy at first glance. They are characteristically alive, find joy in the tiniest of pleasures and know their good apples from their bad. Difficult childhood circumstances can make them either too forceful or too timid, until they learn to strike a healthier balance. Like their male counterparts, they are also undermined. Speaking about her career as a young woman, Raquel Welch said, "They discounted me as empty-headed: some little piece of fluff without any brain that happened to come along... I was participating; it was physical, and I was independent. I wasn't that pushover kind of a girl." Like most Dragon combinations, they tend to be more conservative than they seem and although can engage in, what some may say is outrageous behavior, they stay on the right side of dignified, because it is really important to them. So when producers for Trisha Yearwood's music video expected her to flirt with a performer, she quickly drew some boundary lines. She said, "I absolutely refused to make out with the gorgeous male model." Whether their temperament is typically fiery or otherwise, they do not make concessions easily and if they do, they can be really hard on themselves in private. More than their capacity for hard work, they have such a potent creativity, often in uncomplimentary areas. Angela Cartwright said, "I have always had to have an outlet for my creativity and when my life became more about raising my family than the bright lights of show business exploring my photo art was a great outlet for me."

Ultimately, these perfectionists know how to be present to each moment and seem to be able to see the simple spirit of life. As previously mentioned, they find huge joy in the smallest of pleasures, because beauty is beauty and they really have their priorities right. Trisha Yearwood has said, "I don't spend time wondering what might be next; I just focus on trying to savor every day." They can find beauty in anything, but they also see the other side of the coin for what it is and usually, far quicker than most others. They are hugely in touch with their inner child and it never leaves them. The Dragon-Virgo knows how to live and love on the surface and love and live below too. Just like children do. It is the only way they know how to be. They grow up, but they never grow old. That is why they are so fun to be around. Roald Dahl has said, "A little nonsense now and then is relished by the wisest men."

Soul Mate:	Rooster-Aries
Challenger:	Dog-Pisces
Siblings:	Dragon-Taurus, Dragon-Capricorn
Best Friends:	Rat-Taurus, Rat-Virgo, Rat-Capricorn, Monkey-Taurus, Monkey-Virgo, Monkey-Capricorn

Keanu Reeves
Patrick Marber
Ronaldo
Roald Dahl
Foxy Brown
Rupert Grint
Blair Underwood
Trisha Yearwood
Jimmy Connors
Randy Jones
Zandra Rhodes
James Coburn
Adam West
Roddy McDowall

Brian De Palma
Raquel Welch
Katrina Bowden
Alexa Vega
Asher Book
Mickey Rourke
David A. Stewart
Holly Robinson Peete
Alexander Skarsgård
Rishi Kapoor
Vivek Oberoi
Ludacris

DRAGON – LIBRA

Chinese Name: LONG
Rank: 5th
Hours Ruled: 7am – 9am
Direction: Southeast
Season: Spring
Month: April
Western Zodiac Equivalent of Dragon: Aries
Aries Western Element: Fire
Eastern Zodiac Equivalent of Libra: Dog
Libra Western Element: Air
Numerology: 55 = 1

My role in society, or any artist's or poet's role, is to try and express what we all feel. Not to tell people how to feel. Not as a preacher, not as a leader, but as a reflection of us all.
– John Lennon

When the Dragon's raging inferno meets Libra's cool breeze, the fire grows and grows to a massive size, yet, because it is so inflated by cool air, the fire is not as hot or as forceful as it looks. The Dragon-Libra tends to be a benign flame; more of a talker than a doer, until that is, this Dragon learns to channel greater firepower from within. The problem is Libra's air negates some of the Dragon's fire power yet amplifies its presence so one is confronted with a majestic being who has the ability and talent for so many things, but one who struggles to perceive itself with the status that others do. When these Dragons operate from a humble place, they allow the fire in their belly to be channeled directly into the physical world and make manifest their beauty in profound ways. John Lennon has said, "My defenses were so great. The cocky rock and roll hero who knows all the answers was actually a terrified guy who didn't know how to cry. Simple."

Clear vision and clarity of mind make a huge difference to this combination as their life begins to take a creative flow of its own when they learn to turn their vulnerabilities into their strength. The more the Dragon-Libra questions its own motives and analyses its own behaviors the more objective it will become which is key to managing self-esteem. The more they align with their higher selves, the more these truths become available to them and the more blessings enter their experience. They then begin to care less what other people think and their priority becomes uplifting their own spirit. Talking about her favored performance projects, Greer Garson said, "I think the mirror should be tilted slightly upward when it's reflecting life – toward the cheerful, the tender, the compassionate, the brave, the funny, the encouraging, all those things."

The men of this combination project a raw masculinity, which comes from that indomitable Dragon spirit. Perhaps that is why John Lennon said, "Nobody controls me. I'm uncontrollable. The only one who controls me is me, and that's just barely possible." They often get put on a pedestal because of their looks, smarts, sexual magnetism, physical prowess and charisma. But with power comes responsibility and that is their early learning lesson. Other people often have more belief in them than they, initially at least, have in themselves. But many of these men have a hidden hero inside of them that comes to the surface when all seems lost. Chris Reeve has said, "Either you decide to stay in the shallow end of the pool or you go out in the ocean."

Despite their inner struggles, they will inevitably push themselves and they grow, they flourish and they often exceed their own expectations. Sit-comp producer Chuck Lorre has said, "I work from a deep sense of insecurity. I have the belief, and I can't shake it, that there are endless reasons to turn the channel... And if you make a bad television show there's no reason for the audience to come back the following week." Once they learn to manage their ego, they blaze out into the world making themselves manifest in the most endearing of ways. With their honesty, desire to uplift and idiosyncratic creativity, they bring attention to complicated matters in ways that people can understand and make sense of. Even though some of their profundity is missed by the masses, their spirit and outputs are very well received. John Lennon has said, "I'm often afraid, and I'm not afraid to be afraid, though it's always scary. But it's more painful to try not to be yourself."

The women of this combination tend to be typically Amazonian looking: tall, tough and a little bit trippy-hippy. Libra gives this Dragoness more balance, more intellect and more edge, which ultimately has the effect of opening them up to esoteric and altruistic pursuits. Actress, animal rights and environmental activist Alicia Silverstone also belongs to this combination. Despite her effortless beauty, exuberance and presence, she said, "I don't feel like a dream girl...in my real life, I'm this weird, dorky girl who just hangs out with her dog." Dragon-Libra women tend to be more naturally aligned with spiritual principles than the men and interestingly, do not struggle with themselves as much. They cultivate a method of being present, being real and being there for others. Despite this natural esoteric connection, these women are known to make the occasional faux pas, which they find both devastating and hilarious at the same time. But they are so adored that people find it endearing more than anything else. Sharon Osbourne is a good example; whatever she encounters, she puts her heart into and trusts her instincts above all else. She has said, "Your gut is always right."

Ultimately, the Dragon-Libra is a bit of a contradiction and the difference between who they present in their adolescent phase and who they become in their post-adolescent phase can be dramatic. They require time, compassion and sometimes they just have to learn the hard way. They have an innate desire to push beyond accepted boundaries and develop every facet possible. As performer Seann William Scott has said, "I don't really necessarily think I'm a funny guy, but I like the opportunity to take on something that I don't feel I'm the best at doing." They do so because they know that throwing themselves in at the deep end is the fastest route to improved abilities and greater self-confidence. They have the capacity to be real champions, but they have to see it in themselves first before anyone else will. Christopher Reeve has said, "A hero is an ordinary individual who finds the strength to persevere and endure in spite of overwhelming obstacles."

Soul Mate:	Rooster-Pisces
Challenger:	Dog-Aries
Siblings:	Dragon-Gemini, Dragon-Aquarius
Best Friends:	Rat-Gemini, Rat-Libra, Rat-Aquarius, Monkey-Gemini, Monkey-Libra, Monkey-Aquarius

John Lennon
Christopher Reeve
Chuck Lorre
Clive Owen
Seann William Scott
Sharon Osbourne
Alicia Silverstone
Cat Deeley
Greer Garson
Pelé
Michael Gambon
Cliff Richard
Janeane Garofalo
Constance Bennett

Peter Finch
Jeff Goldblum
Monica Bellucci
Guillermo del Toro
Harry Hill
Ryan Reynolds

DRAGON – SCORPIO

Chinese Name: LONG
Rank: 5th
Hours Ruled: 7am – 9am
Direction: Southeast
Season: Spring
Month: April
Western Zodiac Equivalent of Dragon: Aries
Aries Western Element: Fire
Eastern Zodiac Equivalent of Scorpio: Boar
Scorpio Western Element: Water
Numerology: 56 = 2

I think that all comics or humorists, or whatever we are, ask questions. That's what we're supposed to do. But I not only ask the questions, I offer solutions.
– Roseanne Barr

When the Dragon's firepower meets with Scorpio's murky waters, the universe is gifted with a ballsy, honest creature who values its integrity and whose empathy cannot be turned off. It seems they are born with a sense of compassion that they themselves might not understand. Dragon brings presence, optimism and force, whereas the Scorpio brings audacity, edge and the ability to understand complexity. Remember that the Scorpio's symbol is twofold: it is at once the scorpion and the golden eagle; so at times this creature may look like the golden eagle but be the scorpion, but more often, they look like the scorpion but are actually regal airborne creatures that soar above with the angels. Perhaps that is why they are so often misunderstood. Speaking about being underestimated, Calista Flockhart has said, "What I say now is that the way the world underestimates me will be my greatest weapon. People pat me on the head, and I go to myself, oh, and aren't they going to be surprised."

Dragon-Scorpios tend to live lives that prove the old proverb that "fact is stranger than fiction" so it is not surprising that they have this fondness for humor; but actually, if one digs a little deeper, the humor is a by-product of the truth which is what they are really seeking. If they be presents, the truth is a gift for the Scorpio and the humor a gift for the Dragon. But because it is the Scorpio that goes searching for it, the truth always comes first, then, the Dragon takes it, applies a little love and turns it into something accessible for the whole world to marvel at. Speaking about her experience working in TV, Roseanne Barr said, "Nothing real or truthful makes its way to TV unless you are smart and know how to sneak it in, and I would tell you how I did it, but then I would have to kill you." It is interesting that CBS News Anchor Walter Cronkite was given the title, "The most trusted man on TV", despite his professionalism, he managed to speak his truths through a veil of objectivity as his famous comment on the end of the Vietnam war attests to, "To say that we are closer to victory today is to believe, in the face of the evidence, the optimists who have been wrong in the past." Much to the Scorpio's dismay, the Dragon is not particularly good at concealing the contents of its pencil case. Emma Stone has said, "I don't think that I've been deft at hiding parts of my personality."

The men of this combination are practical idealists. They (as Roseanne said in the opening quote) not only pose difficult questions but also offer solutions. Walter Cronkite has said, "The first priority of humankind in this era is to establish an effective system of world law that will assure peace with justice among the peoples of the world." Presenting a calm image belies their inner outrage at the injustices that they observe, especially when they observe hypocrisy and ignorance. Dragon-Scorpio men are more emotional than their female counterparts but do not show it. The women cannot help but release, if in a public forum, then so be it. In fact, so much the better if their eruption sheds some light on ignored issues.

Generally speaking, the women do not find it easy to connect with others in meaningful ways. This is because they are complex creatures and not what they project so most people do not know how to categorize them. They also do not feel the need to conform. Calista Flockhart has said, "I'm close with my parents. I have a lot of acquaintances, but my very good close friends are few I can count my very good friends on one hand. And that's how I like it to be." Those of an astrological persuasion know that when you add Dragon's fire with Scorpio's water will create bold campy characters expressed through beautiful and charming vessels. Emma Stone has said, "I don't know where this loud, ballsy, hammy ridiculousness came from." In conservative India, speaking about her search for a partner, Bollywood diva Malika Sherawat said, "I am single, waiting for a man who has more balls than me." What the Dragon-Scorpio woman knows is that power is power; that anyone can assume it because the scepter is resting next to the throne; one just needs to have the "balls" to go get it. Roseanne Barr has said, "The thing women have yet to learn is nobody gives you power. You just take it."

Despite being more attractive than most, it is personal character they place their emphasis on and they set high standards for themselves. Most of the time they live up to them because they can be relentlessly single minded, but if things do not pan out in the way they envision, they sometimes project inwards. Emma Stone has said, "When I look back, I don't have regrets. In the moment I am really, really hard on myself, I'm definitely my own worst critic and can be my own worst enemy, and I'm trying very hard not to be that." They are aware of how pointless self-attacks are so they take the lessons and they move on using the Scorpio's resilience and the Dragon's confidence to boost them onwards like a rocket. Stagnation is not an option for them individually, Patrick Warburton has said, "The greatest risk is really to take no risk at all. You've got to go out there, jump off the cliff, and take chances."

Soul Mate:	Rooster-Aquarius
Challenger:	Dog-Taurus
Siblings:	Dragon-Cancer, Dragon-Pisces
Best Friends:	Rat-Cancer, Rat-Scorpio, Rat-Pisces, Monkey-Cancer, Monkey-Scorpio, Monkey-Pisces

Calista Flockhart
Roseanne
Emma Stone
Mallika Sherawat
Walter Cronkite
Patrick Warburton
Tinie Tempah
Mark Philippoussis
Lorna Luft
Marion Ross
Terry Gilliam
Amjad Khan
Art Malik
Liza Tarbuck
Diana Krall
Sandra 'Pepa' Denton
Nadia Sawalha
Yasmin Le Bon
Piper Perabo
Tevin Campbell

DRAGON – SAGITTARIUS

Chinese Name: LONG
Rank: 5th
Hours Ruled: 7am – 9am
Direction: Southeast
Season: Spring
Month: April
Western Zodiac Equivalent of Dragon: Aries
Aries Western Element: Fire
Eastern Zodiac Equivalent of Sagittarius: Rat
Sagittarius Western Element: Fire
Numerology: 57 = 3

The woman's vision is deep-reaching, the man's far-reaching. With the man the world is his heart, with the woman the heart is her world.
– Betty Grable

When the Dragon lends its fire to add to the Centaur's fire, it creates one massive raging firestorm. Although the qualities of the two brands of fire are different, they burn together perfectly serving and encouraging each other. With the Dragon's presence, abundance of energy and love of activity coupled with Sagittarius's intellect, non-self-judgment and thirst for knowledge, this combination is set up to achieve success through hard work and a continual self-improvement. They understand the universe's invisible language and spend much time observing it. As Bruce Lee said, "Notice that the stiffest tree is most easily cracked, while the bamboo or willow survives by bending with the wind." With sharp analytical minds that prefer to learn through experience, they do not easily accept other people's opinions without exploring their notions through some sort of physical experiment. Chess and martial arts international champion Joshua Waitzkin has said, "I love the play between the conscious and unconscious minds in the creative moment, and for me chess and the martial arts are both about developing a rich working relationship with your intuition."

It is interesting to note that Joshua Waitzkin was first known as a child chess champion and became an International Master at the age of 16, and then he went on to become an International Tai Chi Ch'uan champion applying the lessons he had learned in his early chess years to martial arts; in a similar way, Bruce Lee applied his early martial arts training to the world of dance becoming Hong kong's cha cha dance champion in 1958. Dragon-Sagittarians develop a winner's psychology because of how they process data and the self-belief that comes with being a Dragon sign. Before he was famous, Bruce Lee famously said, "You just wait. I'm going to be the biggest Chinese Star in the world." Similarly, comedian Richard Pryor had said, "Even when I was a little kid, I always said I would be in the movies one day, and damned if I didn't make it." Both have gone on to have a legendary status in their respective fields inspiring new generations decades after their deaths.

The men of this combination tend to be exceptionally smart, driven and determined. They have a tendency to neglect the external world because they get so drawn into the specifics of their passions. Bruce Lee said, "Ever since I was a child I have had this instinctive urge for expansion and growth. To me, the function and duty of a quality human being is the sincere and honest development of one's potential." Although naturally attractive, magnetic even, they just have this belief that if one takes care of the inside, the outside takes care of itself; while there is much truth to this, they sometimes need a bit of advice and encouragement with how to manage their appearance. What matters is self-improvement, self-honesty and self-actualization.

Joshua Waitzkin has said, "The key to pursuing excellence is to embrace an organic, long-term learning process, and not to live in a shell of static, safe mediocrity. Usually, growth comes at the expense of previous comfort or safety."

The women of this combination tend to be powerhouses who take the reins without needing permission; they know that they are in charge and so does everyone else. Attractive, captivating with the typical Dragon presence and clout, they are queens of the social world and great fun to be around if you are in their good books; if you are not, this Dragoness is less fun to be around. Honest and sometimes forceful with it, the Dragon-Sagittarius lady lives her life on the surface and has a need to get everything she feels out on the table. Perhaps that is why Betty Grable said, "There's no mystery about me." Like most Dragon women, this lady takes it upon herself to look after, protect and nurture everyone, even when it is an imposition; her heart is in the right place but sometimes her affection can be suffocating and intrusive. There are no shortages of contradictions here either, she presents like she is vulnerable when she is really on top form and portrays strength when she is at her lowest. There is much Dragon pride here. As Vanessa Hudgens has said, "I do always have a wall up. But I feel by doing it, I keep myself safe… Confidence is key. Sometimes, you need to look like you're confident even when you're not." Just let her be her crazy little egomaniacal self without judgment and she will be quite happy.

Ultimately, the members of this combination are masters of learning and can grasp complicated skills much faster than others. It is strange, then, that they are not particularly academic. Traditional methods generally do not suit the Dragon-Sagittarius because they are quite idiosyncratic with very particular ways. They also are born with belief in their superiority so they find it difficult to be taught by lesser minds. It is important for them to find their passions early and to spend much time devouring the details because this is what they excel in and this is what they love. That is why they become masters in their field. Bruce Lee said, "I fear not the man who has practiced 10,000 kicks once, but I fear the man who has practiced one kick 10,000 times." Learning the rules of their preferred game, chess, martial arts, dance or whatever, they apply the lessons to life in general. They know that whatever it takes to win a game is what it will take to win in the game of life so they give it the same attention, same amount of analysis and come at it with the same amount of fervent ardor. And then, they win. Bruce Lee said, "If you always put limit on everything you do, physical or anything else. It will spread into your work and into your life. There are no limits. There are only plateaus, and you must not stay there, you must go beyond them."

Soul Mate:	Rooster-Capricorn
Challenger:	Dog-Gemini
Siblings:	Dragon-Aries, Dragon-Leo
Best Friends:	Rat-Aries, Rat-Leo, Rat-Sagittarius, Monkey-Aries, Monkey-Leo, Monkey-Sagittarius

Josh Waitzin
Bruce Lee
Richard Pryor
Teri Hatcher
Vanessa Hudgens
Betty Grable
Kirk Douglas
Adam Shankman
Don Cheadle
Steve Austin
Michael Gough
Dan Blocker

Donna Mills
Frank Zappa
Dionne Warwick
Mandy Patinkin
Bappi Lahiri
Marisa Tomei
Robson Green
Alistair McGowan
Anna Faris
Amy Acker
Ryan Kwanten
Dominic Monaghan
Zoe Isabella Kravitz
Emily Browning
Esmée Denters

DRAGON – CAPRICORN

Chinese Name: LONG
Rank: 5th
Hours Ruled: 7am – 9am
Direction: Southeast
Season: Spring
Month: April
Western Zodiac Equivalent of Dragon: Aries
Aries Western Element: Fire
Eastern Zodiac Equivalent of Capricorn: Ox
Capricorn Western Element: Earth
Numerology: 58 = 4

Cowardice asks the question, 'Is it safe?' Expediency asks the question, 'Is it politic?' And vanity comes along and asks the question, 'Is it popular?' But conscience asks the question, 'Is it right?'
– Martin Luther King

When the Dragon's firepower meets Capricorn's dense earth, this character is somewhat akin to a volcano, albeit, mostly a dormant one. There is much power here, but this particular Dragon prefers to lead through diplomatic discussion and persuasion. This volcano is a thing of natural beauty and should be seen up close, but when it erupts, the fire-earth elements composing this creature can be formidable. With presence, power and generosity from the Dragon and steadfastness, stubbornness, and quiet dignity from the Capricorn, this subject will serve unselfishly for the good of mankind in their own special way and are prepared to put themselves on the line when they need to. This Dragon puts its money where its mouth is. It is not that they go out looking for causes, they just take it as a personal affront to their intelligence if they are lied to and cannot help but take action to redress the injustices that they perceive. Martin Luther King Jr. said, "Injustice anywhere is a threat to justice everywhere."

These people do not court fame, they are drawn to work that impacts the heart, soul and spirit of others, that opens minds and gets them questioning accepted limits. Above all, they strive to be as objective and as fair as they humanly can; this applies firstly to themselves and then to other people. Edgar Allen Poe described this well when he said, "In criticism I will be bold, and as sternly, absolutely just with friend and foe. From this purpose nothing shall turn me." They often serve as a form of human conscience for their friends and will offer as impartial advice as anyone is likely to find. Being of the quiet, humble and hyper-analytical variety, they recognize that in order to function profi-ciently in the general world, one needs to be able to project a certain, task-appropriate image, which they do whilst maintaining a consistent ethical core. Even former bad boy footballer turned Hollywood Actor Vinnie Jones has said, "I'm a Conservative, but I talk for the ordinary working classes. I get on with the boys at the pub, but I can also mix with Prince Andrew. I understand both levels."

The men of this combination tend to be more analytical than they are academic or intellectual or creative. It is their ability to analyze down to the see the minutiae that is their divine gift. This is also what makes them such quick learners. Actor Orlando Bloom has said, "I read this thing that said when you are in a relationship with a woman, imagine how you would feel if you were her father. That's been my approach, for the most part." Combining this with their heightened sense of compassion and empathy, he presents as a sensitive macho man most of the time, but knows how to switch masks when he needs to. Actor James Nesbitt has said, "We all have different masks we put on for different occasions. As much as we all want to lead decent lives, we're also attracted by the idea that something dark may lurk within us." The Dragon-Capricorn man is not without his darkness; after all, he is a volcano trying his best not to erupt. Vinnie Jones has said, "We all carry our past. But it is a case of getting on with your life and improving it, if you want to."

The women of this combination have that Dragon workaholic thing but because they are usually in charge, they often get their employees to do the lackey work, while they handle the more complicated, more glamorous side of their vocation. These ladies are masters of compartmentalization and also how to don appropriate masks where required. Joely Richardson has said, "It's very difficult when there are pictures taken on the red carpet. I find those things so terrifying that another persona just kicks in. I don't recognize myself." With similar analytical and objective super-powers to the male of their species, they know how to work smart, fuelled by the Dragon's self-confidence, they move towards their goals with what seems like effortless ease. The need for this fore mentioned compartmentalization is because they find it difficult to leave their humble beginnings behind. As Faye Dunaway has said, "I'm still the little southern girl from the wrong side of the tracks who really didn't feel like she belonged." But they have learned what behaviors are appropriate even if they do not come naturally to them. In short, these women are not as conventionally feminine as they seem and are more sensitive than they project.

Ultimately, the Dragon-Capricorn's analytical abilities allow them to develop their skills in any which way they choose to a high level but they usually excel in self-employed business ventures and the arts. This is because they learn from their mistakes and make adjustments as they go. They also seem to be able to access their subconscious better than most and enjoy losing themselves in their imagination. Edgar Allen Poe has said, "Those who dream by day are cognizant of many things that escape those who dream only at night." Although they are drawn to politics, they instinctively know that they are too honest and in order to do themselves justice, they will need time to explain the whys behind their decisions, which will turn off the masses and is unlikely to find a medium in the first place. Political rhetoric has its place, but the public deserve concrete answers. Perhaps that is why Joan Baez has said, "Hypothetical questions get hypothetical answers." Hypocrisy, ignorance and above all, unfairness, bothers them to their core, so in their own individual, idiosyncratic way, they spend their lives highlighting these things wherever they may lurk in order to alleviate the heaviness in their hearts. Martin Luther King said, "Darkness cannot drive out darkness; only light can do that. Hate cannot drive out hate; only love can do that."

Soul Mate:	Rooster-Sagittarius
Challenger:	Dog-Cancer
Siblings:	Dragon-Taurus, Dragon-Virgo
Best Friends:	Rat-Taurus, Rat-Virgo, Rat-Capricorn, Monkey-Taurus, Monkey-Virgo, Monkey-Capricorn

Martin Luther King
Orlando Bloom
Vinnie Jones
Faye Dunaway
Joely Richardson
Joan Baez
Edgar Allan Poe
Nina Dobrev
James Nesbitt
Joe Manganiello
Julia Ormond
Danny McBride

Hayao Miyazaki
Dustin Diamond
Amber Benson
Bill Bailey

DRAGON – AQUARIUS

Chinese Name: LONG
Rank: 5th
Hours Ruled: 7am – 9am
Direction: Southeast
Season: Spring
Month: April
Western Zodiac Equivalent of Dragon: Aries
Aries Western Element: Fire
Eastern Zodiac Equivalent of Aquarius: Tiger
Aquarius Western Element: Air
Numerology: 59 = 5

I don't hide out. If you build a wall around yourself it draws people to invade it. Fear is the enemy.
– Matt Dillon

When the Dragon's sunshine meets the Aquarian's humanitarian hurricane, these two powerful forces must learn to work with each other rather than against. This combination has power without awareness so it has to be cultivated consciously even though this Dragon finds it very hard to look at itself with emotional objectivity. Learning this is a lifelong lesson. With the Dragon's fortitude, love of activity and work ethic, coupled with the Aquarian's eccentricity, humane heart and ability to exist in a bubble, members of this combination are often workaholic loners. At the same time, the Dragon has a deep desire to be surrounded by people so it is important for them to learn how to be comfortable in social settings. Doing so in a professional setting is second nature because it is "work." So it is very common for this combination to focus all of their energy in the professional arena where they most excel. Comedian Chris Farley said. "I used to think that you could get to a level of success where the laws of the universe didn't apply. But they do. It's still life on life's terms, not on movie-star terms. I still have to work at relationships. I still have to work on my weight and some of my other demons."

It is interesting that these two naturally dynamic and altruistic signs merge to create a personality that struggles with its self-esteem, perhaps it is a prerequisite for the inspirational personalities that they become in their later years. These individuals have individual voices and they find it hard to blend in with the general society, so many of them end up on the fringes, determined to be seen, heard and valued. So they work and work and work! The problem is, some of their burning issues are not easily extinguished, especially that of the way that they look as it is one of the most obvious reasons for rejection. Christopher Eccleston has said, "My bony face is like a car crash. I haven't got good looks, just weird looks, enough to frighten the fiercest monster." Even the stunning Shakira has said, "I think I look like a chipmunk." The more open and compassionate they are with themselves, the more the universe reciprocates and brings people reflecting the same compassionate loving energy into their experience. Shakira goes on to say, "We're never content with the way we are and the way we look. But, if you start loving yourself the way you are, and accepting yourself the way you are, your outlook totally changes."

The men of this combination tend to be highly opinionated yet sensitive creatures that wear a very strong protective mask. They cannot help but be affected by the criticism they get for their opinions. In a professional context, they get used to it, accepting it as part of their job, but personally it can be debilitating. They must learn to apply their work ethic to understanding how the social world operates and learn to become comfortable with uncertainty. Perhaps that is why Chris Farley said, "The point is, how do you know the Guarantee Fairy isn't a crazy glue sniffer."

Finding work in an environment that has a strong social aspect is very good option for them as they subconsciously fertilize their social lives with their professional focus. The best thing about this union of Dragon and Aquarius is their resilience and ability to turn their weaknesses into strengths. Once they realize that work will not give them the love that they seek and they refocus their attention upon the mountain that will, the hard part for them will be done. Matt Dillon has said, "I work on my self-destructive behaviors. I try to get past them. There've been times when I'm very prone toward anger. And if I look at my anger, there's usually fear behind it."

The women of this combination tend to be frisky, firecrackers with an effortless sex appeal. They have also struggled with their insecurities in their early years and tend to have to fight with their superiors to be seen and valued. They instinctively know what is right for them and like their male counterparts, have strong convictions. Speaking about the rights of women, Shakira has said, "I always believed that women have rights and that there are some women that are intelligent enough to claim those rights... In this life, to earn your place you have to fight for it." In matters of the heart, they are softer, gentler creatures. They require strong men who are capable of being openly affectionate. As long as the potential lover has the capacity to keep up with their ever-increasing desires, their flame of love will burn bright. Shakira has demanded, "I expect my beloved to be kind, generous, I expect him not to lie so I can look him straight in the eyes, and I expect him to fall in love with me 10 times a day."

Ultimately, this combination has much to contend with in order to develop their awareness and strengths quickly, because the universe relies upon them to take on a lot of responsibility from a young age. They have a fear-busting, weakness-converting, mountain climbing sort of perspective compounded by a powerful appreciation for life. Isla Fisher has said, "I've always had no trouble feeling extremely grateful. So even though, comparatively, I wasn't doing so well, I thought I was on top of the world." Being unconventional people with unconventional desires, it is better that they listen to their inner voices rather than a conventional outsider's. Talking about being balanced and present, Shakira has said, "I want to learn how to live in the present with my eyes open. Because, you know, we always go through the present blindfolded with our hearts in the past and our minds in the future. And that way we never enjoy the here and now."

Soul Mate:	Rooster-Scorpio
Challenger:	Dog-Leo
Siblings:	Dragon-Gemini, Dragon-Libra
Best Friends:	Rat-Gemini, Rat-Libra, Rat-Aquarius, Monkey-Gemini, Monkey-Libra, Monkey-Aquarius

Isla Fisher
Chris Farley
Christopher Eccleston
Matt Dillon
Shakira
Neil Diamond
Diane Lane
Abhishek Bachchan
Randy Crawford
James Ingram
Smokey Robinson
Charlie Day
Janet Varney
Jeanne Moreau
Kerry Washington

Justin Hartley
Brandon Lee
Mary Steenburgen
Plácido Domingo
Jean Simmons

DRAGON – PISCES

Chinese Name: LONG
Rank: 5th
Hours Ruled: 7am – 9am
Direction: Southeast
Season: Spring
Month: April
Western Zodiac Equivalent of Dragon: Aries
Aries Western Element: Fire
Eastern Zodiac Equivalent of Pisces: Rabbit
Pisces Western Element: Water
Numerology: 60 = 6

He who rejects change is the architect of decay. The only human institution which rejects progress is the cemetery.
– Harold Wilson

When the Dragon's soul fire is met by the potency of Pisces's water, rather than dampened, we are given a fire that's fuelled further by its antagonistic element and an ocean of boiling water. Strong, determined and sometimes blunt, they are quite reactive in nature, which causes some issues. They take their innate power and that which is entrusted to them and run wild with it. It takes some time for this Dragon to develop its discernment muscle. However, they are generous and open-minded so they listen when respected friends offer advice and slowly, their self-awareness muscles start growing. The Dragon-Pisces is an unrelenting force that lives life fully until the very last second. Bruce Forsyth has said, "Even though I'm 81, when I walk on to a studio floor, I feel 30... I don't want to grow old gracefully. I want to put up a bit of a fight." Natural performers, they often find themselves in the spotlight and they know exactly what to do to thrill the audience and how to manage it. Comedian Lee Evans said, "Breathe! 'Cause if you're still breathing, you've still got a chance!"

These are the sort of people who attract success wherever they go for the simple reason that they work all the hours and will do whatever it takes to get it. Dragons are known for their work ethic and ability to handle the workload of three people. Wanda Sykes has said, "I work hard. The staff and crew see how much energy I put into this project, and it makes them step up... If you're passionate about your work, it makes the people around you want to be involved too." From the outside, it may look like they have it easy, but only they know the hours that have gone into it. Even Chuck Norris has said, "Whatever luck I had, I made. I was never a natural athlete, but I paid my dues in sweat and concentration and took the time necessary to learn karate and become world champion."

The men of this combination tend to be creatively gifted in all areas and you often find many "triple threats" (actors, singers and dancers) born under this combination. As long as they keep their ego in check and seek out the lessons from the early part of their lives, they will be able to attune themselves to the universal powers and feel connected for the rest of their lives. In a side note, they often have bony faces with chiseled chins. They do not seek out the limelight for the wrong reasons; in fact they are often repelled by undignified people or situations. Freddy Prinze Jr. said, "People just stayed away, which was good because I didn't like what they stood for or believed in." Those born with this combination have an interesting life journey in that they arrive with a well-developed sense of themselves, their abilities and what their worth is. However, it tends to be somewhat egocentric rather than a healthy self-regard. Their paths are therefore littered with ego diminishing events including a number of difficult relationships early in life until they open the door to genuine humility. When this happens, they rebuild themselves with a psychological armory that makes them unstoppable. Go Dragon-Pisces! Observing such triumphs in their own lives, they learn to value human heroism rather than hero-worship which Christopher Eccleston said was "Dangerous because it's very unrealistic to elevate people to heroic status." Rob Lowe has said, "I like the tradition of ordinary men in extraordinary circumstances and how they react to events which force them to be heroic in a way that is not in their natures."

The women of this combination tend to be quite Amazonian (which is quite typical for Dragon women anyway), tall and firmly built with a strong self-protection system already installed. They are sexier than they are beautiful and they have great access to their emotions. Fiery and sparky, they are not particularly predictable. Rihanna, has said, "I like the risk, I like the edge. That's the thrill for me." These are some of the most creative Dragon women of all. Surprisingly approachable, passionate and stylish, once they understand their worth, they open themselves to all the pleasures around them. Laura Harring said, "Let them give you the jewels, go around with your bodyguard, let them dress you...don't be afraid of glamor." Anything that they do, they do for the right reasons, fun being a primary one. When they allow their inner self to direct them, their ego quieted and their universal humanity takes over. Juliette Binoche said, "If a star is someone who gives light, then I can be a star. But if a star is someone who goes after money and magazine covers then it's sick and I don't want it!"

Ultimately, with their work ethic, eternal good humor and Dragon magnetism, they are most definitely stars. You do not even have to look at a Dragon-Pisces to sense their presence. They themselves might never entirely comprehend just how brightly they shine but their frisky personalities and eternal zest for life keep them young forever. Juliette Binoche said, "I live for the present always. I accept this risk. I don't deny the past, but it's a page to turn." They learn new ways of observing themselves and their world, which forces them to confront the mistakes they have made previously. Although it is not easy, it is really helpful for them and eventually liberating because they are able to figure out what is truly significant for them and then they focus specifically on these things that bring joy to them. That is when they organize their lives in a way that works for them. Rihanna has said, "When you realize who you live for, and who's important to please, a lot of people will actually start living. I am never going to get caught up in that. I'm gonna look back on my life and say that I enjoyed it – and I lived it for me."

Soul Mate:	Rooster-Libra
Challenger:	Dog-Virgo
Siblings:	Dragon-Cancer, Dragon-Scorpio
Best Friends:	Rat-Cancer, Rat-Scorpio, Rat-Pisces, Monkey-Cancer, Monkey-Scorpio, Monkey-Pisces

Rashida Jones
Kelly Macdonald
Ali Larter
Chuck Norris
Rob Lowe
Danny Masterson
Freddie Prinze Jr.
Sasha Grey
Brittany Daniel
Rihanna
French Stewart
Peter Berg
Joshua Bowman
Juliette Binoche
Laura Harring

Mark Dacascos
Raul Julia
Daniel Gillies
John Pyper-Ferguson
Paul Schneider
Jake Weber
Robin Ruzan
Peter Fonda
Corey Stoll
Luke Mably
Patrick McGoohan
Markéta Irglová
Wanda Sykes
Gore Verbinski
Bernardo Bertolucci
Lee Evans
Neil Jackson
Prince Edward
Dr. Seuss
Harvey Weinstein

THE SNAKE

THE SNAKE

I am the mentor, the political philosopher, the teacher. My life is my example to inspire you. My great ego endows me with power, influence and persuasive prowess but I must choose my path; for karma afflicts me powerfully and my deeds are read from the circumstances of my life. I am the mysterious strategist and there are only ladders for me to climb as I am the snake that can bring others down, or, if I choose, I can also be a ladder to support the growth of others. Though I am quiet, calm and wise, my anger, when released, creates earthquakes. Though my mystique is well acknowledged, my weakness is my need to be admired, seen as the ultimate sophisticated being. My words are sometimes tools and sometimes weapons, be my friend or my foe, you will be affected by my rhetoric. I breathe, I sweat and I bleed power – there is always more inside me than I release and I will never give it up until the time comes for me to shed my current skin and renew myself once more.

I am the Snake.

Wise and mysterious, you are a master of self-control and image creation. With your enigmatic charm and philosophical banter, you inspire respect and are looked up to by many. You can be thorough and pedantic when things are not to your taste. Although you wouldn't like it to be known, you can be a perfectionist and work hard to have everything the way you like it, though it seems you do nothing at all. The Chinese see snakes as supreme strategists. You are deep, intellectual and well read. Into art and culture, you have impeccable taste and can make money with your ability to spot talent, or bargains in any form.

Career-wise, Snakes are teachers, mentors and spiritual thought leaders. They are often multi-talented and have an ego that needs some feeding so as long as their job provides them with immediate adoration, they are satisfied. Despite their superior intelligence and innate wisdom, they are actually a little bit lazy and prefer to work smart, rather than work really hard. They also like abstract theories, politics and strategy so jobs that require this sort of thinking also appeal. They are also exceptional at spotting bargains, recognizing good ideas at their inception point and finding talent, so they often work as a middleman, selling something they have found on for a higher price. In addition, they like graphic arts, crafts, design, psychology, finance, dance, real estate, science research and technology.

Compatibilities

Soul Mate: Monkey
Challenger: Boar
Best Friends: Ox & Rooster
Good Relations: Rat & Dog

SNAKE – ARIES

Chinese Name: SHÉ
Rank: 6th
Hours Ruled: 9am – 11am
Direction: South-Southeast
Season: Spring
Month: May
Western Zodiac Equivalent of Snake: Taurus
Taurus Western Element: Earth
Eastern Zodiac Equivalent of Aries: Dragon
Aries Western Element: Fire
Numerology: 61 = 7

I'm just an uptight mutt at the top of his game. Welcome to
*Hollywood, b***h!*
– Robert Downey Jr

When the potent earth of the Snake is met by Aries's aggressive fire, wisdom meets constant forward motion. This is one unstoppable force. It is the sort of combination that is always alert and always at work. They never step off duty or fully allow themselves to relax because their next goal is all consuming. Snake-Aries is one of those combinations that can be successful, controversial yet remain hugely popular at the same time and often receive affectionate support rather than judgment if they ever err. People place them on a pedestal but having to live up to such high expectations takes its toll, try as they may, sometimes, the ego just wants its way. Speaking about his struggle with narcotics Robert Downey Jr. said, "Sometimes it's necessary to compartmentalize the different stages of your evolution, both personally and objectively, for the people you have to love and tolerate. And one of those people, for me, is me."

Snake's introversion fights Aries's extroversion here and one cannot say which side will win out. However, it is likely that they will present as Extroverts, while being naturally introverted. Julie Christie has said, "I am very quiet and would much prefer to talk to a few people rather than a crowd." Generally, their views tend to be quite conservative, in that regard, they are the way they look. They like to be seen as well-to-do and popular. They are masters of subtlety. Joan Crawford was repelled by the blatant sexuality of contemporary Hollywood. She said, "I find suggestion a hell of a lot more provocative than explicit detail. You didn't see Clark Gable (Rat-Aquarius) and Vivien Leigh (Ox-Scorpio) rolling around in bed in Gone with the Wind (1939), but you saw that shit-eating grin on her face the next morning." The Snake-Aries however, does not seem to mind being quite direct with its words.

The men of this combination tend to have a strong belief in themselves, even if they are not entirely sure who that self is. They have a quiet yet overpowering sexuality that is appealing although one cannot put their finger on just quite what it is about them. They are not always traditionally attractive. Maybe it is the fact that they know, that every single characteristic that exists, exists in them and that it is nothing to be ashamed of. They understand that the light can only exist because of the dark and they manage their polarities well. Robert Downey Jr. said, "There's a little bit of a—hole in every nice guy, and there's a little bit of genius in every moron." Despite the chaos that appeals to them, the unconscious pull towards spiritual connection with their higher self is also constantly active within them. This gives them an acute perception of themselves, of the external environment and of life in general. Robert Downey Jr. has said, "Worrying is like praying for what you don't want to happen... I don't worry, but I observe where my mind tends to go." Similarly, Michael Fassbender said, "I'm just following my gut instinct."

Usually, petite firecrackers with a professional work ethic, the women of this combination seem available to everybody, yet open themselves truly to only a select few. Sarah Jessica Parker said, "As a woman, I have an inherent need to be all things to all people, to make certain everybody's taken care of." Snake women are some of the most intriguing of all 12 signs, adding Aries to the mix makes them especially distinctive. There is a reason so many of them are cast as leading ladies. They have a vulnerability that they are constantly trying to overcome and turn into a strength. In order to maintain an image of strength, they harden the exterior. Maybe this is why so many of them have played unlikeable, yet sympathetic characters in their careers. Joan Crawford said, "I love playing bitches. There's a lot of bitch in every woman – a lot in every man."

Snake Aries women do not feel inferior to any man, in fact, they do not feel inferior to anyone at all and set about taking charge of their own destiny. Joan Crawford said, "You have to be self-reliant and strong to survive in this town. Otherwise you will be destroyed... Be afraid of nothing." Sarah Jessica Parker said, "I understand why a lot of actresses are producing now; I understand how seductive it is and how hard it is not to have control."

Ultimately, the Snake-Aries is one ambitious creature and they have an innate understanding of what they are built for. They are also happy to listen to the universal guidance that is constantly speaking in their ear. Of course, in order to achieve big, one must have big desires, a sense of worthiness and necessarily, a big ego. They work exceptionally hard to hit their heights and openly accept the rewards of their labor. Joan Crawford said, "If you've earned a position, be proud of it." The primary issue that the Snake-Aries have to deal with is how to take the professional face off in order to rest and recuperate. All they know is how to work;

they even play through their work; the chances are they met their partner through their work. They need strong partners, usually Ox or Monkey signs who have the ability to make them laugh, thereby tricking them out of their serious work mode. When they learn how to manage this side of their personality, their mood lightens, their personal lives become their priorities and they feel free to explore simple pleasures that they denied themselves for no reason.

Soul Mate:	Monkey-Virgo
Challenger:	Boar-Libra
Siblings:	Snake-Leo, Snake-Sagittarius
Best Friends:	Ox-Aries, Ox-Leo, Ox-Sagittarius, Rooster-Aries, Rooster-Leo, Rooster-Sagittarius

Robert Downey Jr.
Michael Fassbender
Sarah Jessica Parker
Sarah Michelle Gellar
Max von Sydow
Alia Shawkat
Aly Michalka
Martin Lawrence
Rick Moranis
Bianca Kajlich
Jon Cryer
Julie Christie
Rob McElhenney
Ana de la Reguera
Mark Pellegrino
Édgar Ramírez
Joan Crawford
Juliet Landau
Barry Sonnenfeld

Dirk Bogarde
Nigel Hawthorne
Paulina Porizkova

SNAKE – TAURUS

Chinese Name: SHÉ
Rank: 6th

Hours Ruled: 9am – 11am

Direction: South-Southeast
Season: Spring
Month: May
Western Zodiac Equivalent of Snake: Taurus
Taurus Western Element: Earth
Eastern Zodiac Equivalent of Taurus: Snake
Taurus Western Element: Earth
Numerology: 62 = 8

I don't get out of bed for less than $10,000 a day.
– Linda Evangelista

When the Snake's mysterious earth meets with the bulls tough terrain, there is consistency, because the land is of the same texture and material; the Snake equates to the Taurus sign and vice versa so in effect, here we have the pure Snake or double Taurus combination. This means that the traits of both of these signs, many of which are shared anyway, are amplified here. The double earth here gives them a powerful presence that speaks louder than they ever do, being naturally quiet souls. They use their Snake minds to dream big, and then they use Taurus's ability to lock in a target, then charge for it constantly gaining momentum until the goal has been reached. Ella Fitzgerald said, "Just don't give up trying to do what you really want to do. Where there is love and inspiration, I don't think you can go wrong." This is an exceptionally tenacious combination; maybe that is why people of this combination achieve the impossible? Audrey Hepburn said, "Nothing is impossible, the word itself says 'I'm possible!'"

Smart, savvy and sexy, the Snake-Taurus is one of those combinations that seems to be good at everything; their minds are highly strategic; they understand the micro as well as macro concerns. The downside is that when they become single-mindedly focused on achieving something, they start making excuses and justifications for their questionable decisions. As Tony Blair said, "I can only go one way. I've not got a reverse gear." This is a universally "Taurus" trait.

This slippery Snake-Taurus knows how to be valuable so that people will pay a premium for the services it can provide. Comedienne Victoria Wood has said, "If you behave normally, people treat you normally. It's only when you act as if you're someone special that they feel obliged to stand on ceremony." People of this combination often do insist that they receive the royal treatment yet will behave so humbly, it's as if the ceremony is embarrassing to their modest core. This is a very smart approach that makes them feel super-special above all else whilst endearing themselves to the masses. For example when Tony Blair was asked what he believed was the most important thing in life, his response was, "You only require two things in life: your sanity and your wife." Similarly, Linda Evangelista said, "When people ask how have I kept on top, I have to say with the help of every photographer, make-up artist and hairdresser I've ever worked with." Smart though this approach is, the reason that Snake-Taureans use it to such effect is that the sentiments expressed are probably more genuine than people can understand.

The men of this combination are sophisticated, sharp and intelligent; this is what they prize more than anything else. They have the ability to firmly be themselves in the face of strong opposition. As Pierce Brosnan said, "When people don't believe in you, you have to believe in yourself." They are attractive in that sophisticated Snake way, but their looks are secondary to their intellectual prowess. However, being that this is the double Snake combination, it is inevitably sensually led and often with a high libido. Although they do not feel the need to exert their dominance particularly, they do make use of their innate authority if one of their core values is being exploited. As Tony Blair has said, "Power without principle is barren, but principle without power is futile." So Principled Power it is. It is common for most double earth combinations to end up in leadership positions, but especially so for this ego-led Snake. Speaking about maintaining boundaries, Tony Blair said, "The art of leadership is saying no, not saying yes. It is very easy to say yes."

The women of this combination are delicious in so many ways. Conventionally beautiful, in fact, they have the ability to be beauty trendsetters going by Linda Evangelista and Audrey Hepburn. Here's the interesting thing about the Snake, it is one of the strongest signs, but also one of the soppiest. So the double Snake combination is going to have these two traits pushed to an extreme and this shows most prominently in the females of this species. Audrey Hepburn said, "I was born with an enormous need for affection, and a terrible need to give it." They also have a great work ethic. Linda Evangelista has said, "When I work, it can be a 16-hour day… On days when I do not work, I am working on my image." And everybody knows how image conscious all Snakes are. Imagine what the double Snake is like.

Controversy often follows these people because of their choices or actions taken when the bull sees red and they may have to work hard to regain the popularity they enjoyed previously. But in time, people forgive and forget, whatever their indiscretions may be. On a spiritual level, the double earth combinations have a close relationship with universal energies and feel its unconditional love with less resistance, meaning that they find it easier to love themselves regardless what they have done in the past.

This lends them universal magnetism that is difficult to resist and that is why people respond to them so powerfully. Audrey Hepburn is a good example of someone who aligned herself with the universal law, letting go of striving, expectations and attempted to remain present to the joy of the moment. She has said, "I decided, very early on, just to accept life unconditionally; I never expected it to do anything special for me, yet I seemed to accomplish far more than I had ever hoped. Most of the time it just happened to me without my ever seeking it." Aligned and non-resistant to the good, all manner of blessings fall straight into their laps.

Soul Mate:	Monkey-Leo
Challenger:	Boar-Scorpio
Siblings:	Snake-Virgo, Snake-Capricorn
Best Friends:	Ox-Taurus, Ox-Virgo, Ox-Capricorn, Rooster-Taurus, Rooster-Virgo, Rooster-Capricorn

Frank Borzage
Henry Fonda
Joseph Cotten
Leila Hyams
David Tomlinson
Celeste Holm
Ella Fitzgerald
Audrey Hepburn
Ann-Margret
Pierce Brosnan
Victoria Wood
Tony Blair
Oleta Adams
Kevin James
Adrian Pasdar
Linda Evangelista

Tom Welling
Melanie Lynskey
Samantha Morton
Lindsey Shaw
Chris Brown

SNAKE – GEMINI

Chinese Name: SHÉ
Rank: 6th
Hours Ruled: 9am – 11am
Direction: South-Southeast
Season: Spring
Month: May
Western Zodiac Equivalent of Snake: Taurus
Taurus Western Element: Earth
Eastern Zodiac Equivalent of Gemini: Horse
Gemini Western Element: Air
Numerology: 63 = 9

When written in Chinese, the word "crisis" is composed of two characters. One represents danger and the other repre-sents opportunity.
– John F. Kennedy

When the Snake's sensuous earth meets Gemini's gentle gale, the old-soul sage meets the two faces of Gemini's innocence and naughtiness. Both signs are powerfully connected to the spiritual world and some may say, somewhat conversely, both like to have the needs of their id met immediately. They have an appetite for life and they go for their desires without hesitation, but if they are met with obstacles or objections, they take it personally. The Gemini aspect of this combination is quite pronounced in that it values its freedom above all else, but what is freedom to them? Jean-Paul Sartre said, "Freedom is what you do with what's been done to you." There is always the choice to choose your response and live from that. One can choose a response that serves them or not. An interesting trait about this combination is how they consistently adopt positive perspectives that lead them to productive places. The Snake's confidence allows them have faith in their own beliefs even if those around them may object; the Snake quietly overrules any contrariness and comfortably follows its own guidance. Bob Dylan has exclaimed, "A hero is someone who understands the responsibility that comes with his freedom."

Tough yet quiet, hard yet relenting, this combination knows when to be firm and when to melt, but rest assured, that whatever external stance they may adopt, they will never give in or submit their will to anyone because they know that there is never any need. Everyone is born an individual and has a right to that individuality. John F. Kennedy said, "I'm an idealist without illusions." It is no surprise that there are many world leaders belonging to this combination. With their feet firmly planted on the ground, their minds find practical methods of improving situations on many levels for many people. Essentially, they believe in human potential and the goodness of human nature. Anne Frank said, "Everyone has inside of him a piece of good news. The good news is that you don't know how great you can be! How much you can love! What you can accomplish! And what your potential is!"

The men of this combination tend to be physically broad, often tall with a contained energy, much like a compressed spring that is waiting to be released. They are quiet and contemplative as most Snakes are and know how to intimidate indirectly. With their clarity of mind and spiritual connection, they are bold and brazen and do not allow much to hold them back. Jean-Paul Sartre has said, "Fear? If I have gained anything by damning myself, it is that I no longer have anything to fear." This lack of fear pushes them onwards and upwards but can also lead them into precarious situations where they may have to rely on their charm and nerve to get them safely home. At the end of the day, they are result oriented so they know how to be productive. As John F. Kennedy said, "Things do not happen. Things are made to happen."

The women of this combination are exceptionally driven. They believe in change and they want to be on the edge with the other pioneers making it happen. Not that they think of it in this way, they are just doing what they feel they must, but they have been endowed with greater awareness, courage and the desire to see the fruits of their labor. So it is important for these women to choose jobs where they really care about the outcome of their work, because that is when they will really see how far they can push themselves. Brooke Shields said, "I realized that my success was directly proportionate to the work I put in."

It is no surprise that born to this combination are people with bold personalities that put themselves on the line even if it could put them at risk personally. But they do it because they have the guts to do so and because they are prepared to die for their ideals. Former Prime Minister of Pakistan and the first female Premier of that country, Benazir Bhutto said, "Democracy is necessary to peace and to undermining the forces of terrorism." Unfortunately, like brother Snake-Gemini John F. Kennedy, she was also assassinated.

Constantly putting themselves on the line, they struggle with sustaining the power of their convictions in private. This can sometimes take them to dark places, which they eventually psychologically unpick and return to balanced *idealism without illusion*. Bob Dylan said, "All the truth in the world adds up to one big lie… Democracy don't rule the world, You'd better get that in your head; This world is ruled by violence, But I guess that's better left unsaid." This is the contradictory roundabout that spins in the Snake-Gemini's mind: reality versus their ideals. It tortures them, forces them into action hoping that their ideals win out. Sometimes they do and sometimes they do not. But when the chips are down, the Snake-Gemini rejects its own naysaying reverting to its core belief best summed up by John F. Kennedy when he said, 'The problems of the world cannot possibly be solved by skeptics or cynics whose horizons are limited by the obvious realities. We need men who can dream of things that never were."

Ultimately, this is an inspirational combination who takes full responsibility for their lives. Even if they choose to laze about and do nothing, they are aware that there is nobody else to be blamed for their lethargic apathy. More often than not though, this snake combination is one that likes to take charge of its life and serve as an example to others. This personality takes adversity and remolds it into hope. As Brooke Shields said, "Don't waste a minute not being happy. If one window closes, run to the next window – or break down a door."

Soul Mate:	Monkey-Cancer
Challenger:	Boar-Sagittarius
Siblings:	Snake-Libra, Snake-Aquarius
Best Friends:	Ox-Gemini, Ox-Libra, Ox-Aquarius, Rooster-Gemini, Rooster-Libra, Rooster-Aquarius

Jean-Paul Sartre
Dean Martin
John F. Kennedy
Anne Frank
Brooke Shields
Elizabeth Hurley
Bob Dylan
Benazir Bhutto
Stephen Frears
Harold Guskin
Delia Smith
Tim Allen

Alfred Molina
Danny Elfman
Sadie Frost
Zachary Quinto
Kanye West
Lucy Hale
Imogen Poots
Nargis

SNAKE – CANCER

Chinese Name: SHÉ
Rank: 6th
Hours Ruled: 9am – 11am
Direction: South-Southeast
Season: Spring
Month: May
Western Zodiac Equivalent of Snake: Taurus
Taurus Western Element: Earth
Eastern Zodiac Equivalent of Cancer: Sheep
Cancer Western Element: Water
Numerology: 64 = 1

You can't stamp out individuality – there's too many of us.
– Cindy Lauper

When the potency of the Snake's earth joins the Crab's silent waters, presence meets creativity giving these creatures the nerve to promote themself and their ideas even when they are ahead of their time and out of the norm. There is much overlap with these two signs; both are cold-blooded creatures that are sophisticated, quietly confident and desire to take charge. The Snake comes from a more cerebral place and the Cancerian, the more sensual, so with two different types of data flowing, the processed information tends to be broad, full and smart. Despite both of these signs being quite ambitious in their own right, the Cancerian's huge heart manages to overrule the more ruthless aspects that often lay dormant, which makes them prioritize romance, love and sensual conquest. It is for this reason, work only takes precedence when they have found and are happy in a romantic partnership. In fact, if they can find a Monkey or a Rooster partner, their work life tends to excel prolifically because they will know how to promote their talents perfectly.

There are many singer song writers of this combination: Cindy Lauper, Jason Mraz, June Carter Cash, Bebe Buell, even Liv Tyler sings; this combination is a soulful creature that feels alive when it is expressing the contents of its heart. Cindy Lauper has said, "When I sing I don't feel like it's me. I feel I am fabulous, like I'm 10 feet tall. I am the greatest. I am the strongest. I am Samson. I'm whoever I want to be." When they feel this empowered, they want to leverage it to lift others to higher state of consciousness or at least open a few minds. Their talent is the way they communicate their message. Author and human guinea pig Tim Ferriss said, "The best entrepreneurs I've ever met are all good communicators."

The men of this combination are interesting to know as they present like they are of the aristocracy, upstanding, well-read, authoritative...but more discerning types soon realize that this is just another Snake projecting another image to be seen to have "value" that they don't actually believe in themselves. It's not that they don't provide value, they do, they just don't believe that they do. In actuality, they are rougher, gruffer and ready to serve their own needs first. Naturally, introverted, they struggle with how they are going to make an impact whilst maintaining their subtle air of cool. Milo Ventimiglia has said, "I'm tough on the outside and soft on the inside [...] I'm really a shy guy...I don't drink, I don't smoke, I don't do anything...but I bowled like a crazy mother..." As previously mentioned, this combination prioritizes love above all else, so it comes as no surprise that Jason Mraz said, "I want to be surrounded by women, I want to be snuggled and cuddled and pampered."

The women of this combination are soft, sensual and charming. Their sense of humor comes as a surprise, especially as they look so cultured and sophisticated; nobody expects them to be as spicy as they are. Singer Cindy Lauper has said, "Humor is a great vehicle for getting a message across. If you get too serious, you could die of starch." Model and Singer Bebe Buell dubbed a "legendary beauty" was the first fashion model to pose for *Playboy* and was fired by Ford Modelling agency for it. Not that it stopped her; she signed with Wilhelmina and continued to work. These women are intelligent, classy and have a raw youthful sex appeal something akin to innocence, without being innocent. Talking about her daughter, Bebe Buell said, "It's so beautiful to watch her 'cause she loves every second of performing and just glows." Liv Tyler takes after her mother in more ways than one: she shares her mother's astrological combination.

When these women really fall for someone, they cannot help but put them completely first; when Liv Tyler found out the truth about her parentage, Buell removed herself from the public forum and functioned behind the scenes. Similarly, when June Carter Cash partnered with Johnny Cash (see Monkey-Pisces for Johnny Cash), she too removed herself. Talking about this she said, "I've been really happy just traveling and being Mrs. Johnny Cash all these years. But I'm also really happy and surprised that someone wanted me to make another album, and I'm real proud of what I've done."

All Snake combinations are born teachers, more specifically, mentors. They get a kick out of altering people perceptions, getting them to believe in themselves and serving as inspirations. Yes, they like to be looked up to too, it is the best way to serve the Snake's ego, but that aside, you cannot argue with their results; they inspire people to get out there, get involved and create change. Talking about her activism, Cindy Lauper said, "I'm a bra-burner from way back!" Following on from fellow Snake Oprah Winfrey (Snake-Aquarius), Tim Ferriss started a book club online where he suggests titles that his entrepreneur-slant audience would find helpful.

Speaking about letting go of one's physical attachments, Jason Mraz said, "Surrender to life itself and you'll just be rewarded with so many things." Despite all of the ego serving behavior, image projection and materialism that Snake signs indulge in, there is also an intrinsic understanding of the futility of these things; it is only when this realization penetrates the paradigm through which they view their daily lives that they let go and experience true freedom. This reconnects them to the cosmic flow of life, that stream of well-being that brings them a constant barrage of blessings whilst highlighting the beauty of all the smaller things that they missed before. Cindy Lauper has said, "You always have to remember – no matter what you're told – that God loves all the flowers, even the wild ones that grow on the side of the highway."

Soul Mate:	Monkey-Gemini
Challenger:	Boar-Capricorn
Siblings:	Snake-Scorpio, Snake-Pisces
Best Friends:	Ox-Cancer, Ox-Scorpio, Ox-Pisces, Rooster-Cancer, Rooster-Scorpio, Rooster-Pisces

Prince George Alexander Louis
Milo Ventimiglia
Liv Tyler
Bebe Buell,
June Carter Cash
Cyndi Lauper
Jason Mraz
Jeremy Kyle
Jaine Murray
Ashley Scott
Alex Winter
Mindy Sterling
Timothy Ferriss

Robert Forster
Robert Pine
George Clinton
David Kelly
Rajendra Kumar
Phyllis Diller
Susan Hayward
Lena Horn

SNAKE – LEO

Chinese Name: SHÉ
Rank: 6th
Hours Ruled: 9am – 11am
Direction: South-Southeast
Season: Spring
Month: May
Western Zodiac Equivalent of Snake: Taurus
Taurus Western Element: Earth
Eastern Zodiac Equivalent of Leo: Monkey
Leo Western Element: Fire
Numerology: 65 = 2

Anything's possible if you've got enough nerve.
– JK Rowling

When the Snake's fertile earth meets the Lion's raging fire, presence meets power, intelligence meets audacity and the strategist merges with the warrior. It is not surprising then that this combination turns out to be a bit of a gladiator of sorts with an endless amount of determination: when they set their minds on a goal, they will see it through to the end. As J.K. Rowling has said, "The moment you are old enough to take the wheel, responsibility lies with you."

Having seen thousands of young actors, it was after Daniel Radcliffe auditioned for the role of Harry Potter that J.K. Rowling said, "That's my Harry!" It's likely that she felt he would innately understand her work and her fictional protagonist because in real life, they are both born under the same astrological archetype; they are both Snake-Leos. This sort of thing happens frequently in casting, especially so with the Snake signs. (See Snake-Pisces for another example.) It is also interesting that the character of Harry Potter is connected to the serpent creatures throughout the series.

As a Snake combination, a certain level of perfectionism is only to be expected and with the Lion's pride in the mix, the need to complete their work to the highest possible standards can also be expected, so it does not come a surprise that Martha Stewart has described herself as a "maniacal perfectionist." Similarly, Daniel Radcliffe has said, "I'm a frighteningly thorough person." The Snake-Leo is one of those flowers that will slowly wilt if there is no passion in their work life; they are made for professional contribution, they enjoy knowing that they can make a difference and that what they do affects the lives of others, so it is important that they put themselves in environments where their passion and values meet. J.K. Rowling said, "I just write what I wanted to write. I write what amuses me. It's totally for myself. I never in my wildest dreams expected this popularity."

The men of this combination usually have a touch of arrogance that has them believe that they are just that little bit better than others. But this is a cultivated belief that they have to have in order to keep pushing the boundaries and to retain a competitive spirit, which they need in order to excel in a professional environment. Jonathon Rhys Meyer said, "Could I imagine myself as king? Of course I could." They are born with regal qualities for a reason and know that they are important, worthy and powerful, but that does not mean that they do not struggle with their insecurities and self-doubts just like everyone else. In fact, the higher you are up the hierarchy, the worse the struggle; that is if one chooses to maintain humility and keep grounded, which the Snake-Leo generally aspires to do. Although, they sometimes do go through periods of believing their own hype...this does not end well. Eventually, they understand the need for balance. Daniel Radcliffe has said, "Being self-critical is good; being self-hating is destructive. There's a very fine line there somewhere, and I walk it carefully."

The women of this combination are typical Snake women with as much strength as vulnerability, beauty, intelligence, deep empathy and a commitment to self-improvement. J.K. Rowling has said, "I think you're working and learning until you die." Similarly, Martha Stewart said, "My new motto is: When you're through changing, you're through." Looking good matters to Snake signs, they know that the external body is a reflection of what is happening on the internal plain. These women seem to be intrinsically connected to spiritual principles and rely on their instinct and intuitive voice to guide them. Even if they find themselves in precarious situations, they are smart enough to navigate the territory to usher the tide towards the result that they want, the result that usually benefits the majority of people involved without damaging any egos. That being said, sometimes, they believe in bruising an overdeveloped ego where necessary and can be overt bulldozers. It's not wise to tell them that something is unattainable or impossible; that word is not in their vocabulary. Oscar winning Actress Viola Davis said, "I didn't see myself any different from my white counterparts in school. I just didn't! I thought I could do what they did. And what I didn't do well, I thought people were going to give me the opportunity to do well, because maybe they saw my talent, so they would give me a chance. I had no idea that they would see me completely different."

Powerfully, they project their differences, their individuality and vulnerable-strength and it supports them to succeed. There is still a bit of that pretention that Snakes come with, but it serves as an ego-booster, which they need. Do not forget, this gladiator fights in a vicious arena where the eyes of the masses are on them all of the time. Jonathon Rhys Meyer has said, "Going after a part in Hollywood is like being a gladiator in ancient Rome." Speaking about getting a movie made, Director Sam Mendes uses a similar image, "Listen, you make a big movie, you're going into the

Coliseum, and people are going to give you the thumbs up or the thumbs down."

Ultimately, the Snake-Leo goes through major highs and lows; Jonathon Rhys Meyer, Robert Mitchum and famously Martha Stewart all did jail time, but all came back stronger and more inspirational. It is only because they fall so low that they can jump so high; they decided on that before choosing to be born in the Snake-Leo skin and actually, they get off on it. J.K. Rowling said, "It is impossible to live without failing at something, unless you live so cautiously that you might as well not have lived at all." When they allow themselves to *be* themselves, they find their feet. These gladiators know how to fight and they know how to win. And win they will, eventually!

Soul Mate:	Monkey-Taurus
Challenger:	Boar-Aquarius
Siblings:	Snake-Aries, Snake-Sagittarius
Best Friends:	Ox-Aries, Ox-Leo, Ox-Sagittarius, Rooster-Aries, Rooster-Leo, Rooster-Sagittarius

Daniel Radcliffe
J.K. Rowling
Hayden Panettiere
Jonathan Rhys Meyers
Sam Mendes
Slash
Robert Mitchum
Viola Davis
Danny Dyer
Martha Stewart
Jeremy Piven
Ali Cobrin
Embeth Davidtz

Jaime Pressly

Edward Furlong

Kyra Sedgwick

Peter Krause

Hulk Hogan

Joe Jonas

Ken Baumann

James Horner

SNAKE – VIRGO

Chinese Name: SHÉ
Rank: 6th
Hours Ruled: 9am – 11am
Direction: South-Southeast
Season: Spring
Month: May
Western Zodiac Equivalent of Snake: Taurus
Taurus Western Element: Earth
Eastern Zodiac Equivalent of Virgo: Rooster
Virgo Western Element: Earth
Numerology: 66 = 3

I identify with Superman. I am adopted, I am an only child, and I love the idea that he comes from another world, that he's the ultimate immigrant. He has all these extraordinary powers, and he has a righteousness about him.
– Bryan Singer

The Snake's earth and the Virgo's earth are of quite different compositions yet they have the same purpose: to nurture, grow and excel. Like most double earth combinations, this one is as tough as steel and as stubborn too. They require a lot of time by themselves to get centered, especially when they are trying to fill their time with things to do. The Snake brings its wisdom, ambition and presence; the Virgo brings its common sense, humility and resilience. Many double earth combinations have a reputation for being unreasonable because of their exceptionally high standards but unfortunately, they also expect a lot from other people. It is also interesting that it is their unreasonableness and reluctance to accept the status quo that ultimately makes them so effective. Country Superstar Shania Twain has said, "I find that the very things that I get criticized for, which is usually being different and just doing my own thing and just being original, is the very thing that's making me successful."

With this potent spirituality, they find it very therapeutic to spend time in nature. Despite having a natural aptitude for academia, many opt to work with the land instead and have their own farm or running their own business that require large amounts of space. Also, they are often have an interest in animal welfare. Greta Garbot said, "If I needed recreation, I liked to be out of doors: to trudge about in a boy's coat and boy's shoes; to ride horseback, or shoot craps with the stable boys, or watch the sun set in a blaze of glory over the Pacific Ocean. You see, I am still a bit of a tomboy."

Snakes are very particular about many things; they know what they like, they know how things are supposed to be done and it irks them when things are not done to their standards. The Virgo and the Snake are two meticulous masters to deal with! Even those who are the politest and most obliging Snake-Virgos cannot help but feel disconcerted when surrounded by messiness, classlessness and general lack of self-awareness. That is why they require solitary time to remember that not everyone is on their level and communicate with the spiritual powers that be who might understand their predicament. Iyanla Vansant has said, "In my deepest, darkest moments, what really got me through was a prayer. Sometimes my prayer was 'Help me.' Sometimes a prayer was 'Thank you.' What I've discovered is that intimate connection and communication with my creator will always get me through because I know my support, my help, is just a prayer away."

The men of this combination present a testosterone charged face to the world while they struggle to reconcile this image with who they feel they are inwardly, which is borderline "god" and "vagabond fraud." Actor Tom Hardy has said, "A lot of people say I seem masculine, but I don't feel it. I feel intrinsically feminine. I'd love to be one of the boys but I always felt a bit on the outside." Snake-Virgo men believe that they really do have superpowers and want to share them but the world seems to say that it is not appropriate, so they try to conform in the most appropriate way that they can which hampers their creativity. It is a strange and uniquely Snake-Virgo issue. In any case, when they feel like this, they ought to meditate or share their ideas with non-judgmental people and avoid extreme behaviors. Charlie Sheen has said, "I'm tired of pretending I'm not a total bitchin' rock star from Mars."

The women of this combination are sophisticated tomboys! It cannot be denied that Snake women of all varieties love to be ladies; they love fashion, make up, color and general feminine frivolity. At the same time, this combination also loves to get their hands dirty, which is surprising as neither of these signs would suggest that separately. Shania Twain has said, "I played a lot of football when I was younger. I'm a good receiver, actually... I have arm-wrestled here and there...guys seem to want to test my strength." They have a Spartan way about them, going about their business highlighting ways to make improve-ments without expressing any weakness externally while beating themselves up inwardly for not doing or being enough. This can be very self-destructive for them. Iyanla Vansant has said, "I gave myself permission to feel and experience all of my emotions. In order to do that, I had to stop being afraid to feel." Similarly, Shania Twain said, "I spent a lot of my life holding back my cries, and I want to change that because it's not good for me."

Ultimately, this is a real powerhouse of a combination. They have vision, can see the bigger picture but also know how to get involved with the details and the everyday chores. These people see themselves as leaders so it is better for them to seek out leadership positions quickly because they just believe that they know better and it sometimes causes friction. When the Snake-Virgo realizes that their noble intentions to help might actually be destructive, they are mortified; at the end of the day, this Snake perceives itself as a mentor, leader and teacher so damaging somebody's esteem is not usually their plan. It is usually at this point that their hyper-self-awareness develops and they manage their moods and behaviors better. At the same time, it is better for them to believe that they are superheroes because it is only through doing so that they are able to affect the world in major ways, so even if they do not share their belief in their superiority, it is not beneficial for them to lose it. Iyanla Vansant has said, "I've seen the good, the bad, and the ugly. Lived it and I'm still here to talk about it and help someone else if I can."

Soul Mate:	Monkey-Aries
Challenger:	Boar-Pisces
Siblings:	Snake-Taurus, Snake-Capricorn
Best Friends:	Ox-Taurus, Ox-Virgo, Ox-Capricorn, Rooster-Taurus, Rooster-Virgo, Rooster-Capricorn

Greta Garbo
Shania Twain
Iyanla Vanzant
Bryan Singer
Tom Hardy
Robin Thicke
Charlie Sheen
Jason Derulo
Ludacris
Yasser Arafat
Sanford Meisner
Stirling Moss
Otis Redding

Kyle Chandler
Moby
Lennox Lewis
Craig McLachlan
Fiona Apple

SNAKE – LIBRA

Chinese Name: SHÉ
Rank: 6th
Hours Ruled: 9am – 11am
Direction: South-Southeast
Season: Spring
Month: May
Western Zodiac Equivalent of Snake: Taurus
Taurus Western Element: Earth
Eastern Zodiac Equivalent of Libra: Dog
Libra Western Element: Air
Numerology: 67 = 4

First they ignore you, then they laugh at you, then they fight you, then you win.
– Mahatma Gandhi

When the potency of Snake's earth meets with the Libra's cool breeze, the earth is gently caressed and shows its gratitude; these two signs work exceptionally well together to create a power-house of a personality. Libra loses its balance here and pushes the Snakes into an amplified state, so its need to project image, need to lead and even its spiritual dimensions are hugely magnified. There is much ego here and it is not easily managed, which is so necessary because of all of their alpha qualities. As Mahatma Gandhi said, "Be the Change you want to see in the world." Snake-Libras must, must, must lead by example, otherwise, they can become a *do as I say, not as I do* types and bring all sorts of karmic chaos into their lives. As a sign with much power, much responsibility is also bestowed. American activist and Politician, Jesse Jackson has said, "Leadership has a harder job to do than just choose sides. It must bring sides together."

With their quiet authority and charged quality, one is always happy when they are happy because to see this firework explode could be terrifying. Everybody sort of fears the release of that tension because, it goes without saying that they have the capacity to create natural disasters in one being: a simultaneous earthquake and storm. And they themselves know this. That is why they have learned how to control their more destructive feelings. Jesse Jackson has said, "I'm too mature to be angry." Even Gandhi has said, "Anger is the enemy of non-violence and pride is a monster that swallows it up." They are still human at the end of the day and when the Snake-Libra cannot always be a monolith of strength. In vulnerable moments, they collapse, not knowing how to handle their emotions and this is why they often seek out meeker, compassionate personalities to partner with who support them through the emotional complexities of life and make allowances for their indiscretions.

The men of this combination are quiet, observant yet free from the constraints that afflict other people. If it wasn't for their need to be perceived as a pillar of the society, this Snake combination would be very similar to an Ox one, in that they firmly believe in their right to rule, in the rightness of their opinion and they refuse to allow any societal conventions or existing rules get in the way of them achieving their goal. This has both positive and negative connotations. On the one hand, you get a Gandhi, but on the other, you get any number of people who flout the law, cheat their friends and abuse even those closest to them in order to have their needs met. This combination has one of the biggest egos of all. Jesse Jackson said, "Great things happen in small places. Jesus was born in Bethlehem. Jesse Jackson was born in Greenville." This ego has them pushing into territory others dare not, because this one Snake-Libra believes it is special enough, that he alone can make a change. They have such self-belief that they go against the public in public and eventually, persuade them of their rightness. As Gandhi has said, "Even if you are a minority of one, the truth is the truth."

The women of this combination are academic, witty and tough. They know who they are, where they are and what they believe. They are tough on the surface, compassionate on the inside and are constantly attempting to grow beyond their conscious perspectives. Anne Rice has said, "We have to become saints. We have to become like Christ. Anything less is simply not enough." The gentle, green, Linda McCartney also belonged to this group. She understood what was important in life, she said, "I don't need a lot of money. Simplicity is the answer for me." Make no mistake, they have their opinions and they are unlikely to sway from them despite how they maneuver themselves. It is all part of their coy manner. But these ladies are strong! They often look for partners they can boss around or who simply fall into line and let the trousers be worn by the boss. In a professional context, these women create waves, because, like their male counterparts, they head down roads that have never been slithered down before. So what else could the inspirational and pioneering Barbara Walters be, if not a Snake-Libra? Speaking about her legacy and how she will be remembered, she said, "I have affected the way women are regarded, and that's important to me."

Ultimately, these creatures are formed with the wisdom and strength of the Snake and the clarity and communication skills of the Libra. Together, they were made to rule the world, or at least alter it so that it suits their own temperament more: Jesse Jackson continuing the fight for race equality in the US, Linda McCartney being a voice for animal welfare and Mahatma Gandhi non-violently bringing down the British rule in India. It is so important that they place themselves on a road that serves humanity and let that serve their own needs, rather than following the call of their id as that often takes them down dirty roads. An ego like this is not given to many, because most are not capable of handling it. It is a gift and a blessing when utilized correctly. The sooner they figure out what cause they believe and how they can pay it forward, the sooner their lives will have meaning and they will enter the spiritual flow. They want their lives to be the lesson that this mega-mentor leaves behind. Mahatma Gandhi said, "You must not lose faith in humanity. Humanity is an ocean; if a few drops of the ocean are dirty, the ocean does not become dirty."

Soul Mate:	Monkey-Pisces
Challenger:	Boar-Aries
Siblings:	Snake-Gemini, Snake-Aquarius
Best Friends:	Ox-Gemini, Ox-Libra, Ox-Aquarius, Rooster-Gemini, Rooster-Libra, Rooster-Aquarius

Mia Wasikowska
Michelle Wie
Kimmie Meisner
John Mayer
Bode Miller
Mario Lemieux
Patrick Roy
Sofia Milos
Scottie Pippen
Shelley Ackerman
Tony Shalhoub
Paul Simon
Brian Lamb
Jesse Jackson
Anne Rice
Chubby Checker
Linda McCartney
Barbara Walters

Joan Fontaine
Dizzy Gillespie
Arthur Schlesinger, Jr.
Thelonious Monk
June Allyson
Allen Ludden
Buddy Rich
Jean Arthur
Andy Devine
Spring Byington
Lillian Gish
Mahatma Gandhi
Alfred Nobel

SNAKE – SCORPIO

Chinese Name: SHÉ
Rank: 6th
Hours Ruled: 9am – 11am
Direction: South-Southeast
Season: Spring
Month: May
Western Zodiac Equivalent of Snake: Taurus
Taurus Western Element: Earth
Eastern Zodiac Equivalent of Scorpio: Boar
Scorpio Western Element: Water
Numerology: 68 = 5

Emancipation of women has made them lose their mystery.
– Princess Grace Kelly

When the fertile earth of the Snake meets the depth of Scorpio's murky waters, the earth becomes even more potent; the Snake's power and presence meets the Scorpio's enigmatic creativity. What places this Snake apart from its Snake siblings is that the Scorpio side encourages deeper exploration of the darker aspects of their nature so any creative undertakings are that much fuller and rounded as a result. Because of this, they do not follow conventional pathways and tend to be unusual in some regards. They use everything that they have experienced, observed, have been and are in everything that they do, maybe that is why there is such compassion in this seemingly cold-blooded creature? Indira Gandhi said, "Forgiveness is a virtue of the brave."

Although, the Snake likes shortcuts and looks for the fastest route to success, it is wise enough to know that the shortcuts are only available to those who are prepared to take them. That is why they work so hard in developing their own skillset. Bjork has said, "I do believe sometimes discipline is very important.

I'm not just lying around like a lazy cow all the time." In fact, this combination in particular is exceptionally detail oriented. Art Garfunkel has said, "I'm more that thorough, meticulous, disciplined nut."

Containing much power, will and a playful friskiness that imbues everything that they do, often, they do not open this side of their personality. The Snake is image-conscious and the Scorpio has a strong need to self-protect, so if this cold-blooded creature gets a whiff of judgment, they tend to close up and project their defensive face, which can be quite terrifying in the right lights; either that or they will challenge the judgmental person with a view to rip their argument and self-esteem to shreds. They understand that there is value in diversity, primarily because they themselves feel so different...okay, the truth is that on some level they feel extraordinary, because of their above average intelligence, talent, attractiveness and most importantly, endless potential. Singer-songwriter Bjork has said, "I get obsessed by little nerdy things in my corner that no one else is interested in." This extraordinariness is both their gift and curse, because they feel arrogant if they accept their innate blessings, but until they do, they tend to coast in their lives. It is better for them to just admit to themselves (not to anyone else) that they really are super-special and get on with their extraordinary existence rather than taking one step forward and two steps back. Enough emotional vacillation: accept your blessings and move forward with confidence...and if necessary, short-term arrogance.

The men of this combination recognize that they cannot be anything other than who they are, so they consciously root out the aspects of themselves are the most congenial and decide to develop and amplify them. This way, they are being authentic whilst making the most of who they are too. Whether they are good looking, talented, rich or whatever, they do not rely on these things for self-esteem; rather they know that their essence is valuable because they exist and therefore are constantly finding ways to be bigger, better and even more prominent in their own eyes, taking it as their duty to make the most of themselves. Bollywood superstar Shahrukh Khan said, "Some people say, 'Shah Rukh, you work so hard. Why don't you sit back with a glass of red wine or go out on the terrace for a smoke?' But that's not me." With their powerful presence, many assume that they do not suffer with insecurities, when they probably suffer more than most. Ever the titans, they turn their pains into strengths in the end.

The women of this combination look like the epitome of a "lady" but with the power of a bulldozer. Often times they try to play down the force of their will, but repressing anything only makes it more powerful and that is what happens here; that is why other women, especially, tend to be suspicious of their intentions. Princess Grace Kelly said, "Other women looked on me as a rival. And it pained me a great deal." Some women of this combination sense such animosity from other very girly women that they end up making friends with unconventional people. Maybe that is because they are somewhat unconventional themselves. Bjork has said, "I am one of the most idiosyncratic people around." These women are drawn to gay men because as a culture, they tend to celebrate feminine strength rather than fear it. Straight men however, must be able to accept this lady's strength if they are going to earn her respect, adoration and love. Grace Kelly said, "I don't want to be married to someone who feels inferior to my success or because I make more money than he does." That is probably why she ended up as a Princess.

Ultimately, people belonging to this combination are often misunderstood, sometimes they care what people are making of their precious image and other times, they don't give a rap. Being a step ahead of the crowd means that they must get used to living on the edge, with their nerves constantly tested. But this is what creates that strength of character. With power comes responsibility and they accept that responsibility admirably. With power also comes scrutiny and they know how to handle that, even if that sometimes means taking what some might deem as controversial actions. Of all things, they do not believe in excessive displays of emotion, especially anger. Princess Grace Kelly said, "Getting angry doesn't solve anything." They remain composed mostly because they have learned how to control their reactive nerves, stopping in the gap between stimulus and response to prevent massacres. Their getting angry causes mass destruction so they have developed techniques of self-management. Indira Gandhi said, "You must learn to be still in the midst of activity and to be vibrantly alive in repose."

Soul Mate:	Monkey-Aquarius
Challenger:	Boar-Taurus
Siblings:	Snake-Cancer, Snake-Pisces
Best Friends:	Ox-Cancer, Ox-Scorpio, Ox-Pisces, Rooster-Cancer, Rooster-Scorpio, Rooster-Pisces

Indira Gandhi
Grace Kelly
Art Garfunkel
Shah Rukh Khan
Björk
Griff Rhys Jones
Famke Janssen
Edward Asner
Joan Plowright
Sally Kirkland
Boney Kapoor
Mads Mikkelsen

Mike D
Maggie Gyllenhaal
Brittany Murphy
Jon Heder

SNAKE – SAGITTARIUS

Chinese Name: SHÉ
Rank: 6th
Hours Ruled: 9am – 11am
Direction: South-Southeast
Season: Spring
Month: May
Western Zodiac Equivalent of Snake: Taurus
Taurus Western Element: Earth
Eastern Zodiac Equivalent of Sagittarius: Rat
Sagittarius Western Element: Fire
Numerology: 69 = 6

It's not a gift of mine, but one given to me, to be able to criticise myself and not be crushed, by myself or by others.
– John Malkovich

When the cerebral yet spiritual Snake earth combines with the Centaur's frisky fire, we get a personality that benefits from its separate components; the Snake lends its intelligence and self-awareness while the Sagittarius brings optimism, fun and its uninhibited nature. The adult teacher meets the unruly child, but in a unified way, so the members of this group tend to be delight-fully joyful yet with their feet firmly planted on the ground. They are able to bring this interesting energetic mix to everything they do and as long as they feel free to be who they are without feeling like who they are is odd or unusual, they tend to excel and exceed expectations. As John Malkovich has said, "If you don't interfere with me, I'll always do something really good."

The blend of these two very different signs also explains the curious way their mind functions. The child's hyper-creativity is channeled by the teacher collecting the fragments as they fly all over the place putting them into some sort of order so that it makes sense. Perhaps that is why Taylor Swift has said, "My imagination is a twisted place." They enjoy the process of creative free flow where they let *whatever* free-fall into their consciousness without judging it, then they apply the grown up perspective. Ryan Murphy has said, "I think I have a pattern of nice and lovely and then dark and twisted."

The men of this combination, like most Snake signs cannot escape their inner geek and they tend to get very passionate about niche topics. Often times, they can be the most handsome or the most intelligent or the most charismatic person in the room, yet they find it difficult to accept acceptance. Ben Stiller has said, "I have a lot of nervous energy. Work is my best way of channelling that into something productive unless I want to wind up assaulting the postman or gardener." As a result of their nervous disposition and their simultaneous need to project strength, status and an image that says this guy is in control, when they feel exceptionally vulnerable, they believe it is better not to say a thing and remain silent. Let the Snake presence do the talking. Nicolas Hoult has said, "Supposedly I'm impossible to talk to. But it's honestly not me being difficult. Sometimes you just don't have a lot to say."

The women of this combination never lose their girly innocent hearts; they often grow into typical Snake Superwomen who take on the world without ever thinking twice, but at the same time, what inspires them continues to inspire them with the same level of potency. Kim Basinger has said, "I still go and sit in the movies like everyone else and look up there and go 'God! Movie stars! Wow!' And I'm in this business. I walk out there just fascinated and I always want to stay like that." Snake women are not one of the girls, they are leaders of the girls; that is why they are so comfortable talking about the girls and their place in that arena. On some level they know that, but they are far too smart to openly state it for fear of being deposed, especially if there are Dragon, or Ox ladies in their midst. In any case, it does not lessen their sisterly support. Taylor Swift has said, "There's a special place in Hell for women who don't help other women."

Despite their own struggles with their own esteem, they are able to use their heightened level of self-awareness to turn their insecurities into strengths and push themselves to grow, to be bigger, bolder and ultimately, better than they were before. Taylor Swift has also said, "It was always my theory that if you want to play in the same ballgame as the boys, you've got to work as hard as them."

The defining characteristic of this Snake is its self-understanding, lessons are learned from mistakes and the experience is mined for every single gem. Because of this, they understand the various levels that life can be lived in; their system receives more information than most to collate which means they are much more aware of the consequences of their actions, how they are perceived or will be perceived if they take a specific action. But because they are so self-aware, they learn to manage what they cannot resolve. John Malkovich has said, "I wouldn't describe myself as lacking in confidence, but I would just say that the ghosts you chase you never catch... If you're too smart it can limit you because you spend so much time thinking that you don't do anything." Eventually, they learn the best ways to get out of their head and out of their own way.

Ultimately, this is a combination that is in harmony with its various energetic levels of functioning. The child absorbs information sensually, the teacher collects and organizes it mentally and the unified whole communicates it back to source. Of all the Snakes, this could be the most visceral. Dougray Scott has said, "I don't like acting things; I like feeling things." They let their senses guide them initially and they learn time and time again that their intuition knows best. Kim Basinger has said, "I feel there are two people inside me – me and my intuition. If I go against her, she'll screw me every time, and if I follow her, we get along quite nicely." Occasionally, that Snake ego voice chirps in pretending to be guidance and wrecks a little havoc. Taylor Swift has said, "In this business you have to develop a thick skin, but I'm always going to feel everything. It's my nature." Yes it is and that is why they become leaders in the social and professional realms, whether that be overtly or covertly, they will direct their own pathways and those of the people they care about most towards their highest evolutionary peaks.

Soul Mate:	Monkey-Capricorn
Challenger:	Boar-Gemini
Siblings:	Snake-Aries, Snake-Leo
Best Friends:	Ox-Aries, Ox-Leo, Ox-Sagittarius, Rooster-Aries, Rooster-Leo, Rooster-Sagittarius

John Malkovich
Kim Basinger
Ben Stiller
Dougray Scott
Jeffrey Wright
Nicholas Hoult
Taylor Swift
Ryan Murphy
Dick Clark
Bill Pullman
Christopher Plummer
Ted Raimi
Berry Gordy
John Osborne
Beau Bridges
Bess Armstrong
Jim Davidson

Andrew Stanton
Kimi Katkar
Emmanuelle Chriqui
Caleb Landry Jones
Ashley Benson
Jordin Sparks

SNAKE – CAPRICORN

Chinese Name: SHÉ
Rank: 6th
Hours Ruled: 9am – 11am
Direction: South-Southeast
Season: Spring
Month: May
Western Zodiac Equivalent of Snake: Taurus
Taurus Western Element: Earth
Eastern Zodiac Equivalent of Capricorn: Ox
Capricorn Western Element: Earth
Numerology: 70 = 7

I am the Greatest!
– Muhammad Ali

When the Snake's sensual earth meets the Capricorn's tough terrain, fertility meets firmness. These two earth signs have much in common; they are both ambitious, secretive and they know how to leverage power. Even the laziest Snake-Capricorn believes in itself and when push comes to shove, this creature quietly makes up for lost time and goes a little overboard with research, preparation and practice to make sure its future success is not probable, but definite. And it looks effortless. As Bollywood Superstar Salman Khan has said, "Have you seen a duck gliding smoothly on water? Does it ever look like it is paddling furiously underneath the surface?"

There is a noted dark side to this Snake, its venom is potentially the most poisonous. If wronged, they will want to seek revenge, even when they know better, it is hard for them to forgive or be the bigger person, there is a part of them that just wants to win, even if the terms of the game have been defined by the competition. This overwhelming need to be the number one is both their gift and their curse because when channeled correctly, it makes legends out of them, but if activated reactively, they may regret their actions later. Muhammad Ali said, "Champions aren't made in gyms. Champions are made from something they have deep inside them – a desire, a dream, a vision. They have to have the skill, and the will. But the will must be stronger than the skill."

The men of this combination tend to present as humble, sophisticated, patient and all things associated to the stereotype of the Snake man. Despite what they say, these men like to put themselves first and they like everyone else to put them first also; they like to get their way. That does not mean that they are being fake, they just like other people to realize that they are dealing with first-class goods and as long as they get that treatment, the humility will continue. Speaking about relationships, Bollywood Superstar Salman Khan has said, "I'm not possessive, I'm caring... Once you realize a person doesn't want that much care, you automatically back off." Although their quiet, intriguing nature coupled with their hyper-masculine ego is attractive to women, their inability to prioritize their women ultimately causes friction and they have to spend much time in behavioral analysis before they figure out what they are doing wrong. Even one of the most famously learned people in the world, Stephen Hawking has said, "Women. They are a complete mystery." It is usually in their forties that they begin to see the impact of what some may consider selfishness and a genuine transformation begins. Sit-com superstar/stuntman, musical theatre and musical movie star Michael Crawford has said, "I think one of the best words in the English language is compassion. I think it holds everything. It holds love, it holds care...and if everybody just did something. We all make a difference."

The women of this combination are the epitome of the stunning femme fatale, with the confidence and frisk to boot and they know how to make full use of it. January Jones has said, "I have that thing in my stomach where I just need to keep striving for things. In my mind, I want the fairy tale." Like father, like daughter is a term oft used, but not often in combined-astrological terms; the chances that one might bear a child in the same astrological combination as themselves is rare, but if anyone was going to manage it, it would be *The Greatest*; Laila Ali, daughter of Muhammad Ali is also born under this combination. And illustrating this indomitable Snake-Capricorn spirit just like her father, she has said, "Impossible is just a big word thrown around by small men who find it easier to live in the world they've been given than to explore the power they have to change it." These women are powerhouses, like all of the double earth combinations; they are able to function with a lower level of fear than most, including that of societal rejection; as a result, they are more likely to step into seriously controversial territory. Infamous Hollywood brothel Madame, Heidi Fleiss said, "Look, I had the party, did the party, threw the party, was the party. I'm partied out." These ladies are multi-faceted, sexy and uber-mysterious. Men want to know more, but these vixens know that less is infinitely more. January Jones has said, "Women should have lots of secrets. It's our right to have secrets."

When the stubborn Snake and obstinate Capricorn meet, their similarities are compounded; but sometimes this can come across as arrogance. Muhammad Ali has said, "At home I am a nice guy – but I don't want the world to know. Humble people, I've found, don't get very far."

Ultimately, like all Snakes, there is a powerful connection to the spiritual world and of their own worthiness. Perhaps that is why they're so self-assured; the world needs powerful teachers and leaders who know what they want and are prepared to take the reins. A. R. Rahman, who incidentally, did open a music school, has said, "I am like a boat without an oar. I let life take its own course." There are those Snakes who know that all they have to do is use their natural gifts and talents and the universe will guide them to where they are supposed to be. Despite their controversial nature, that of an athlete that wants to succeed at all costs, their ego abates in time and the universe makes them see what is really important and how to use natures laws for successful living, not just professional success. As Muhammed Ali has said, "Service to others is the rent you pay for your room here on earth."

Soul Mate: Monkey-Sagittarius
Challenger: Boar-Cancer
Siblings: Snake-Taurus, Snake-Virgo
Best Friends: Ox-Taurus, Ox-Virgo, Ox-Capricorn, Rooster-
                  Taurus, Rooster-Virgo, Rooster-Capricorn

Heidi Fleiss
January Jones
Salman Khan
Michael Crawford
A.R. Rahman
Muhammad Ali
Laila Ali
Stephen Hawking
Patrick Dempsey
Olivier Martinez
Vidya Balan
Liam Hemsworth
Howard Stern
Anthony Minghella
Lucy Punch
Jane Levy

Katey Sagal
Liam Aiken
James Remar
Tippi Hedren
Laila Ali
Vernee Watson-Johnson
Trudie Styler
Eddie Cahill
America Olivio
AJ Maclean

SNAKE – AQUARIUS

Chinese Name: SHÉ
Rank: 6th
Hours Ruled: 9am – 11am
Direction: South-Southeast
Season: Spring
Month: May
Western Zodiac Equivalent of Snake: Taurus
Taurus Western Element: Earth
Eastern Zodiac Equivalent of Aquarius: Tiger
Aquarius Western Element: Air
Numerology: 71 = 8

All my life I have known that I was born to Greatness.
– Oprah Winfrey

When the potency of the Snake's earth meets the lofty heights of
Aquarius's, they have one foot firmly planted in reality and the
other resting on a cloud. The image of the temperance tarot card
comes to mind where the hermaphrodite angel straddles the
physical and non-physical realms. When the Snake gets an
infusion of the air element, it creates a daring leader that is not
afraid to speak out against the masses. Although Snake-
Aquarians live in the real world, they have unreal expectations
that they manage to manifest against all odds. In Eastern
astrology, the Snake is revered for its wisdom, knowledge and
foresight; in Western astrology, Aquarius is also known for its
wisdom and inquisitive nature so when these two signs come
together, it creates the sort of person who has vision enough to
see the end goal along with the tenacity to get there step by step.
Oprah Winfrey has said, "Follow your instincts. That's where
true wisdom manifests itself."

As the teacher, mentor and spiritual counselor of the cycle,

Snake signs attached to many different Western signs will advocate the importance of education and literacy, but none with more vehemence than the Snake-Aquarius. To them, books are living, breathing companions that set them free to imagine a world outside of their current circumstances. Virginia Woolf said, "Lock up your libraries if you like; but there is no gate, no lock, no bolt that you can set upon the freedom of my mind." Self-education never stops either and the Snake-Aquarius is nothing if not an eternal student. Abraham Lincoln said, "The things I want to know are in books; my best friend is the man who'll get me a book I ain't read."

The men of this combination tend to be quiet, but with a presence larger than themselves which makes others feel safe. They can be sometimes be perceived as cocky, but this is usually done in fun. As a mentor-teacher type, they are also highly intelligent and see through prevalent false premises to bring knock some common sense back into the world. Comedian Chris Rock has said, "When I hear people talk about juggling, or the sacrifices they make for their children, I look at them like they're crazy, because 'sacrifice' infers that there was something better to do than being with your children." In the 1830s when Abraham Lincoln was but in his 20s, he openly voiced his opinions against slavery even though he was in a minority. He said, "Whenever I hear anyone arguing for slavery, I feel a strong impulse to see it tried on him personally." Generally speaking, because of their educated mind and empathic nature, they know that they know nothing and there will always be more to learn. Charles Darwin stated, "Ignorance more frequently begets confidence than does knowledge: it is those who know little, and not those who know much, who so positively assert that this or that problem will never be solved by science."

The women of this combination tend to be hyper-professional, perfectionists and may channel all of their energy into their work. Even those without a high level of education tend to rise to senior positions because they know how to deconstruct the journey and what to do to get to their goal. Oprah Winfrey said, "Think like a queen. A queen is not afraid to fail. Failure is another stepping-stone to greatness." Knowing their value in a professional context, it is common for them to focus on this arena because it gives them a sense of control, but not necessarily the happiness they are seeking.

With their level of self-awareness, they usually know what is happening, but there is sometimes a delay in jumping the track from *success* to authentic living that they are actually striving for. When they finally make that jump, there is no looking back. Virginia Woolf said, "The man who is aware of himself is henceforward independent; and he is never bored, and life is only too short, and he is steeped through and through with a profound yet temperate happiness."

Despite their lightness, levity and loveliness, the Snake-Aquarius has its intense moments and struggles in silence. They also have that need to project an image, for them in particular, they want to be an inspiring personality that is fun and successful. But, they can get very low, very serious and beat up on themselves. When they feel an insecurity attack coming on, they remove themselves from public view quickly. It is not easy handling the power that they yield and when things go wrong, they cannot help but take them personally. Abraham Lincoln has said, "Nearly all men can stand adversity, but if you want to test a man's character, give him power."

Ultimately, the Snake-Aquarius knows that life is led moment to moment and the only moment is now. Oprah Winfrey said, "Doing the best at this moment puts you in the best place for the next moment." Learning to be as present as possible, they open their eyes to nature and all its little workings. There is something

akin to a spiritual scientist about this combination. It's interesting that when Sidney Sheldon was asked who his personal
hero was, he said, "Abraham Lincoln because he was a man filled
with great compassion who believed that all men are created free
and equal, and was not afraid to stand on that platform. The way
Lincoln lived his life has served me well in mine." Inspired by a
fellow Snake-Aquarius. It's not surprising really, they generally
are pretty inspiring and their journeys are not particularly easy.
But what they know is that there are spiritual laws that govern
the basics of life. If one attunes to them, they can be more prolific
than they ever dreamed, make more money than they know
exists and have more influence than they are capable of understanding. Once they get a handle on the invisible laws of life,
their success is astounding. Franklin Roosevelt said, "Physical
strength can never permanently withstand the impact of
spiritual force."

Soul Mate:	Monkey-Scorpio
Challenger:	Boar-Leo
Siblings:	Snake-Gemini, Snake-Libra
Best Friends:	Ox-Gemini, Ox-Libra, Ox-Aquarius, Rooster-Gemini, Rooster-Libra, Rooster-Aquarius

Elizabeth Olsen
Jeremy Sumpter
Dr. Dre
Chris Rock
Maura Tierney
Brandon Lee
Princess Stephanie
Sherilyn Fenn
Oprah Winfrey
Rick Warren
Peter Tork

Carole King
Dick Cheney
Edwin "Buzz" Aldrin
John Forsythe
Sidney Sheldon
Zsa Zsa Gabor
Ernest Borgnine
James Joyce
Franklin D. Roosevelt
Virginia Woolf
Abraham Lincoln
Charles Darwin
Nicolas Copernicus

SNAKE – PISCES

Chinese Name: SHÉ
Rank: 6th
Hours Ruled: 9am – 11am
Direction: South-Southeast
Season: Spring
Month: May
Western Zodiac Equivalent of Snake: Taurus
Taurus Western Element: Earth
Eastern Zodiac Equivalent of Pisces: Rabbit
Pisces Western Element: Water
Numerology: 72 = 9

I do what I feel is right. I am not scared to walk on the new path and take risk.
– Aamir Khan

When the Snake's sensual earth meets the potency of Pisces's water, it creates a wonderfully potent mix of power and creativity, intelligence and intuition, the need to dominate yet knowing when to relent. The Snake Mentor energy is very present in this double yin combination and they may feel that their biggest contribution is that of inspiring the next generation to positively update their belief systems. Psychologically aware, blessed with an acute mind for business and academia, there is little they cannot turn their hands to and become successful at. That being said, they never quite feel like they are part of any group because the way they think seems to require them to stay on the fringes of society. Paul Haggis said, "Artists need to be outsiders in order to really view what's going on."

Their greatest gift and Achilles heel is that they have a great ability to influence people. Sometimes for selfish motives (which ultimately backfires) and sometimes for the benefit of the whole, but in any case, this is their rare power. Bollywood actor, director, producer, chat show host and philanthropist Aamir Khan said, "I am a very idealistic kind of person. I believe that even people who are part of the problem can become part of the solution." Aamir Khan also created Chat Show *Satyamev Jayate* in India which has been likened to *The Oprah show.* Oprah Winfrey is a Snake-Aquarius, the combination before this one; that spiritual and altruistic mentor energy persists here. They sees all people as children who are still learning and developing better ways of living. They see everyone as equal and do not talk down to anyone. Even teen screenwriter and producer Kevin Williamson said, "I don't look at teens as teens. I think maybe that's the whole trick to what I do, is that they're just smart, sophisticated adult characters. And they happen to be 15."

The men of this combination tend to be fairer than normal, light-colored hair or skin with sophisticated, intelligent looks. One can sense that these are well read individuals. Quiet and subtle, they can say what they want to without opening their mouths. James Van Der Beek said, "It's a free country and I can keep my mouth shut whenever I want." They innately know to *not speak unless they can improve the silence.* But when this Snake mentor does speak, its words have the capacity to cause mini revelations. The spiritual dimension to the men is highly pronounced. They seem to naturally understand the laws of the universe and are not afraid to listen to that deeper inner part of themselves. Aamir Khan has said, "For me, it has always been whether my gut feeling, my instinct or my heart is allowing me to agree to do a film or not." An interesting side note is when Kevin Williamson was casting the lead role for Dawson's Creek (which was based on himself) he saw hundreds of young men but settled on James Van Der Beek, who shared his astrological combination of Snake-Pisces. And what was the character? He is an overachieving, precocious young man, over developed psychologically and underdeveloped emotionally. That pretty much sums up the Snake-Pisces man at least until they reach their 40s. Speaking about his getting married very young, William Petersen said, "I was only 21, and there were many things I didn't know. I was trying to be a man and I wasn't ready for it."

The women of this combination are sophisticated, cultured and feminine looking with forceful personalities that they feel they must keep locked in a cage. When they let them out, their special beauty is both overpowering and overwhelming. They can be soft yet strong, flirty and in charge, they like to play the game on their terms without ever losing their feminine charm. Kristin Davis has said, "At one point, they offered me this part to play a drug-dealing, gun-selling butch lady...she had like a crew cut and stuff. I was like, 'Is this a joke?' And they said, 'No, we think it would be great because everyone would be like, "Oh, look at what we've done to Charlotte."' I was like, 'Well I can't do that!'" They are also spiritually inclined and are especially connected to crystals, stones and colors. They tend to change their spiritual beliefs in their early years as they are endowed with a strong sense of who they are. It is this connection with their true source that leads them to great success later on. Or even in those early years. Two times, world champion gymnast, Shannon Miller said, "When I go in to compete, whether it's gymnastics or anything else, I do my own thing. I compete with myself."

Ultimately, the Snake-Pisces is a gentle seeming person with the presence of a rock. Their softness is part of the Snake package, as is the big ego, but without it, they would not be as prolific. These are perhaps the mushiest of Snakes and love to be loved and touched and held, although most people need some sort of interpretation manual to understand what their actions mean, they need to be shown categorically how much they are loved. Their amazing skillset is one of broad vision and any action that they take considers the larger impact. Gymnast Shannon Miller said, "I think it's really important to look at the big picture instead of just one competition." Regardless of the occupation they choose or where they find themselves stationed in life, they will find a way to inspire other people to find the beauty in who they are and share it. Because it is in bringing light to others that their true joy is located. Aamir Khan said, "I also believe that an entertainer has a much larger role to play in society, one that perhaps only he/she can play best and that is to bring grace to society, to help build the moral fiber of society, to instill higher values in young children."

Soul Mate:	Monkey-Libra
Challenger:	Boar-Virgo
Siblings:	Snake-Cancer, Snake-Scorpio
Best Friends:	Ox-Cancer, Ox-Scorpio, Ox-Pisces, Rooster-Cancer, Rooster-Scorpio, Rooster-Pisces

Anton Yelchin
Lily Collins
Paul W.S. Anderson
William Petersen
Sterling Knight
Scout Taylor-Compton
James Van Der Beek
Kristin Davis
Jake Lloyd
Brittany Ashton Holmes
Ron Eldard
Ron Jeremy
James Hong
Daniella Monet
Aamir Khan (Actor)
Jorma Taccone

Bree Turner
Chris Martin
Isabelle Huppert
James Wan
Paul Haggis
Corbin Bleu
Kevin Williamson
Shannon Miller
Michael Bolton
Anthony Burgess
Andres Segovia
Lord Baden-Powell

THE HORSE

THE HORSE

I am the humanitarian rebel, the brave savior, the noble fighter. I am swift and agile and need space to roam. I crave freedom; therefore obtain it for others. With my external yang spirit and internal yin life, I present to the world an eternal contradiction, even though I maintain nature's perfect balance. I am 100 percent instinct! That is why I present such an inconsistent front. I require sole exploration. I want to know who I am without prior definition. I want to live life with blood coursing through my veins a million miles per hour because it suits me, because I know I'm the only one who can handle it, because anything other than that is death. That is why I have this raw instinct, invisible antennae and reflexes: I was born with speed so I can live on the edge because that is where I belong! Pushing my own boundaries and that of society. If that pushes your buttons at the same time, deal with it! My job is to equalize the status quo, not make you comfortable.

I am the Horse.

Fast, furious and cool, with reflexes as sharp as they come. You rely on your instinct and nuances to feed you all the information you need to get by. Intellectual, stubborn and egotistical, you like to have everyone's attention without seeming like an attention seeker. You are also one of the hardest workers out there. With a great sense of humor and comic timing, you keep everyone entertained with your stories and views. Bursting with energy and life, you are always in demand, maybe that's because you're never around for long. There's always another sunset for you to chase.

Career-wise, the Horse is a good team player and is happy to do whatever is expected. Also, if there is no leader, or a weak leader, the Horse will step up and take charge doing a pretty good job as they are not dictatorial and know how to appeal to the team's sense of fun. However, the downside is that they are not particularly psychological and may not provide emotional space for people to be people. They are also value driven so may not want to manage those whose views differ. In political environments, they play the rebel of course and seek to highlight issues for the little people. Their instinct and heightened personal sensitivity seems to be perfect for drama and the world of acting. They also excel in sports, engineering and adventurous, groundbreaking environments. Horse people often have the highest IQs and the lowest EQs. But they are fearless and want to leave the world a better place for them having been in it. They also enjoy working in science, technology, business management, law, travel and communications.

Compatibilities

Soul Mate:	Sheep
Challenger:	Rat
Best Friends:	Tiger & Dog
Good Relations:	Dragon & Boar

HORSE – ARIES

Chinese Name: MA
Rank: 7th
Hours Ruled: 11am – 1pm
Direction: Directly South
Season: Summer
Month: June
Western Zodiac Equivalent of Horse: Gemini
Gemini Western Element: Air
Eastern Zodiac Equivalent of Aries: Dragon
Aries Western Element: Fire
Numerology: 73 = 1

I'm crazy, but I'm not stupid
– Jackie Chan

When the Horse's hurricane joins with Aries's constant blaze, it creates a personality that defies definition for the contradictory Horse nature becomes even more contradictory. Shy, retiring and intelligent one second, wild, soulful and plain right foolish the next, this personality is difficult to grasp. The reason for this is quite straightforward really and it is the key to understanding a Horse native. They are almost purely instinctual. They receive their information through their horse antennae and process it in their gut, taking action based on that. This is also why they are so significantly affected by their environments making them go from shy to wild in a matter of minutes.

They are also hugely affected by the energies of different people. They have a nose for the truth and can psychically pick up on other people's intentions. The Horse Aries has an amazing ability to deconstruct what is happening in any situation despite not knowing the people involved or the details. With that superpowerful antennae feeding them facts missed by most people, they are like master psychologists although their mental process is not particularly psychological. This makes them seem a little odd or unconventional by social standards. This is why there are so many mature child artistes of this combination, as were, Kristen Stewart, Emma Watson and Alex Pettyfer.

This unconventionality leads to the biggest contradiction of this personality; they have a huge desire to fit in, to be accepted by the core group of any social setting whilst sternly refusing to conform or sacrifice what they consider to be their moral values. Kristen Stewart has said, "You get criticized for being honest and criticized for being nervous. So that's kind of annoying. I do a whole day of press and then I get calls from publicity people that are like, 'you might want to be a little bit more bubbly'. And I'm like, 'no'."

It is surprising how many Horse-Aries people have the same story of their childhood development; they tend to be lonely independent children who spend much of their time lost in daydreams and fantasies. They tend to be denied the open affection they needed because their behavior or temperament suggested that they did not need or crave it. But like all children, they do. So they create fantasies where their emotional needs can be met. People of this combination make excellent actors. With their instinct and experienced imagination combined with their compassionate nature and empathy, they make truly engaging performers. They also like painting. James Franco said, "I needed an outlet in high school and came across painting. I've actually been painting longer than I've been acting." Similarly, Emma Watson has said, "I love painting and have a need to do it."

The men tend to be typically attractive with sharp facial features. One second they are tough and butch and all things male, the next, they are crying to their barrage of platonic female friends about the current drama. Then they'll be hanging with the boys again talking football, drinking beer and picking up girls. But in the morning they will go into their creative occupation possibly with a political slant and make use of their artistic skills along with their higher than average IQ. Alex Pettyfer has said, "You hear a lot of people say they want to make art in this industry, but so few people actually fucking do it. I was disillusioned by [Hollywood] at the time, but now I've come to accept that's just the way things are: it's called show business, not show art." James Franco has three degrees and even taught drama at New York University.

The women of this combination tend to be naturally pretty and like a lot of Horse women, do not wear a lot of make-up. They tend to feel easily ostracized so keep away from groups preferring to get to know people on a one to one basis. They are not particularly "girly" they verge towards neutral until they are hit by a certain stimulus which draws them to another new guise altogether. Kristen Stewart has said, "It took me a long time to realize that I was a girl as a teenager. At that point I never really believed it. I looked like a boy for a long time. Now, finally, I feel like a woman." They are however highly sensitive and can be easily affected by harsh words or situations. They are individuals who understand their own complexity even if nobody else does. They eventually leave their self-criticism behind and find internal validation.

Choosing the truth above all else, they prefer to live lives of honesty and will always take the option that feels "right" to them and their sensitively tuned system. This is precisely why they are so often misunderstood. Often times they are a source of aggravation to other people because it can seem like their minds are impenetrable to certain advice or information. Often, they have grown way beyond the person giving the advice and have a much broader perspective, even as children, so they know that the advice or information is coming from a limited source, so although they listen, they will do what they think best. And time often proves them right.

When they achieve personal authenticity, like everyone, they thrive and are happy to serve in any way they can. Jackie Chan has said, "I never wanted to be the next Bruce Lee. I just wanted to be the first Jackie Chan." They have a strong sense of their own individuality, more so than of any firmly fixed or defined identity; they need space and non-judgment because they will make what seems like strange decisions, but go with it. Steve McQueen describes the Horse-Aries well when he said, "When I believe in something, I fight like hell for it." They can be formidable opponents even if their face does not show the aggression they are capable of. They are not selfish people, although many (of the men mostly) have problems managing their ego and if other people want to make them the center of their lives, they are all too happy to let them. But with their beauty, intelligence and spiritual connection, who can resist these sparkling unicorns?

Soul Mate:	Sheep-Virgo
Challenger:	Rat-Libra
Siblings:	Horse-Leo, Horse-Sagittarius
Best Friends:	Tiger-Aries, Tiger-Leo, Tiger-Sagittarius, Dog-Aries, Dog-Leo, Dog-Sagittarius

Kristen Stewart
Emma Watson
James Franco
Robin Wright
Alex Pettyfer
Jackie Chan
Britt Robertson
Dennis Quaid
Matthew Goode
Steve McQueen

Ellen Barkin

Lorraine Nicholson

Keisha Castle-Hughes

Cynthia Nixon

Peter MacNicol

Michael York

Scott Wilson

Daniel Mays

Rani Mukherjee

Cassie Scerbo

Richard O'Brien

Mike Newell

Mary-Margaret Humes

Lara Dutt

HORSE – TAURUS

Chinese Name: MA
Rank: 7th
Hours Ruled: 11am – 1pm
Direction: Directly South
Season: Summer
Month: June
Western Zodiac Equivalent of Horse: Gemini
Gemini Western Element: Air
Eastern Zodiac Equivalent of Taurus: Snake
Taurus Western Element: Earth
Numerology: 74 = 2

People who read the tabloids deserve to be lied to.
– Jerry Seinfeld

When the Horse's hurricane meets with Taurus's tough earth, the humanitarian rebel is further nurtured by the bull's confidence creating a super-ballsy stallion with a really powerful neigh! This combination creates political provocateurs, people like Michael Moore, Jerry Seinfeld and Stephen Baldwin. They have strong opinions, even when they have been raised in families with different views, they will have their slant and they will be more than ready to share their views. The Horse by itself is the rebel, but with the Taurean bull fuelling it, this ballsy creature may actually go out to look for causes to fight. The Horse-Taurus likes everyone to agree with their point of view and they can be unrelenting in their verbal battering. Most people end up letting them believe that they are on the same page, just so they get left alone. But it irks the Horse-Taurus when people just follow the mainstream opinion without considering the alternatives. How can people be so blind? Simple? Base? Jodi Picoult has said, "People are always afraid of the unknown – and banding together against the 'thing that is different from us' is a time-honored tradition for rallying the masses."

There is a side to this personality that thrills putting itself on the line, time and time again. Despite the potential backlash, many Horse-Taurean celebrities were openly critical of George W. Bush. Discussing "Nipple-gate" when a wardrobe malfunction led to a bared breast during a Super Bowl halftime show, Janet Jackson said, "I truly feel in my heart that the president wanted to take the focus off himself at that time and I was the perfect vehicle to do so at that moment." On winning an Oscar for documentary expose, "Dude, Where's My Country?" Michael Moore said, "We live in the time where we have fictitious election results that elects a fictitious president. We live in a time where we have a man sending us to war for fictitious reasons. Whether it's the fiction of duct tape or fiction of orange alerts we are against this war, Mr. Bush. Shame on you, Mr. Bush, shame on you." Even Barbara Streisand has said, "We have a president who stole the presidency through family ties, arrogance and intimidation, employing Republican operatives to exercise the tactics of voter fraud by disenfranchising thousands of blacks, elderly Jews and other minorities." Whatever they perceive as "unfairness" or "inequality" affects them hugely and they will be active in their stance to rectify the situation.

The men of this combination live from their gut; they utilize their intellectual abilities to analyze a situation quickly then respond instinctively, trusting purely in that inner guidance. Maybe that is why people like Jerry Seinfeld and Michael Moore are so successful in their fields, the former having the "Most Successful Sitcom" (source: nowthatsnifty) and the latter having the highest grossing documentary of all time for *Fahrenheit 9/11*. Michael Moore has said, "You know why I'm a multi-millionaire? 'Cause multi-millions like what I do. That's pretty good, isn't it? There's millions that believe in what I do." These men listen to their inner guidance whether they know it or not and end up inching towards the life they always wanted. They are open to ideas that serve their already established belief system and if something seriously challenges their previous ways, they might go with it, changing dramatically in ways that people are never prepared for. More often than not, they know who they are, where they are going and they stick to it. As Jerry Seinfeld said, "Sometimes the road less traveled is less traveled for a reason."

The women of this combination are extremely ballsy also. They refuse to be seen as anything less than equal in every environment and more often than not end up taking charge whether they have authority to or not. They also pride themselves on being grounded, authentic and real. Barbara Streisand has said, "You have got to discover you, what you do, and trust it." Similarly, Janet Jackson has said, "Self-expression is my goal; I want to be real with my feelings. Singing and dancing – and all the joy that goes with performing – come from my heart. If I can't feel it, I won't do it." Yes, they have feminist qualities, sometimes, in your face feminist qualities when they feel it is necessary, but mostly, they like to do it in an unobtrusive, subtle way because there is more dignity in it. (And all Horses must have a need to maintain their dignity at all times!) Just like the men, they feel indignities, unfairness and inequality powerfully in their gut that they too get involved in socio-political altruism. Jane Campion has said, "To deny women directors, as I suspect is happening in the States, is to deny the feminine vision."

The Horse sign is often difficult to pinpoint because they have a tendency to take 90-degree turns every now and then, giving them what people consider inconsistent personalities. Some may even say, hypocritical personalities. The reason for this is that they live by their gut, they let their instinct, emotions and current mental state dictate the immediate decisions being made, despite the hours, years and decades of intellectual study. Sometimes they may go completely against their years of study, purely on a gut feeling. And they may get criticized for doing that, but what some consider "foolish" can sometimes be "blind courage"! They do it because their intrinsic nature will not let them take any action that does not feel authentic, even if it is divisive, dogmatic or even dictatorial. These are powerful politically provocative people who use their creativity to open eyes and in doing so will necessarily court criticism but they can handle it. Jodi Picoult has said, "It's certainly my honor to be able to, hopefully, change the world a tiny bit, one mind at a time."

Soul Mate:	Sheep-Leo
Challenger:	Rat-Scorpio
Siblings:	Horse-Virgo, Horse-Capricorn
Best Friends:	Tiger-Taurus, Tiger-Virgo, Tiger-Capricorn, Dog-Taurus, Dog-Virgo, Dog-Capricorn

Margaret Rutherford
Mary Astor
Eddie Albert
Joan Sims
Barbra Streisand
Sandra Dee
John Shrapnel
Tammy Wynette
David Keith
Jerry Seinfeld
Michael Moore
Pia Zadora
Jane Campion
Jeffrey Dean Morgan
Stephen Baldwin

Janet Jackson
Jodi Picoult
Malin Akerman
Jim Sturgess
Jason Biggs
Dev Patel

HORSE – GEMINI

Chinese Name: MA
Rank: 7th
Hours Ruled: 11am – 1pm
Direction: Directly South
Season: Summer
Month: June
Western Zodiac Equivalent of Horse: Gemini
Gemini Western Element: Air
Eastern Zodiac Equivalent of Gemini: Horse
Gemini Western Element: Earth
Numerology: 75 = 3

I tried being reasonable, I didn't like it.
– Clint Eastwood

When the Horse's hurricane meets with Gemini's gentle gale, they merge into one powerful force moving swiftly together, complimenting each other perfectly: this is because they are of the same essence, as the Horse sign equates to the Gemini and vice versa, so this is the double Gemini or pure Horse combination. The Horse is the political rebel and the Gemini is the detached social butterfly; both signs are highly intelligent and academic. This combination is known for its refusal to budge from its ideological stance and unrelenting fight for equality. As Clint Eastwood has said, "Sometimes if you want to see a change for the better, you have to take things into your own hands." With an almost identical sentiment, Kathleen Turner said, "It never occurred to me that I couldn't change things that needed changing or couldn't have what I wanted if I worked hard enough and was good enough."

As the pure Horse sign, the Horse traits will be amplified so their toleration of pretentious behavior will be exceptionally low, as Kathleen Turner has said, "The older I get, the less I suffer fools gladly." This combination has never been very good at dealing with what they consider to be *insincerity* or *shameless opportunism*. Speaking about her career and Hollywood, Helena Bonham Carter said, "With the number of people I ignore, I'm lucky I work at all in this town." Valuing honesty, integrity and compassion above all else, these people strive for dignity in everything they do. They do not bend to public opinion or general consensus as they prefer to make up their own minds looking at the facts and listening to their instinctual kick.

This is the most typically "Horse" of all combinations, so caging this noble steed in a small space is never wise, they need to feel very free, they require constant creative and emotional expression and must feel like they are contributing to the expansion of some sort of humanitarian aid. In fact, this is one of the most activist combinations of all, with people like Josephine Baker and Harvey Milk belonging to this club, one can understand why. A common "Horse" tendency is to gather information, facts and figures, pass it over to their subconscious mind, then let their instinct guide them into action. Many Horse-Geminis come across as more intelligent than they are (even though this is a highly intelligent combination), simply because of the actions they take as directed by their exceptionally loud internal guidance system. They never lose touch with their soul's essence and in many ways live out their inner child's fantasies for the rest of their adult life. Helena Bonham Carter has said, "It's easy for me to go back to being a kid. You know how kids can be like savages before they get civilized?"

The men of this combination tend to be naturally quite secure in their masculinity, so much so, that it is often common for the straight males to have really close friendships with gay men because they do not judge based on superficialities. They are seen as highly attractive, many are conventionally attractive, but it is their bright boyish spirit that seeps through charming everyone. They can often intimidate others by accident because of their super-intellect and knowledge. Although they can be self-deprecating, they are aware of their own skills and their value. As Clint Eastwood has said, "Respect your efforts, respect yourself. Self-respect leads to self-discipline. When you have both firmly under your belt, that's real power." Sometimes they are pulled towards occupations or callings that are quite unusual but fight with themselves as they may, they will ultimately give in to their inner urges and follow that inner guidance. Maybe that is why Paul McCartney said, "I used to think anyone doing anything weird was weird. Now I know that it is the people that call others weird that are weird."

The women of this combination tend to fit the Horse stereotype; this being the double Horse sign, it is only to be expected. They tend to be tomboys with a natural elegance who do not need to wear a lot of make up as their skin and coloring is quite naturally attractive. They do not care so much about feminizing up for a man; in fact, many may even view it as demeaning or insulting to do so. Usually their vehement feminism phase comes to an end at some point and they are able to strike a healthy balance. Helena Bonham Carter said, "It took me ages to grow into being a woman, into being happy with it." They also learn that feminine power is not in the feminine form, it comes from within, from the spirit and they know how to unleash it upon the world. Kathleen Turner said, "Being a sex symbol has to do with an attitude, not looks. Most men think it's looks, most women know otherwise."

Ultimately, this combination is instinctual, intelligent, intellectual and for the most part, non-judgmental. When these traits merge with the Horses conscience, the activist within them emerges powerfully. They may not like political movements, but are also aware that in order to change things they need to take action.

Kathleen Turner said, "I'm not very active politically. The causes I work on offer immediate, practical, accessible help, and politics has never meant that to me." What they really want is fairness and equality for all and this is what they work towards with everything that they do. Clint Eastwood said, "I mean, I've always been a libertarian. Leave everybody alone. Let everybody else do what they want. Just stay out of everybody else's hair." They are logical, persuasive and like most Horses are prepared to put themselves on the line. That is what makes them so powerful.

Soul Mate: Sheep-Cancer
Challenger: Rat-Sagittarius
Siblings: Horse-Libra, Horse-Aquarius
Best Friends: Tiger-Gemini, Tiger-Libra, Tiger-Aquarius,
                  Dog-Gemini, Dog-Libra, Dog-Aquarius

Josephine Baker
Clint Eastwood
Paul McCartney
Helena Bonham Carter
Kathleen Turner
Harvey Milk
Ben Johnson
Barbara Parkins
Roger Ebert
Brian Wilson
Muammar Gadaffi
Gena Rowlands
Edward Woodward
Sunil Dutt
Dennis Haysbert
James Belushi
Julianna Margulies

Jason Patric
Lisa Edelstein
Eric Cantona
Heston Blumenthal
Zoe Saldana
Shane West
Joshua Jackson
Dominic Cooper
Bill Hader
Daniel Brühl
James Corden
Katie Price
Adam Rickitt
Frank Lampard
Brian Dowling
Aaron Johnson
Chris Colfer

HORSE – CANCER

Chinese Name: MA
Rank: 7th
Hours Ruled: 11am – 1pm
Direction: Directly South
Season: Summer
Month: June
Western Zodiac Equivalent of Horse: Gemini
Gemini Western Element: Air
Eastern Zodiac Equivalent of Cancer: Sheep
Cancer Western Element: Water
Numerology: 76 = 4

Any man or institution that tries to rob me of my dignity will lose.
– Nelson Mandella

When the Horse's hurricane meets the sensual waters of the Cancerian crab, the noble steed's need for adventure struggles against the crab's constant need for security. Rebelliousness meets compassionate calm and edgy raw passion meets sophisticated artistry. These are two very different signs that merge to create an interesting and, like most horses, contradictory characters. The defining difference here though, is that this Horse is aware that it needs to monitor its own functioning in order to grow. Well, to be more accurate, they learn this while on their journey. In their early days, they are known to have taken controversial actions and it is through seeing the consequences of their actions that they adjust their behavior. The way Ingmar Bergman puts it is, "My basic view of things is – not to have any basic view of things. From having been exceedingly dogmatic, my views on life have gradually dissolved."

Both the Horse and the Cancerian are sensitive to their

surroundings but they have different needs; the cancer needs to know its world, where everything is, that creature comforts are readily available and that they can accommodate their friends and family if need be, whereas the Horse needs acres of space, physically and mentally. Ideally, this personality needs a house small enough that they could manage solo if necessary, but with a large expanse of land. City living will be fun for them for about three months to a year, then they will wonder what the fuss is about and find a sanctuary in the country or at minimum, the suburbs. Superstar Harrison Ford has said, "My land gives me an opportunity to be close to nature, and I find spiritual solace in nature, contemplating our species in the context of the natural world." Similarly, Actor Matthew Fox has said, "I enjoy a four-seasonal climate and wide-open spaces, so being on an island 2,500 miles into the South Pacific made me feel a little claustrophobic." All Horses need space! If you have Horses in your life, it is wise to tattoo that one into your memory banks.

Speaking about Harrison Ford and Matthew Fox, it is interesting to note just how many similarities that these two Horse-Cancer gentlemen have: they both own homes surrounded by a lot of space, both love cars and both fly planes. In fact, they both live in the mountainous US state of Wyoming, the tenth most extensive yet least populated state: heaven for the Horse-Cancer!

Beyond the superficial way that these creatures choose to live their lives, they are also deep thinkers with those well-developed humanitarian muscles, just as one would expect from a Horse of course. Horse signs are blessed with invisible antennae through which they receive their universal messages and it is this that makes them hyper-instinctive. Add that to the fact that the crab uses feelers to navigate its world, this combination gets an explosion of emotion when they perceive injustices. Perhaps that is why Nelson Mandela said, "I should tie myself to no particular system of society other than of socialism."

The men of this combination tend not to consider their own attractiveness because in their minds, they are such nerds. Their masculine spice is in their attitude more than their looks, although when you consider that Harrison Ford, Matthew Fox and Josh Hartnett belong to this clan, it is quite obvious that they are blessed with looks as well as brains. Despite the gift of handsomeness, they live their lives without really benefitting from it because, unfortunately, they really are geeks with a somewhat cranky disposition. Harrison Ford has said, "I think I did have a reputation for being grumpy. I don't think I'm grumpy. I have opinions. I have an independent vision. I am a purposeful person." J.J. Abrams has said, "When I was a kid, it was a huge insult to be a geek. Now it's a point of pride in a weird way." Incidentally, J.J. Abrams cast fellow Horse-Cancer Matthew Fox as the lead character in his break out show Lost.

The women of this combination, like most Horse women tend to be tomboyish, tough and feisty. Nicole Sherzinger has said, "I've never seen myself as sexy. I see myself as a goofball." That being said, these women are always sexy and always goofballs. They have that silly childish sense of humor that stems from having an extended relationship with their inner child and also their intellectual sensibilities. Yes, they are academics too, they just have minds for it. Michelle Rodrigues has said, "Basically I was a rebel growing up. I got kicked out of six schools. But I don't think that it makes you less of an intellect. You know, if you ever crave knowledge, there's always a library." And why should the Horse-Cancer lady be anything less than she can be? Nicole Sherzinger has also said, "If believing in yourself and going after what you want in life and realizing your worth is ruthless and selfish, then I'm definitely ruthless and selfish." Often, they can appear icy and cold, but what they really want is for someone to melt them down. As Michelle Rodriguez has said, "I do have a delicate side."

Ultimately, Horse-Cancers do not relax easily unless they can dictate the terms and the environment. They just need to be left alone and eventually, they will ease themselves into the situation, whatever it is. They have to be judged by their actions more than their surface personality, because often they are not prepared to play nice just for the sake of it. Authenticity is the most important thing to them, not niceness and they will strive to be whom and what they are at every point. As Nelson Mandela has said, "There is no passion to be found playing small – in settling for a life that is less than the one you are capable of living."

Soul Mate:	Sheep-Gemini
Challenger:	Rat-Capricorn
Siblings:	Horse-Scorpio, Horse-Pisces
Best Friends:	Tiger-Cancer, Tiger-Scorpio, Tiger-Pisces, Dog-Cancer, Dog-Scorpio, Dog-Pisces

Nelson Mandela

Harrison Ford

Ingmar Bergman

J.J. Abrams

Matthew Fox

John Cusack

Nicole Scherzinger

Mary Stuart Masterson

Michelle Rodriguez

Topher Grace

Mike Tyson

Josh Hartnett

Freddie Prinze

Tamera Mowry

Tia Mowry

Neil Tennant

Marton Csokas

Greg Grunberg
Gil Birmingham
Don Stark
Alice Krige
Wolfgang Becker
Richard Roundtree
Mick Fleetwood
Roger McGuinn
Sally Ann Howes
Robert Evans
Polly Bergen

HORSE – LEO

Chinese Name: MA
Rank: 7th
Hours Ruled: 11am – 1pm
Direction: Directly South
Season: Summer
Month: June
Western Zodiac Equivalent of Horse: Gemini
Gemini Western Element: Air
Eastern Zodiac Equivalent of Leo: Monkey
Leo Western Element: Fire
Numerology: 77 = 5

Mystery creates wonder and wonder is the basis of mans desire to understand.
– Neil Armstrong

When the Horse's hurricane meets the Leonine fire power, smart ideas are effectively put into action quickly and easily converted into magic. This is one of those combinations where one is left astounded at what they achieve and cannot entirely understand how. How did Neil Armstrong become the first man on the moon? How did Halle Berry become the first black actress to win the Oscar for best Actress, how does James Cameron continuously break records with how much he spends on making his movies, but also with his profits? James Cameron said, "Curiosity – it's the most powerful thing you own. Imagination is a force that can actually manifest a reality." The lion has the confidence to take the Horse's instinctive ideas and apply the collaborative intellect to come up with something that perfectly fits the bill.

Give them a task and they will just know how to approach it so that it gets done to the highest standard and will please pretty much everyone, and "get it RIGHT." This is not a common trait.

It is very rare. James Cameron has said, "People call me a perfectionist, but I'm not. I'm a *rightist*. I do something until it's *right*, and then I move on to the next thing." Similarly, but speaking about acting roles, Jennifer Lawrence has said, "I worry about them – if someone else gets the part, I'm afraid they won't do it *right*; they'll make the character a victim or they'll make her a villain or they'll just get it wrong somehow." One can argue with their methods, but not with their results.

Horse-Leos know when to avoid conflict and when to stand up for themselves but because they are often victims of jealousy, they begin to lose their patience with the appropriate expected decorum and just do what will get them to their results quickly without catering to the emotional needs of those around them. Of course, this gives them a reputation for being difficult themselves. Speaking in an interview, Jennifer Lawrence said, "I could see my publicist in the background, mouthing things to say. They want you to be likable all the time, and I'm just not." What they are all of the time, like most of the Horse combinations, is *real*!

The men of this combination tend to be tall, introverted and detail oriented. They do not like to rely on other people and prefer to do as much as they can by themselves so are constantly learning new skills and surrounding themselves with people who are experts in their field so that they can absorb their knowledge by osmosis. This could be a reason why Horse-Leos tend to need careers where there is constant research required or something where there is much variety. Actor turned Writer turned Director John Huston said, "I've lived a number of lives." These men need to, or their passion for life wanes and they become miserably difficult to live with and can often be picky fault-finders. Actually, they are anyway. But they are also pioneers in the sense that they go places that no men have gone before, yes, that means the moon, but also in other ways. John

Huston was the first person to do a documentary exploring the effects of post-traumatic stress on soldiers after they returned from war and he also explored risqué topics such as homosexuality that no director had previously dared to touch. The world needs the horse-lion to barge through walls to allow lesser mortals to access the treasure they find and build upon it.

The theme of being a pioneering does not cease with the men as their female counterparts will not be outdone. Halle Berry broke down the race barriers when she became the first black American to enter the Miss World competition, the first black American woman to win the academy award for best actress and she is currently (in 2014) one of the highest paid actresses in Hollywood. She has said, "I spent a lot of time with a crown on my head."

Jennifer Lawrence also broke some waves being the second youngest person to win an Oscar for best Actress. She also graduated high school two years early. Halle Berry was a member of the honor society, editor of the school paper and class president; yes they were both smarty pants; they both play super-powered mutants in the X-men movie franchise (along with Lucas Till, another Horse-Leo compatriot), and they also have their clumsiness in common; Halle Berry is often injured on the sets of her movies and Jennifer Lawrence has a tendency to trip over during public events. Horse-Leo women have the typical horse traits; great sense of humor, elegance, socially they are usually high up in the hierarchy and they have highly feminist views. Adding Leo, they become even more dignified and their need for adventurous experiences increases, yet, they become more conservative and traditional than other Horse women. Jennifer Lawrence has said, "I'm excited to be seen as sexy. But not slutty."

Ultimately, the Horse-Leo is one of those combinations that likes to make the impossible possible. They set ridiculous targets for themselves that most people would think are unachievable. Before setting off for the journey, this foal knows that it has the ideas, the skills and the know-how to make its dream a reality. Jennifer Lawrence has said, "I like when things are hard; I'm very competitive. If something seems difficult or impossible, it interests me... I came home and announced, 'I'm going to move to New York,'... Then when I did, they [friends] kept waiting for me to fail and come back. But I knew I wouldn't. I was like, 'I'll show you.'" It thrills them to take such risks fearlessly because it is the only way to be present *in* the moment and *to* the moment when the universe might spark and the Horse-Leo can pull some more ambrosia into this mortal world. James Cameron has said, "And no important endeavor that required innovation was done without risk...failure is an option, but fear is not."

Soul Mate:	Sheep-Taurus
Challenger:	Rat-Aquarius
Siblings:	Horse-Aries, Horse-Sagittarius
Best Friends:	Tiger-Aries, Tiger-Leo, Tiger-Sagittarius, Dog-Aries, Dog-Leo, Dog-Sagittarius

Jennifer Lawrence
James Cameron
Halle Berry
John Huston
Neil Armstrong
Princess Margaret
Martina McBride
Jack O'Connell
Dean Cain
Lucas Till
Chris Sarandon
Maureen O'Hara
Robert Culp

Walter Brennan
Lee Ann Womack
Stieg Larsson

HORSE – VIRGO

Chinese Name: MA
Rank: 7th
Hours Ruled: 11am – 1pm
Direction: Directly South
Season: Summer
Month: June
Western Zodiac Equivalent of Horse: Gemini
Gemini Western Element: Air
Eastern Zodiac Equivalent of Virgo: Rooster
Virgo Western Element: Earth
Numerology: 78 = 6

I keep waiting to meet a man who has more balls than I do.
– Salma Hayek

When the Horse's hurricane meets the fertile earth of the Virgo, heaven's clouds try to merge with mortal soil; gods meet monsters of the human variety and all sorts of drama ensues. This creature is blessed and cursed with an acute perception that sees through hype and smoke screens straight to the point allowing them to come up with simple practical solutions that most others refuse to believe are possible. That humanitarian Horse heart continues to hold out its hoof so that it can pull others up and out of the mess they call their lives, but most people perceive them as wild stallions chasing sunsets they'll never catch.

So when the Horse-Virgo realizes that others cannot accept anything bigger, better and brilliant, they just decide to trot off solo to show them how it's done. Warren Buffett, who is widely considered to be the most successful financial investor of all time is a good example of this, he has said, "There seems to be some perverse human characteristic that likes to make easy things difficult... I don't look to jump over 7-foot bars: I look around for 1-foot bars that I can step over."

With strong personalities, they don't come across as humble as they have controversial voices that are hard to ignore. Intelligent, passionate and benevolent, they like to get involved on the ground roots level so that they can establish what issues actually exist rather than obtain the information second hand, in diluted form. They trust their own judgment before all else and want to get the information from the source, i.e. straight from the Horse's mouth. Discussing how she has always been involved with social causes within her community, Salma Hayek has said, "I think that it's important for every single person, no matter what they do in life, to participate in the well-being of humanity and the planet."

The men of this combination do not need to be conventionally attractive to exude a raw sex appeal. In fact, more often than not, they have a clean-cut, nerdy exterior with a sexy glint in their eyes. It's a good combination and it works for them. Adam Sandler has jestingly said, "God gave me some weird, beautiful scent that makes men and women go crazy. People compare it to Carvel. It is a whale of a smell." Being blessed with the sort of clarity that the Horse-Virgo has can sometimes be difficult to manage because it has them constantly facing the truth; being confronted with the weaknesses of others is one thing, but to constantly be aware of your own is another thing. These exceptionally sharp minds have them living at the point of power at all times, i.e. in the moment, not in the past or in the future; perhaps that is why they are not particularly sentimental or nostalgic, it just seems like a waste of energy because they intend to live their lives fully until their last breath. Sean Connery has said, "I've never kept a record of anything. I gave away everything: all the posters, the memorabilia that would have been helpful – and financially rewarding."

The women of this combination have the typical horse traits, tough tomboys with feminist views who act as the political rebel fighting their own and the causes of their community for equality. Shirley Manson has said, "Until we command the exact same salary as every male counterpart, I feel a political desire to stand by other women. If we don't stand together, that equality will never be fully realized, and that bothers me." The Horse-Virgo women can often be even stronger than their male counterparts, because their struggle for equality has strengthened their psychological muscles. Salma Hayek has said, "I think that a lot of women that know they're going to be part of history somehow decide to have a character to be remembered by."

They feel an intense affinity with their female sisters and spend much of their time encouraging them to break through barriers that have been holding them back. Salma Hayek has said, "I don't see women and think of them as competition or with judgment. Women really move me. I feel connected to all kinds of women." So when the media tries to stir some sort of animosity to get a story, many people have fallen victim to the manipulation, not the Horse-Virgo. Shirley Manson has said, "I refuse to step inside the ring and fight like a gladiator against my own. I'm not playing that game. Any woman who has survived a year or more of making music has my undying respect."

Ultimately, the Horse-Virgo is the next step along from the pioneering Horse-Leo sign, so much of that energy is present here, perhaps a little less daring because of the lack of Leo fire but more directly altruistic which comes as a result of the Virgo earth. Elegant and attractive creatures, they really care about people even if they do not say it. Their sense of humor is another defining characteristic, which is enjoyed not just by those around them, but primarily, by themselves. Salma Hayek has said, "If you're feeling blue, lock yourself in a room, stand in front of a mirror, and dance – and laugh at yourself and be sexy. Dance the silliest and ugliest you've ever danced. Make fun of yourself and try to recover your sense of humor." No matter what befalls them, they will never be down for long. Their love of life and knowledge of their own power will draw them back into the game time and time again until every ounce of life has drained from their body. As Sean Connery has displayed as he received his AFI Life Achievement Award, "Though my feet are tired, my heart is not." This Horse's heart never ever tires! Period!

Soul Mate:	Sheep-Aries
Challenger:	Rat-Pisces
Siblings:	Horse-Taurus, Horse-Capricorn
Best Friends:	Tiger-Taurus, Tiger-Virgo, Tiger-Capricorn, Dog-Taurus, Dog-Virgo, Dog-Capricorn

Sean Connery

Warren Buffett

Adam Sandler

Salma Hayek

Shirley Manson

Wes Bentley

Kobe Bryant

Werner Herzog

Michael Michele

Ben Folds

Elvis Costello

Anne Diamond

Devon Sawa

Ben McKenzie

HORSE – LIBRA

Chinese Name: MA
Rank: 7th
Hours Ruled: 11am – 1pm
Direction: Directly South
Season: Summer
Month: June
Western Zodiac Equivalent of Horse: Gemini
Gemini Western Element: Air
Eastern Zodiac Equivalent of Libra: Dog
Libra Western Element: Air
Numerology: 79 = 7

Sometimes I feel illusions are more of life's essence. I can trust them more that real life that is full of deceit and covering-up.
– Ang Lee

When the Horse's hurricane meets Libra's little cyclone, they fuel and support each other higher and higher into the stratosphere to such an extent that they can hardly be seen. It is part of their nature to be beyond and out of reach. Like all Horses, they have invisible antennae that feed them detailed information that allows them to function largely by instinct. It is their preferred method of living. However, this combination also has a tendency to overthink things, which often gets in the way of what their instinct is trying to tell them. The upside of this is their fantastic ability to narrow in on one single subject and draw it to themselves quickly. If they have contradictory feelings, it just takes longer, but because of their obsessive focus and consistent action, they tend to get what they want eventually. As Singer Usher Raymond has said, "Strivers achieve what dreamers believe."

First and foremost, this Horse needs space! Most Horse signs do but this sign needs to feel like the horizon is always available to them. This is a difficult need to navigate because they want to feel accepted and to give that acceptance whilst maintaining their own personal universe. In romantic relationships, they often feel trapped, inhibited and forced to be something that they are not, especially the women, when they feel that the man is trying to be the "man" by taking charge. Some even have debilitating social anxiety or acute shyness that keeps them removed from the company they might otherwise choose. Speaking about her youth, Bollywood Icon, Rekha has said, "I was never a kind of person who voiced my impressions or my feelings. I never told anybody what I feel. I was very shy, to open my mouth when there are men around." Unfortunately, many Horse-Libras see only two options; either sacrificing a certain share of freedom and part of themselves to enter a relationship or truly maintaining a sense of who they are, but never fully committing to someone mind, body and soul. Director Ang Lee has said, "I'm a drifter and an outsider. There's not one single environment I can totally belong to."

The men of this combination like to get straight to the point and do not always consider the emotional repercussions of their actions. Richard Harris said, "I was a sinner. I slugged some people. I hurt many people. And it's true, I never looked back to see the casualties." It's not that they don't care, actually, they care too much. With a heightened sensitivity they take all the energy in any interaction on board and end up taking things personally that were never meant in that way. Eventually, they realize this and either become more aware of their own functioning and chill out, or they just remove themselves from situations where there is a risk of this happening. They reach a point where they stop trying to be accepted by their peers or society and instead just stick to the people who have always been in their corner and doing the things that they are most interested in. And of course, that is when they receive the affirmation they always sought. Jon Favreux has said, "I have to be really engaged, and then I go straight from lazy to obsessive. I couldn't study chemistry, but I could memorize all the books for Dungeons and Dragons. It was ridiculous. The trick is to find what I like to do."

The women of this combination are real examples of that hurricane flying higher and higher until it is outside of the vision or understanding of the current culture that they live in because, frankly, they tend to be ahead of their time. Most Horse women are tomboys and this combination is no different. They also do not see why they cannot enjoy the same lives that their male counterparts do and they set out to live such lives. Unfortunately, society is not as quick as them and does not always accept their choices or ways of being. Speaking about the sort of man that she is attracted to, Britt Ekland has said, "I just like someone who satisfies me sexually and is fun, but puts no demands on me and who disappears out of my life when I like them to disappear out of my life." In a country as conservative as India, very few women choose to remain single, it's extremely rare even today (2014), so when Rekha and Asha Parekh, two of the biggest Bollywood actresses in the 60s and 70s did so and did not have children, it cannot have been easy. But they are tough, independent and can be a little bit scary with it. Speaking about her reputation on film sets, Asha Parekh said, "Whenever I entered the studio everyone would run for cover."

Ultimately, the modest, arty and introverted Horse-Libra learns to manage its moods in social environments by choosing friends who understand and open them up. Their true love is their art and nothing quite compares. As the most famous man in Bollywood of all time, Amitabh Bhachan has said, "That hunger and those butterflies in the stomach are very essential for all creative people." This modest Horse applies its passion and discipline to everything it attempts. They grow and grow and fly higher and higher which is what they want but it is not what they want. All Horses are contradictory creatures. But their love of life is infectious and they tend to travel a lot in their lives; many have a knack for languages and settle in countries that are foreign to them. One thing that is for sure, the Horse-Libra cannot be anything other than that which it is and when they accept themselves, they find external acceptance is quick to come. Luckily, they are more than committed to their own growth and development. As Ang Lee has said, "You can't move forward without changing, and that's why I try to stay open to new perspectives. I want to keep learning. If there's one thing I've learned, it's that you can never learn enough."

Soul Mate:	Sheep-Pisces
Challenger:	Rat-Aries
Siblings:	Horse-Gemini, Horse-Aquarius
Best Friends:	Tiger-Gemini, Tiger-Libra, Tiger-Aquarius, Dog-Gemini, Dog-Libra, Dog-Aquarius

Rita Hayworth
Amitabh Bachchan
Britt Ekland
Richard Harris
Harold Pinter
Ang Lee
Usher Raymond
Jon Favreau
Rekha
Ray Charles
Robert Walker
Anne Haddy
Ian McShane

Michael Crichton
Asha Parekh
Eric Benét
Trevor Donovan
Shannyn Sossamon
Devon Gummersall
Mya
Alesha Dixon
Soha Ali Khan
Jonathan Lipnicki

HORSE – SCORPIO

Chinese Name: MA
Rank: 7th
Hours Ruled: 11am – 1pm
Direction: Directly South
Season: Summer
Month: June
Western Zodiac Equivalent of Horse: Gemini
Gemini Western Element: Air
Eastern Zodiac Equivalent of Scorpio: Boar
Scorpio Western Element: Water
Numerology: 80 = 8

I don't like looking back. I'm always constantly looking forward. I'm not the one to sort of sit and cry over spilt milk. I'm too busy looking for the next cow.
– Gordon Ramsay

When the Horse's heavenly clouds meet the Scorpio's murky waters, it merges the good, the bad and the not so ugly into one single being. Adding Scorpio to any combination brings a level of mystery and intrigue; adding it here creates the Dark Horse combination. Being smarter than average as a child, they tend to outshine their siblings or friends and may even be given preferable treatment, if they choose to play by the rules; if they do not, they may be shunned or ignored by the very people whose love they need. Even in their younger years, they have a strong sense of their personal identity, a good grasp of what their talents may be and most importantly, what feels right to them. That is why they, like most Horse combinations, place great emphasis on instinctual living. Gordon Ramsay has said, "I act on impulse and I go with my instincts."

Horses receive information in an intellectual way, even though they live by their instincts, whilst the Scorpio uses its senses to process everything; when these two signs converge, the resulting personality digests a lot of information before making a decision, usually very quickly because it does not like to hang around or waste time. Usually, they tend to be gifted at many things so naturally they will choose those things to conquer that challenge them most. David Schwimmer has said, "If there's something I want, I go for it. I just think about how I'm going to go for it."

Although inwardly, they may question their decisions, they do not like this to be known. They want to be seen as someone who knows what they are doing and where they are going. Actually, they are and they do, but when they feel that they sacrificed their integrity, they struggle with themselves and it tends to be quite visible. This is often the result after they have been engaged in an argument where their defenses go up and they end up saying whatever comes into their heads, whether they believe it or not. Then they regret it and beat up on themselves in private. This happens more frequently than they would like because they are exceptionally passionate people. But when this very same passion is channeled into their professional lives, the resultant drive serves them very well. Calvin Klein has said, "When I started the business, I hardly went home. I became very driven about work and about my career."

The men of this combination are opinionated, boisterous and sexy. They tend to learn early how to manage their fears and push themselves to keep stretching outside of their comfort zones. This is why people like Gordon Ramsay and Calvin Klein belong to this combination, people who start their own enterprises, then continue to pump energy into them until they succeed. Despite their external appearances, they have a good blend of intellectual and creative mental function. David Schwimmer has said, "I spend half my time just living my life, and the other half analyzing it." Generally speaking, these men advocate freedom of expression and self-empowerment. The humanitarian Horse experiences freedom in a way unlike any other sign and so wants to help everyone feel how it feels to run wildly towards the sun. Jeff Buckley has said, "I'm against the arbitrary organization of God as a concept. We should all experience it all individually and purely."

The women of this combination are equally as fierce, if not fiercer than their male counterparts. This powerful Horse-Scorpio will come disguised in a feminine, dainty package, but make no mistake this mare is a beast with a desire to be seen for everything she is, not just her physical beauty. Horse signs of all combinations tend to have an interest in politics, especially if they can help to alleviate unfairness and promote equality. Horse-Scorpio women can be feminine but there is something a tad graceless, or clumsy about them. This actually increases their charm rather than it diminishing. It is that Scorpio mystique rubbing up against the Horse's tomboy spirit that makes them so attractive, yet intimidating at the same time. They like their views to be respected without their femininity getting in the way. And if you dare to treat her in a way unequal to a male peer? Stefanie Powers has said, "Unfortunately, sometimes people don't hear you until you scream." That spirited and volatile Horse-Scorpio nature rears its head once more!

Ultimately, the Horse-Scorpio is sensitive, sensual and serious. They know that they should "relax" more, but they just have an inbuilt need to keep working, get better and be exceptional. In their youth, they will have had that phase where the Dark Horse unashamedly served its ego; playing around without considering the feelings of other people, gained at the expense of others and created regrets that they carry with them for the rest of their lives. These experiences broaden their perspective and their fiery reactive behaviors tone down. They realize that they have been taking everything too seriously and that life is not a game where someone must lose for another to win. Instead, their priorities change and they lighten up, learn to chill out and lose themselves in uncompetitive play. As Martin Scorsese has said, "And as I've gotten older, I've had more of a tendency to look for people who live by kindness, tolerance, compassion, a gentler way of looking at things."

Soul Mate:	Sheep-Aquarius
Challenger:	Rat-Taurus
Siblings:	Horse-Cancer, Horse-Pisces
Best Friends:	Tiger-Cancer, Tiger-Scorpio, Tiger-Pisces, Dog-Cancer, Dog-Scorpio, Dog-Pisces

Martin Scorsese
Jeff Buckley
Matthew Morrison
Rachel McAdams
Stefanie Powers
Condoleezza Rice
Gordon Ramsay
Calvin Klein
David Schwimmer
Eve
Prithviraj Kapoor
Teresa Wright
Peter Hall
Linda Evans
Marcia Wallace
Larry Flynt
Chris Noth
Kamal Hassan
Adam Ant
Rocco DiSpirito

Adam Horovitz
Sisqó
Vanessa Mae
Bob Hoskins

HORSE – SAGITTARIUS

Chinese Name: MA
Rank: 7th
Hours Ruled: 11am – 1pm
Direction: Directly South
Season: Summer
Month: June
Western Zodiac Equivalent of Horse: Gemini
Gemini Western Element: Air
Eastern Zodiac Equivalent of Sagittarius: Rat
Sagittarius Western Element: Fire
Numerology: 81 = 9

I don't do anything in order to cause trouble. It just so happens that what I do naturally causes trouble. I'm proud to be a troublemaker.
– Sinead O'Connor

When the Horse's hurricane meets the Centaur's frisky fire, two of the most instinctive signs come together; the intelligent, independent, rebel merges with the philosophical, nomadic vagabond. Performance, storytelling and general entertaining are natural gifts for these people. On the surface, they tend to be quiet and gentle, this they are, but no matter how passive they might look, they have strong opinions, a stubborn streak and an unusual brand of wisdom, an instinctual knowledge of the natural order of things which is why they feel so strongly about injustices, humanitarian and environmental concerns. Their natural tendency is to live their life with their big horse-heart on their sleeve, being very upfront about everything. Everything! As a Horse sign, directness is to be expected, but this Horse does not know how to censor itself. Katherine Heigl has said, "There are some things that, if you say them out loud, will hurt the other person's feelings. I tend to say them anyway. It's better to be honest."

This combination takes criticism exceptionally well; like wind of a raging stallion's back, primarily because they interpret it constructive advice, therefore, in the same vein, it is their natural assumption that others will not only be able to handle their words, but welcome their "constructive advice." Many just state their opinion in a raw way. This is why many have a reputation for being harsh or cold. But they are not. It is their natural way of being. They are honest with themselves and honest with the rest of the world. Writer Hanif Kureishi has said, "I am determined to live without illusions. I want to look at reality straight. Without hiding."

The men of this combination tend to be exceptionally pretty. Long eyelashes tend to be a distinctive feature. Rob Lowe, Gael Garcia Bernal, Ian Somerhalder and Jesse Metcalf are examples of the Horse-Sagittarius brand of *pretty*. Despite being quite aloof and some would say, remote, they actually really like to get to know people and help them to find the humor in life's little trials. Comedian Billy Connolly has said, "Before you judge a man, walk a mile in his shoes. After that who cares? He's a mile away and you've got his shoes!" They choose to stick to the people whose value systems most resemble their own because they know that their views are likely to rile the more conservative of folk. Ian Somerhalder has said, "I have a million acquaintances but just two or three true friends. I can't hide anything from them."

Both of the signs here are masculine energy yang signs, yet, because of their instinctive connection with nature, they know how to let their softer side surface when they choose to. Ray Liotta has said, "I'm emotionally in tune with my feelings and what people mean to me, and I have no trouble saying it and relating to it." When one gets to know them properly, they realize that they are gentle, compassionate men with open hearts that love to bring their lightness to everything they do. Gael Garcia Bernal has said, "I go with the flow. Whatever music you play for me, I'll dance."

The women of this combination are typical Horse tomboy types with the usual Horse woman proclivities; the need for physical, emotional and psychological space, with sharp, witty, observations and full of humanitarian concern. They also have that defense mechanism in place to deal with the jealousies all Horse women experience from other women, yet at the same time, being the biggest champion of them as a gender. As Katherine Heigl has said, "I'm not out burning bras, but I'm very opinionated about women owning their power." These mares just instinctively know how to function in the man's world because, as far as they are concerned, they are on the same playing field. Actually, their own nature is quite masculine. Instinctive rather than empathic, imaginative more than contemplative and impulsive rather than considered, they are also not particularly girly and have many platonic male friends. They are also mentally cluttered because of the haphazard way they go about their lives. Katie Holmes has said, "I'm definitely a messy person... I know where everything is but I just can't organize... It's bad, I really need to take control." They will be their charming tomboy selves but allow themselves the freedom to paint over their core with whatever color suits them on any particular day, the rest of the world will just have to wait and see what turns up. Nelly Furtado has said, "Some days I'm brainy, some days I'm funny, some days I'm sexy, and sometimes, I just want to dance."

A favorite humanitarian concern for the Horse-Sagittarian is the continued sustenance of the earth and especially the development of alternative energy so that the current polluting methods can be replaced. This comes from that heightened instinctive connection to the world and their love of unspoiled open spaces, which just seems to thrill some inner part of themselves. Speaking about he preferred choice of profession, Actor Ian Somerhalder said, "I don't know how to do anything else other than be an actor. If I wasn't in this, I would be in alternative energy and conservation." They revel in their passion and let that lead them, so their priorities shift regularly, almost cyclically, but one thing is for sure: if they care about something, they will do something about it eventually. Actor Gael Garcia Bernal has said, "I think we're all political, in a way. What has happened recently in my case is that, fortunately, I've been able to get more in touch with the things I can change and do." At the end of the day, they are quietly caring souls who do not like grand displays emotion, so they let people perceive them in whatever way they choose without much resistance, but that does not stop how fervently they feel about the people in their lives and their causes. Perhaps that is why Jimi Hendrix counseled that, "When the power of love overcomes the love of power, the world will know peace."

Soul Mate:	Sheep-Capricorn
Challenger:	Rat-Gemini
Siblings:	Horse-Aries, Horse-Leo
Best Friends:	Tiger-Aries, Tiger-Leo, Tiger-Sagittarius, Dog-Aries, Dog-Leo, Dog-Sagittarius

Hanif Kureishi
Chris Evert
Kiefer Sutherland
Billy Connolly
Jimi Hendrix
Ray Liotta

Sinéad O'Connor
Ian Somerhalder
Katherine Heigl
Katie Holmes
Gael García Bernal
Jesse Metcalfe
Nelly Furtado
Ronnie Corbett
Gemma Jones
Jean-Luc Godard
Jean-Louis Trintignant
Joel Coen
Geeta Dutt
Jermaine Jackson
C. Thomas Howell
Vincent Cassel
Billy Burke
Gary Dourdan
Summer Phoenix
Kayvan Novak
Sarah Hyland
Diego Boneta

HORSE – CAPRICORN

Chinese Name: MA
Rank: 7th
Hours Ruled: 11am – 1pm
Direction: Directly South
Season: Summer
Month: June
Western Zodiac Equivalent of Horse: Gemini
Gemini Western Element: Air
Eastern Zodiac Equivalent of Capricorn: Ox
Capricorn Western Element: Earth
Numerology: 82 = 1

Don't compromise yourself. You are all you've got.
– Janis Joplin

When the Horse's hurricane meets Capricorn's dense earth, the stubborn stallion tries to use its speed and coarse surface to sand down the rock like earth it meets into something softer and more malleable, but the Capricorn's earth is as stubborn as the Horse's air. Although they have that in common, they are very much different characters: the super fast, super cool rebellious Horse verses the quiet, slow, purposeful Capricorn goat. That contradictory Horse personality becomes even more so here; they are equal parts politician, artist, activist, pacifist, intellectual, commoner, parent and forever child. All people juggle various roles and doing so alters ones priorities, but when the Horse-Capricorn goes from one role to the next, they inhabit the persona so completely that they forget who they were before. Eventually, they learn that life is so complex that straightforward ideas or answers do not exist, so they learn to absorb information through their unicorn horn or antennae and let themselves be guided by their instinct. Annie Lennox has said, "I don't have clear-cut positions. I get baffled by things. I have viewpoints. Sometimes they change."

Where the Horse is complicated, the Capricorn is simple; when the Horse courts drama, the Capricorn seeks the quiet life. Merged together, they have an uncanny ability to understand what the public will respond to. It's not even a commercial mindset, it's that Horse instinct coupled with the Capricorn's simplicity. Rowan Atkinson has said, "I think I have an inner confidence that my tastes are pretty simple, that what I find funny finds a wide audience." Similarly, talking about his music, R. Kelly has said, "I wouldn't be able to do the songs as long as I've been doing if I didn't feel the pulse of the world... I feel like I know how they are, because I am the people. And I just have a gift." Part of their gift is knowing that the priority is the product, not the packaging, substance not just style.

The men of this combination are manage to turn their geekiness into the coolest thing going; Mr. Bean is an unusual eccentric, but there's something about his "I don't care attitude" that his alter ego Rowan Atkinson shares, that's pretty cool too! Rowan Atkinson has said, "People think because I can make them laugh on the stage, I'll be able to make them laugh in person. That isn't the case at all. I am essentially a rather quiet, dull person who just happens to be a performer." Outside of their work life, they are surprisingly simple, humble people as the Horse-Capricorn only knows how to be personally honest, if you ask them for the truth, they will speak their truth, even if nobody else agrees. They are the everyman with everyday priorities. Denzel Washington has said, "Acting is just a way of making a living, the family is life."

The women of this combination tend to be slight and small in frame and fiercely feminist! Then, she is an activist. Because, like their male counterparts, they are extremely value driven, unconventional and are often accused of being manly. This androgyny somehow allows them to be taken seriously in a man's world. Annie Lenox has said, "I have a reputation for being cold and aloof, but I'm so not that woman. I'm passionate. I love my girls, being with my girlfriends, getting involved with issues that affect other women and children who are suffering." They do not go with the public census because they are usually a little ahead. Instead, they listen to their instinct that guides them to artistic places where they then employ that quality ethic that ensures a certain level of success. Janis Joplin said, "I always wanted to be an artist, whatever that was, like other chicks want to be stewardesses. I read. I painted. I thought."

Ultimately, the Horse-Capricorn's journey is to go from self-criticism to self-acceptance. Despite how hard they work, they never feel like they have done enough or that they have lived up to what they set for themselves. There is a bit of that perfectionism there, but this is more of an emotional-dysmorphia. Rowan Atkinson has said, "I have always worried about things more than I should."

They spend a lot of time in solitary contemplation about what they ought to do in order to be more acceptable. Then, that Horse part rebels against itself telling the rest of the world to go leap off a cliff. They are even more beautiful when they release their inhibitions and just be. The truth is, they are as funny, as talented and as superstar-ish in real life as they are on the stage, but they only feel able to open themselves to nurturing friends. They are not easy people to get to know as a result of this. But it is *who* they are that has everyone mesmerized! They tend to step back and let their work speak for them, because it is easier than abusing the limelight. They live their ideals with greater and greater intensity as they age and spend their lives in pursuit of equality and justice for all. Khalil Gibran has said, "Life without liberty is like a body without spirit." This is a typical Horse sign manifesto and

through this mission, they learn to relax into their skin and
realize what everyone else already knows: that this everyman is
actually one of a kind. Khalil Gibran also said, "Knowledge of
the self is the mother of all knowledge. So it is incumbent on me
to know my self, to know it completely, to know its minutiae, its
characteristics, its subtleties, and its very atoms."

Soul Mate: Sheep-Sagittarius
Challenger: Rat-Cancer
Siblings: Horse-Taurus, Horse-Virgo
Best Friends: Tiger-Taurus, Tiger-Virgo, Tiger-Capricorn,
                 Dog-Taurus, Dog-Virgo, Dog-Capricorn

Denzel Washington
Kevin Costner
Rowan Atkinson
John Legend
Janis Joplin
R. Kelly
Annie Lennox
Khalil Gibran
Gayle King
Anwar Sadat
Irrfan
Robert Duvall
Dave Matthews
James Earl Jones
Sarah Polley
Emily Watson
J.K. Simmons
Tyrese Gibson
Tia Carrere
Aaliyah
Paul Freeman

Bipasha Basu
Rajesh Khanna
Pixie Lott
Steve Earle
Akosua Busia

HORSE – AQUARIUS

Chinese Name: MA
Rank: 7th
Hours Ruled: 11am – 1pm
Direction: Directly South
Season: Summer
Month: June
Western Zodiac Equivalent of Horse: Gemini
Gemini Western Element: Air
Eastern Zodiac Equivalent of Aquarius: Tiger
Aquarius Western Element: Air
Numerology: 83 = 2

Dream as if you'll live forever. Live as if you'll die today.
– James Dean

When the Horse's hurricane meets the lofty clouds of Aquarius, they merge and become one huge cloudy storm. Mystery, intrigue and sex appeal are rife when these two air signs come together. The rebel Horse lends its intellect, instinct and edgy "cool" while unconventional Aquarius brings a sort of lost-child innocence, a connection to subconscious worlds and just a hint of obliviousness. What they both have in common is their mutual concern for mankind: where the Horse wants to abolish inequality and highlight hypocrisies, the Aquarian wants to puts its arm around the world and uplift it by being an inspiration. Actor and Entrepreneur Ashton Kutcher said, "Life can be a lot broader... when you realize one simple thing: everything around us that we call *life* was made up by people who were no smarter than you... So build a life. Don't live one."

These people are smart, really smart, but people tend to see their sexiness and not their "smartiness." This could be because they cultivate an air of the himbo and bimbo. Ashton Kutcher has said, "There's something advantageous about having people underestimate your intellect, insomuch as a lot of things are revealed to you." Members of this combination do tend to look, for lack of a better word, *dim*, but they are not! In fact, it is at this part of the astrological cycle where scientists and academic geniuses are born. Even Ashton Kutcher was studying biomedical engineering. Ashton Kutcher also said, "I wanted to figure out what the codon sequence was that causes replication in a cardio myopathic virus. That was my goal." They also lead with their cheeky, sexy, sass, which also encourages people to think that their wit, audacity and vivaciousness is all they have. It's not that they are purposely trying to mislead anyone, it's more that they like to have fun and keep the energy they create, light and frisky. Celebrated mystery writer Ruth Rendell has said, "I've had two proposals since I've been a widow. I am a wonderful catch, you know. I have a lot of money."

The men of this combination are an interesting juxtaposition between young and old. They have that carefree youthful Horse attitude along with the ageless Aquarian wisdom that taps into the heart of universal consciousness. Perhaps that is why John Travolta has said, "I have this dichotomy where I'm either, like, super young or feel like I'm coming to the end of my years." They are smart, gorgeous and nice. They are also instinctive risk takers who are prepared to put themselves on the line in order to push boundaries and explore new territory. As the original rebel without a cause, James Dean has said, "Death can't be considered, because if you're afraid to die there's no room in your life to make discoveries." They love life more than most because of the thrill they get by living on the edge of it. Even Ashton Kutcher has said, "I woke up many mornings not knowing what I'd done the night before. I'm amazed I'm not dead." At the end of the day, these men have a sensitivity that belies their competitive, masculine spirit. They are boys who never really grow up.

They like their boy's toys and they like to spend much of their time in the company of their buddies doing boys stuff, in a messy, muddy and uninhibited way. Ashton Kutcher has said, "I'm a guy's guy. I don't comb my hair unless I have to, and I don't use lotions or fancy shampoos."

The women of this combination are like beautiful dolls who struggle with the way that they look and how the world perceives them. They cannot help but present themselves as these beautiful dolls because the attention they get serves their inner need for adoration, affirmation and their need to create an image of something unobtainable. Emma Roberts has said, "If there wasn't mystery, people wouldn't have anything to ponder. If you already knew everything, you wouldn't have anything to think about and life would just be really boring." If the world perceives them as beautiful but dumb, that is their problem! However, the Horse-Aquarian lady needs to be appreciated for her capabilities too, that is why many of them go into professional positions, even though they are drawn to the arts: dance, literature and painting specifically. There is a noted tendency to change to a creative career in their late twenties or early thirties, which is part of their journey to find self-acceptance. Stacey Dash has said, "I'm trying to fall in love with myself. And hopefully after I do that, I'll be able to fall in love and stay in love with someone else." This they learn to do relatively easily when they realize that thinking patterns can be changed by practicing new ones.

Ultimately, the Horse-Aquarius is the sort that wants to get involved with life in every aspect; from a mental, practical, physical, psychological and esoteric way. They just want to get inside of everything they do, not just to understand but to appreciate the beauty of the simplicity of the complexity. Because not many people can, but they can and they know it. It is the reason for their insatiable drive. Ashton Kutcher has said, "I don't believe that old cliché that good things come to those who wait. I think good things come to those who want something so bad they can't sit still." How does anyone expect this subject to sit still when there is so much to do to make the world a better place? They love life and are able to find joy in the smallest things. They know that finding happiness is an inside job and it is important to be at peace with oneself. Ashton Kutcher has said, "I'm happy wherever I go, whatever I do. I'm happy in Iowa, I'm happy here in California."

Soul Mate:	Sheep-Scorpio
Challenger:	Rat-Leo
Siblings:	Horse-Gemini, Horse-Libra
Best Friends:	Tiger-Gemini, Tiger-Libra, Tiger-Aquarius, Dog-Gemini, Dog-Libra, Dog-Aquarius

Gene Hackman
James Dean
John Travolta
Ashton Kutcher
Stacey Dash
Ruth Rendell
Emma Roberts
Sara Rue
Tatyana Ali
Neal McDonough
Dexter Fletcher
Rick Astley
Rene Russo
Robert Wagner
Will Young
Chris Parnell
Bobby Deol

John Wesley Shipp
Blythe Danner
Rip Torn
Claire Bloom
Les Dawson
Sean Kingston

HORSE – PISCES

Chinese Name: MA
Rank: 7th
Hours Ruled: 11am – 1pm
Direction: Directly South
Season: Summer
Month: June
Western Zodiac Equivalent of Horse: Gemini
Gemini Western Element: Air
Eastern Zodiac Equivalent of Pisces: Rabbit
Pisces Western Element: Water
Numerology: 84 = 3

I regret that I wasn't wilder. I was working and I was nervous. I was the one in the corner with the book being responsible.
– Cindy Crawford

When the humanitarian Horse's hurricane connects with Pisces quiet stream, the academic intellectuality joins dreamy creativity; the difference being that with this amazing mind, plans are easily created to achieve goals so this personality's dreams are very much reachable. It is at this part of the astrological cycle that many academic geniuses are found. There is a real attraction to intellectual pursuits and many born under this sign are gifted with extraordinary memories. Have a look at the academic achievements of the following Horse-Pisceans: nineteenth century French pianist/composer Frédéric Chopin was a renowned child prodigy, Jensen Ackles was on track to study sports medicine before choosing the performing arts, Cindy Crawford graduated as valedictorian of her high school and won a scholarship to study chemical engineering at Northwestern university, Jennifer Grant went to Stanford to study history and political science, Donal Logue also studied history but at Harvard and Ben Miller's PhD thesis at Cambridge was on 'novel quantum effects in quasi-zero dimensional mesoscopic electrical systems'. Donal Logue said, "Follow your deepest dream, the one you had as a kid...but stay focused."

That many of them leave their academic pursuits behind to chase down a creative career is also no surprise as Horses like to be seen, they just don't want to be seen making a fuss about it. The Pisces influence brings additional flair but also an over the top soppy side that seems not to mesh with the other sides of this personality. The truth is, most Horse signs are not so great at handling their emotions (believe it or not, the women are worse than the men) especially when it comes to expressing their feelings, so if they find what they consider an appropriate outlet for their affection, they will shamelessly vent as much as they can. Generally speaking, they prefer to rely on their wit and words until their defenses are broken down by loved ones and their inner child can then be openly accessed to be lavished with cuddles and love.

The men of this combination are known for their high morals, intelligence and the strange ability to get sexier and sexier the longer one looks at them. In the TV show *Buffy the Vampire Slayer*, there were two full time "Watchers" of Slayers, sort of Guardians who train and "watch" over their wards. The roles required them to be bookish, tough and paternally nurturing whilst possessing a sex appeal attractive to viewers; both of the Actors portraying Watchers, Anthony Stewart Head and Alexis Denisoff belong to this combination albeit 12 years apart. Men of this combination are quiet, private and push themselves to improve on a daily basis. Anthony Stewart Head said, "Don't fall back on the parachute (my safety net). Go outside the zone of confidence and find out what's on the other side." Their intelligence and drive to be better leads them to great heights. Ron Howard said, "I wanted to become a leader in the business." In many respects, Horse-Pisceans are quite typical Horses in that they are more instinctual than anything else. They like to live according to their feelings and make their own assessments of any situation. Billy Zane said, "With me it's always about first impressions. I trust my instincts. I love to prepare if it's something that requires training. But I don't like to prepare the psychology too much."

The women of this combination are usually elegant, regardless of their height, size or shape; they have a way of carrying themselves like ladies despite being one of the "boys." It is characteristic of Horse women to have a lot of male friends, gay or otherwise. They are not traditionally feminine and have more quirks and idiosyncrasies than they would like to reveal but they cannot stand the unfairness of living in a man's world. Catherine O'Hara said, "It wasn't supposed to be ladylike for a girl to joke. To this day, I've found that it doesn't matter what a guy looks like if he's really funny. His sense of humor makes him attractive. On the other hand, you don't hear men saying, 'No she's not pretty, but is she ever funny!'" Horse women do not mix with particularly "girly" girls who often make them the subject of their jealous fixations, this starts in high school but its effects are often lasting. However, this doesn't prevent them from being highly popular, they just seek out non-judgmental people who are surprised by their down to earth nature. Cindy Crawford said, "The other models looked at me with a little too much awe like, "Oh my God, I've been your biggest fan for over 20 years!" And I'm like, 'How old are you? Shut up!'"

Merging the intellectual side with the freedom seeking instinctual creature makes for a high achiever connected to the physical world but also the non-physical world. They set their standards exceptionally high and so the rest of the world seems to hold them to this standard, which annoys the Horse Pisces to no end. Cindy Crawford has said, "Even I don't look like Cindy

Crawford in the morning." Unfortunately, what this does is create a nervous tension inside them and a worry that they are not doing their best or letting people down. Joanne Woodward said, "I'm going to have to stop giving interviews because I'm always saying the wrong thing. I don't want that to happen."

Ultimately, they strive to live according to their ethical standpoint and try to find friends and partners who are aligned with their values. This is very important to them. Catherine O'Hara said, "I think the success of my work stems from being truthful." Similarly, Baltasar Kormákur said, "I'm not tempted to sell out. If I'm going to become well known, I want it to be for something I'm proud of." They live lives of honest hard work. Many are drawn to science, math and technology because of their pioneering ideas and exceptional mental faculties. But whatever they choose to do, they will put 100 percent of their heart into it.

Soul Mate:	Sheep-Libra
Challenger:	Rat-Virgo
Siblings:	Horse-Cancer, Horse-Scorpio
Best Friends:	Tiger-Cancer, Tiger-Scorpio, Tiger-Pisces, Dog-Cancer, Dog-Scorpio, Dog-Pisces

Jensen Ackles
Zack Snyder
Ron Howard
Téa Leoni
Billy Zane
Catherine O'Hara
Madison Riley
Anthony Head
Geoffrey Arend
Jennifer Grant
Lauren Ambrose

Alexis Denisof
Jay Hernandez
Baltasar Kormákur
Ben Miller
Donal Logue
Andrea Bowen
Nick Zano
Brooke Burns
Cindy Crawford
Joanne Woodward
Mia Michaels

THE SHEEP

THE SHEEP

I am the social artist, the subconscious scientist, the compassionate innovator. My calmness, tender countenance and warmth invite all to love me. That is why I am often family favorite, the golden child, the chosen one. Though I may seem docile and malleable, I let you think what you want so that your needs are met and I can be free to be unconventional me. I experience the greatest *me* in my daydreams, for it extends the self in this tangible realm. I am not easily understood for what I understand is the un-understandable. I am the connection to subconscious worlds, to unknown realms and to divine plans. I feel it, I sense it, and then I know it. I pull magic from my dreams and manifest it into tangible reality. I take my intuitive esotericism and add it to my emotional awareness to become the ultimate human behavior expert. Though I can be spoilt, frivolous and expensive, you will never feel more at home than when I am there, for I am *home*, I am comfort, I am your woolen security blanket...and I'm worth it.

I am the Sheep!

Warm, gentle and caring, you are the heart of the twelve signs. Sophisticated and cultured with a great flair for aesthetics. Naturally insecure, you need love and encouragement to truly excel. Domestically oriented, yet you have extensive creative abilities as a result of being the sign most connected with the subconscious. Non-confrontational, innocent and hypersensitive, some may feel like they need to treat you with kid gloves, this isn't necessary. Always on the look out for bad intentions, you use your heightened powers of objectivity to figure out someone's true goal and assess their personality on that. Smart and well groomed, you are never short of admirers or protectors.

Career wise, the Sheep is a highly tuned dreaming machine

that serves by bring new ideas into this real world by channelling the gods. Sometimes they do this consciously, but most of the time, it is an unconscious process so they do so through their art, especially in their written work. Highly sensitive and natural nurturing, they also make great social workers and caretakers. Arts, technology, social work and the esoteric are the places these non-confrontational creatures feel most comfortable. They like to be in groups but also recognized for their individual creative contributions. Despite their work environment, as long as you treat everything a Sheep person does as art, they will be putty in your hands. In conventional workplaces, the Sheep is often undermined or overlooked because their processes are not the same as other peoples. They are relationship builders and know how to leverage them to improve their productivity. But more conventional signs may miss their contributions and try to push them to conform which only dissipates the magic they can otherwise create.

Compatibilities

Soul Mate:	HorseA
Challenger:	Ox
Best Friends:	Rabbit & Boar
Good Relations:	Dragon & Snake

SHEEP – ARIES

Chinese Name: YÁNG
Rank: 8th
Hours Ruled: 1pm – 3pm
Direction: South – Southwest
Season: Summer
Month: July
Western Zodiac Equivalent of Sheep: Cancer
Cancer Western Element: Water
Eastern Zodiac Equivalent of Aries: Dragon
Aries Western Element: Fire
Numerology: 85 = 4

Son, give 'em a good show, and always travel first class.
– Walter Huston

Aries's fire is very welcome to push the creative, watery Sheep onwards and upwards. This combination acknowledges the virtues of its talents and knows how to apply them. Aries gives the combination more self-belief and drive to get out there to use any special abilities without letting their inner voice be a fierce obstruction. Many of them are introverted, intelligent and artistic and their physical appearance reflects this. Refined, smart and opinionated, they allow people to think that they can bend and mold them into any form, whilst their true self lives on unscathed, happily inside. This is until a line is crossed then this Ram's horn starts getting ready for a brawl. Generally though, it is the Sheep's low burning candlelight and generous heart that typifies this combination. Leonard Nimoy said, "I believe in goodness, mercy and charity. I believe in casting bread upon the waters."

If you know this combination well, you will know that they often seem a little spoiled, being the darlings of the family structure, they are often given gifts, accolades and pet names that others in the family are not. It is not their fault they are so wonderful that they elicit this response. But if you really, really know this combination, you will know that they do not care about the extra frivolities they are often showered with outside the basics: food, shelter and love. Truth be told, they don't really even need the food and shelter as long as they get the love. They can live on love alone. Despite outward appearances, they have a huge amount of empathy for all types of people, regardless of their wrong doings, especially for animals and children. They themselves manage to retain something of their own childlike innocence even into their old age and never entirely allow external influences to encroach upon their personal bohemian little world. Kate Hudson has said, "I'm a hippie at heart. I wear the clothes, and they're the best. And the music is incredible, too." Similarly, Norah Jones said, "I'm not melancholy; I'm a happy-go-lucky person, kind of silly…I tend to like music that's mellow, though."

Keeping with this theme, Christopher Walken has also revealed his hippie side as he has said, "Guns make me very nervous. They're dangerous. I'm more of a pacifist than anyone could imagine." The watery Sheep side of this personality that encourages peace, harmony and raw living may take the lead more often than Aries forceful fires.

There is a balancing act that takes place as this personality understands the power that image and reputation has, but at the same time fights for authenticity without perceived loss of face or potentially revealing their level of insecurity. So the ideal thing to do is to say very little and do not affirm anyone's specific idea. Keep them guessing and even if they guess right, they'll never know for sure. This is one technique they have learned to umbrella them from the scrutiny of others that they fear so much. Claire Danes has said, "Extreme self-doubt is only attractive when it's fictionalized." Yet, the Aries side of their personality does not cease pushing out there because it believes that if they are not improving, they are regressing. Heath Ledger said, "I like to be afraid of the project. I always am. When I get cast in something, I always believe I shouldn't have been cast. I fooled them again. I can't do it. I don't know how to do it. There's a huge amount of anxiety that drowns out any excitement I have toward the project."

Planning their diaries is better handled by someone else as they naturally prefer to live in the moment and leave organizing the future until it arrives. Heath Ledger said, "I'm not good at future planning. I don't plan at all. I don't know what I'm doing tomorrow. I don't have a day planner and I don't have a diary. I completely live in the now, not in the past, not in the future." And if they do try and get their dates in order, the universe does not like to comply. Claire Danes has said, "I'm trying not to make any plans, because when I do, everything goes wrong." Similarly, Christopher Walken said, "At its best, life is completely unpredictable." That's how Sheep-Aries prefer to live, expecting surprises every new day.

The men of this combination tend to be tall, slim, some may say a "weedy" and usually dark haired. Tender generous and creative hidden in a crispy thin shell that is easy to crack through. That Sheep sensitivity is somewhat protected by Aries need for movement and progression, so the men of this combination get hurt but stay in motion anyway. Life is a mystery and they just want to get inside it. Heath Ledger said, "I just want to stay curious." An interesting note is that both Leonard Nimoy and William Shatner of Star Trek belonged to this combination.

The women are hyper-feminine beauties with exceptional self-awareness who charm everyone with their intelligence and star quality. Their sexiness comes from their authenticity they do not try to be anything they are not. Reba McEntire has said, "Being a strong woman is very important to me... I can get kind of spunky or I can get tough, you know that kind of tough, sexy look. But sexy? No, I don't think so. Just what you see is what you get on me. And it's never been anything of a sexual nature."

Ultimately, the Sheep-Aries is not created to carry out routine work, as long as there is a level of autonomy and a creative component, they tend to do very well in any work environment, even corporate environments which do not generally suit the Sheep temperament. In fact, Sheep-Aries are often found at the higher end of the hierarchical structure. The reason for this? They are easy to get along with, present as exceptionally capable and they know when to keep their mouths closed. Plus...Reba McEntire has said, "To succeed in life, you need three things: a wishbone, a backbone and a funny bone... Be different, stand out, and work your butt off."

Soul Mate:	Horse-Virgo
Challenger:	Ox-Libra
Siblings:	Sheep-Leo, Sheep-Sagittarius
Best Friends:	Rabbit-Aries, Rabbit-Leo, Rabbit-Sagittarius, Boar-Aries, Boar-Leo, Boar-Sagittarius

Claire Danes
Heath Ledger
Maria Bello
Lake Bell
Kate Hudson
Christopher Walken
Lee Pace
Brendan Gleeson
Leonard Nimoy
Amanda Michalka
William Shatner

Michel Hazanavicius
Natasha Lyonne
Lindy Booth
Matthew Ziff
Lena Olin
Jamie Lynn Spears
Marina Sirtis
Reba McEntire
Jonathan Firth
Kristine Sutherland
Norah Jones
Paul Nicholls
David Janssen
Walter Huston

SHEEP – TAURUS

Chinese Name: YÁNG
Rank: 8th
Hours Ruled: 1pm – 3pm
Direction: South – Southwest
Season: Summer
Month: July
Western Zodiac Equivalent of Sheep: Cancer
Cancer Western Element: Water
Eastern Zodiac Equivalent of Taurus: Snake
Taurus Western Element: Earth
Numerology: 86 = 5

When the reviews are bad I tell my staff that they can join me as I cry all the way to the bank.
– Liberace

When the Sheep's sea of serenity washes over Taurus's tough rough earth granules, the result is a soft fertile ground in which any seedling flourishes; the Sheep's creativity is given a firm hand so this Sheep native is more disciplined than many others so is able to develop its craft to an exceptionally high standard without losing any of its innate innocent charm. They make their decisions from their heart but employ their earthy common sense when making their action plan. Add to that the bull's resilient spirit that would prefer to die rather than not reach its goal; the Sheep-Taurus seldom fails at anything. Smart, savvy and sincere, the people belonging to this combination do not attempt to be anything other than what they are. They do not need to be. Their power lies in their simple being; they just need to be because that is when they shine…as long as they ignore that inner critic that might try to convince them that they are not enough. Maybe that's why Katherine Hepburn had said, "I never lose sight of the fact that just being is fun."

Taking this notion further, it seems that their way of life is not something that they develop by accident; it is actually more of a conscious construct; they train themselves to remain as present as possible, feel as alive as they can and to enjoy every second they are blessed with. Because this way of life is relatively unfiltered by social conventions, they are often intuitively led to unconventional places and by societies norms, may live within somewhat eccentric circumstances. Luckily for them, they soon become accustomed to being unusual so learn to manage their individual situation. Bollywood superstar Madhuri Dixit has said, "I'm not interested in living up to the expectations and fantasies of 900 million human beings. If someone thinks I'm cold, fine. I'm not here to clarify anyone's assumptions about me." Similarly, Katherine Hepburn had said, "Never complain. Never explain." They do not feel the need to explain their behavior, to do so would be to indirectly suggest that there was something wrong with it. Remember they are consciously aware of themselves, how they are being perceived and how everybody else in the room is doing. It's a very Sheep thing!

They are also intelligent types and often do well in academia although, inevitably, they return to do what inspires them. People of this combination, more than most, must do something that they are passionate about otherwise their lives become stale, boring and small – all the color drains from their lives and they feel like zombies; they must-must-must do something that they love otherwise their life becomes unbearable. As Katherine Hepburn said, "Life is to be lived. If you have to support yourself, you had bloody well better find some way that is going to be interesting."

The men of this combination tend to be open, warm and typically "good boys." James McAvoy has said, "I was talking to one of my aunties at Christmas and she said she didn't think it was ever in my nature to go against the grain, that I was always a good boy. I think she was right – I did always want to be good." Despite what they look like on the surface, they usually have a soft mushy core over which they layer a personality of strength and control that fools nobody. These "boys" are clearly tenderhearted individuals who have a lot of love to give but don't know how to give it without submitting to the will of their partner. Whether they are heavy metal rock musicians or flamboyant Liberaces, it must be said, music tends to play an important role in this Sheep's existence. There are many, many Sheep-Taurus musicians and they tend to be pretty successful. Elaborating on his famous saying, Liberace said, "You know that bank I used to cry all the way to? I bought it."

The women of this combination are feminine, fiery and feisty. The Taurean earth gives this Sheep woman a need to be sophisticated, independent and in charge of their faculties. Bollywood superstar Madhuri Dixit has said, "Depend on yourself and you will never be let down." They also carry out their work to the highest possible standards using their imagination to find innovative ideas that delight and surprise the masses. Donatella Versace said, "Creativity comes from a conflict of ideas." They like to work with the best in any industry and are not afraid to take charge when necessary, doing so with unwavering focus and power. This is a gentle Sheep lady fused with and fuelled by the powerful Taurean Bull! Eva Peron said, "I know that, like every woman of the people, I have more strength than I appear to have."

Ultimately, the Sheep-Taurus has sharper corners than other Sheep combinations. There is a latent aggression that rears its head unexpectedly and like the Bull, intends to destroy its target. Usually this behavior comes as a defense or when they feel undermined. But ultimately, this is one of those combinations that learns to manage its esteem, prioritizes according to its hearts true desires and chases down its dream in a premeditated way. Success is inevitable. That is why Debra Winger has also said, "I am one of the happiest people I know. And that's a weird place to have arrived at from being a depressed Jewish kid." They wait and watch and learn the game in detail. Then they prepare in silence whilst continuing to wait and watch until an opening appears that makes their intuition chime; that's how they know that the time has come to take action. Once in the game, they climb the ladder quickly, yet quietly. One wonders what they did, when they did it and how did they do it so fast. The Sheep-Aries is not a patient creature, despite presenting as such, once the goal has been decided; the bull is off while the Sheep holds on for dear life. As Katherine Hepburn said, "If you obey all the rules you miss all the fun."

Soul Mate:	Horse-Leo
Challenger:	Ox-Scorpio
Siblings:	Sheep-Virgo, Sheep-Capricorn
Best Friends:	Rabbit-Taurus, Rabbit-Virgo, Rabbit-Capricorn, Boar-Taurus, Boar-Virgo, Boar-Capricorn

Katharine Hepburn
Fred Zinnemann
Liberace
Eva Perón
Michael Palin
Bill Paxton
Debra Winger
Yun-Fat Chow
Donatella Versace
Lynne Spears
Sherri Shepherd

Tim McGraw
Ana Gasteyer
Madhuri Dixit
James McAvoy
Rosario Dawson
Jaime King
Jordan Pruitt
Rudolph Valentino

SHEEP – GEMINI

Chinese Name: YÁNG
Rank: 8th
Hours Ruled: 1pm – 3pm
Direction: South – Southwest
Season: Summer
Month: July
Western Zodiac Equivalent of Sheep: Cancer
Cancer Western Element: Water
Eastern Zodiac Equivalent of Gemini: Horse
Gemini Western Element: Air
Numerology: 87 = 6

If you've got them by the balls their hearts and minds will follow.
– John Wayne

When the serene waters of the sensitive Sheep meet Gemini's hectic hurricane, the sophisticated woolly artist meets the tangy twins, fusing this personality, with intelligence, conscience and spunk. They feel compelled to make something of their natural talent because they just know their energy can bring light to the masses and could have a positive impact. So they plod along taking a number of unnecessary detours, bit by bit, as they struggle with their esteem, history and their wonderfulness until they finally achieve their dream...only to experience nothing more than a fleeting victory. The Sheep-Gemini knows that reality is a mixed bag, there is light and dark in every bean and life moves on without ceremony. Sir Laurence Olivier said, "Living is strife and torment, disappointment and love and sacrifice, golden sunsets and black storms."

Yet they remain Jolly and cheerful, they thrive in social settings and are often the life and soul of the party. But there is much more to them than just the party animal that people see. Noel Gallagher has said, "I'm a happy-go-lucky character. I'm not that miserable. But I can never let anyone into my world." Perhaps not the best example, as Sheep-Geminis are usually smiley people with a glint in their eyes, but scratch beneath the surface and you will find a sensitive heart that longs for connection. One assumes that they are more open than they actually are because of their willingness to discuss their own lives, but push a little and you will realize that the shutters were down all along; exploration of their inner selves just isn't as dangerous to them as it is for other people. So what is dangerous to them? Sheep signs are the most connected to their subconscious world and that is why there are so many artists, psychics and pioneers belonging to this sign, this tendency gives them greater access to information and it is this that keeps them pushing for growth and development in cutting-edge ways. Tim Berners-Lee is credited with creating the internet and he belongs to this clan. Staying on top of that development is what thrills and intimidates this combination. As John Wayne said, "Courage is being scared to death...and saddling up anyway." The reason for this is that there is no better or faster way to grow and most importantly, live with a sense of integrity.

Being so sensitive, they sometimes struggle with making difficult decisions; they could to and fro endlessly and write an eternal 'pros and cons' list so the universe teaches them the lesson of *surrender* early on in their journey. Nicole Kidman has said, "When you relinquish the desire to control your future, you can have more happiness." Yes, there is a potent spirituality that some Sheep-Geminis choose to develop while other repress it altogether. Usually, the Sheep-Gemini is an energy giver, but sometimes they have a tendency to take beyond what is appropriate, a few even earning "parasite" status.

The men of this combination are highly sensitive, sensual beings which gives them their natural affinity for performance art. Despite the jolliness on the surface, they have a tendency to focus on the negative and may have intermittent spells of pessimism. Meditation can help lift them out of their funk. One of the most prominent actors of all time Sir Laurence Olivier belongs to this combination; he said, "I take a simple view of life: keep your eyes open and get on with it." That could almost be the Sheep-Gemini male's manifesto. It may come as no surprise that people of this combination have a natural talent for mimicry and picking up accents. Sir Laurence Olivier said, "We ape, we mimic, we mock. We act." They love physical play, whether theatrically, vocally or in sport. They can access energetic forces from other worlds so have a greater need to release or channel it, so they will be drawn to methods that suit them best.

The women of this combination tend to be slight, dainty with sparkling innocent eyes and radiant smiles. There is an effortless sex appeal and femininity that other girls do not find threatening, possibly because they value their intelligence more than their looks. They are classy, generous and loving. Their impact is subtle yet strong and they strive for authenticity in everything they do, even though they may not always succeed. Nicole Kidman has said, "You don't have to be naked to be sexy." This could be changed to: you just have to be a Sheep-Gemini to be sexy! Like all Sheep signs, they are highly sensitive and struggle with the powerful currents of feeling that flow through their veins. Nicole Kidman has said, "I would describe myself as emotional and highly strung. If something upsets me, it really upsets me. If something makes me angry, I get really angry. But it's all very upfront. I can't hide it." This is another reason why so many are drawn to spiritual pursuits as it helps them to moderate their overflowing feelings. Whatever happens, they are never short of people to turn to as these women attract protectors throughout their lives, even though they don't really need them.

Despite their seeming ease in the social realm, they do not always consider themselves successful in this area as they secretly feel odd, strange and unusual. Maybe that is why Barry Manilow said, "Misfits aren't misfits among other misfits." Artists often speak about feeling misunderstood and tend to find friends who share their predilections. They do know that they are blessed with certain talents and gifts; when they consciously choose to honor their blessings, the heavens open, the seas part to support them in their goal to achieve the highest artistry possible. Barry Manilow said, "Yeah, I'm old as the hills and you would think I'd be out to pasture someplace because I've done everything, but nothing has changed."

Soul Mate:	Horse-Cancer
Challenger:	Ox-Sagittarius
Siblings:	Sheep-Libra, Sheep-Aquarius
Best Friends:	Rabbit-Gemini, Rabbit-Libra, Rabbit-Aquarius, Boar-Gemini, Boar-Libra, Boar-Aquarius

John Wayne
Laurence Olivier
Nicole Kidman
Barry Manilow
Laurie Metcalf
Noel Gallagher
Uta Hagen
Jack Albertson –
Rosalind Russell
Betty Garrett
Richard Todd
Gene Barry
Carroll Baker
Malcolm McDowell

Sharon Gless
Leslie Uggams
Henry Hill
Cilla Black
Arlene Phillips
William Forsythe
Dana Carvey
Sandra Bernhard
Rosanne Cash
Kiron Kher
Paul O'Grady
Dale Winton
Paul Giamatti
Dan Futterman
Paul Gascoigne
Morena Baccarin
Tim Berners-Lee

SHEEP – CANCER

Chinese Name: YÁNG
Rank: 8th
Hours Ruled: 1pm – 3pm
Direction: South – Southwest
Season: Summer
Month: July
Western Zodiac Equivalent of Sheep: Cancer
Cancer Western Element: Water
Eastern Zodiac Equivalent of Cancer: Sheep
Cancer Western Element: Water
Numerology: 88 = 7

I have an underdog spirit in me, and now it feels weird to
kind of get my own way more often than not.
– Mindy Kaling

When the Sheep's gentle river meets Cancer's quietly ferocious rapids, they merge together effortlessly because they are two separate sides of the same coin; the Sheep is the Eastern equivalent of the Cancer and vice versa. When the potency of this same sign compounds, power, confidence and an uninhibitedness is added to the basic Sheep character. The regular Sheep traits are amplified also, so they have even greater emotional intelligence, greater sensitivity and even greater creative ability. Writer, actress and comedienne Mindy Kaling has said, "I never want to be called the funniest Indian female comedian that exists. I feel like I can go head-to-head with the best white, male comedy writers that are out there. Why would I want to self-categorize myself into a smaller group than I'm able to compete in?"

This Sheep is also not so afraid to take charge, genuinely attempting to serve in a way that benefits the majority; however, most Sheep signs do not have the courage of their convictions and let other people take the lead, only to regret it later. That tendency is still here with the Sheep-Cancer, but because they think ahead as well as in between the cracks and edges of the potential consequences of their decisions, they figure, that they might as well be at the decision table seeing as their thinking process is more advanced and their decisions are likely to be better thought out than everyone else's...so why not put them on the throne? Better them than some egotistical half-wit! This thinking process is what makes them powerful. All Sheep are led by their intuition; the Sheep-Cancer is led by its intuition times 100! Will Ferrell has said, "I used to worry that I wasn't crazy enough to succeed in comedy. Or troubled enough. In the beginning, people were surprised that a seemingly mild-mannered person could bring a script or a character to life."

The men of this combination are big children, in a positive and in a negative sense. They are so in touch with their inner child, they know how to be present and spend most of their lives in a form of play creating a light, happy, joy-filled environment to be in. Actor Willem Dafoe has said, "My impulses are the impulses of a child. I like being the thing itself... It's just that my real pleasure, where I feel vital and everything drops away, is when I'm in the middle of doing it, and I look for that opportunity untainted by other responsibilities." Conversely, despite being able to think at a level most others are not, when it comes down to it, this spoilt boy wants what it wants and wants it now! This ram is both very masculine and very feminine but not simultaneously. When the situation requires it the yang will surface otherwise, they prefer to allow the yin side to be more prominent generally. And this is especially true the older they get. Vin Dielsel has said, "With age, you get to a place where you don't want to knock people out. You just want to give people a hug."

The women of this combination are hyper-feminine-princesses.

The Sheep is the most feminine sign in the Chinese cycle and this is the double Sheep or double Cancer sign; however you look at it, this combination has more feminine yin energy than any other. That is why the ladies belonging to this clan are uber-feminine, busty, with beautiful thick long hair and childbearing hips. Like the men, they also find it difficult to say *no* to immediate gratification, despite the consequences. They struggle with themselves as a result, but that does not detract from their self-knowledge and desire to inspire others, especially other women. Pamela Anderson has said, "The true meaning of feminism is this: to use your strong womanly image to gain strong results in society." The Sheep-Cancer woman knows the meaning of friendship and really enjoys being able to play emotional caretaker, counselor and psychiatrist to her loved ones. Perhaps that is why Mindy Kaling has said, "Personally, I, Mindy Kaling want to spend like 80 percent of my life hanging out with women."

Ultimately, the Sheep-Cancer is an ambitious creature with great confidence in its own abilities. This they develop in private and may be slow to expand upon, even though their powerful inner guidance is encouraging them early on in their lives. Cancer does two things to the Sheep that are contradictory; it amplifies its insecurities but gives it the tools to manage them. Speaking about an internal tension that he struggles to deal with, Willem Defoe has said, "It's just this intense tickle in the back of my throat. It's like I'm on the verge the whole time I'm walking over that bridge, and I'm not going to get a release until I jump." When they think, they tend to overthink, so they learn to do the thinking during the preparation phase so that they can create parameters within which they are free to roam because that is where the fun of life is for them. They also learn to become comfortable with their discomfort and push themselves to grow. Despite their skills, their talent and their power, they like to present themselves as just someone in the crowd, but they do recognize that what they bring to the table is exceptionally valuable. That is why they are prepared to work so hard. They do not like to let others or themselves down. At the same time, they take themselves and life with a pinch of salt because, with that exceptionally perceptive mind, they see the truth of life – that we are all connected, we are all one and life is fun, if you let the fun be had. Will Ferrell has said, "I'm no tortured, anger-stoked, deeply neurotic comic. Just a pretty low-key normal guy. 'Hey, the glass is half-full,' kind of a guy. But please keep it quiet, or I may never work again."

Soul Mate:	Horse-Gemini
Challenger:	Ox-Capricorn
Siblings:	Sheep-Scorpio, Sheep-Pisces
Best Friends:	Rabbit-Cancer, Rabbit-Scorpio, Rabbit-Pisces, Boar-Cancer, Boar-Scorpio, Boar-Pisces

Vin Diesel
Will Ferrell
Willem Dafoe
Pamela Anderson
Jayma Mays
Mindy Kaling
Shane Filan
Gil Bellows
Fred Norris
Kurtwood Smith
Edward Herrmann
Busy Philipps
Rosemary Forsyth
Wendy Richard
Geraldo Rivera
Robert Arnold
Harvey Miller

SHEEP – LEO

Chinese Name: YÁNG
Rank: 8th
Hours Ruled: 1pm – 3pm
Direction: South – Southwest
Season: Summer
Month: July
Western Zodiac Equivalent of Sheep: Cancer
Cancer Western Element: Water
Eastern Zodiac Equivalent of Leo: Monkey
Leo Western Element: Fire
Numerology: 89 = 8

My secrets must be poetic to be believable.
– Mick Jagger

When the Sheep's gentle river meets the lion's raging inferno, a fight ensues; the water tries to tame the fire and the fire wants to consume the water. But the Leo fire is more prominent here and is like a greasy, sticky fire that does eventually control the water, fuelling the fire further, somewhat negating the water element's influence; the creativity, sensitivity and empathy of the water element remains but adds to the aggressive proactivity of the fire. This is why this specific Sheep combination is known for creating legends like Mick Jagger, Robert Dinero and Supermodel Iman. Being that the Sheep is the patron of the arts and is driven to serve its sensual desires and the Leo's ego requires constant attention, a life in the performing arts is common for this combination. They are drawn to the mass adoration, affirmation and opportunity to showcase their innate talents. They are also drawn to the decadent, hedonistic lifestyle in which they happily indulge. As Mick Jagger has said, "Anything worth doing is worth overdoing."

It is safe to say that the Sheep-Leo is pretty anti-establishment and they have a laissez faire attitude to life...until they have children and then they start seeing 360 degrees of the sphere. But even then, this special brand of water-fire gives them the confidence to air their individual voice and make what are deemed, socially controversial choices, yet they are forgiven, remain popular and unanimously adored. Billy Bob Thornton has said, "...I'm not real crazy about the Hollywood system. So the fact that they embrace me is a shock to me because I tell them to kiss my ass all the time. I don't understand why they haven't thrown me out on my ear."

The men of this combination tend to have big bulbous lips with a cheeky lost boy attitude. This could actually be one of the most sexy male combinations. The Sheep side knows how to make one feel at ease, while that Leo side is all animal. They also know how to provide for themselves and their family because they are money-motivated and they are not afraid to say it. Mick Jagger has said, "I came into music just because I wanted the bread. It's true. I looked around and this seemed like the only way I was going to get the kind of bread I wanted." Money is freedom to the Sheep-Leo, they will worry their woolly socks off until they have so much in the bank that they do not have to think about it anymore; then they will allow that inner child to have all the toys its dreamed of. It suits Sheep signs (male and female) to have money and they just know how to attract it into their life. Robert Di Nero has said, "Money makes your life easier. If you're lucky to have it, you're lucky."

The women of this combination are effortlessly elegant, unusually attractive and psychologically strong. They take the talents of the Sheep and add the Leo's confidence; they take the strengths of the Leo and add the Sheep's sensitivity; all in all becoming broadly rounded characters with great psychological understanding. Both signs are generous and know how to serve others, so in the female form, this need to give becomes quite pronounced and they need to consciously learn to come to a state of balance regarding it. Actress Rose Byrne has said, "I'm allowing myself to be a bit more selfish, for want of a better word, just that it's OK to focus and that I don't have to be nice to everybody." Both signs are strong in different ways, but when they come together these strengths are complimentary and allow them to excel in a variety of different environments. This lady is no fool and she does not present herself as one either. She is feisty, funny yet open enough to reach anybody on any level if she so chooses to. The Sheep-Leo lady knows that her energy is valuable so shares it only with people she deems worthy of her time. Speaking about dating, Evangeline Lily has said, "I'm very picky when it comes to men. I come across a man who I'm really attracted to about once every five years."

Considering the number of Sheep-Leos who have reached the pinnacle of their careers, usually that others use as the yardstick, the members of this clan remain relatively humble about it. Perhaps not immediately, but eventually as they realize the futility of fame. Robert Di Nero has said, "I do not consider myself some sort of acting legend, just an actor doing his best with the material that is there at the time." Speaking about remaining present so that new creative discoveries can be continuously made, Mick Jagger said, "I am not a librarian of my own work. It's a good thing not to be too involved with what you have done."

Ultimately, the Sheep-Leo is gentle seeming personality that is hugely ambitious. Like all Sheep signs, they must follow their passions because they will lose interest in anything that they don't love and will eventually fail at it. Speaking about his early days as an Actor, Philip Seymour-Hoffman said, "Not only couldn't I get a job as an actor, I couldn't hold down the temporary non-acting jobs I managed to get. I got fired as a waiter in restaurants and as a lifeguard at a spa." But when Sheep-Leos choose their passion, deal with their insecurities and allow themselves to accept their own greatness, success comes to them from all angles. They learn, they grow and they flourish when they allow their creative persuasions to take a lead. Anything less diminishes their artistic soul and cages this beast when all it wants to do is roam wild, play and share its light. The Sheep-Leo just wants to have fun with everyone, let it, because if it doesn't follow its heart, if it cannot play, if it cannot be artistic, a piece of it dies and their light dims. As Mick Jagger has said, "Lose your dreams and you might lose your mind." Dream dear Sheep-Leo and show the world how dreams are made manifest!

Soul Mate:	Horse-Taurus
Challenger:	Ox-Aquarius
Siblings:	Sheep-Aries, Sheep-Sagittarius
Best Friends:	Rabbit-Aries, Rabbit-Leo, Rabbit-Sagittarius, Boar-Aries, Boar-Leo, Boar-Sagittarius

Robert De Niro
Philip Seymour Hoffman
Billy Bob Thornton
Matt LeBlanc
Rose Byrne
Evangeline Lilly
Iman
Mick Jagger
Carrie-Anne Moss
Ty Burrell
Adewale Akinnuoye-Agbaje
Peter Gallagher
Paul Greengrass
Sylvester McCoy

SHEEP – VIRGO

Chinese Name: YÁNG
Rank: 8th
Hours Ruled: 1pm – 3pm
Direction: South – Southwest
Season: Summer
Month: July
Western Zodiac Equivalent of Sheep: Cancer
Cancer Western Element: Water
Eastern Zodiac Equivalent of Virgo: Rooster
Virgo Western Element: Earth
Numerology: 90 = 9

When I was in seventh grade my mom caught me smoking cigarettes and punished me by making me smoke the entire carton. All it did was piss me off because I was out of cigarettes.
– Pink

When the Sheep's gentle river meets Virgo's fertile earth, the ewe's powerful creative currents are handled by the virgin's powerful mental processor. As soon as a creative impulse hits, it's like they just know what to do with it, where to take it and how to turn it into *art*. However, most Sheep signs are susceptible to outside influences. It is wise for them to be encouraged, cajoled and pushed to try as many different creative pursuits as possible from a young age in order help them find their passion. They are more than capable of making money from their creative skills. Harry Connick Jr. has said, "Everything I do is part of my passion. I do the things I like to do. It's sort of a bigger version of having more than one hobby. I love to play piano, sing, and act. I love to do all those things."

This combination is much less unconventional than other

Sheep signs and they strive to live as full a life as they can by observing how their peers live and choosing what they like most rather than listening to their gut early on. It takes them some time to acclimatize to who they really are because that Virgo critic sometimes gets too much airtime. Although they are Sheep signs, they don't always have that scatty, high and lost disposition because they are smart enough to get someone to handle those things for them. Harry Connick Jr. has said, "I mean, you know, you're looking at a guy who has a manager, who's created a life for me that – I mean, I don't pay phone bills and electric bills. I have somebody to do that for me."

Dignified, loving and emotional, it is important for them to make their relational bonds early and commit to them. That is because they seek stability first and foremost, if they have that in a relationship, they are content as everything else is secondary icing. Anne Bancroft said, "If you marry the wrong person for the wrong reasons, then no matter how hard you work, it's never going to work." Those with artistic inclinations usually suffer with fluctuating esteem so they need a rock that will love them and save them from todays new demon. When they find that someone who knows how to manage them at their self-pitying worse, they will commit. Larry Hagman said, "I have been married for 58 years to the same woman. Our secret? Separate bathrooms."

The gentlemen tend to be tall and alpha looking, but they are not, actually they are much more feminine that the first glance would suggest. Their intellect, gentleness and creative spirit can be sniffed a mile off. They also have the Sheep's esoteric wisdom and Virgo's poise. More emotional than one might expect, they understand complicated situations and are surprisingly nurturing for men. Harry Connick Jr. said, "I've raised my girls in a sort of genderless fashion. I mean, I'll take them to get their nails done – I actually love doing that – but I also play ball with them. As a result, my girls are tough and athletic and game for everything." They are tenderhearted and do not handle rejection easily so may avoid putting themselves on the line to begin with. Blending in with their social group is such a big deal for them because inwardly, that Sheep spirit is a strange one. But Virgo needs social affirmation, so the Sheep-Virgo treads an awkward line of wanting to blend in and wanting to be seen as special. This is why they sometimes fall into a pattern of projecting images of what they think people want. Confident, in-control and cool in particular. Larry Hagman said, "Well I think they broke the mold when they made me and being humble is one of my great assets."

The ladies of this combination are just that, ladies with a sexy, feisty attitude that belies their insecurity, uncertainties and woes. Singer Pink has said, "People are always so surprised when they meet me. Firstly, that I'm 'so tiny,' and secondly that I'm 'so sweet'. They seem surprised that they're not scared of me." Sheep-Virgos are beautiful, multi-talented and blessed with distinctive voices. Many born with this combination are also prominent singers, many act and dance too. Multi-talented and multi-faceted, these types have star quality but they tend to be shy about it so they might not shine as bright as they could without outside intervention and esteem building. Speaking about self-acceptance in Hollywood, Anne Bancroft said, "I was at a point where I was ready to say I am what I am because of what I am and if you like me I'm grateful, and if you don't, what am I going to do about it?" It is not easy to manage the two signs contained here as they are very different. One is dreamer living in Neverland and the other wants to climb the ladder of success rung by rung, without causing a commotion.

Ultimately, the Sheep-Virgo is a tenderhearted creature that prioritizes its personal life before its professional one, which is both a gift and curse as some may take any job just to pay the bills being that they are fulfilled by their romantic and family life, but this prevents their creative magnificence to ever be see the light of day. They are also likely to have a greater level of emotional intelligence than most because of the Sheep will bring forth all of this emotional data which the Virgo will analyze and categorize accordingly. This of course lends itself to spiritual understanding also. When they learn the art of surrender, this Sheep flows straight to success, albeit with a little joyful dillydallying along the way. Pink has said, "The willow is my favorite tree. I grew up near one. It's the most flexible tree in nature and nothing can break it – no wind, no elements, it can bend and withstand anything."

Soul Mate:	Horse-Aries
Challenger:	Ox-Pisces
Siblings:	Sheep-Taurus, Sheep-Capricorn
Best Friends:	Rabbit-Taurus, Rabbit-Virgo, Rabbit-Capricorn, Boar-Taurus, Boar-Virgo, Boar-Capricorn

Ariana Richards
Pink
Chad Brannon
Faith Hill
Jim Abbott
Harry Connick, Jr.
Maria Bartiromo
Robin Yount
Jeanne Robertson
Maria Muldaur
Lola Falana
Mickey Hart
Roger Waters

Valerie Perrine
Jean-Claude Killy
David Soul
Tuesday Weld
Larry Hagman
Anne Bancroft
George Jones
Fay Wray
Jesse James

SHEEP – LIBRA

Chinese Name: YÁNG
Rank: 8th
Hours Ruled: 1pm – 3pm
Direction: South – Southwest
Season: Summer
Month: July
Western Zodiac Equivalent of Sheep: Cancer
Cancer Western Element: Water
Eastern Zodiac Equivalent of Libra: Dog
Libra Western Element: Air
Numerology: 91 = 1

I don't believe in frontiers, and I don't believe in races or nationalities.
– Julio Iglesias

When the Sheep's gentle river meets Libra's cool breeze, genteel sophistication and good grace meets sharp perception and discipline. The Sheep brings its innocence, emotional intelligence and nurturance to the mix while the Libra brings its idealism, practicality and wit. Both signs are known for their open nature, ability to really listen and for their ethereal good looks. This part of the 144-combination cycle is both classy and cool so the combined signs here have a lot going for them; smart, attractive, understanding, quick learners, people's people and they have huge hearts too. They feel more, explore more and understand more, yet they do not judge…well they do, but they recognize their own judgments as a vulnerability of the human condition, so they separate these judgments into a box in their minds and keep a tab on them. This thinking process is what allows them to expand their understanding to the exceptional degree that they manage, why people feel so comfortable in their presence and why they have such amazing clarity. Yo-Yo Ma has said, "You have to keep both things in your head at once – the biggest possible picture and the most minute one – the 'right now'. Then you have access to both objective and subjective narratives, you have perspective, so you don't get lost."

What starts in their mind impacts their entire life and eventually, the lives of others. But their thought process requires greater exploration in order to understand this complicated combination. They are highly intelligent, sophisticated and super-empathic people, so empathic that it can be detrimental. The further they dig, the more questions they unearth and they become comfortable in the knowledge that there are no simple answers to anything. After trying to open people's eyes a few thousand times, they find that most people like to live in the dark. Speaking about his movie Kinsey based upon the life of biologist Alfred Kinsey (Horse-Gemini) who was the first person to undertake a scientific study into the varying shades of sexuality, director Bill Condon has said, "The idea of bisexuality, that everyone is somewhere along that sliding scale, is incredibly threatening today."

The Sheep-Libra questions everything, especially themselves, their own actions and their own intentions. This continues to develop their exceptional emotional intelligence at the same time as keeping them forever on the edge of their own self-esteem. It is unfortunate that these two aspects are the two sides of the same coin; you cannot have one without the other, they are mutually exclusive. Actor Guy Pearce has said, "You meet these people who are confident all the time. They annoy me. And I wonder if it's because I'm envious or if it's because they're shallow."

The men of this combination tend to be attractive in looks and personality. They are respectful, charming and delicate creatures who take great care to care greatly. Also, the way they look is not necessarily reflective of who they actually are. Speaking about his nickname since he was a child, Liev Schreiber has said, "It's not easy being 6' 3" and being called 'Huggy'." They have big hearts full of affection but which also need reciprocation. Having a strong partner who provides emotional security is important to them, despite how together or strong they might try to present. Plus, romance is the be all and end all for this woolly ram. Julio Iglesias has said, "I am a lover for sure. I love to be loved... Attraction is always the first thing, no? But love must be more than that. It must be magic." There is also something very old-skool about them. They are like beautiful human anachronisms, transported directly from the Victorian era into a world that sees them as relics, even though their minds are light years ahead. Liev Schreiber has said, "Style, no matter how outrageous it is, is still an expression of someone's personality. And my personality is somewhere stuck in the classics."

The women of this combination are the epitome of feminine grace. They are beautiful, elegant and gracious creatures who love nothing more than to be treated as such. This lady may present as if highly-strung and high maintenance, but actually, she is not. All she wants is for someone to love her regardless of her whines, insecurities and petty little games. Ignore them or call them out for what they are and she'll be impressed. Catherine Denueve has said, "People who know me know I'm strong, but I'm vulnerable." Although Libra is a Yang sign, the Sheep is the most Yin of all, so there is a lot of feminine energy here so she will be drawn to dominant masculine partners who can take charge whilst respecting her moral principles. Mira Sorvino has said, "There's a side of my personality that goes completely against the East Coast educated person and wants to be a pin-up girl in garages across America."

Ultimately, the Sheep-Libra is a complicated personality that is often misunderstood and finds itself being drawn into battles that it was not made for. Ironically, they often look like the instigating *troublemaker* when in actuality, they are anything but. It's just that they are so much more spiritually advanced that most people do not understand them. Also, because of their heightened spirituality, they are easy targets. However, the Sheep-Libra gets used to being misconstrued and develops their psychological muscles to deal with this and are prepared to fight back where necessary. But even these adversarial experiences open and unwrap this beautiful spirit further, until you can almost smell divinity. Yo-Yo Ma has said, "As you begin to realize that every different type of music, everybody's individual music, has its own rhythm, life, language and heritage, you realize how life changes, and you learn how to be more open and adaptive to what is around us."

Soul Mate:	Horse-Pisces
Challenger:	Ox-Aries
Siblings:	Sheep-Gemini, Sheep-Aquarius
Best Friends:	Rabbit-Gemini, Rabbit-Libra, Rabbit-Aquarius, Boar-Gemini, Boar-Libra, Boar-Aquarius

Bill Condon
Catherine Deneuve
Julio Iglesias
Yo-Yo Ma
Guy Pearce
Liev Schreiber
Chris O'Dowd
Mira Sorvino
Brandon Routh
Davina McCall
Desmond Tutu

Penny Marshall
Diana Dors
Angie Dickinson
Shammi Kapoor
Chevy Chase
Tanuja
Michael Morpurgo
Tanya Roberts
John Krasinski
Rachael Leigh Cook
Tyler Posey
Shawn Ashmore
Aaron Ashmore
Jedward

SHEEP – SCORPIO

Chinese Name: YÁNG
Rank: 8th
Hours Ruled: 1pm – 3pm
Direction: South – Southwest
Season: Summer
Month: July
Western Zodiac Equivalent of Sheep: Cancer
Cancer Western Element: Water
Eastern Zodiac Equivalent of Scorpio: Boar
Scorpio Western Element: Water
Numerology: 92 = 2

True love doesn't come to you it has to be inside you.
– Julia Roberts

When the Sheep's gentle stream meets Scorpio's murky river of mysteries, the Sheep's purity is diluted by its co-sign's darker nature. This is one of the more dominant Sheep combinations along with its sibling combinations (Sheep-Pisces and Sheep-Cancer), although this combination manages to keep its innocence, sophistication and emotional access, these creatures also more comfortable taking a leadership role. With the Sheep's ability to access the subconscious world and heightened skills of self-reflection coupled with the Scorpion's ambition, this combination will eventually be noticed and taken very seriously. The younger they take themselves seriously, the better, but whatever age they are, when they find the way that their heart most likes to serve, they will become obsessed by it. Director Mike Nichols has said, "There's nothing better than discovering, to your own astonishment, what you're meant to do. It's like falling in love… The reason you do this stuff – comedy, plays, movies – is to be seized by something, to disappear in the service of an idea."

Sheep signs are known for their artistic talent and almost all of them can learn to sing if they choose, but this combination, packed full of artists of various descriptions contains a significantly large number drawn to the musical arts; Joni Mitchell, Keith Urban, Ike Turner, David Guetta, Sharleen Spiteri, Sophie B. Hawkins, Tina Arena, even Vanilla Ice is a Sheep-Scorpio. Many of the actors are also musicians and singers also such as Juhi Chawla and Steve Zahn.

The men of this combination are drawn to the gentler, sophisticated and creative aspects of life. Where they will really excel is in occupations that require creativity and a large dose of psychological strength which they have developed through living with that tortured poet soul. This has the interesting by-product of keeping them on edge most of the time; yet, they seem to function best in this mode, or at least, find themselves at their most creative. Bill Gates has said, "In this business, by the time you realize you're in trouble, it's too late to save yourself. Unless you're running scared all the time, you're gone." Even music producer David Guetta has discussed this professional mode of functioning, he said, "When you're too relaxed it's not good to create."

Whether they recognize their emotional intelligence as a strength, it is most definitely so as it allows them to make smart decisions that bring them long term happiness that many other men seem incapable of achieving. Actor Mark Ruffalo has said, "I think of marriage as a garden. You have to tend to it. Respect it, take care of it, feed it. Make sure everyone is getting the right amount of, um, sunlight." It also lets them channel their masculine energy in productive ways because yin knows how to manage the masculine yang ego. They remove themselves from those who *talk the talk, but not walk the walk*, because they do not see the value they can contribute. They respect people who put themselves on the line. Borris Becker has also said, "I don't really care what the man on the street thinks. I never did anything to please him in the first place, and I'm not going to start now."

The women of this combination are the sweethearts of the land they inhabit. It is likely that they are the favored beauty, the darling of the family or the girl who seems to get special treatment from the people who matter. At the same time, they can be prickly creatures, because they have particular tastes and they are not afraid to speak up if their comfort or luxury is threatened in any way. But they are still Sheep signs: the nurturers of the cycle, so as long as their needs are met, they will be more than happy to support, encourage and love anyone within their sphere of influence. Speaking about a relationship, Hollywood superstar Julia Roberts has said, "You know it's love when all you want is that person to be happy, even if you're not part of their happiness." As this is a double water combination, they are endowed with great persuasive skills and the ability to reframe situations to illustrate alternative points of view with clarity and weight so they are often very effective speakers or campaigners. Tennis Champion Billie Jean King has said, "I wanted to use sports for social change... When they take surveys of women in business, of the Fortune 500, the successful women, 80 percent of them, say they were in sports as a young woman."

Ultimately, this is another innovative Sheep sign that goes about its business with its passionate heart loudly pounding, alerting everyone to this crazy person in the room making huge statements with a small gentle voice. The Scorpio brings confidence without judgment to the mix here so the Sheep goes about its business with less dilly dallying and additional focus. This allows every ounce of the Sheep's passion to be channeled into passing the finish line. The reason they achieve these heights is, as Billie Jean explained, "Champions keep playing until they get it right." But these people surpass their teachers and their peers leading them to a bit of quandary, as Borris Becker pointed out, "Where do you go when you're the best in the world? What's next?" It's down to the Sheep-Scorpio to either find a new mountain or create a whole new one altogether. One thing they will never do is accept that the game is up. Whoopi Goldberg has said, "I am where I am because I believe in all possibilities." And their possibilities are endless. Through pushing themselves and remaining on the edge, as they grow and change, they subconsciously and often times, consciously, inspire those around them to do the same. Bill Gates has said, "As we look ahead into the next century, leaders will be those who empower others."

Soul Mate:	Horse-Aquarius
Challenger:	Ox-Taurus
Siblings:	Sheep-Cancer, Sheep-Pisces
Best Friends:	Rabbit-Cancer, Rabbit-Scorpio, Rabbit-Pisces, Boar-Cancer, Boar-Scorpio, Boar-Pisces

Joni Mitchell
Whoopi Goldberg
Julia Roberts
Mike Nichols
Bill Gates
Mark Ruffalo
Billie Jean King
Keith Urban
Boris Becker
Vanilla Ice
Steve Zahn
Juhi Chawla
Joely Fisher
Ike Turner
Sam Shepard
Martin Campbell

Maria Shriver
Rufus Sewell
Courtney Thorne-Smith
Lisa Bonet
David Guetta
Letitia Dean
Sharleen Spiteri
Sophie B. Hawkins
Tina Arena
Olga Kurylenko
Dania Ramirez
Shailene Woodley

SHEEP – SAGITTARIUS

Chinese Name: YÁNG
Rank: 8th
Hours Ruled: 1pm – 3pm
Direction: South – Southwest
Season: Summer
Month: July
Western Zodiac Equivalent of Sheep: Cancer
Cancer Western Element: Water
Eastern Zodiac Equivalent of Sagittarius: Rat
Sagittarius Western Element: Fire
Numerology: 93 = 3

I love it when someone insults me. That means that I don't have to be nice anymore.
– Billy Idol

When the Sheep's gentle stream meets with Sagittarius's burning flame, a sexy, colorful and highly literate personality emerges. They are fun and light with a lively sarcastic twist to them. At the same time, they have an inconsistent personality because these two signs are so different, with different priorities and different needs; each side allows the other the benefit of the doubt and whilst inwardly fighting each contrary decision. The Sheep feels its way through life, while the Centaur intellectualizes every-thing. Mostly, the Sheep side wins out so that sensitive, creative, youthful personality will be what they present to the world, yet at the same time, the Sagittarius side will resent the Sheep side for selling out, for being too "nice" when, in the centaur's opinion, they should be more "honest." That is why these person-alities are both open and warm-hearted, yet also, spicy and saucy whose opinions can come out of the left field and seemingly contradict who the have presented before. Singer-songwriter Sara

Barreilles has said, "I think I have some anger-management issues, and they end up coming out in these passive-aggressive songs that sound happy."

Self-expression is so important to this combination and much time goes into their appearance. Remember that the Sheep sees itself as a Prince or Princess so the more one recognizes their regality the more they will be rewarded. With a reputation for being highly fashionable, they also have the ability to predict (and or set) trends. Let's not forget, 80s icon Billy Idol also belongs to this clan. They also tend to be on the leading edge of what is popular, knowing what is happening, where to go and where bargains are to be found. Interestingly, they would rather have a large group of friends around them, even if they do not like or respect the members. The Sheep-Sagittarius needs an audience. But what do they attribute their attractiveness to? Kelly Brook has said, "Sex keeps me fit and healthy. What can be better than that? It's not about crazy diets or gym workouts."

The men of this combination have a raw sexual appeal, they are pretty, yet they give off a vibe that suggests they are also rough. With Sagittarius in the mix here, they do not let their inhibitions get the better of them and are not hindered by overthinking in quite the same way as other Sheep combinations are. Jamie Foxx has said, "If you look at how long the Earth has been here, we're living in the blink of an eye. So, whatever it is you want to do, you go out and do it." Leading with their wit and humor, they are often underestimated or undermined by those who are not capable of perceiving the complex creature that they actually are. Even Billy Idol has said, "The biggest misconception people have about me is that I'm stupid." In a strange sort of way, they have an internal mechanism that is self-judgmental in a similar way but it keeps this rock 'n' roll Prince humble.

The women of this combination share much with their male

counterparts, especially being undermined for the way that they look; Kelly Brook has said, "People think you can't be clever if you have breasts." But they are clever, common sense is also common and they cannot tolerate too much posturing or pretense. Something inside them just wants to explode, but they want to be "nice." Most of the time, they are as Sara Barreilles puts it, "I would never intentionally want to hurt someone's feelings" yet it irks them something chronic to put up with emotional dishonesty and they have to get away from it to get some fresh emotional air. The Sheep-Sagittarius lady likes to be feminine, she loves her little expensive luxuries, has a very colorful palette for all her design needs. This lady loves to be spoiled by everyone around her. She is a grounded Princess who chooses to forge a life on her own...with a few assistants who might undertake the donkeywork for her as she is way too delicate a creature and is not made for manual labor. Kelly Brook has said, "I've always wanted to be independent and answer for myself. That probably is the part of me I would class to be feminist. I'd like to have children; *marriage* I have a bit of an issue with." The Sheep-Sagittarius lady needs space just like the male does, but their idea of personal space differs from most – so it is important to establish their boundaries with them, even though they might not be able to help you out consciously; most will learn what their boundaries are when they are crossed.

Ultimately, the Sheep-Sagittarius is a quiet and subtle combination that sparkles because of their unusual qualities that they learn to love and turn into something sexy. When they stop judging themselves and other people, they start to excel and can allow themselves to go to places they inwardly sense they belong. Jamie Foxx has said, "I knew that I was meant for a different destination. I think that the minute I was born, there was something inside telling me where I would go, it's like energy – an intangible destiny." With all of their humor, heart and creative flair, they have the opportunity to become shining beacons, to help others find their way also, as long as they choose to be so; otherwise, they also have the capacity to become self-destructive and damaging to others, in which case, they can create cages for themselves where their spark dims. Luckily, this is rarely the case, for that struggle between compassion and judgment becomes less pronounced as they age with their loving nature increasingly coming to the fore. The more freedom they create for themselves, the more freedom they subconsciously encourage and spread. As Billy Idol has said, "If your world doesn't allow you to dream, move to one where you can."

Soul Mate:	Horse-Capricorn
Challenger:	Ox-Gemini
Siblings:	Sheep-Aries, Sheep-Leo
Best Friends:	Rabbit-Aries, Rabbit-Leo, Rabbit-Sagittarius, Boar-Aries, Boar-Leo, Boar-Sagittarius

Keith Richards
Billy Idol
Jamie Foxx
Sara Bareilles
Howie Mandel
Kelly Brook
John Kerry
Nick Stahl
Anna Nicole Smith
Mo'Nique
Simon Amstell
Peggy Ashcroft
Om Prakash
Rita Moreno
Lionel Blair
Terrence Malick

Kevin Conroy
Jane Kaczmarek
Robert Wahlberg
Nestor Carbonell
Joel Kinnaman
Konkona Sen Sharma
Flo Rida

SHEEP – CAPRICORN

Chinese Name: YÁNG
Rank: 8th
Hours Ruled: 1pm – 3pm
Direction: South – Southwest
Season: Summer
Month: July
Western Zodiac Equivalent of Sheep: Cancer
Cancer Western Element: Water
Eastern Zodiac Equivalent of Capricorn: Ox
Capricorn Western Element: Earth
Numerology: 94 = 4

I'm not trying to be new school and I'm not old school – I'm classic.
– LL Cool J

When the Sheep's gentle stream meets with Capricorn's dense earth, the water nurtures, caresses and loves each granule to a place of fertility, power and strength. The Chinese equivalent of Capricorn is the Ox, which is the Sheep's opposite sign. Although that means there tends to be a certain level of internal friction, these two signs actually work together well and make up for each other's weak points. The Sheep brings the creativity, sensitivity and an open heart, while the Capricorn brings a work ethic, long-term vision and resilience. If things do not work out, the earthy Capricorn side will delve into the details utilizing the Sheep's well of emotional awareness to figure out what happened and where the system broke down, then will come up with a concrete, actionable solution to rectify the issues and get to a place of readiness for when the next opportunity presents itself. As LL Cool J has said, "Once the referee throws the ball in the air, it's either your ball or their ball and you have to just take your shot."

This is one driven Sheep. As Broadway superstar Ethel Merman said, "I have been ambitious to be a somebody from the time I was five years old." Naturally gifted, they work to further develop their skills so that when they perform, they shine. They really struggle if they start questioning their own importance so it actually serves them to believe in their own hype jus a tad. LL Cool J has said, "I am a rapper first. Man, I just love what I do. I am just the greatest and I can't help it. I'm sorry man... I think I'm the best, of course. How could I not?" Sometimes, others try to talk them out of it by calling them egotists or narcissists but one cannot argue with their results. They have only two settings, confident superstar or insecure wreck. That is why it is better for them to be a little bit arrogant than not, because once that button is pushed, they can find themselves self-sabotaging and heading towards self-destruction. Mel Gibson has said, "I got to a very desperate place. Kind of jump-out-of-a-window kind of desperate... But when you get to that point where you don't want to live, and you don't want to die, it's a desperate, horrible place to be."

The men of this combination have sex appeal in spades. Sometimes they will come off as over-zealous to prove themselves because they fear that people will not see what they can do or what they bring to the table. They also have a zest for life that they try hard to downplay because they want to be taken seriously, not seen as a child, even though, their ability to connect with that inner child is very important to them. Ben Kingsley has said, "I think that all of us either lose touch with the child inside us or try and hold onto it because it so precious to us and it's such an extraordinary part of our lives." Secretly, they are die hard ;) romantics and place more importance on their relationships than anything else. When asked what is the most important thing in life, Diego Luna said, "That's easy: having someone to love and being loved. And having the chance to work with people I admire. Those are my priorities." Although most Sheep-Capricorn men would claim that they are what they are, they do have a need to project an image of masculine prowess. They like to be taken seriously, believe that their opinion matters and have a need to be seen and heard. Cuba Gooding Jr. has said, "I'm not a prude. On the set, they called me 'Butt Naked.'"

The women of this combination are quirky and unusual. They are as soft and gentle and loving and disarming as you would expect any Sheep lady to be, but there is also an edge to them. Ethel Merman said, "I am known to be able to take care of myself when I become angry. I don't mince words." Like their male counterpart, they want to be seen, heard and expect their contribution to make a difference. Zooey Deschanel has said, "The fact that people are associating being girlie with weakness…that needs to be examined… Are we bitches because we have our own opinions?" At heart though, they are Sheep women through and through. They love first and ask questions later, they are highly creative and perceive themselves as walking pieces of art, they are drawn to children and animals and want nothing more than to put their arms around the world and just hug it to death. Even with a cerebral earth sign attached to this Sheep, she just cannot help but be a free spirit and be drawn to the bohemian world. Imelda Staunton has said, "At the time of Woodstock, I was just 13, but I used to see these exotic hippy creatures and I did look on with envy."

Ultimately, the Sheep-Capricorn is a smart hippy, but one that does not always want to be seen as one because of the way that the world will label and categorize them, so they often present themselves as guarded, solemn and egotistic. In actuality, they are way more open, playful and genuine than anyone might immediately suspect. Zooey Deschanel has said, "I'm into sincerity in music and sincerity in art. If it doesn't feel true, I don't want to do it." Their edginess makes them more intimidating so people are more likely to maintain a distance and respect their boundaries, which many other Sheep combinations struggle with. They are not restricted to a scientific or solely rational worldview nor is their head in the clouds all of the time. Straddling the lines, they benefit from both, the esoteric Sheep and the earthy Capricorn. It is for that reason this ambitious, creative and effective personality continues to break through their personal limitations throughout their lives. As LL Cool J has put it, "Dreams don't have deadlines."

Soul Mate:	Horse-Sagittarius
Challenger:	Ox-Cancer
Siblings:	Sheep-Taurus, Sheep-Virgo
Best Friends:	Rabbit-Taurus, Rabbit-Virgo, Rabbit-Capricorn, Boar-Taurus, Boar-Virgo, Boar-Capricorn

Zooey Deschanel
Imelda Staunton
Ethel Merman
Mel Gibson
Ben Kingsley
Cuba Gooding Jr.
LL Cool J
John Denver
Diego Luna
Harry Shearer
Noomi Rapace
Jason Segel
Logan Lerman
Rachel Nichols
Sarah Shahi

Rachael Harris
Eden Sher
Joey Lauren Adams
Oscar Isaac
Vanessa Johansson
Sam Riley

SHEEP – AQUARIUS

Chinese Name: YÁNG
Rank: 8th
Hours Ruled: 1pm – 3pm
Direction: South – Southwest
Season: Summer
Month: July
Western Zodiac Equivalent of Sheep: Cancer
Cancer Western Element: Water
Eastern Zodiac Equivalent of Aquarius: Tiger
Aquarius Western Element: Air
Numerology: 95 = 5

I think... I'm perceived as an every-person. There is no
pedestal. I'm no different from anybody else.
– Sarah McLachlan

When the Sheep's gentle stream meets the lofty clouds of Aquarius, supernatural creativity meets idealism, emotional intelligence combined with objective clarity and both of these signs fuel this combination with the attributes to see into the future and pull fragments into the present so that the world can progress to that very point. Yet, they are not big headed or arrogant despite their achievements, though they worry that they might be seen as such. Remember that the Sheep sign is the sign most connected to its subconscious world and nobody quite knows which world the Aquarius inhabits, so this is one combination that will drum to its own beat. Perhaps that is why this is often seen as a visionary. And as Federico Fellini put it, "The visionary is the only true realist."

With members such as inventor Thomas Edison, one can see how the visionary label fits. It is interesting to note that more than the realm of science, there are a large number of prominent writers of this combination, Lord Byron, John Grisham and Toni Morrison to name a few. Toni Morrison has said, "As you enter positions of trust and power, dream a little before you think." There are also a number of prominent singer-songwriters; people such as Sarah McLachlan, Brandy Norwood and most recently, Ed Sheran. Even Ed has said, "Be original; don't be scared of being bold!"

There is something very childlike about the Sheep-Aquarius, in their optimism, naiveté and never-ending faith in people. They cannot help but maintain their esoteric happiness throughout their life. It does not seem to matter what happens to them, before long, they are back to being all smiles, jokes and openhearted communication. As Comedian George Burns said, "A young mind in a healthy body is a wonderful thing. Especially for an old man with an open night." Incidentally, this combination is also known for not letting limiting conventional ideas infiltrate their minds allowing them to break new ground. George Burns finally winning an Oscar aged 80 and actress Geena Davis who narrowly missed out on getting into the 2000 Olympics for archery. Federico Fellini, "Put yourself into life and never lose your openness, your childish enthusiasm throughout the journey that is life, and things will come your way.

The men of this combination tend to be cute, cuddly and non-threatening. Essentially put, they are "good boys" that try to stay on the right side of the line in their own unconventional sort of way. Ed Sheeran has said, "I'd like to say that I'm a rock star, but I'm not – I'm honestly more of a relationship kind of guy. I'm a guy you could take home to meet your mum rather than a guy your mum wouldn't like." Similarly, Backstreet Boy Nick Carter has said, "I try to be bad, but nobody will let me." It's interesting that these men have a tendency to take responsibility, not just for their own lives, but for the lives of other people too. This causes no end to the frustration; they must learn to say *no* and be firm.

They are even hard on themselves feeling as if they have not done enough, learned enough or are talented enough. Benicio Del Toro has said, "I like to keep growing. I haven't gotten anywhere, as far as I'm concerned." Honest, with a conscience the size of a planet and the heart of giggling a toddler, they cannot escape from being the most bright eyed, bushy tailed lamb in the barn, even though it takes time for them to recognize this. Nathan Lane has said, "Sure I think it is healthy to speak the truth, and be who you are, and be proud of that."

The women of this combination have much in common with their male counterparts, primarily, being as responsible, as forthright and equally as "good." Sarah McLachlan has said, "I'll answer anything... I'm brutally honest, actually, which gets me in trouble... I've learned to trust myself, to listen to truth, to not be afraid of it and to not try and hide it." With all of that ethereal Sheep energy, they have faith in themselves, in their ability to handle whatever comes up because they access a feeling of universal protection. That is why they are not afraid to take chances. As Geena Davis has said, "If you risk nothing, then you risk everything." Yet, at the same time, all Sheep ladies are classy creatures who love dressing up and playing the Princess. Beauty is important, money is paramount and luxury is everything. Well, it's not...but it is. Christina Ricci has said, "I could easily exist on less money, but I like the way I live now." Essentially, the Sheep-Aquarius lady likes to serve in an advisory capacity, either directly or indirectly through her art. As long as she is occasionally spotlighted, heard and her message considered, she is quite happy to remain in the background. But when she realizes that there is nobody with her humanitarian heart ready and able to take the reins in order to benefit the majority, she will reluctantly take charge. As Toni Morrison has said, "Somebody has to take responsibility for being a leader."

Ultimately, the Sheep-Aquarius is a combination that, although full of self-doubt, insecurities and seemingly living with the fairies, they are actually, highly moral, constantly striving to better themselves and are psychically connected to their spiritual source. Sarah McLachlan has said, "I have the ability, no matter what's going on in my life, to find something – my cup is always half full." There are many storytellers of this combination, of various mediums and they turn their pain into something beautiful. Toni Morrison has said, "If there's a book you really want to read, but it hasn't been written yet, then you must write it." That is why, I, Sheep-Aquarius Astrologer Zakariya Adeel wrote this book.

Soul Mate:	Horse-Scorpio
Challenger:	Ox-Leo
Siblings:	Sheep-Gemini, Sheep-Libra
Best Friends:	Rabbit-Gemini, Rabbit-Libra, Rabbit-Aquarius, Boar-Gemini, Boar-Libra, Boar-Aquarius

Ziyi Zhang
Benicio Del Toro
Ed Sheeran
Christina Ricci
Nick Carter
Sarah McLachlan
Geena Davis
Nathan Lane
Federico Fellini
Toni Morrison
Eva Gabor
George Burns
Joe Pesci
James Altucher

John Grisham
Brandy Norwood
Janice Dickinson
Wilmer Valderrama
Mena Suvari
Rosamund Pike
Jesse Spencer
Rachelle Lefevre
Laura Dern
Nicolas Sarkozy
Christopher McDonald
Jeff Daniels
Jack Palance
Cesar Romero
Mimi Rogers
John Lydon
Rutger Hauer
Margaret Avery
Piper Laurie
DeForest Kelley
Pran
Zakariya Adeel ;)

SHEEP – PISCES

Chinese Name: YÁNG
Rank: 8th
Hours Ruled: 1pm – 3pm
Direction: South – Southwest
Season: Summer
Month: July
Western Zodiac Equivalent of Sheep: Cancer
Cancer Western Element: Water
Eastern Zodiac Equivalent of Pisces: Rabbit
Pisces Western Element: Water
Numerology: 96 = 6

That's been one of my mantras — focus and simplicity.
Simple can be harder than complex: You have to work hard to
get your thinking clean to make it simple. But it's worth it in
the end because once you get there, you can move mountains.
– Steve Jobs.

When the Sheep's gentle stream meets with Pisces's creative waters, one can be forgiven for expecting an extra docile, super passive Sheep native who locks themselves in a barn painting masterpieces in isolation, then undersells them on a market stall for tuppence. But, two water signs meet, they contain within them the power of the ocean; these people are like giant powerful waves that do not stop until they have reached their final destination. Creative, persuasive and artistically motivated, physical expression is as important to them as breathing. They also take into consideration the political ramifications of everything that they are involved in which often leaves them feeling stunted. David Cronenberg has said, "I'm not a big fan of political correctness. It's very detrimental to art in general. An artist's responsibility is to be irresponsible. As soon as you start to think about social or political responsibility, you've amputated the best limbs you've got as an artist."

Similarly, Mike Leigh refuses to sacrifice his artistic integrity and "will not talk about a film, even if there is a massive budget, if there are strings attached about casting." He has his own organic process that he prefers to stick with. Generally speaking, they dislike overbearing systems unless they can orchestrate some way to benefit from them.

It is still at that part of the cycle where the collective unconscious is given more space to breathe so this combination is full of innovators and creative geniuses via whom all receive gifts from the godly powers that be. Like the preceding combination, Sheep-Aquarius, which boasts Thomas Edison as a member, the Sheep-Pisces can boast one of the most celebrated innovators of recent times, Steve Jobs. "Creativity is just connecting things. When you ask creative people how they did something, they feel a little guilty because they didn't really do it, they just saw something. It seemed obvious to them after a while." This ability to see what others cannot comes from an early alternative worldview that Sheep signs as a whole, tend to have. The esoteric has always appealed to them because they are more connected to their subconscious than most other signs and the patterns they find seem eerily familiar. Sheep-Pisceans, are not money motivated, they are naturally service oriented beings who like to do what they like to do and will do it until they drop. The late Steve Jobs was typical in that regard. They must lead lives full of passion.

Men of this combination are sensitive, cultured, intelligent, part geek, part rock star and completely what the universe sent them to the Earth as. They do not know how to be anything other than what they are, though they have an ability to amp up the sex appeal at will. At the same time, they tend to have quite dramatic lives, usually caused by a constant fight with their conscience.

They are gifted persuaders and if necessary, manipulators, but the Sheep conscience doesn't allow them to take ethically questionable actions without inwardly focused reprimands. This creates an inner tension and uncertainty that they prefer to keep hidden overcompensating with an exaggerated image. Kurt Kobain said, "It just so happens that there's a bunch of people that are concerned with what I have to say. I find that frightening at times because I'm just as confused as most people." However, what they do have bucket loads of is pride and a strong sense of direction. Kobain also said, "Wanting to be someone else is a waste of the person you are…I'd rather be hated for who I am than loved for who I am not." Showing admirable self-awareness, Bruce Willis has stated, "I don't think my opinion means jack shit, because I'm an actor. Why do actors think their opinions mean more because you act?"

Many of the women decide that their home life is their passion and set about creating a haven for their entire family. They tend to be typical Sheep women with curvaceous, fertile looking bodies with a good girl charm. On discussing her assets, Jennifer Love Hewitt has said, "I just accepted them as a great accessory to every outfit." These opinionated, yet tender women like to seek out a man with balls, emotional intelligence and ideally, a fully loaded wallet as they have expensive tastes and like to be treated like the Princesses they are.

Ultimately, the Sheep-Pisces knows how to use its natural gifts to bend the world to its own mold. They look innocent, vulnerable and gentle, but they are not; they are calculating, opportunistic and slippery. Do not underestimate how persuasive these creatures are, as they will have you doing their bidding until you wake up from the enchantment they cast upon you. Somehow, they know how to reframe circumstances to always make them right. Mundane work or regular routines dampen their spirits and affect their self-esteem. Kelsey Grammer said, "I got fired when I was a dishwasher at Denny's. That set me back a little bit. You don't realize how important dishwashers are until you do the job." This combination needs a lot of freedom to explore their creative talents and develop them in their early years so that their product can be effectively marketed as soon as possible. Without passion for what they are doing, they lose focus, energy and their drive dissipates quickly. They need to work in an environment that nourishes their fertile imagination. They need to create. If you employ one, put them in an environment where they can assume responsibility for a creative project and watch them come alive. They can be astonishingly brilliant and even if you do not say it, if you believe in them, their loyalty will be yours for life. Because, as Mike Leigh has said, "Everyone who knows me knows I do what I do with the greatest integrity."

Soul Mate:	Horse-Libra
Challenger:	Ox-Virgo
Siblings:	Sheep-Cancer, Sheep-Scorpio
Best Friends:	Rabbit-Cancer, Rabbit-Scorpio, Rabbit-Pisces, Boar-Cancer, Boar-Scorpio, Boar-Pisces

Bruce Willis
Shalim Ortiz
Jennifer Love Hewitt
Danneel Ackles
John Barrowman
Lauren Graham
Steve Jobs
Chris Klein
Connie Britton
David Cronenberg
Mark Boone Junior
Sarah Bolger

Bianca Lawson
Lili Taylor
Edi Gathegi
Gary Sinise
Kelsey Grammer
Dominic Chianese
Ben Indra
Adam Levine
Freema Agyeman
Patrick Renna
Devon Werkheiser
Ornella Muti
George Eads
Gilbert Gottfried
Rhys Coiro
Glenne Headly
Bill Duke
Marc Warren
Kurt Cobain
Mike Leigh
Anupam Kher

THE MONKEY

THE MONKEY

I am the most evolved of the cycle, I see the obvious and I turn it into comedic music, for I am the agile imp, the cheeky chimp, the naughty nymph. Naughtiness is present in my every gesture, my eyes wink without moving and I project sexiness without trying. But I am more than just a passing fancy, for within me is balance that all my astrological siblings lack; some may share my wit, attractiveness, a few have a presence I do not, but what they lack is a firm, grounded common sense and that I have in spades. I know what needs to be done and I do it, not because I feel it is the right thing to do, even I question my moral colors at times, but because I can see the results of the potential outcome if I do not take the action. It is not discipline that keeps me moving, it is my need for monkey motion and foresight. I want paradise for my own and I know what to do to get there.

I am the Monkey.

Sexual and naughty, these cheeky imps have a witty response for everything. With one of the fastest minds on the circuit, you have intelligence and skills other people cannot match and being a bit of a show off, you let them know it. Aggressive and unpre-dictable, you can be tough opponents in any game, which is just as well because you're extremely competitive. Your sense of humor is what makes you so popular and you make a brilliant impersonator.

Career wise, Monkeys have such versatile talent they can succeed in any career but they tend to be drawn to positions where they can play the intermediary and make sense of compli-cated information. They are very good at translating other people's genius so that the masses can understand the appli-cation of new technologies. In the performance world, they are drawn to comedy as one would expect, but they are often triple threats: singing, dancing and acting with equal force. Interestingly, they often play promiscuous roles despite being quiet reserved types in real life. Other working environments that suit them are sports, design, publishing, PR, science and technology.

Compatibilities

Soul Mate: Snake
Challenger: Tiger
Best Friends: Rat & Dragon
Good Relations: Ox & Dog

MONKEY – ARIES

Chinese Name: HOU
Rank: 9th
Hours Ruled: 3pm – 5pm
Direction: West – Southwest
Season: Summer
Month: August
Western Zodiac Equivalent of Monkey: Leo
Leo Western Element: Fire
Eastern Zodiac Equivalent of Aries: Dragon
Aries Western Element: Fire
Numerology: 97 = 7

I always had the will to win. I felt it baking cookies. They had to be the best cookies anyone baked.
– Bette Davis.

When the special brand of the Monkey's sparkly fire meets with Aries's bush fire, of course there is the forward thrust that always comes with a double fire combination, but there is also an abundance of talent, humor and irrepressible charm. The most notable characteristic is that this combination is just that little bit over-dramatic. Bette Davis said, "Acting should be bigger than life. Scripts should be bigger than life. It should ALL be bigger than life...I have been uncompromising, peppery, intractable, monomaniacal, tactless, volatile and often times disagreeable. I suppose I'm larger than life!" The women tend to openly accept this aspect of themselves more readily than their male counterparts who are subtler with their drama-queen nature. David E. Kelley said, "I tend to be a little grand in terms of storytelling, I've never been limited by anybody's sense of reality."

Monkey-Aries' are more talented than they are ambitious in their early years and it is when they develop a greater appreciation for their own gifts that they begin to really make use of them. They are also surprisingly domestic and find much joy in creating a family where they fully partake as much as they can. Lucy Lawless has said, "I don't even consider myself usually. Soccer mom, that's what I consider myself." Similarly, Celine Dion has said, "My life is to be a mom. It is what I enjoy the most. It is my most amazing reward." Their career aspirations often take second place but they work on them slowly and practically until they reach their desired destination.

Without realizing it, they work harder than those around them picking up skills by osmosis that other people struggle to learn at all. They can learn anything and relatively quickly, although, the traditional school system does not allow for the freedom they require to truly excel: it stifles their creativity, which often encourages them to "act up." Lucy Lawless said, "I remember the moment I realized the value of comedy is when I was eight years old and I was sitting in class and I realized that if I just acted really stupid, I could get away with a lot of stuff. And it would diffuse a lot of tension and the teachers would focus on you." They naturally lean towards the arts, singing, dancing, acting and writing. They are also drawn to the law enforcement and policy.

The men of this combination exert their masculinity in a typically unconventional Monkey fashion. Through their wit, hyper-intelligence and ability to tell concise side splitting stories, they entertain, tickle their captive audience and end up dominating the scene. They may be aloof, weedy and somewhat geeky in appearance but do not be deceived, these men are highly coveted. David E. Kelley has said, "If you interview people or friends who work with me, they would say I'm private or internal or don't emote a lot. Yet I do it every day for 10 million people. I just don't do it for the 30 people I'm in the room with." Smart, sharp and surprisingly competitive, enter into a contest with them at your peril. Do not be deceived by their soft pliable looks, Monkey-Aries men play to win. And they win a lot. Often their words can come across as harsh and insensitive but most of the times, they say it like they see it and expect people to be able to take it. Still, they are masters of placation as it comes with experience. Whether it is their wit or their cheeky grin, it is very hard to stay mad at them for long.

The women of this combination tend to project a bawdy strength pushed further by their frisky personalities that delight and arouse. They have an overt sexuality and they know how to use it. Bette Davis has said, "From the moment I was six I felt sexy. And let me tell you it was hell, sheer hell, waiting to do something about it." It is almost as if their parent's give birth to adolescent children on the cusp of rebellion – these children are vocal about their likes and dislikes. They are more mature then their peers on a commonsensical level, not particularly an intellectual one. These are the children that provide the playground sex education for all the other kids through funny stories and entertaining exaggerations. Bijou Philips said, "I never had innocence." These women also tend to have many gay men as friends; in fact they are prototypical "fag-hags." Although they are naturally popular, they often don't allow themselves to be. They have an unusual tendency to set restrictive parameters for themselves to abide by that limit their own freedom out of a misplaced sense of loyalty or kinship. That being said, they consider themselves more than merely equal to their male partners but put their familial duties above all else including their men. Speaking about her son, Celine Dion said, "He's the only guy who intimidates me." Regardless who you are, treat them with the respect they demand, otherwise you will be directly told where to go, most probably with two words.

Ultimately, the forward motion that the union of two fire signs create takes the lead in this personality and they are compelled to continuously take action propelling them further and further in their life journey. The sooner they life their self-imposed restrictions, the better as they cage the creativity that wants to burst from them. If they do not allow themselves the expression they crave, they could become bitter in their later years. When they are inspirational beacons, they are joys to behold. Especially since they pepper everything they do with that famous impish humor. When they open the door to their own creative inspiration, all manner of angels enter to support them in their endeavors. The motivation is innate. All they need to do is allow themselves to take action. Diana Ross said, "You can't just sit there and wait for people to give you that golden dream. You've got to get out there and make it happen for yourself."

Soul Mate:	Snake-Virgo
Challenger:	Tiger-Libra
Siblings:	Monkey-Leo, Monkey-Sagittarius
Best Friends:	Rat-Aries, Rat-Leo, Rat-Sagittarius, Dragon-Aries, Dragon-Leo, Dragon-Sagittarius

Charlie Hunnam
Lucy Lawless
Ashley Judd
Nicholas D'Agosto
Anthony Michael Hall
Eric Roberts
Katee Sackhoff
Andy Garcia
Debbie Reynolds
Patricia Arquette
Timothy Dalton
Nick Krause
Bijou Phillips

Omar Sharif
Bette Davis
Anthony Perkins
Laura Mennell
David E. Kelley
Jaye Davidson
David Lean
Sandra Hess
Diana Ross
Celine Dion

MONKEY – TAURUS

Chinese Name: HOU
Rank: 9th
Hours Ruled: 3pm – 5pm
Direction: West – Southwest
Season: Summer
Month: August
Western Zodiac Equivalent of Monkey: Leo
Leo Western Element: Fire
Eastern Zodiac Equivalent of Taurus: Snake
Taurus Western Element: Earth
Numerology: 98 = 8

I don't know if I'm very complicated at all. I wish I was. I wish I was one of these deep, intricate people. But I just love having fun really.
– Channing Tatum

When the Monkey's fiery flame meets with Taurus's tough earth, action joins contemplation; the Monkey's momentum pushes forward the bull's intentions; noisiness meets subtle power. These two signs are complementary and create a personality that loves quietly, but does not have the need to express it for showy purposes. Its love is genuine and real, so cherish it if you get it, because the Monkey-Taurus is quite picky about where to channel its powerful emotive force.

It's hard to say whether the Monkey takes charge of the Bull in this combination or the other way around, actually, there are personality overlaps that people may not expect. Both signs have a need to see any responsibilities through to the end, although the Monkey encourages shortcuts while the Taurus supports more organic methods; neither can tolerate too much nonsense and mostly, both signs like to have fun on their own terms regardless what the world thinks about it. It must be said though, with the Taurus's discipline, this Monkey does not take as many shortcuts as other Monkey combinations, but rather makes a point that working hard builds character in a way that nothing else can match. Pope John Paul II said, "Young people are threatened...by the evil use of advertising techniques that stimulate the natural inclination to avoid hard work by promising the immediate satisfaction of every desire." Similarly, Geoge Lucas has said, "Working hard is very important. You're not going to get anywhere without working extremely hard."

That being said, the Monkey is not one to hang around once the party is over and likes to get things done quickly and move on. Even James Stewart said, "If I had my career over again? Maybe I'd say to myself, speed it up a little." The problem that this combination encounters is that once they establish a routine, they can get stuck in it. Luckily, they are self-aware enough to know this so they create routines that serve their growth rather than allow complacency to settle in. Besides, they have to find something to do with all of the Monkey's fire fuel. Channing Tatum has said, "I've always had way too much energy so I'm always looking for new things to do to channel that energy." It is also true that this combination loves to do many things to satisfy the cheeky Monkey's voracious appetite for life.

As per the previous quote by Channing Tatum, the men of this combination usually have an excess of energy, even Tony Hawk was thought to have ADD as a child but it emerged he was just gifted and psychologically advanced for his age; eventually he found skating as an outlet for his abundance of energy. Tony Hawk has said, "I won't quit skating until I am physically unable." Yes these men are intelligent though they do not neces-sarily chase down an academic profession because living a life of fulfillment is more important. Talking about his education and choice of career, James Stewart said, "I graduated with a degree in architecture and I had a scholarship to go back to Princeton and get my Masters in architecture. I'd done theatricals in college, but I'd done them because it was fun."

The women of this combination have a quiet front that contains the wit heart that they are really made of. These women love to laugh and have a camp sense of humor. Traci Lords said, "Be good or don't get caught." Just like the previous combination of Monkey-Aries, these women also have many gay male friends whom they cherish and adore. A noted tendency is that they are overly protective of their heart and don't always know how to open up and say how they feel. They find it easier to be assertive in a work context, but when it comes to affairs of the heart, the Monkey-Taurus woman is more vulnerable than she would like to be. In one of her poems, Traci Lords wrote, "You consume me, I don't even fight, Oh, I feel intoxicated... But beware I bite." Discussing her career versus being a stay a home mother, Catherine Tate has said, "I don't think that would have been the choice for me because I like to work. Especially if you're lucky enough to do something you love."

Ultimately, the Monkey-Taurus wants to live life for the pure joy of it while keeping their feet firmly on the ground. This combination is more sensible than anything else, probably because self-honesty is an important part of their psychological construction. They do not lie to themselves and recognize how destructive it is in general life. Lars Von Trier has said, "If one devalues rationality, the world tends to fall apart." Similarly, Pope John Paul II said, "An excuse is worse and more terrible than a lie, for an excuse is a lie guarded." This honesty keeps them open, productive and successful but as a by-product, as they get older, they often become more and more insular which is not helpful for them. It is wiser that they continue to push themselves further into a social scene because it prevents the

Monkey cynic to become any more pronounced. Channing Tatum has said, "Everyone's a nerd inside, I don't care how cool you are." Not being fooled by image or perception, they are well aware of their own abilities and skill set and once they learn to channel their excessive energy, the Monkey-Taurus excels at pretty much everything. Which is lucky, since they want to attempt just that: everything!

Soul Mate:	Snake-Leo
Challenger:	Tiger-Scorpio
Siblings:	Monkey-Virgo, Monkey-Capricorn
Best Friends:	Rat-Taurus, Rat-Virgo, Rat-Capricorn, Dragon-Taurus, Dragon-Virgo, Dragon-Capricorn

James Stewart
Eve Arden
Saul Bass
Pope John Paul II
Geraldine McEwan
Robert Osborne
Valentino Garavani
Danny Trejo
John Rhys-Davies
George Lucas
Joe Cocker
Lars von Trier
Bob Saget
Nicholas Hytner
Timothy Olyphant
Catherine Tate
Traci Lords
Tony Hawk
Al Murray

Channing Tatum
Jordana Brewster
Taio Cruz

MONKEY – GEMINI

Chinese Name: HOU
Rank: 9th
Hours Ruled: 3pm – 5pm
Direction: West – Southwest
Season: Summer
Month: August
Western Zodiac Equivalent of Monkey: Leo
Leo Western Element: Fire
Eastern Zodiac Equivalent of Gemini: Horse
Gemini Western Element: Air
Numerology: 99 = 9

I have to go 150 percent or nothing at all.
– Patti Labelle

When the Monkey's lazer flame meets Gemini's hurricane storm, two different but powerful forces combine to create a mischievous creature that is much stronger than it seems. Because they can be quiet and subtle, people do not realize just how rooted they actually are in their belief systems and in the knowledge of what they can achieve. Learning who they are is an ongoing process as they change and evolve over the years, but observing how others perceive them gives them much information. The Monkey-Gemini is just trying to do its thing, uncover joy, moment to moment; so why does the world have to make so much of their actions? Sometimes controversial, sometimes understated; this combination is always visible... because they like to be.

This is a very active combination; one that feels compelled to keep moving, keep achieving and climbing upwards, because to stop actively doing so would give them the feeling of end-ness, nothingness of premature old age. It's also a very quick combination; their minds are very sharp and sometimes it's a feat to keep up with themselves. Director Robert Rodriguez said, "I kind of like working fast."

They are intrinsically youthful creatures and have no desire to let their bodily age dictate what they "should" be doing with their lives at any point. They also have an inner guide that sets a sort of standard that they must live up to; but for the Monkey-Gemini, this is a much more physical standard than many other combinations may set for themselves. Singer Peggy Lee has said, "Retire? Not on your life. I have no plans to stop singing. What are you going to do when you love music? It's a terrible disease. You can't stop. Of course, I'd like to get off the road." Similarly, Patti Labelle has said, "I'll perform all the way to the grave." It is very common for them to use their hobbies as a channel to talk about themselves and/or choose to work in a job, which actually makes them a talking point.

There are many iconic people born under this combination, especially those who are adopted by the gay community as their own; people like, Patti Labelle, Gladys Knight, Kylie Minogue and even her early partner, Jason Donovan. What makes people of this combination interesting is that although they can make everything they do look so effortless, they are exceptionally committed and hard working behind the scenes. Patti LaBelle has said, "A diva is someone who is a perfectionist, who does her best in her craft… So if diva means giving your best, then yes, I guess I am a diva."

The men of this combination are known for their virility and looks, sensuality, masculinity and nerve. Interestingly, they often keep their hair long in their youth, possibly to symbolize their artistic bent at the time. With voracious sexual appetites in their earlier years, many of these spirited Monkey's cannot help but go a little wild; some remain in the shadows of who they were in their youth because it tends to be when they felt most powerful and alive. Some may say that they peak early, but that is only because some allow their youthful beauty to overshadow the new doors that actually lay open to them if they choose to see them. When they humble themselves and recognize the new phase of life the universe is ushering them towards, they find that what they had previously valued so dearly, was a form of fantastic farce rather than the genuine happiness that was becoming available to them as they opened to their true selves. This is a common male Monkey-Gemini journey. As Robert Rodriguez has said, "Changing the game is a mindset." And when they do, they flourish in a whole new way that is much more suited to their actual temperament, which is soft, tender and instinctive. Kenny G said, "I really create everything I do from the heart."

The women of this combination may seem introverted, yet have a need to be seen and heard. With Gemini's social spirit added to the Monkey's need to exert its supremacy, these ladies are likely to be spunky, sexy and totally prepared to share that with the world. Kylie Minogue has said, "I'm just a natural flirt, but I don't see it in a sexual way. A lot of the time I'm like an overexcited puppy." Often, they are quite open with their sexuality and do not see it as anything to be ashamed of, rather to be expressed and enjoyed. Miss Minogue continued to say, "I've fancied other women, but I haven't done anything about it... Part of me is a sexual exhibitionist." Like all Monkey women, they have a great sense of humor, have witty responses for everything and forever retain that special twinkle in their eyes.

Ultimately, the Monkey-Gemini is a natural performer and doesn't really know how to turn it off. They can contain their ego, but they want to know that they can pull focus if they choose to. Ray Davies said, "I like surfers; their imagery, it's great," perhaps because they catch the waves and ride them; instinctively adjust when necessary and continue to ride, chasing the thrill and when they get wiped out, they just get back on their board and start all over again, excited and enthused by the next big wave. This is very Monkey-Gemini! They love the thrills, they love the game and they love to do it where there's an audience. What they want is not easy to attain, but they up for the challenge, so they chase it knowing those with equal nerve will be at their tail. So if they are challenged, expect them to be enthralled by the prospect of it rather than intimidated. Monkeys of every description are tough opponents because if they play, they play to win; and that they do. As Robert Rodriquez has said, "Don't be told something is impossible. There's always a way."

Soul Mate:	Snake-Cancer
Challenger:	Tiger-Sagittarius
Siblings:	Monkey-Libra, Monkey-Aquarius
Best Friends:	Rat-Gemini, Rat-Libra, Rat-Aquarius, Dragon-Gemini, Dragon-Libra, Dragon-Aquarius

Peggy Lee
Patti LaBelle
Gladys Knight
Kylie Minogue
Kenny G
Ray Davies
Robert Rodriguez
John Drew Barrymore
Antonio Reid
Padmini
Frank
Oz
Sondra Locke
Rudolph W. Giuliani
Keith David

Brian Benben
Lisa Niemi
Tom Irwin
La Toya Jackson
Mani Ratnam
Joe Montana
Jason Donovan
Scott Wolf
Yasmine Bleeth
Jon Culshaw
David Gray
Oliver James
Preeya Kalidas

MONKEY – CANCER

Chinese Name: HOU
Rank: 9th
Hours Ruled: 3pm – 5pm
Direction: West – Southwest
Season: Summer
Month: August
Western Zodiac Equivalent of Monkey: Leo
Leo Western Element: Fire
Eastern Zodiac Equivalent of Cancer: Sheep
Cancer Western Element: Water
Numerology: 100 = 1

My worst fault is that I keep things to myself and appear
relaxed. But I am really in a room in my own head and not
hearing a thing anyone is saying.
– Tom Hanks

When the Monkey's laser flame meets Cancer's creative stream, the Monkey's innovation and drive meets with the Cancer's shy and reserved nature, the result is someone who wants to achieve a lot, but not seem like they do. Their humor hides their drive and they manage to achieve a lot under everybody's nose. Because of their lighthearted nature and famous quick wit, people assume that their outlook must be equally as light and positive but that is not entirely accurate. Tom Hanks has said, "I understand the concept of optimism. But I think with me what you get is a lack of cynicism." And sometimes, you get a bit of the old cynic thrown in too. This combination is often at the forefront of the technological revolution and is usually the first to implement new gadgets or understand the practical consequences of new ideas. Gisele Bündchen has said, "I'm one of these people that likes adrenaline and new things, like extreme sports. It makes me feel alive." Yet, despite their advanced perspective technologically, there is something very traditional about them and they believe in good old fashioned, hard work. Chris Isaac said, "I'm not the kind of guy to talk about angels: I'm a very pragmatic kind of guy."

This pragmatism extends to most areas of their life including the management of their purse strings. They like to live streamlined lives where they only have the basic necessities, although these tend to be luxury necessities. Nelson Rockerfeller has said, "The secret to success is to own nothing, but control everything." But even those without Rockerfella's bank balance have a natural tendency to save their pennies and dimes, mostly because the material lifestyle seems so indulgent and pointless. Plus, the money saved increases their feeling of internal security. Chris Isaac has said, "I don't live beyond my means. I have real cheap tastes. My only expenses are probably guitar strings and records."

The men of this combination are known for their sensitivity, humor and quick wit. They are also highly intellectual. Being slightly naïve for an extended part of their youth, their social development can be somewhat stunted. They learn best from experience, but they are much more sensitive then they would like to reveal so they hold back until their desire overpowers them and they are compelled into action. With their quiet compassion, they listen first and if they judge, will do so inwardly without projecting. Chris Isaac has said, "When people ask me really stupid questions or get it really wrong, I feel embarrassed for them. I don't really feel angry at them." Many struggle with insecurities when it comes to asserting their intellectual authority, especially if they have not attended higher education. This is usually because they are intellectually superior to the majority even if they do not have the qualifications to back them up. Montel Williams has said, "I have based my life on being strong enough to do anything." Although they are not always conventionally masculine, they are never the less extremely appealing and they are wise enough to know that little happinesses scattered through the days are what add up to full lives of meaning. Tom Hanks has said, "I want to have a good time myself. I don't want to dread going to work no matter what the gig is. I think, selfishly, I will make sure that I have a good time; how about that?"

The women of this combination are some of the world's most beautiful and are highly coveted. Supermodel's Jerry Hall, Gisele Bundchen and Stephanie Seymour belong to this group. Jessica Simpson and Kristen Bell also. Jerry Hall has said, "I think if I weren't so beautiful, maybe, I'd have more character." Said unfairly in jest of course, along with their beauty comes a naughty, saucy personality that people cannot resist. Taking Tom Hanks's quote above further, Gisele Bündchen has said, "If I honor my needs first, I will be the best wife, the best mum, the best sister, the best friend. I have to come first, because then everyone benefits." Like their male counterparts, the ladies also like to save for a rainy day, so use what they have to make a lot. Monkey-Cancers generally are good moneymakers and savers, but prying a penny out of their palm could prove difficult. At the same time, fashion appeals to them. Jessica Simpson said, "I never thought I'd be some fashion mogul!" Because of their beauty, it is easy for them to attract partners, but generally speaking, they are not interested in the dating game and just want to get to know one person in detail. Kirsten Bell said, "I've always been a serial monogamist."

Ultimately, being advanced in some respects and lagging behind in others gives them an inconsistency that is hard to explain. They are clever, astute and sharp, but choose to be blind to the world's natural order. Despite what happens, they never lose their sense of humor even if they are down in the dust, when they make someone else laugh, their mood brightens and before they know it, their recovery has begun. They are also wise enough to have other tactics up their sleeve to break them out of unhelpful modes. Tom Hanks said, "Everybody has something that chews them up and, for me, that thing was always loneliness. The cinema has the power to make you not feel lonely, even when you are." In time, they learn to accept that there are some things they cannot choose to ignore and recognize that it is important to face them head on. It is common for them to point a finger at the human race for the atrocities that man causes and they quite seriously consider removing themselves from society to go live with nature. Gisele Bündchen has said, "I want to get a farm where I am going to live for the rest of my life. I like the idea of a secluded place."

Soul Mate:	Snake-Gemini
Challenger:	Tiger-Capricorn
Siblings:	Monkey-Scorpio, Monkey-Pisces
Best Friends:	Rat-Cancer, Rat-Scorpio, Rat-Pisces, Dragon-Cancer, Dragon-Scorpio, Dragon-Pisces

Selena Gomez
Jennette McCurdy
Gisele Bündchen
Kristen Bell
Jessica Simpson
Michelle Kwan
Eric Stretch
Barry Sanders
Michael Connelly
Tom Hanks
Montel Williams
Alan Ruck

Chris Isaak
Joe Penny
Jan-Michael Vincent
Erno Rubik
Gary Busey
Jeff Beck
Roosevelt Grier
Pat Morita
Isaac Stern
David Brinkley
Milton Berle
Nelson Rockefeller
Thurgood Marshall
Roald Amundsen
Calvin Coolidge
Lizzie Borden
Gracy Singh
Amrish Puri
Stephanie Seymour
Zayed Khan

MONKEY – LEO

Chinese Name: HOU
Rank: 9th
Hours Ruled: 3pm – 5pm
Direction: West – Southwest
Season: Summer
Month: August
Western Zodiac Equivalent of Monkey: Leo
Leo Western Element: Fire
Eastern Zodiac Equivalent of Leo: Monkey
Leo Western Element: Fire
Numerology: 101 = 2

Sex appeal is all about confidence, and that comes from self-knowledge.
– Kim Catrall

When the Monkey's laser flame meets with Leo's forceful blaze, they effortlessly merge and become one raging fire. The Monkey is the Chinese sign equivalent of the Leo and vice versa, so these two signs have many traits in common. When two fire signs come together, the resulting personality tends to be focused, organized and active so any interruption to their plans bothers them. This double Monkey or pure Leo combination takes that a little bit further, they kind of expect other people to also place the same level of importance to their plans. The cheeky imp brings mental acuity, speed and common sense whereas the regal lion brings presence, power and clout. And sex appeal like you would not imagine! Both signs can be controversial, make lots of mistakes and have a tendency to burn bridges, but they always come back stronger afterwards. Singer-songwriter Demi Lovato has said, "I think scars are like battle wounds – beautiful, in a way. They show what you've been through and how strong you are for coming out of it."

The Monkey-Leo does not have a high tolerance for stupidity and their sarcasm smoothly surfaces along with a cheeky, sly grin when faced with it. Amusing themselves with their own wit is a secret pass time too. They believe in finding easy happiness and do not like to be dragged down by the past or held prisoner by what has happened. That being said, when confronted by highly strung, chaotic types who make their personal drama everybody else's problem, the Monkey-Leo just wants to runaway, they have an aversion to energy drainers. Peter O'Toole said, "If you can't do something willingly and joyfully, then don't do it. If you give up drinking, don't go moaning about it. Go back on the bottle. Do. As. Thou. Will."

It's safe to say that the Leo believes itself to be the King or Queen of the jungle, but what the Lion doesn't know is that the Monkey does not subscribe to any such nonsense and believes himself to a be a completely free agent. And if the Lion ever expected to pull rank, the Monkey would bludgeon the Lion to death by throwing coconuts at its head from the trees above. The point being, that these two signs both believe in their own superiority and there is something infinitely appealing about their confidence. This is why the combination of these two signs creates such a sexy creature. Model-Actor Julian McMahon said, "I'd say without a doubt I've had the most sex scenes in any television show, ever. Last season I did eight sex scenes in one day – I haven't topped that yet." Also, super-sexy vixen in the city, Kim Catrall belongs to this combination, she has teased, "I'm a trysexual. I'll try anything once."

The men of this combination are known for their presence, intellect and mischievousness. Though they may be quiet, they are emphatic. Often, their silences speak more loudly. They are master manipulators when they want to be. They can almost make one want to give in to them and serve their desires. Perhaps because they make everything so much fun, even losing the game. Speaking about his childhood, Julian McMahon has said, "I was pretty young when my father was prime minister… My folks were away a lot…but it never struck me as odd. If anything it allowed me to get into all sorts of mischief." It is also interesting to note, that they keep their friends close and their enemies closer. They have an innate desire to lead, to control or at least, be the primary influencer. Work is a game of chess to these guys, that is why they avoid working with close friends who they do not want to lose. However, outside of work, they are quite different. They are affectionate with their actions and words without being physically tactile. For someone who is as ambitious as they are, they are also surprisingly domestic. Eric Bana has said, "I love being at home, being with friends and family. I'm of European stock, brought up in Australia. I'm a passionate guy. I just love life."

The women of this combination are known for their presence, intellect and mischievousness, just like their male counterparts. This woman is likely to be an alpha female, even though this is not immediately visible. Monkey-Leos like to hide their greatness, it makes the impact of their reveal that much greater. This Monkey lady has so much going for her, her sexiness, her intellect, her humor…she is a one-woman sitcom! That being said, she believes her insights to be, clever, smart and funny rather than cheap, idle ridicule. Kristin Chenoweth has said, "There's a difference between making fun of something and having fun with something." It is a fine line and the Monkey-Leo lady knows which side she is on when she is on it. There is much more to her however, than just saucy smarts, she is also of the inspiring variety and understands the spiritual rewards of giving back. Jackee Harry has said, "My goal is to give young girls confidence in this world so they can be more like men in the decision-making process."

Ultimately, the Monkey-Leo is a quietly alpha personality who is most comfortable in the role of sexy joker and encourage others to find their own inner sexy self. They like to remain as neutral as possible in public, though they do need to vent in private. In most regards they are exceptionally open people and apply the same standards to themselves that they apply to others. Demi Lovato has said, "I don't have many deal breakers. I've done so much in my life; it doesn't feel right to judge other people." But they continue to push themselves, mentally, spiritually and often physically so that they can inspire through their own individual talents and show others how it is done. Kristin Chenoweth has said, "If you can learn to love yourself and all the flaws, you can love other people so much better. And that makes you so happy."

Soul Mate:	Snake-Taurus
Challenger:	Tiger-Aquarius
Siblings:	Monkey-Aries, Monkey-Sagittarius
Best Friends:	Rat-Aries, Rat-Leo, Rat-Sagittarius, Dragon-Aries, Dragon-Leo, Dragon-Sagittarius

Eric Bana
Kristin Chenoweth
Peter O'Toole
Kim Cattrall
Debra Messing
Jackée Harry
Demi Lovato
Julian McMahon
Helen McCrory
Sam Elliott
Gillian Anderson
Michael Biehn
Daniel Dae Kim
Maureen McCormick
Shelley Winters

MONKEY – VIRGO

Chinese Name: HOU
Rank: 9th
Hours Ruled: 3pm – 5pm
Direction: West – Southwest
Season: Summer
Month: August
Western Zodiac Equivalent of Monkey: Leo
Leo Western Element: Fire
Eastern Zodiac Equivalent of Virgo: Rooster
Virgo Western Element: Earth
Numerology: 102 = 3

Mediocrity scares me. It's the fear of not being as good as you want to be. If you give over to that fear, it will sabotage you. As much as I can, I try to use that fear to guide me.
– Chris Pine

When the Monkey's mischievous flame meets with Virgo's fertile earth, the result is an observant, introverted and imaginative imp. They tend to be creatively gifted, yet they do not necessarily feel the need to pursue their creative pursuits beyond what they do for fun. Many choose to go into professional or trade jobs for the security even though they might know that they have greater talent than others who do work in the uncertain world of art. The Monkey is a pragmatic realist and the Virgo is practical above all else, so they figure that they would rather work to live than live to work. Ironically, guess what they do with the majority of their spare time? However, when their artistic inclinations become all consuming, they often make the leap and enter the universe in which they really belong. The coming together of these two signs does create a personality that is unusual, offbeat and often misunderstood. Actor Chris Pine has said, "When you feel like an oddball, it never really leaves you. Even now, I'm better around people who are uncomfortable with themselves – the misfits."

It's interesting that many people belonging to this combination do not feel that they are good at relationships or in social interactions in general. Actress Julia Sawalha said, "I've got a string of disastrous relationships behind me. I don't think I'm an easy person to live with." They feel socially clumsy and feel that they never entirely say or do or be the "right" thing. This Monkey combination is also connected to its spiritual side and tend to be drawn to new age thinking utilizing these methods to keep their minds energized, youthful and productive. Julia Sawalha has said, "I'm into the law of attraction and quantum physics. Like cosmic ordering. It's all about thinking lovely things that you would like in life, and feeling good about them before they manifest, so that by the time they do, you don't want them because you're on to your next desire." Being as well read as they tend to be, they can see beyond the physical, the psychological and current societal norms. Michelle Williams has said, "Everything's connected, and everything has meaning if you look for it."

The men of this combination tend to be taller than average, more handsome than average and more talented than average. However, this does not do much to increase their own sense of self-esteem particularly; instead, it is developed over the years when they push themselves to overcome their own self-imposed restrictions. They are sweet natured, sensitive and funny, although, you may have to see beyond that tunnel-vision gruffness that they adopt when in work mode. Chris Pine said, "Women think that men don't talk about their feelings with guys. We do talk to friends about relationships, but it's succinct – 10 minutes, then we move on." They also know how to use their subconscious minds to unearth mysteries from the universe's deep well, as magician David Copperfield discussed when he said, "I discovered something amazing, which has caused a lot of controversy – the fountain of youth. I have to keep it a secret!" This combination does not commit easily, but when it does, it takes its responsibilities very seriously. Barry White said, "I kept my babies fed. I could have dumped them, but I didn't. I decided that whatever trip I was on, they were going with me. You're looking at a real daddy."

The women of this combination look like ladies, but their energy is quite boyish. That's not to take away from their attractiveness or femininity; they are beautiful, funny and witty women with very little tolerance for girly nonsense. Julia Sawalha has said, "I'd hate to be a sex symbol. Because you're always having to live up to an image. I haven't got time to sit around doing my nails." These "girls" run about looking for fun things to do, or fun things to read or fun people to mess with. They can sometimes dominate the energy of their entire social group and all of the members might all err or the side of unconventionality as a result and be quite comfortable with it...either that, or they will let her dominate in public, then meet in private to pick out her eccentricities. They dare not do it to her face though, as she can be quite a formidable creature when roused. Perhaps that is why Patsy Cline has said, "Anybody that'll stand up to The Cline is all right."

Ultimately, Monkey-Virgos are attractive, quiet little creatures that struggle with their *weirdo* title. For whatever reason, Monkey-Virgos cannot *fit in;* instead, they accidentally amplify their quirks eventually realizing that their *weirdness* is what makes them so special in the first place. Chris Pine has said, "I think the most dangerous word in the English language is 'should.' 'I should have done this.' Or 'I should do that.' 'Should' implies responsibility. It connotes demand. Which is just not the case. Life ebbs and flows." Learning to catch the waves of this universal flow is a life lesson that they can become masters of. They are gifted with talents that the universe asks them to develop and when they choose to, this Monkey will be guided onwards and upwards, branch by branch to greater and greater heights. With that Monkey's fire behind them, there is no shortage of fuel and they just keep going until they achieve their desires. Once they do, they move the finish line further and further so that their progression is endless. Even when Patsy Cline had already become famous in her genre, she said, "I'm gonna be something one of these days." When will they realize, they always were *something else* all along!

Soul Mate:	Snake-Aries
Challenger:	Tiger-Pisces
Siblings:	Monkey-Taurus, Ox-Capricorn
Best Friends:	Rat-Taurus, Rat-Virgo, Rat-Capricorn, Dragon-Taurus, Dragon-Virgo, Dragon-Capricorn

Patsy Cline
Michelle Williams
Diane Warren
Chris Pine
David Copperfield
Barry White
Julia Sawalha
Guy Ritchie
Rachael Ray
Gary Cole
Marta Kauffman
Jacqueline Bisset
Saira Banu
Eileen Brennan
Macaulay Culkin

Ben Savage
Kareena Kapoor
Marc Anthony
Ricki Lake
Anastacia

MONKEY – LIBRA

Chinese Name: HOU
Rank: 9th
Hours Ruled: 3pm – 5pm
Direction: West – Southwest
Season: Summer
Month: August
Western Zodiac Equivalent of Monkey: Leo
Leo Western Element: Fire
Eastern Zodiac Equivalent of Libra: Dog
Libra Western Element: Air
Numerology: 103 = 4

The difference between involvement and commitment is like
ham and eggs. The chicken is involved; the pig is committed.
– Martina Navratilova

When the Monkey's mischievous flame meets with Libra's light hurricane, ambition meets discernment, the Monkey's drive is met by the Libra's ability to adjust itself to any circumstance and both signs keep the end goal in mind. They understand that sacrifices are necessary when working towards a bigger picture, so they are very careful to choose something they are passionate about. Even if that means climbing an Everest; the way they see it, few people are prepared to put themselves through the ringer, so they might as well. Leave it to the Monkey-Libra to do what others deem impossible. Will Smith has said, "Life is lived on the edge."

Being early developers when it comes to nature's urges, but late developers when it comes to learning the lessons of love. They can be easily defensive, manipulative and greedy; they want it all and they want it now, but what they get as a result tends to be lackluster and of temporary satisfaction. Perhaps that is why Micky Rourke has said, "Love wears off too quickly." In their early years, they tend to be extremely focused on fulfilling their own needs, it is only when they adjust their attitude to *giving* what they want, that they end up being the recipient of the blessings they were so greedily trying to attain by force. Obtaining older friends or mentors helps them shortcut their development. Nick Cannon has said, "People have always said I have an old soul, and all my best friends are 10 to 15 years my senior." Nick Cannon also sought out a mentor, one who shares his exact astrological combination: Will Smith. Nick Cannon has said, "To be compared to Will Smith is probably one of the coolest things because that's who I came up admiring."

As previously mentioned, this is one of the most competitive Monkey combinations, which one can understand when they realize that Martina Navratilova belongs to this group. She has said, "Whoever said, 'It's not whether you win or lose that counts,' probably lost." Sharing the sentiment somewhat more directly, Hugh Jackman has said, "I'm quite a competitive person, so I do quite like to win." But what happens is the Monkey-Libra soon realizes that winning in a given, organized, controlled environment becomes increasingly less interesting and they start looking outside of the box. They realize that these established ideas were set up by man and they can be altered by man, especially if the resulting notions can be more productive to society at large. Physicist, Author and Public Speaker Bruce Lipton has said, "Nature is based on harmony. So it says if we want to survive and become more like nature, then we actually have to understand that it's cooperation versus competition."

The men of this combination tend to be tall, amiable and extroverted. Everybody needs solitary downtime, as do they, but there is something quite showman about them and they do love to have an audience to perform to. They tend not to lose their youthful zest for life and enthusiasm for life's sensual pleasures which makes them seem younger than their actual years. As Mickey Rourke said, "I was a 14-year-old boy for 30 years." It is this same enthusiasm and youthful energy that allows them to pour themselves into their work so completely, so much so, it is easy for them to lose themselves in it. When they commit to something, they are committed forever. Speaking about his work ethic, Will Smith has said, "I've always considered myself to be just average talent and what I have is a ridiculous insane obses-siveness for practice and preparation." In their later years, they learn to find balance so allow themselves time to create happiness in all areas of their life, but they do not quell that relentless search for excellence. Capable, innovative and sexy, they just know how to live a life with youthful wonder. As Micky Rourke put it, "There may be a little snow on the mountain, but there's a lot of fire in the furnace."

The women of this combination are sultry, sumptuous and strong. Although they are generally feminine creatures, there tends to be a masculine energy here that one feels. Both the Monkey and the Libra are Yang signs. Naomi Watts has said, "I'm a tomboy now. I always wanted to fit in with my brother's group, so I climbed trees and played with lead soldiers. But I'm a woman's woman. I never understood women who don't have woman friends." These women live to empower their sisters, but do not have much tolerance for women who sell out or refuse to learn from their lessons. At best, they might sympathize, but if you're a fool, do not expect admittance at the Monkey-Libra inn. They have had to learn the hard way (which they recommend) and it has turned them into the formidable creatures that they are. Linda Hamilton has said, "I just have to trust in the perfection of my instincts: that wherever I am or wherever I'm going to go is exactly where I'm supposed to be." These women are inspiring, no nonsense and pioneering. Arguably the most famous female tennis legend of all time, Martina Navratilova has said, "I think the key is for women not to set any limits."

Ultimately, the Monkey-Libra is a spiritual combination that has reverence for life, nature and time. They sit with the big questions of life without letting the lack of definite answers inhibit their progress. They know that belief and expectation is everything, so they work to get themselves to place where they believe they deserve the object of their desire and before long, it is theirs. Bruce Lipton has said, "Through consciousness, our minds have the power to change our planet and ourselves. It is time we heed the wisdom of the ancient indigenous people and channel our consciousness and spirit to tend the garden and not destroy it."

Soul Mate:	Snake-Pisces
Challenger:	Tiger-Aries
Siblings:	Monkey-Gemini, Monkey-Aquarius
Best Friends:	Rat-Gemini, Rat-Libra, Rat-Aquarius, Dragon-Gemini, Dragon-Libra, Dragon-Aquarius

Bruce Lipton
Mickey Rooney
Linda Hamilton
Martina Navratilova
Will Smith
Nick Cannon
Hugh Jackman
Naomi Watts
Kim Kardashian
Dwight Yoakam
Michael Douglas
Carrie Fisher
Danny Boyle
Josh Hutcherson

Carole Lombard
Danny O'Donoghue
Walter Matthau
Jim Caviezel
Montgomery Clift
Mehmood
Udo Kier
Kulbhushan Kharbanda
Anne Robinson
Jane Krakowski
Luke Goss
Matt Goss
Ziggy Marley
Shelby Lynne
Ashanti
T.I.
Sofia Vassilieva

MONKEY – SCORPIO

Chinese Name: HOU
Rank: 9th
Hours Ruled: 3pm – 5pm
Direction: West – Southwest
Season: Summer
Month: August
Western Zodiac Equivalent of Monkey: Leo
Leo Western Element: Fire
Eastern Zodiac Equivalent of Scorpio: Boar
Scorpio Western Element: Water
Numerology: 104 = 5

Every human has four endowments – self awareness, conscience, independent will and creative imagination. These give us the ultimate human freedom... The power to choose, to respond, to change.
– Stephen R Covey

When the mischievous Monkey's flame meets with Scorpio's murky, mysterious rivers, this personality can go one of two ways; that of the Monkey-Scorpion, which uses the powers of both signs to be self-serving and money grabbing or that of the Monkey-Golden Eagle (a lesser known symbol of the Scorpio sign), which uses the Monkey's intelligence and the Scorpio's connection to the heavenly realms to serve unselfishly for the benefit of mankind. They get to choose. On some unconscious level, the Monkey-Scorpio gets this and they usually morph into that golden eagle in their 30s and start heading down the road of spiritual service. That is when they really begin to achieve a level of success they may never have anticipated. What this combination does better than most is understand that the universe functions through vibration, so if they get a grasp on their own vibration, they can leverage a certain amount of control over their own life experience. The starting point is to get over those negative thought patterns that create roadblocks. Country singer Dwight Yoakam has said, "However you arrive at the ability to ignore self-doubt – if you can acquire it or possess it or find it or discover it – move beyond self-doubt." The next step is to create the life you really want. Writer of the epic self-help, psychology and business management book: the seven habits of highly effective people, Stephen R. Covey has said, "Live out of your imagination, not your history."

Methodical, detailed and disciplined, they are also creative with a great understanding of the human condition. Whether they choose to be compassionate or not is up to them, but the more they are, the more sweets the universe gives them. Actor Ben Foster has said, "Sincerely, the real root of things is love and sacrifice. Everything else is an illusion...there are so many great secrets in the world, so many signs. It's when we stop for a moment and listen that the world gets interesting." And the more they are rewarded, the more they want to share their understanding, life lessons and blessings. British screenwriter Richard Curtis has said, "I think it's a responsibility of people who have had very lucky lives indeed to try to spread some of that around."

The men of this combination tend to have larger than average builds with plain facial features that are charged with sexual energy by these two very sexual signs. The imp's cheekiness is clearly visible in their eyes and they need play in many different forms in order to utilize the excessive energy they have.

Sex is very important for men of this combination, it just is. The Monkey is highly sexual, the Scorpio is highly sexual; bring the two together and we got us a little sex bomb over here. Sexual energy is also life giving and life affirming, that is why these men have such a thirst for life. Actor Owen Wilson has said, "At about the same age as I was interested in petrified wood, I was just fascinated with this dumb idea that we only used 10 percent of our brains. I was always thinking, Man, if I could only use 20." They learn to allow the ego enough freedom to exist while preventing it from running wild. This they manage through maintaining spiritual connection and recognizing that they do not have all the answers. When they surrender their will to the universal powers that be, miracles are possible. Ryan Gosling has said, "I've learned it's important not to limit yourself. You can do whatever you really love to do, no matter what it is."

The women of this combination also tend to be taller or broader than most. They have a look about them that suggests that they do not tolerate fools gladly. These are not women one messes with. Being highly opinionated, firm and with a need to lay out their boundaries, they need to know who they are and want others to know too. Singer Petula Clark said, "There are definitely people who are stuck in the '60s and there are definitely people who think I am and it's just not true. I was performing for a long time before the '60s and I'll be doing exciting interesting things for along time to come." Generally, they are open-minded but if they have made a decision to subscribe to a set of beliefs, they expect their ideals to be respected and not questioned. They, themselves are the only people allowed to question them. Actress Monica Arnold has said, "My image is me. I talk for myself. I didn't become this person others wanted me to be." Although there is more masculine yang energy here than feminine yin, these ladies love to express themselves in lavish colors and designs. They may even have a ridiculous number of handbags. Make no mistake: this female is a lady! Bo Derek has said, "Whoever said money can't buy happiness simply didn't know where to go shopping."

Ultimately, the Monkey-Scorpio is a complicated, difficult, yet entertaining personality that needs to know itself, where its sanctuary is and who will be prepared to lay down their life for them. They are aware that everyone's basic desires are simple and easy to achieve. Perhaps this is why they are so family orientated. As Stephen R. Covey has said, "The main thing is to keep the main thing the main thing." This Monkey does not need to be center stage in any grand fashion; in fact, as long as they are surrounded by loved ones (preferably a decent sized group), that Monkey need for an audience is easily met. This combination does struggle with ego, but they soon learn how to maintain perspective through their spiritual study and head out to become principle-centered personalities who lead by example, because, as Stephen R. Covey has said, "What we are communicates far more eloquently than anything we say or do."

Soul Mate:	Snake-Aquarius
Challenger:	Tiger-Taurus
Siblings:	Monkey-Cancer, Monkey-Pisces
Best Friends:	Rat-Cancer, Rat-Scorpio, Rat-Pisces, Dragon-Cancer, Dragon-Scorpio, Dragon-Pisces

Steven R. Covey
Ryan Gosling
Danny DeVito
Owen Wilson
Richard Curtis
Bo Derek
Juliet Stevenson
Ben Foster
Monica Arnold
Dwight Yoakam
Petula Clark
Tim Rice
Gene Tierney

Sam Rockwell
Kelly Rutherford
Eddie Kaye Thomas
Isaac Hanson
Vanessa Minnillo

MONKEY – SAGITTARIUS

Chinese Name: HOU
Rank: 9th
Hours Ruled: 3pm – 5pm
Direction: West – Southwest
Season: Summer
Month: August
Western Zodiac Equivalent of Monkey: Leo
Leo Western Element: Fire
Eastern Zodiac Equivalent of Sagittarius: Rat
Sagittarius Western Element: Fire
Numerology: 105 = 6

I'd rather do what I love and get tomatoes thrown at me than get up there and be fake and get applause. I've got to be me.
– Christina Aguilera

When the Monkey's mischievous flame meets the centaur's blaze, these two very different brands of fire find it difficult to merge together easily so resign themselves to doing so over time. It is a double fire combination, so they are likely to be organized, naturally talented and endlessly ambitious. With a need to prove themselves, to show the world who they are, this ample dose of ambition comes in handy. Often though, they still need to manage their youthful insecurities as the smallest gesture can make them feel as if they are seven years old again being told they can't sit with the cool kids at the school dinner table. So what does this Monkey do? It decides, *I don't care what anyone thinks, I'm going to be me amplified by 100 and show the world how original and special I am!* That is why the likes of Christina Aguilera and Miley Cyrus are born under this combination. Christina Aguliera has said, "I like to be edgy, I like to be different. I'm a little bit of rebel."

Combining these two fire signs creates a complex personality, whose perspective is unusual and ahead of its time. They can see life's various shades of grey and do not label their experiences as Miley Cyrus illustrates here when she said, "There's no right or wrong, success or failure. I don't look at things as black or white. My life won't be a series of either/ors – musician or actor, rock or country, straitlaced or rebellious, this or that, yes or no. The real choices in life aren't that simple." Instead, they remain present with each moment and remember to remember every one to see what the long-term outcome is: they are interested in seeing what the eventual necklace of life will look like with all of the beads of experience threaded together. Brendan Fraser has said, "I guess darkness serves a purpose: to show us that there is redemption through chaos. I believe in that. I think that's the basis of Greek mythology."

The men of this combination actually look like man-monkeys with their big lips, big eyes and overgrown hair. They are also super-smart, super-funny and with an amiable yet tough exterior. They are reflective yet are quick enough to make immediate mental connections and see all dimensions of the sphere. Like many Monkey signs, there is an excess of energy here, in this case, it is fire energy, which needs to be contained. Exercise, meditation and journaling can help. Casper Van Dien has said, "I bounce off four walls, 24 hours a day, seven days a week, because I only sleep those four hours a day." Getting a good nights sleep might also help! It's interesting to note that both Brendan Fraser and Casper Van Dien have both played man-monkey Tarzan. There is an impish charm to these guys that makes them extremely popular. Actor Simon Helberg said, "Well, I think that everybody is kind of a nerd at heart."

The women of this combination tend to struggle with their own image, their need to be seen verses their need to be honorable and live an exemplary life. They actually have a greater than average need for attention and they have a greater than average level of talent which does nothing but piss off their peers in their early years. The Sagittarius fire manages to stoke the Monkey's flame and it amplifies some of the Monkey's traits, this need to be seen and taken seriously is one of them and for some reason manifests itself more voraciously in the Monkey-Sagittarius women. It also amplifies their sex appeal and penchant for raunchiness. Christina Aguilera has said, "Be a strong female – don't be afraid of the flack that goes along with that... Confidence is the hugest thing – once you exude that, guys catch on." This sometimes overshadows their other skills and it is a real annoyance for these ladies. However, they are the types that refuse to disappear quietly, in fact, they refuse to disappear ever! Speaking about getting older in Hollywood, Ellen Burstyn has said, "It's unfortunate but our society is such that, for women in Hollywood, you get to a certain age and just fall off a cliff. But in my case, I refuse to die. I will hang on, by a little finger if necessary." They are tough Monkey monsters when they need to be and one just gets the sense that there is a fearsome creature living in the (usually small or petite) body, so people know to tread carefully, lest they awaken the beast. But this beast is one that plans on growing at every point in their life journey and making the most of every experience. Lucy Liu has said, "You can't look back; you have to keep looking forward."

Despite their humor and likeable personality, the Monkey-Sagittarius does not lead an easy life. They have had to traverse their own difficult selves and create a personality that they are proud of. Nobody can teach that; they had to learn how to do it themselves and because of that, there is a certain amount of self-confidence they have earned. Along with this, they learn many other important life lessons, which deepens their perspective and makes them broader personalities. Ellen Burstyn has said, "The main way you grow is in deepening compassion. Somehow when you go through painful experiences you're more sympathetic to other people's experiences." But this compassion also needs to be projected inwards. In fact, it needs to be projected inwards before it can be applied to others. Brendan Fraser has said, "I believe you have a responsibility to comport yourself in a manner that gives an example to others. As a young man, I prayed for success. Now I pray just to be worthy of it." Simply put, the more the Monkey-Sagittarius loves itself, the more it is able to bring out that love and share it with others, through their work, through their person and through their continuous contribution to society at large.

Soul Mate:	Snake-Capricorn
Challenger:	Tiger-Gemini
Siblings:	Monkey-Aries, Monkey-Leo
Best Friends:	Rat-Aries, Rat-Leo, Rat-Sagittarius, Dragon-Aries, Dragon-Leo, Dragon-Sagittarius

Brendan Fraser
Lucy Liu
Casper Van Dien
Rachel Griffiths
Jonathan Knight
Jake Gyllenhaal
Christina Aguilera
Miley Cyrus
Montell Jordan
Ellen Burstyn
Simon Helberg
Little Richard
Bernard Hill
Jeroen Krabbé
Tim Reid

William Fichtner
Stephen Dillane
Dina Meyer
Michael Vartan
Nina Wadia
Jenna Dewan-Tatum
Ashley Cole

MONKEY – CAPRICORN

Chinese Name: HOU
Rank: 9th
Hours Ruled: 3pm – 5pm
Direction: West – Southwest
Season: Summer
Month: August
Western Zodiac Equivalent of Monkey: Leo
Leo Western Element: Fire
Eastern Zodiac Equivalent of Capricorn: Ox
Capricorn Western Element: Earth
Numerology: 106 = 7

People only hate what they see in themselves.
– Marilyn Manson

I'd worked so hard that by the time I was 20, I wanted to play hard. And I did that really well.
– Jason Bateman

When the Monkey's mischievous flame meets with Capricorn's dense earth, the fire burns the earth into ash so the nutrients are left on the surface. That is what this Monkey is like: a raw creature with all of its goodies visible, available and as a result, vulnerable. Though Monkeys do not like to project weakness, the Monkey-Capricorn believes that honesty is the most important thing, if they are vulnerable and that's the truth, then let it be seen; nature knows what it is doing and it has made them a certain way so they will be that way in its purest form. This brutally honest nature is both their gift and their curse as they take it upon themselves, not to just highlight hypocrisy, but to seek it out! In doing so, they displease many, but they are truth finders to the end. Christy Turlington has said, "I like the big questions." Ingenuity meets discipline here; the Monkey's speed is met by the Capricorn's reflective nature; so the Monkey is encouraged to sit its attention-deficit-self down and work on one thing in detail. This specific Monkey is perhaps the best at specializing in one topic rather than being a jack-of-all-trades. Perhaps that is why Jason Bateman has said, "Marathons are good training goals."

Many Monkeys are smart enough to learn from the experiences of others and if they are unsure about some advice or situation, they take it upon themselves to apply it within their lives to get the results for themselves so that they know for sure. They do not merely follow the masses. Christy Turlington has said, "So much of religion is exegesis. I would rather follow in the footprints of Christ than all of the dogma." What is sacred to others is just a stone in the ground to this modern Monkey. They do not see why something should be cherished out of tradition or habit if it does not warrant genuine commendation. Speaking about what he deems worthy of praise, Marilyn Manson has said, "I think art is the only thing that's spiritual in the world. And I refuse to forced to believe in other people's interpretations of God. No one person can own the copyright to what God means."

The men of this combination have a casual prettiness about them. They are like the boy-next-door type, but get more and more attractive the more one is around them. Their eyes sparkle, their smile hides secrets that one wants to unearth and there is an interesting yin-yang balance inherent to this combination that allows them to be both masculine and feminine at the same time. Perhaps it is because they are so comfortable being their Monkey selves that they do not feel the need to conform. Jason Bateman has said, "I don't worry about people misinterpreting my kindness for weakness." Their example speaks louder than anything that they can say. Perhaps that is why Marilyn Manson created such an extreme persona to highlight the absurdity of the entertainment world, he has said, "Find out what's really out there. I never said to be like me; I say be like you and make a difference." What is honest is beautiful to them and they are not influenced by mere superficialities. Although, they are contro-versial, non-conformist and happy to be strange if that's the label society chooses to use, they are die hard romantics! Because it is real, because it is honest and because, like all Monkeys, they love to be loved! Rod Stewart has said, "I'm a romantic and like a one-on-one situation, candlelight and foreplay, all the old-fashioned things."

The women of this combination tend to be beautiful with the same edginess that the men have, but somehow, they are more "cool!" There is feistiness here also which may keep other women at a distance from them. This is not necessary as they are intel-ligent women with open minds and are not superficial, despite many of them looking like (and being) beauty queens. Christy Turlington has said, "When you are balanced and when you listen and attend to the needs of your body, mind, and spirit, your natural beauty comes out." This is all part of their need to remain honest in all aspects of their lives. Helena Christensen has said, "A beautiful person is someone who stays true to themselves and their spirit; someone who is self-confident and can make you smile." That is why they are so very open, but like most Monkey women, do not tolerate fools gladly. They would rather stick to their inner core of two or three good friends than masquerade as the quintessential courtesan to a hundred people. And that is the approach they always take, no matter their status, position or occupation. Katie Couric has said, "I've always tried to stay true to my authentic self... You can't please everyone, and you can't make everyone like you."

Ultimately, because of their need to be honest and push an

extreme version of their truths so that the masses might dislodge destructive misconceptions, it is important for them to have a balanced perspective of reality, even as it evolves, so they take it upon themselves to know what is really happening and rally other truth seekers on common causes. They have the bigger picture imprinted upon their inner mind like a screensaver and keep their eye on the ball on both macro and micro levels. Katie Couric has said, "The competition is one aspect of the job, but I think if you're too busy worrying about the competition, you don't focus enough on what you're doing." It is not an easy journey for the Monkey-Capricorn because they set such high standards of living that they feel they must live up to. They just feel there is too much bullshit in the world and that a redress is required. Marilyn Manson has said, "The burden of originality is one that most people don't want to accept. They'd rather sit in front of the TV and let that tell them what they're supposed to like..."

Soul Mate:	Snake-Sagittarius
Challenger:	Tiger-Cancer
Siblings:	Monkey-Taurus, Monkey-Virgo
Best Friends:	Rat-Taurus, Rat-Virgo, Rat-Capricorn, Dragon-Taurus, Dragon-Virgo, Dragon-Capricorn

Jason Bateman
Marilyn Manson
Christy Turlington
Pitbull
Helena Christensen
Katie Couric
Rod Stewart
Naveen Andrews
Eliza Dushku

Norman Reedus
Julia Dietze
Genevieve Padalecki
Bitsie Tulloch
David Grohl
Jesse L. Martin
Ray J

MONKEY – AQUARIUS

Chinese Name: HOU
Rank: 9th
Hours Ruled: 3pm – 5pm
Direction: West – Southwest
Season: Summer
Month: August
Western Zodiac Equivalent of Monkey: Leo
Leo Western Element: Fire
Eastern Zodiac Equivalent of Aquarius: Tiger
Aquarius Western Element: Air
Numerology: 107 = 8

There's nothing wrong with shooting for the stars.
– Justin Timberlake

When the Monkey's mischievous flame meet the lofty clouds of Aquarius, the cheeky imp meets the class weirdo; the result is an eccentric character with a glint in its eye! Aquarians revel in their own strangeness, they like being unique and different because it makes them feel special, but they do not understand why they are judged by others for it, primarily because they do not judge others. The Monkey, however, is not as naïve and knows how people work, so when these two rocks collide, there is lots of ready compromise and understanding that takes place. The Monkey-Aquarius is going to be its wonderful, colorful and talent-ful self anyway! Elijah Woods has said, "There is nothing noble in being superior to your fellow men. True nobility lies in being superior to your former self."

The Monkey is world-wise, the Aquarius is not, it lives in the clouds, in the heavens with the angels and fairies, so that is why it dreams big, it dreams in colors not many people have seen and it dreams visions of the future that will soon come to fruition; but it is not the most practical of signs. Luckily, the Monkey is! So what happens is the Monkey takes all of the magic that the Aquarian brings and acts as an alchemist to take it from concept to concrete form. Aquarius loves to learn and wants to constantly improve itself in every which way that it can so supports the Monkey's pragmatic approach wherever it can. That is why there are so many prominent artistic pioneers of this combination. Writer-Poet Alice Walker has said, "I'm entirely interested in people, and also other creatures and beings, but especially in people, and I tend to read them by emotional field more than anything."

The men of this combination tend to look younger than they are, more experienced than they are and more conventional than they are. They have a tendency to end up in situations that they look "right" for but are completely wrong for. Speaking about working in politics, Jerry Springer has said, "I treat politics kind of like my religion. It's something I believe in, but I don't want to have to make a living at it, because if you make a living at it, you somehow become dishonest." One doesn't see the eccentric straight away in this gentle-crazy-man until one spends a weekend with him. That is when his bizarre insights and sense of humor will either endear him or make one run a mile. It is when they follow their own unique interests, then will be able to commit to completing the entire journey. Justin Timberlake has said, "If you put out 150 percent, then you can always expect 100 percent back. That's what I was always told as a kid, and it's worked for me so far!" Although they struggle with their demons, that ever practical Monkey nature always pulls them through and keeps them moving towards their desires. Arsenio Hall has said, "I am consumed with the fear of failing. Reaching deep down and finding confidence has made all my dreams come true."

The women of this combination use their observational skills to see through the mist to what is really going on. Interestingly enough, people seem to think they see through rose-tinted glasses, but that's not really the case. Sometimes, it serves their family members to cling to this view of them, because they may have been that way in their past, but as they mature, these women learn the lessons the hard way and have the scars to prove it. Jennifer Aniston has said, "People who avoid the brick walls – all power to ya, but we all have to hit them sometimes in order to push through to the next level, to evolve." Try as they might not to live with their heart on their sleeves, they do not know any other way. Alice Walker has said, "For me, writing has always come out of living a fairly to-the-bone kind of life, just really being present to a lot of life." But this changes when they decide to love, nurture and honor who they are. When this self-love becomes their focus, their lives improve dramatically and quickly as they attract love in all its forms into their experience. Alicia Keys has said, "I've learned to love my curves, my womanliness. I used to hide it, to downplay it. But now I revel in it."

Ultimately, this sensitive soul has a number of personal struggles but is quickly rescued by it its rational side and reminded that self-doubt, worry and guilt are too destructive to be given too much attention. It is better to distract oneself or focus on what is going right, being grateful for the blessings and ignoring the ego chatter that is so prevalent in the world. This chatter never makes sense to the Monkey-Aquarius, but they wonder whether it should, whether it is something that they are missing, but if they listen too long, their lives begin to go south, so they realize, it is better to just shut it out as their instinct is guiding them to do. Josh Brolin has said, "I've heard "Who do you think you are?" so many times in my career for the sole reason that I just didn't want to do what somebody else thought I should do." With their own opinions, they navigate the world, conscious of the fact that they might alienate people with their "controversial" views but at the same time, they recognize that who they are counts, so it is important for them to be heard all the same. They listen to their own inner guidance and do what they feel is right for them, despite the consequences, despite the rumble and despite the potential rejection; they know that it is only by being true to themselves. The Monkey works with the Aquarius here in innovative and magical ways to create a beautiful world that others are unlikely to understand, but wish they could experience. Elijah Wood has said, "Dream the impossible because dreams do come true."

Soul Mate:	Snake-Scorpio
Challenger:	Tiger-Leo
Siblings:	Monkey-Gemini, Monkey-Libra
Best Friends:	Rat-Gemini, Rat-Libra, Rat-Aquarius, Dragon-Gemini, Dragon-Libra, Dragon-Aquarius

Alicia Keys
Jennifer Aniston
Molly Ringwald
Alice Walker
Josh Brolin
Arsenio Hall
Jerry Springer
Justin Timberlake
Elijah Wood
Darren Aronofsky
Kelly Hu
Gary Coleman
Stockard Channing
Chynna Phillips
Lisa Marie Presley

Alan Parker
Roger Lloyd-Pack
Taylor Lautner
Buster Crabbe
Amrita Arora
Michael Sheen
Mary McCormack
Bobby Brown
Subhash Ghai
Bob Marley
Mia Farrow
Tom Selleck
Donna Reed

MONKEY – PISCES

Chinese Name: HOU
Rank: 9th
Hours Ruled: 3pm – 5pm
Direction: West – Southwest
Season: Summer
Month: August
Western Zodiac Equivalent of Monkey: Leo
Leo Western Element: Fire
Eastern Zodiac Equivalent of Pisces: Rabbit
Pisces Western Element: Water
Numerology: 108 = 9

I found out that there weren't too many limitations, if I did it my way.
– Johnny Cash

The cheeky imp's fire burns quietly next to the threat of Pisces's water potentially putting it out creating a more cautious and introverted Monkey type. They spend much of their time in observation of the external world attempting to learn how they best fit into it. The Monkey and Pisces mix is an interesting one; Pisces checks the Monkey's ego and Monkey offers Pisces a healthy dose of practicality; Pisces will set an ambitious goal and the Monkey will go get it.

Technologically advanced like their sibling combinations (Monkey-Cancer and Monkey-Scorpio), they are often the go to person in order to understand a new gadget or computer program as they have a good level of patience (actually, they don't but they hide it well) and have an ability to explain it in an accessible way. They understand the application of new technology before others recognizing how it could impact society at large…

With their capacity to understand complex stances and offer balanced advice, they often have a smaller number of very good friends rather than a large number of acquaintances. They tend to prefer one on one sessions rather than group events although this does give that Monkey with a chance to pop out. This also makes them more open-minded than most. Johnny Cash said, "Ain't nothin' too weird for me. People call me wild. Not really though, I'm not. I guess I've never been normal, not what you call Establishment. I'm country."

An interesting side note about Monkey-Pisces is that Jeri Ryan and Majel Barrett both played computers in Star Trek. Performers belonging to this combination have given life to a number of animated characters, especially for the Marvel universe: Tim Daly and Dana Delaney played Superman and Lois Lane respectively.

Gifted with masculine features, Monkey-Pisces men are attractive and have a quiet geeky charm. Even if they have traditionally "hunky" looks, as many of them do, their introversion and unconventional view of the world stemming from their heightened observational skills, prevents them from fitting the popular guy stereotype. Their depth gives them great perseverance and amplifies their insistent spirit. Johnny Cash said, "You build on failure. You use it as a stepping-stone. Close the door on the past. You don't try to forget the mistakes, but you don't dwell on it. You don't let it have any of your energy, or any of your time, or any of your space." Daniel Craig said, "Competition is so important, even when you're an artist. And if you deny that there's competition, then you're a liar. That's what gives you your ambition." Monkey-Pisces men have a calculated confidence, a jumper they wear at work or in certain situations that require it, a learned or developed self-assurance rather than a natural one. They also might secretly like to experience the popularity one assumes would come with their attractiveness, but shy away from all of the hassle that comes with it.

The women often have surprisingly strong bodies, whether they are petite or slightly larger frame. They are known for their sauciness and acceptance of their own sexuality. Dana Delaney said, "There's something liberating about walking around half undressed and not really caring about what people think." Sometimes speaking about the physical side of things is actually easier for them than discussing more mundane items, purely because of the boredom aspect. Open, fun and sexy, there are few bedroom boundaries. Dana Delaney also said, "I love to talk dirty during sex. I've been told to shut up before." Despite their sexy appeal, they are not particularly girly; they teeter on the edge of tomboy territory. Elizabeth Taylor said, "I could drink everyone under the table and not get drunk. My capacity was terrifying." Speaking about an acting role, Laura Prepon said, "I'm the tomboy so I got to be a little butch." Emily Osment said, "I'm a soccer fanatic, so I'm very competitive. I'm always ready to play, and I'm always asking, 'Why isn't everyone ready to play?'"

This rough and ready attitude strikes a chord with "the guys" and it is not unusual to find the Monkey-Pisces females with a number of male close friends. Laura Prepon said, "Even in real life, I'd rather hang out with guys." Dana Delaney said, "Younger men are just more fun. I like their energy. I've always been kind of young for my age."

With an intuitive understanding of the spiritual laws, they are lead to a deep understanding so that their ambitious goals can be turned into tangible reality. Elizabeth Taylor said, "I believe in mind over matter and doing anything you set your mind on." Bryan Cranston said, "Ever since I stopped worrying about finances, I've made more money than I ever thought I'd make in my life." Aaron Eckhart discussed his ideas on metaphysical manifestation saying, "I believe if you contextualize something then it will manifest in your life. I have done that with houses, cars, jobs. It absolutely works and it's not hocus-pocus. I believe everything in life has a spiritual component and everything's fair game."

Monkey-Pisces' tend not to be what people expect and defy pigeonholing. Laura Prepon said, "When people meet me, they think I'm going to be outgoing, but I like things low-key. I don't like people to think I'm bragging." Although they are not overtly insecure, they spend much of their time managing their self-esteem. Sophia Myles said, "I sometimes think that if someone spoke to me the way I speak to myself, I would kick them." It is when they stop the self-criticism and self-undermining that they find the freedom to really excel in the way everyone around them already expect them too. And when they allow their inner artist expression, magic occurs.

Soul Mate:	Snake-Libra
Challenger:	Tiger-Virgo
Siblings:	Monkey-Cancer, Monkey-Scorpio
Best Friends:	Rat-Cancer, Rat-Scorpio, Rat-Pisces, Dragon-Cancer, Dragon-Scorpio, Dragon-Pisces

Daniel Craig
Bryan Cranston
Aaron Eckhart
Matthew Gray Gubler
Laura Prepon
Kaya Scodelario
Jeri Ryan
Dana Delany
Emily Osment
James Frain
Elizabeth Taylor
Moira Kelly

Sophia Myles
Tim Daly
Joshua Fredric Smith
Katie Morgan
Dennis Farina
Majel Barrett
Brandon Beemer
Ezra 'Buddha' Masters
Mercedes McNab
Megan Follows
Johnny Cash

THE ROOSTER

THE ROOSTER

I am the critical calculator, the cerebral conservative, the quality controller. I am the last to sleep and the first to rise for my service is necessary and my goals, paramount. Of course, I am a special child of nature, less the common farmyard bird and more the peacock. My head-comb is shines so bright, it can blind, my wings are perfectly brushed and my feathers are stunningly fanned! I have to look perfect so the world recognizes my superiority. I need to be "on" all of the time, I need to be available, I have to be perfect! When I am not happy, you will know, for I am a cocky, cocksure, cockerel. I know what I'm cockadoodledooing about...even when I don't! I am not critical, I am discerning! I am not impulsive, I'm confident. I listen to my head over my heart because my heart is an impudent child in an adult's world. Discipline is necessary in all areas leaving the rest of me to dazzle and attract without any of my peacock-eyes leaving sight of the goal!

I am the Rooster.

Flirty, flamboyant and colorful, you tell it like it is and expect it the way you like it. With high expectations of yourself and of others, some find you hyper-critical and insensitive when you are genuinely trying to help. Not everybody is capable of adopting your work ethic. Vain and talkative, roosters have a reputation for being self-obsessed. Once again, misunderstood, this is one of the most sensitive signs, you wear a heavy mask to protect your ego from scrutiny, so in order to project confidence you talk, and talk and talk. Efficient, alert and effective, you can be highly organized and your mind is like a dictionary.

Career-wise, the Rooster is a dream employee...for a deaf boss. If one could separate their work from their mouth, it would make many people more content, but unfortunately, it is just the way of it that the Rooster comes with a critical bent and the office is just the place for them to vent. Although, they can be the most professional when required to be, they have high standards, an aggressive nature and a tendency to put their beak into others affairs, especially if it might impact them in some way. However, their work tends to be of the highest quality, gets done before it is required and they often take the initiative creating lists, or databases to make everyone's work life easier...just make sure that they are complimented, recognized and praised for their efforts and they will never leave. They are good at anything that requires detailed, specific knowledge. They are also drawn to quirky designs, colors, numbers, medicine, science and the world of beauty augmentation. Marketing is also a natural talent.

Compatibilities

Soul Mate: DragonA
Challenger: Rabbit
Best Friends: Ox & Snake
Good Relations: Monkey & Boar

ROOSTER – ARIES

Chinese Name: JI
Rank: 10th
Hours Ruled: 5pm – 7pm
Direction: Directly West
Season: Autumn
Month: September
Western Zodiac Equivalent of Rooster: Virgo
Virgo Western Element: Earth
Eastern Zodiac Equivalent of Aries: Dragon
Aries Western Element: Fire
Numerology: 109 = 1

Life is one constant search for betterment for me
– Jayne Mansfield

When the fine granules of the Rooster's earth unite with the raw power of Aries's fire, it creates a spicy personality with a sharp mind. The fire here contributes to an independence of spirit and they are unlikely to conform to society's standards, instead, they may like to dictate their own through persuasive arguments backed by facts, figures and dates. Such intelligence in small children is often met with friction as not everyone has the mental acuity to spar with them, or the strength to overcome their alpha nature. Or their innate bossiness. Bethany Joy Galeotti said, "I had a lot of creative energy when I was young...I was always challenging what the teachers were saying, rather than just accepting it." These are the types of children who always seem older than they are. Jessica Chastain has said, "I was a difficult child because I wanted to be the mom." They also have an uncanny ability to calculate events, true motivations and potential resistances to figure out the end outcome in advance. This is an ability that continues to develop as they age. Peter

Ustinov has said, "World government is not only possible, it is inevitable; and when it comes, it will appeal to patriotism in its truest, in its only sense, the patriotism of men who love their national heritages so deeply that they wish to preserve them in safety for the common good."

Respect for themselves and therefore respect for all of life is also very important. They use their Rooster-Aries confidence to bring light to situations that they care deeply about. Jessica Chastain has said, "I don't normally get into this, but I'm a vegan...I don't want to torture anything. I guess it's about trying to live a life where I'm not contributing to the cruelty in the world..." Similarly, Hayden Christianson said, "I just want to care very much about what I do and be kind to everyone in the process. It's important that I can feel that. That's happiness."

As Jayne Mansfield said in the opening quote of this combination, the Rooster Aries is on a constant search for betterment. The best way to learn is to Do! Learn from the successes and from the failures. Jessica Chastain said, "I'm going to fail sometimes. And that's OK. Because when you fail, you learn more." Their ability to examine both sides of the spectrum gives them a reliable point of view. They apply this same ability for self-analysis, thereby learning who they are in great detail, which is a prerequisite to knowing other people. Christopher Lambert said, "It may be a mistake to say this, but I know my limitations as an actor and I know what I can and cannot do... What I'm attempting to do is develop my ability as an actor and try to be the best I can be in the fantasy/action genre."

Rooster's natural tendency to project the image that they are infallible, fully in control and loving it is somewhat tempered here because adding Aries always creates a more open vulnerability. These two traits serve the Rooster very well as the honesty allows them to access help, even if they have not directly solicited it and their vulnerability is a channel to hyper-creativity; it also grounds them more. Hayden Christianson said,

"Actors are observers. They're trying to have an understanding of human sensibility. And how do you have that accurate observation if you regard yourself as someone of great importance?"

The men are usually conventionally attractive, highly intelligent and unafraid to challenge the status quo. Michael Pit has said, "There's this double standard with nudity. You can show a woman's full anatomy, but it's threatening and uncomfortable with guys...I don't agree with those values at all." Peter Ustinov has said, "The habit of religion is oppressive, an easy way out of thought... Beliefs are what divide people. Doubt unites them." Their intelligence and independence of spirit has its downside though as their internal drive to be authentic can sometimes read as over-zealous which intimidates or scares people away. It can also be a bit draining to be around all of the time. Eric Clapton has said, "My dedication to my music has driven everyone away. I've had girlfriends, but I always end up on my own. I don't particularly like it, but I don't see a way 'round it."

The women of this combination tend to be quite typically Rooster, so hyper-feminine, flirtatious and unashamed of their sexuality. Bethany Joy Galeotti said, "I'm a girlie girl. I just like being feminine." Similarly, Jayne Mansfield said, "I like being a pin-up girl, there's nothing wrong with it... Sex appeal is a wonderful, warm, womanly, healthy feeling...it comes only from inside...it's an effervescent desire to enjoy life." Often times, the only thing that takes them off track are strong men who appeal to their sensual side otherwise their careers are the most important thing in their life. These are strong, alpha females with particular tastes and they are not afraid to share them. They like to take charge and they like to give orders. Even those that put up a fight usually submit to their will and the Rooster-Aries loves nothing more than achieving a difficult conquest.

Ultimately, these people can sometimes be a bit in your face, which causes friction and makes them withdraw like a hermit. Requiring time to think their thoughts through in great detail, they quite like solitude and are comfortable in their own company. They always have lots of loving friends and family available to them whenever they need it. Despite all of their ranting and raving, they are exceptionally sensitive. Just because they can give it, it doesn't mean they can take it. But this is just another learning lesson for them. Everything requires their observation and they need time and space to do it. It also gives them the chance to formulate their plan to achieve their next big coup. As Jayne Mansfield has said, "If you want the best things in life you have to earn them for yourself."

Soul Mate:	Dragon-Virgo
Challenger:	Rabbit-Libra
Siblings:	Rooster-Leo, Rooster-Sagittarius
Best Friends:	Ox-Aries, Ox-Leo, Ox-Sagittarius, Snake-Aries, Snake-Leo, Snake-Sagittarius

Jessica Chastain
Paul Rudd
Taylor Kitsch
Julia Stiles
Hayden Christensen
Michael Pitt
Pauley Perrette
Katy Mixon
Christopher Lambert
William Smith
Bethany Joy Galeotti
Philip Winchester
Jayne Mansfield
Peter Ustinov

Brett Ratner
Ajay Devgan
Jesse James
Eric Clapton

ROOSTER – TAURUS

Chinese Name: JI
Rank: 10th
Hours Ruled: 5pm – 7pm
Direction: Directly West
Season: Autumn
Month: September
Western Zodiac Equivalent of Rooster: Virgo
Virgo Western Element: Earth
Eastern Zodiac Equivalent of Taurus: Snake
Taurus Western Element: Earth
Numerology: 110 = 2

Don't you find that work, if you love it, is actually really invigorating?
– Cate Blanchett

When the fine granules of the Rooster's earth joins with Taurus's tough terrain, the two different brands of earth seem to stabilize each other. The Rooster becomes even more in control of its faculties. Resilient, resourceful and rigorous, the Rooster is quite a tough cookie all by itself, but when Taurus is added to the mix, you can expect these traits to be multiplied to the power of ten. As a double earth combination, the desire to achieve perfection is also present. Whatever they decide to do, they will do it with energy, focus and passion. Jessica Alba has said, "You have to be the best of whatever you are, but successful, cool actresses come in all shapes and sizes."

Discussing how she has and continues to take charge of her life, Carol Burnett said, "Only I can change my life. No one can do it for me." This sort of thinking is typically Taurean and is immensely conducive to personal growth and development. Rooster-Taureans take responsibility for everything that happens in their lives, perhaps that is why many are often attracted to new age thinking where they learn conscious methods to direct their own future. Willie Nelson said, "Once you replace negative thoughts with positive ones, you'll start having positive results." Going against the Rooster grain a little here, they do not like to plan too far into the future preferring to remain open to the current energies to direct them as and when necessary. Cate Blanchett has said, "I think that's what I love about my life. There's no maniacal master plan. It's just unfolding before me."

More often though, this spiritually aligned way of living happens almost by accident, providing this inhabitant with signs or messages from the universe that guides them to their current destination. The road might not be easy, but it is the route to their dream so they will take it and manage the repercussions admirably. The Taurean Bull understands that in order to succeed, one has to charge onwards regardless of the obstacles, even if one falls. Carol Burnett said, "You have to go through the falling down in order to learn to walk. It helps to know that you can survive it." Similarly, Cate Blanchett has said, "I don't understand a way to work other than bold-facedly running towards failure."

Being a double earth combination, idealizing, perfectionism and being highly productive are likely to be common traits. Even if a tragedy befalls them, they will squeeze it for its juice or focus on something more fruitful. Talking about her love life, Renee Zelleweger said, "I believe in love, but I don't sit around waiting for it. I buy houses."

The men of this combination tend to be hairy and disheveled, but usually by design as Rooster men are known to be vain followers of fashion. However, the Taurus side does kick the "pop" fashion out in lieu of a more edgy look, so facial hair and the unkempt look, whether it's on purpose or not, tends to be their thing. As Willie Nelson has said, "I'm a romantic slob!" Yes these men are romantic, they love the whole event side of it, making a mini drama out of the situation so that they can express just how much they care. That's the upside of every man born under the sign of Taurus, he may be a taciturn little misery guts but when they're in love, don't they just love their romantic expressions of affection?

The women of this combination are tough as tarmac and hard as nails. Even if that Rooster need for attention has them wearing the face of a fragile dainty Cinderella, do not be fooled; her strength is more akin to the wicked stepmother and her heart more like Buttons, but, Cinderella, she is not! They are driven and determined and do not like to admit defeat. As Carol Burnett has said, "When you have a dream, you've got to grab it and never let go." If there's something they do not know how to do, they will learn, if it is something they do not want to learn, they will find someone who knows how, charm them and get a huge discount. If there's something they want but don't know how to get it, they will throw themselves into the situation and wing it! Their success rate is high because they do not stop until they succeed. Jessica Alba has said, "My theory is that if you look confident you can pull off anything – even if you have no clue what you're doing." Financially, although they have their little luxuries, these women are far too frugal and sensible to be wasteful with their money, they prefer to invest rather than spend. Renee Zellweger has said, "I don`t have the appetite for a decadent lifestyle."

Ultimately, the Rooster-Taurus is effortlessly super-efficient and super-practical. That is what happens when two earth elements converge. They create an ideal that they aspire to, take huge action to start their way towards it and do not stop until they have achieve it. There might be babies along the way, discarded relationships, friends, feuds and fatalities, but the Rooster-

Taurus will get what it wants. Jessica Alba has said, "I wish there were two of me and 48-hour days so I could get everything done. But for me, I have to not try and think that everything has to be 100 percent perfect all the time and leave room for error." Their emotional relationships are important to them of course, but there is some sort of internal programming that these people have; give them a goal and they cannot rest until it is achieved; sometimes, achieving their goals do come at the detriment of their emotional connections but it is what they choose to prioritize. This does begin to shift later on in their lives where they relax a lot more and learn to chill out. As Willie Nelson has said, "When I started counting my blessings, my whole life turned around."

Soul Mate:	Dragon-Leo
Challenger:	Rabbit-Scorpio
Siblings:	Rooster-Virgo, Rooster-Capricorn
Best Friends:	Ox-Taurus, Ox-Virgo, Ox-Capricorn, Snake-Taurus, Snake-Virgo, Snake-Capricorn

James Mason
Margaret Sullavan
Satyajit Ray
Janet Blair
Carol Burnett
Willie Nelson
James Brown
Björn Ulvaeus
Daniel Day-Lewis
Richard E. Grant
Alan Ball
Sid Vicious
Cate Blanchett
Renée Zellweger

David Boreanaz
Darcey Bussell
Jessica Alba
Kunal Nayyar
Craig David
Zara Phillips

ROOSTER – GEMINI

Chinese Name: JI
Rank: 10th
Hours Ruled: 5pm – 7pm
Direction: Directly West
Season: Autumn
Month: September
Western Zodiac Equivalent of Rooster: Virgo
Virgo Western Element: Earth
Eastern Zodiac Equivalent of Gemini: Horse
Gemini Western Element: Air
Numerology: 111 = 3

Publicity can be terrible. But only if you don't have any.
– Jane Russell

When the fine granules of the Rooster's earth meets with the twin's hurricane, something akin to a sandstorm occurs where all that is real is concealed behind a dramatic façade, all constructed to protect this personality's delicate ego. Like all Roosters, this combination is far more sensitive and self-critical than they would like to be known, so they use any number of techniques to divert the focus away from their vulnerabilities by heightening their own traits; their humor; their sexuality; their audacity. So at times, they may come across as caricatures or almost like cartoon-creatures to serve a social purpose, all because they dread not being useful or not being genuinely liked...which they almost universally are. With the addition of Gemini, this Rooster's natural flamboyancy is pushed to a higher level. Stories, metaphors and other artistic symbols help them assimilate academic information so that it resonates with their inner humanity and explains their success in these fields. Natalie Portman said, "Overall, to get a real deep, nuanced understanding of human behavior, art is the best way."

There is something very youthful about them that remains, deeply embedded in their personalities, even into old age. The men are little boys lost and the women are famous for growing old disgracefully, yet fabulously. Joan Collins said, "Age, in my opinion, has no bearing at all, that is unless, of course, one happens to be a bottle of wine." In addition to all of their humor, enthusiasm and frisk for life, there is a simplicity that they seldom reveal; being an earthy Rooster, they are often very connected to the earth, greenery and nature. Actor Chris Evan's has said, "The point is that when I see a sunset or a waterfall or something, for a split second it's so great, because for a little bit I'm out of my brain..." This combination is notorious for being too cerebral and when they learn from their mistakes of being too superficial, they go to the other extreme and take in more information: sensually, intellectually and empathically. Then they attempt to bridge everything together to create the broadest perspective possible. However, to assimilate this information takes longer to do because there is ten times more data to process. Even Natalie Portman has said, "I was in a relationship recently with someone who yelled at me for being too much in my head, you know?"

The men of this combination are more openly sensual creatures; Congressman Charlie Wilson, nicknamed "Good Time Charlie" for his playboy shenanigans; his mantra was to "take his job seriously, without taking himself seriously." Although, most Rooster-Gemini men do not have a superiority complex, there are those that seem to think it is an amusing mask to wear. Prince Philip is known to have made many politically incorrect comments such as telling a bunch of British students who were studying in China that "If you stay here much longer, you'll all be slitty-eyed" or asking an Australian Aborigine, "Do you still throw spears at each other?" Most likely an attempt at humor, it stems from a need to be seen and to get everybody's attention even though this sort of behavior backfires. Most of the time their intentions are honorable, it is just that their mouth is a fraction faster than their mind. In all actuality, they are exceptionally sensitive and their many public faux pas disturb them greatly in private, even if they pretend otherwise.

The women of this combination tend to present themselves like glamorous princesses but with warrior spirits. Hollywood icon Jane Russell described herself as, "The girl with the summer-hot lips...and the winter-cold heart." There may be truth in jest, but even this is a defense mechanism. One must be Alpha, good at what they do and be well regarded in society to gain their attention, but even then, one wonders if they will be able to handle this bird. As Joan Collins has said, "I've never yet met a man who could look after me. I don't need a husband. What I need is a wife." They often collect admirers as they project the beautiful Princess image, but that is why it can be easy for them to start believing their own hype. Many Rooster-Geminis learn this lesson the hard way. Not all of them of course: Natalie Portman has said, "The moment you buy into the idea you're above anyone else is the moment you need to be slapped in the face." Like them or loathe them, one has to respect what these women are capable of and the vigor with which they live their entire lives; they just never give up and refuse to let their age be a barrier. Comedienne Joan Rivers said, "They all come up to me and say, 'Without you, I couldn't be here, the barriers you broke down.' I say, 'Get the f*** away from me. I still could take every one of you with one hand behind my back.'"

Some may consider this combination as socially controversial. They often cloak themselves in their cliques and often do not peek outside their own little worlds and that is why they can sometimes be perceived as *ignorant*. But those that have been burned by their own social awkwardness and give it due attention rather than proclaiming it *everyone else's problem*, become highly well-adjusted and admirable people. Learning from their lessons inevitably makes you a teacher, leader and inspirer and there are many examples of people like that belonging to this category. It's just that their beauty is often so in-your-face and larger-than-life caricature personalities are so much more colorful that their noble deeds get completely overshadowed. It is just too easy to stereotype them, to categorize them and to label them one color when they are in fact the complete spectrum; but they do themselves a disservice when they play up to their own caricature. As the eternally effervescent Joan Collin's has said, "The compartment that's easy to put me in is 'freethinking, sexy broad with a dirty mouth, who pretty much does what she wants.' But there's more to me than that."

Soul Mate:	Dragon-Cancer
Challenger:	Rabbit-Sagittarius
Siblings:	Rooster-Libra, Rooster-Aquarius
Best Friends:	Ox-Gemini, Ox-Libra, Ox-Aquarius, Snake-Gemini, Snake-Libra, Snake-Aquarius

Jane Russell
Joan Collins
Joan Rivers
Natalie Portman
Chris Evans
Justin Kirk
Jessica Tandy
Errol Flynn
Prince Philip
Hal David
Gene Wilder

Seabiscuit
Charlie Wilson
Adrienne Barbeau
Priscilla Presley
Ted Levine
Judge Reinhold
Phyllida Lloyd
Dimple Kapadia
Siouxsie Sioux
Ice Cube
Peter Dinklage
Anne Heche
Brian McKnight
Larisa Oleynik
Amrita Rao
Anna Kournikova
Brandon Flowers
Jade Goody

ROOSTER – CANCER

Chinese Name: JI
Rank: 10ᵗʰ
Hours Ruled: 5pm – 7pm
Direction: Directly West
Season: Autumn
Month: September
Western Zodiac Equivalent of Rooster: Virgo
Virgo Western Element: Earth
Eastern Zodiac Equivalent of Cancer: Sheep
Cancer Western Element: Water
Numerology: 112 = 4

Being hot never hurts!
– Debbie Harry

When the fine granules of the Rooster's earth mix with Cancer's serene stream of secrets, the personality that emerges is a prickly one. On the one hand, the Rooster strives for perfection in all things, while the Cancer dreams increasingly bigger dreams so that there is forever more to achieve. Although both sides need space to recuperate, neither ever let up, so they keep each other moving and striving, even when both are desperate for some time off. This tends to keep them on edge and they require outside perspective to help them to chill. This is one of the more excessive combinations and their pendulum tends to swing further out than most so they are used to dealing with extreme ends of the spectrum. Despite what happens, that irrepressible Rooster spirit will always find the humor in the drama. Jon Lovitz has said, "My dad would always say, 'What can you do to make the world a better place?' Well, I can make people laugh."

As a result of the tension mentioned before, the Rooster-Cancer enters the world with a tiniest chip on their shoulder, which they must consciously work on to remove. Most do that pretty early on, but, if they do not, an unhelpful attitude can prevail. It's interesting that the most talented Rooster-Cancers are the ones who use this attitude as a defensive tactic to try and prevent people from seeing their fragile esteem and crying inner child. They learn to manage it in time and are usually a joy to behold. Kelly McGillis has said, "For a long time I thought I could deal with my anger and hostility on my own. But I couldn't. I denied that it had affected me, and yet I was so frantic on the inside with other people: I needed to be constantly reassured." Similarly, speaking about how he turned his struggle into a strength, Josh Holloway has said, "There's definitely an intense anger that I have inside, and I don't know where it came from, I've had it all my life. My mum was always like, 'You're going to end up in jail with that temper!' Now I use that to help me."

The men of this combination have an edgy sexiness, the sort of looks that would suit a quiet, brooding sort: brooding, yes, but quiet, not so much. This polarizes them in groups where some love their brazenness and guts to put themselves on the line, whereas others just see them as reckless. The wiser Rooster-Cancer men have learned to let that brooding image be and say as little as possible to get in the way of it. Josh Holloway has said, "I'm an outdoorsman kind of person, so I don't like the buzz of the crowd, crowd, crowd and all that so much. I mean I don't mind it, but I don't seek it out." But there's a part of them that just cannot hold back and they have to let it rip regardless of the outcome. Jon Lovitz has said, "Sometimes the best way to make 'em laugh is to show 'em how you honestly feel... Apparently, I said what a lot of people are thinking and a lot of people have thanked me." It is their spirit that is the most sexy thing about them and it never ages, so it is not unusual to find Rooster-Cancer men in their 50s with a stunning babe in her 20s on their arm. Even TV's Batman, Burt Ward said, "Maybe it was all those wild times that kept me young."

The women of this combination have an equally edgy sex appeal as Debbie Harry, Carly Simone and Kelly McGuiness attest to. Interestingly, although both signs of this combination are Yin signs, these ladies have a need to prove themselves in masculine environments and as a result, they consciously try to project more of a Yang energy. Kelly McGuiness has said, "There's a part of me that wants to be stoic and very strong." Debbie Harry took it even further by saying, "The only person I really believe in is me." The more they learn to trust the universe and know that they are eternally provided for, they relax into who they really are and can let themselves be vulnerable without defensive mechanisms to protect themselves. As Carly Simon said, "A really strong woman accepts the war she went through and is ennobled by her scars."

Ultimately, the Rooster-Cancer's journey is to let go of habits that cause them stress, complications and strife. Dealing with the internal issues takes them a while to orient, but when they do, their perspective broadens in such a way that they are able to see how to un-complicate more complex situations. Jon Lovitz has said, "Instead of making people victims of people who are successful, we should be telling people, 'Look, you are having a hard time, I feel bad for you. Let's look at what you're doing, let's teach you how to succeed.'" They recognize issues that others feel but are not able to articulate. Speaking about the power of not judging any situation and instead, attempting to feel through it, Josh Holloway has said, "When our minds as people normally starts to wrap around things, we start to attach all these ideas to it that really aren't that necessary to the core of it, if you just experience it and kind of go through it." The more they channel their tension, smart brains and creative energy to undertake the work their soul urges them towards, the happier and more successful they become. And the more they do so remaining in the moment, the better. Just listen to Debbie Harry's advice and allow your inner child the freedom to play, she has said, "I thought I'd live to a ripe old age, because I always felt there was a lot to do. I had a driven feeling. I always thought in the present."

Soul Mate:	Dragon-Gemini
Challenger:	Rabbit-Capricorn
Siblings:	Rooster-Scorpio, Rooster-Pisces
Best Friends:	Ox-Cancer, Ox-Scorpio, Ox-Pisces, Snake-Cancer, Snake-Scorpio, Snake-Pisces

Josh Holloway
Jon Lovitz
Burt Ward
Kelly McGillis
Deborah Harry
Carly Simon
Cameron Crowe
Ryan Hansen
Taylor Kinney
Clive Standen
Tahar Rahim
Clive Standen
Sheridan Smith
Gale Harold
RZA
Jason Clarke
Lisa Nicole Carson
Frances McDormand
Tim Kring
Paul Merton
Fern Britton

Ron Glass
Kim Carnes
Marty Feldman
Cormac McCarthy
Brad Harris

ROOSTER – LEO

Chinese Name: JI
Rank: 10th
Hours Ruled: 5pm – 7pm
Direction: Directly West
Season: Autumn
Month: September
Western Zodiac Equivalent of Rooster: Virgo
Virgo Western Element: Earth
Eastern Zodiac Equivalent of Leo: Monkey
Leo Western Element: Fire
Numerology: 113 = 5

Life, like poker has an element of risk. It shouldn't be avoided.
It should be faced.
– Ed Norton.

When the fine granules of the Rooster meet with Leo's raging fire, we are undoubtedly faced with an awe-inspiring creature destined for a life of drama. They just cannot help it, wherever these outrageous characters go, thrills always follow. The upside is that they experience more than most and draw from their past to move onwards. The courage of the lion meets the confidence of the Rooster; some may expect an explosion of arrogance: yes and no. Rooster gives the Leo discipline, which manages to contain its ego whilst Leo provides a fiery presence. It creates a powerful person who is self-assured, efficient and organized. People of this combination tend to be inspirational and are often put on a pedestal as examples to aspire to. Tennis legend Roger Federer has said, "When you do something best in life, you don't really want to give that up – and for me it's tennis."

Rooster-Leos are also known for their sense of humor but have a tendency to use this humor to cover up their true feelings.

Matthew Perry of *Friends* fame has said, "When I was younger, I used humor as a tool to avoid getting too serious with people – if there was deep emotional stuff going on, then I would crack a joke to defuse the situation." The confident, determined and organized Rooster mixing with the commanding, ambitious and bold Leo encourages this being to head straight for success. This is one of the most disciplined combinations of all. Jennifer Lopez said, "I had a natural discipline from early on. I was always training for something." Even if they are struggling, when the chips are down, the Rooster-Leo is in 100 percent. Roger Federer said, "What I think I've been able to do well over the years is play with pain, play with problems, play in all sorts of conditions."

The men of this combination tend to be slender, with a kind of geek-chic look. But that doesn't mean they are geeks in any way. Once again, humor plays a big role in their lives and they take their levity very seriously. Steve Martin said, "I did stand-up comedy for 18 years. Ten of those years were spent learning, four years were spent refining, and four years were spent in wild success." On the surface, they can seem unconventional as they are colorful and unusual beings, but if you look at the construction of their deep character, they are security conscious and therefore employ methods that have stood the test of time. Hard work, tunnel vision and keeping the end in mind are starting points. But because they do work harder than most, sacrifice more and they feel like they contribute more, it can sometimes create a little attitude. Matthew Perry said, "I've certainly had a lot of experiences in my life where I was much too self-centered." But these feelings are also by-product of their extensive and complicated needs that often keep them feeling tense. Christian Slater said, "As I've gotten to know myself over the years, I realized I'm kind of a sweet, sensitive guy, a shy guy, and communication is not something I'm so good at." Many choose to work in inhibiting professional environments but the

Rooster-Leo needs cathartic outlets. Edward Norton said, "All people are paradoxical. No one is easily reducible, so I like characters who have contradictory impulses or shades of ambiguity." An interesting side note is that there are many drag queens of this combination.

The women of this combination tend to be blessed with naturally provocative bodies whether they like it or not, but the way they carry themselves makes them even more attractive. Make no mistake they plan to come across as strong and fully in charge of their lives because they need to project strength even if they are floundering. That is the strength and the downfall of the Rooster and is why their compassionate friends are so important to them. Jennifer Lopez said, "Oh my God, my girlfriends are everything to me. They celebrate with you, they cry with you, they hold you when you need to be held. They laugh with you. They're mean with you! They're always there, and it's just a priceless thing to have." There is an inner struggle also where the Rooster wants stability but the lion wants excitement, so rather than compromising on the need, it's more likely that each side gets allotted airtime where one experiences stability, then the other gets excitement. Helen Mirren has said, "I still have a Gypsy sense of adventure." Despite the sensitivity and vulnerability, both of these signs have a mouth on them and know how to turn on the confidence button so they go through their worlds achieving all sorts of feats. Making mistakes does not inhibit this bird, no, she knows that setbacks are temporary, but inner growth is forever. Julie Newmar said, "You can't fail. The further you fall, the greater the opportunity for growth and change." That is why the Rooster-Leo is a beautiful, vocal, colorful beast-bird of sorts.

Ultimately, the Rooster-Leo is someone with a need for creative expression. They have a natural way with spoken words and are exceptionally quick witted. Learning to be direct is not easy and learning to ask for help, a herculean task for this trouper. But it gets easier and they learn to stop hiding behind their smartness and humor. Melanie Griffiths said, "I don't walk around with fear. I walk around with strength. I believe in cause and effect." They learn to manage their Achilles heel and manage their nerves. Jennifer Lopez said, "Doubt is a killer. You just have to know who you are and what you stand for." Slowly, they turn their weaknesses into strengths where they can and manage what they cannot applying a heavy dose of healthy mind, body and spirit techniques. Roger Federer said, "I'm a very positive thinker, and I think that is what helps me the most in difficult moments." Exceptionally popular, highly effective at everything they attempt and endearing, they have the potential to earn legendary status in their chosen area of expertise.

Soul Mate:	Dragon-Taurus
Challenger:	Rabbit-Aquarius
Siblings:	Rooster-Aries, Rooster-Sagittarius
Best Friends:	Ox-Aries, Ox-Leo, Ox-Sagittarius, Snake-Aries, Snake-Leo, Snake-Sagittarius,

Alyson Stoner
Taylor Momsen
Bradley McIntosh
Roger Federer
Vanessa Amorosi
Summer Glau
Matthew Perry
Christian Slater
Edward Norton
Erik "Everlast" Schrody
Donnie Wahlberg
Triple H
Jennifer Lopez

Denis Leary
Melanie Griffith
Steve Martin
Jim Davis
Rick Wright
Helen Mirren
Roman Polanski
Julie Newmar
Edd "Kookie" Byrnes
Amelia Earhart
H.C. Oersted

ROOSTER – VIRGO

Chinese Name: JI
Rank: 10th
Hours Ruled: 5pm – 7pm
Direction: Directly West
Season: Autumn
Month: September
Western Zodiac Equivalent of Rooster: Virgo
Virgo Western Element: Earth
Eastern Zodiac Equivalent of Virgo: Rooster
Virgo Western Element: Earth
Numerology: 114 = 6

When I was writing the Destiny's Child songs, it was a big thing to be that young and taking control. And the label at the time didn't know that we were going to be that successful, so they gave us all control. And I got used to it.
– Beyonce

When the fine granules of the Rooster meet with the Virgo's fertile soil, they intermingle easily as they are of the same consistency. The Rooster is the Chinese Astrological equivalent of the Virgo and vice versa so it is the double Roster or pure Virgo combination. With so much concentrated Rooster or Virgo energy, it will come as no surprise that this combination has the biggest desire to achieve perfection than any of the 144 combinations. They have a superior work ethic and good enough does not exist in their vocabulary: if it is not a superior piece of work to every one of their peers, it simply will not do. They are still Roosters too so will want to stick out too, be appreciated for their eccentricities and be seen, heard and taken seriously. Superstar Beyonce Knowles has said, "I can never be safe; I always try and go against the grain. As soon as I accomplish one thing, I just set a higher goal. That's how I've gotten to where I am."

With their capacity for hard work and putting in the hours necessary to excel beyond everyone's expectations, they also tend to be born with a lot of natural talent. Comic Actor Jack Back has said, "I think of myself as an entertainment arsenal. Like I have my acting bazooka and my music machete. And you don't know what I'm going to come at you with."

In their desire to achieve perfection, they often need external affirmation to prove what they did was exceptionally more advanced than their peers. Little digs and psychological projections, start becoming commonplace and it is important for them to know that it is not their fault. Stephen Fry has said, "I have spent much of my life trying to please people, trying to be what they wanted me to be rather than what I actually wanted to be." As they begin to notice this pattern they release the need for anyone to affirm them and keep others words in perspective. Beyonce Knowles has said, "When you love and accept yourself, when you know who really cares about you, and when you learn from your mistakes, then you stop caring about what people who don't know you think."

The men of this combination tend to be either taller or shorter than most, there's no average anything with the Rooster-Virgo. They do not like to rely on other people and asking for help is like admitting a weakness so they work on becoming as self-sufficient as possible. Despite their intellect, abilities and status, they do not lose touch with their inner child; they feel very free around children and have an innate understanding of them. Jack Black has said, "I'd rather be the king of kids, than the prince of fools." The kinder they are to themselves, the easier it is to cope with the cross of being Mr. Perfect. Determined to their last breath, they will put everything they have into achieving their goals...if that means proving some people wrong along the way, that's just fine with them. Tyler Perry has said, "You close the door on me and tell me

I can't, I'm gonna find a way to get in... You can never be upset with the people who forced you into your dream or up higher."

The women of this combination are known to be prominent, powerful and present to their lives, no matter what part of the world you investigate. With an amazing work ethic, they put in more hours than anyone else, refuse to let any obstacle get in their way and talk and debate and argue until they get what they want. Gloria Estefan has said, "In the United States, if you believe in yourself and you're determined and persevere, you're going to succeed." Even Indian singing Superstar, Asha Bhosle said, "I worked tirelessly and that is why no one could snatch what was due to me." Beyonce Knowles is a one of a kind superstar that typifies the pure perfectionist Rooster-Virgo traits perfectly, she has said, "My focus is my art, and that's what I love to do. I have to be really passionate in order to do something. I've turned down many things that I just didn't believe in." In the movie version of Dreamgirls, another performer shined equally to Beyonce without her credentials, but what astrological combination could ever stand up to the perfect Rooster-Virgo combination? Only another Rooster-Virgo! As Jennifer Hudson has said, "I accept any challenge."

Ultimately, the Rooster-Virgo combination is one of the most focused, driven and successful combinations of all. This is the cockerel that gets up first to wake up all the other cockerels to go wake up the rest of the world. They let themselves be lifted and moved by whatever inspiration comes their way and then follow it to see where it leads. Jack Black has said, "I don't have any real spirituality in my life – I'm kind of an atheist – but when music can take me to the highest heights, it's almost like a spiritual feeling. It fills that void for me." At the end of the day, the Rooster-Virgo combination manages to combine the cerebral aspects of their sign with a personal spirituality that does not blindly follow the masses. This combination most definitely belongs to themselves and that is why they are so inspirational to everyone else. Stephen Fry has said, "I am a lover of truth, a worshipper of freedom, a celebrant at the altar of language and purity and tolerance."

Soul Mate:	Dragon-Aries
Challenger:	Rabbit-Pisces
Siblings:	Rooster-Taurus, Rooster-Capricorn
Best Friends:	Snake-Taurus, Snake-Virgo, Snake-Capricorn, Ox-Taurus, Ox-Virgo, Ox-Capricorn

Van Morrison
Stephen Fry
Jack Black
Tyler Perry
Jason Priestley
Asha Bhosle
Gloria Estefan
Jennifer Hudson
Beyoncé Knowles
Harry Secombe
David McCallum
Karl Lagerfeld
Bruce Spence
Nick Cave
Johnathon Schaech
Rachel Hunter
Shane Warne
Alexis Bledel
Rachel Bilson
Chad Michael Murray
Jonathan Taylor Thomas
Nicole Richie

ROOSTER – LIBRA

Chinese Name: JI
Rank: 10th
Hours Ruled: 5pm – 7pm
Direction: Directly West
Season: Autumn
Month: September
Western Zodiac Equivalent of Rooster: Virgo
Virgo Western Element: Earth
Eastern Zodiac Equivalent of Libra: Dog
Libra Western Element: Air
Numerology: 115 = 7

I used to go around looking as frumpy as possible because it was inconceivable you could be attractive as well as be smart. It wasn't until I started being myself, the way I like to turn out to meet people, that I started to get any work.
– Catherine Zeta Jones

When the Rooster's fine granules meet the Libra's cool breeze, it is like they were made to work with each other, they unite to create a beautiful and powerful sandstorm unlike any other. It is light and smooth and soft yet forceful; it knows when to be stationary and when to move at pace in order to achieve its objective with efficient ease and effortless control. Like all Rooster combinations, this one has a lot to offer, a lot to advise and mostly, a lot to say as candidly as possible. Comedienne Dawn French has said, "I'm known among my friends for saying things I probably shouldn't sometimes, but I have to get things out in the air." Unlike other Roosters though, Libra lightens them and their energy is not so heavy, in fact, they also have the ability to lighten others with their humor and wit whilst letting their penchant for highlighting the truth spark the way. Comic Bernie

Mac said, "Bernie Mac just says what you think but are afraid to say. Bernie Mac don't sugarcoat."

The men of this combination are essentially quite happy doing their own thing without needing to conform to what is expected of them. They are just being themselves, in fact, sometimes they are oblivious to society's expectations and other times, they just don't care. Simply put, they are most comfortable in their own company. Bernie Mac said, "I've always been a reserved cat. When I play sports, there's people used to get mad at me because I didn't hang out and things like that... I've never been posse, and all that. I'm a quiet storm." They have that "clown" side to them too and they love to be given the floor so that they can pump humor, emotion and life into crowds of the undead. They have the ability to bring light to dark places, even if they themselves are secretly in the darkest of rooms. Conversely, they are also able to highlight darkness through their light. Director Steve McQueen has said, "I'm essentially quite happy, but, for some reason, I have done a lot of stuff that is dark. I don't know why that is and I don't question it. I don't really think you have a choice where you go as an artist." Like most Roosters they are uninhibited and do not let their inner struggles, insecurities or conscience hold them back for too long. They either philosophize an argument that allows them to make their preferred choice (even if it is ego based) or they don't think about it too much and just take action. This is the key to their hyper-productivity.

The women of this combination are some of the world's most beautiful, but it's interesting that the reason for this may not necessarily be the way they actually look, but because of the confidence with which they carry themselves. Dawn French has said, "For me, whatever age or size I've been, I have rather liked myself. The shell is not the thing at all." Speaking about accepting and learning to love the way she looks, Serena Williams has said, "Since I don't look like every other girl, it takes a while to be okay with that. To be different. But different is good." They are classy birds, with classy minds and they know how to dress with classy panache that makes a statement yet maintains a certain level of intrigue. Catherine Zeta Jones has said, "I like to feel sexy… But I don't go out half-naked with 'sex' written across my back."

These ladies tend to be alpha females, whether their surface is gentle or otherwise, they are born with a need to lead and be around powerful men who can also lead. Sometimes, these ladies feel that they have an obligation to the world to project happiness and provide levity, whilst they are crying inside. But as they mature, they learn to moderate their own imbalances and become so much more compassionate with themselves and others. Dawn French has said, "I'm constantly astounded by how amazing women are. And as we go through all these different stages of life as long as you share them with others and say, 'Well, this is bloody weird,' you can get through everything."

Ultimately, the Rooster-Libra knows how to manage itself in order to be productive in a world that is so externally based. They know how to manage their mental resources in order to manifest the results they are looking for. Discipline, hard work and performing under pressure come relatively easily so imbues them with an admirable self-confidence. Dawn French has said, "Other than my memory being a bit woolly and my knees being a bit creaky, I don't really think there's anything I can't do." That is why this combination contains so many high achievers and champions. Serena Williams has said, "I always say that when I'm playing well, no one can beat me. I'm not just saying that to sound full of myself or anything, but it's true." They are also givers, but givers, even if they don't look it. They are not particularly soft or frilly, especially the women, even if they try to be milder, their energy tends to remain tough and forceful. It's just the way they are made. That does not mean that they do not care, they do and they like to give back in their own individual way. Bernie Mac said, "I don't have no story. Everybody wants this Hollywood story, but the world don't owe you nothing, man. It's what you owe the world."

Soul Mate:	Dragon-Pisces
Challenger:	Rabbit-Aries
Siblings:	Rooster-Gemini, Rooster-Aquarius
Best Friends:	Ox-Gemini, Ox-Libra, Ox-Aquarius, Snake-Gemini, Snake-Libra, Snake-Aquarius

Bernie Mac
Deborah Kerr
John Lithgow
Dawn French
Catherine Zeta-Jones
Steve McQueen
Gwen Stefani
Serena Williams
Dominic West
Bryan Ferry
Michael Madsen
Don McLean
Will Sampson
Cissy Houston
Divine
Fran Drescher
Mira Nair
Zach Galifianakis
Wyclef Jean
Rupert Friend
Christina Milian

ROOSTER – SCORPIO

Chinese Name: JI
Rank: 10th
Hours Ruled: 5pm – 7pm
Direction: Directly West
Season: Autumn
Month: September
Western Zodiac Equivalent of Rooster: Virgo
Virgo Western Element: Earth
Eastern Zodiac Equivalent of Scorpio: Boar
Scorpio Western Element: Water
Numerology: 116 = 8

Youthfulness is connected to the ability to see things new for the first time. So if your eyes still look at life with wonder, then you will seem young.
– Goldie Hawn

When the Rooster's fine earth granules meet with Scorpio's murky waters, the conservative meets the dark hedonist. The Rooster side wants to live the perfect life, whereas Scorpio wants unadulterated sensual fun; this combination flits from being highly cerebral and disciplined to being highly emotion-led and pleasure seeking. Remember that there are two iconic symbols for the Scorpio: the dark scorpion and the royal golden eagle. When the golden eagle picks up the otherwise earthbound Rooster, this combination serves to be a huge inspiration. It is also at this part of the 144-combination cycle that the Rooster allows its inner child out to play which continues through to the Rooster-Aquarius combination. Whatever they do, they bring an amazing work ethic and a sense of play. Goldie Hawn has said, "So curiosity, I think, is a really important aspect of staying young or youthful... Find the light in your life that you had when you were a little girl or little guy that made you happy."

Despite trying their best to live up to the image of themselves that they create in their mind, they will be knocked off track by their desire to live, to play and to have fun. Both Gerard Butler and Matthew McConaughey trained as lawyers but ended up in Hollywood. Matthew McConaughey said, "I was about 21 when I started. I dropped out of law school to go to film school – the idea of practicing law for my whole life seemed a little boring." But the heaviness of professional positions doesn't suit them, art or occupations where they can play are better, as they amplify the best traits of both the Rooster and Scorpio. Let the Scorpio's water enthuse the Rooster's plans and execute them with the childlike gusto. P. Diddy has said, "I'm like a child inside and I really get excited, so sometimes when I'm trying to go to bed, I'm so excited about the next day that I can't go to sleep." Larry King always enjoyed his job as talk show host, about it, he said, "I'm having as much fun today as I did when I made $55 a week, because it is as much fun."

The men of this combination are both the conservative prince and the dark knight; both positions are unique and solitary, so naturally, they often feel like others cannot understand them. They need to mull in their own energy and let their own thoughts amuse them. Gerard Butler has said, "I love to spend a lot of time on my own. I can seriously go into my own head and often love to let myself travel where I don't know where I'm going." There is a part of these guys that feel inhibited by the presence of other people, because they like being strange and they fear that nobody will accept their eccentricities, so they find a place to be alone to accept themselves in private. Matthew McConaughey has said, "I'm a loner and proud of it. I can be the world's most sociable guy... But being alone is where it's mostly at for me. Nothing beats the feeling of taking off on my own and driving to wherever the road takes me." There is an aspect of both the Rooster and the

Scorpio that needs to control its environment, but because they cannot do this to the extent that they require, they prefer to remove them every now and then so that they can exist in a world of their mental making. It is a happy place where they can be extraordinary all by themselves. Dolph Lundgren has said, "My problem is that people get intimidated by someone big and beautiful like me. They hate to think I can be smart as well."

The women of this combination are much like their male counterparts in that they also need alone time especially since the feminine aspect of the Rooster-Scorpio has a greater need to serve the needs of other people. But where the Scorpio lives in extremes, the Rooster is wise and manages to strike a balance for a few seconds...before the Scorpio pulls it to an extreme again. Echoing statements made earlier, Ivana Trump said, "Love what you do. There's always going to be someone else who's smarter than you, but there's no substitute for passion. People who are passionate always work the hardest, and that sets them apart!" With all of that sexy passionate Scorpio energy and Rooster's big personality, it makes sense that these women are so disarming as well as professionally successful. They are experts at using their personal skills in a professional environment. Goldie Hawn has said, "I'm not afraid of my femininity and I'm not afraid of my sexuality."

Ultimately, the Rooster-Scorpio rides the line between traditional pillar of the community and hedonistic outcast; they are complicated people to understand and it is through detailed observation of their behavior that any sort of personality pattern will emerge. But because of their dual nature, there is much wisdom present here which comes through a somewhat childlike mask. They know that they can never know enough so plan to be life-students for the rest of their lives. Larry King has said, "I remind myself every morning: Nothing I say this day will teach me anything. So if I'm going to learn, I must do it by listening." Both the Rooster and the Scorpio contain wisdom, but of different brands; the Rooster's wisdom is that of long-term vision and the Scorpio's is that of emotional awareness. When they combine here, they understand their own needs and desires enough to set themselves on a pathway that will lead them to their hearts desire, no matter how long it takes; they are in it for the long haul. Matthew McConaughey has said, "Be the lean horse for the long ride. I figure I am in the third round of a 15-round fight."

Soul Mate:	Dragon-Aquarius
Challenger:	Rabbit-Taurus
Siblings:	Rooster-Cancer, Rooster-Pisces
Best Friends:	Snake-Cancer, Snake-Scorpio, Snake-Pisces, Ox-Cancer, Ox-Scorpio, Ox-Pisces

Larry King
Goldie Hawn
Neil Young
Dolph Lundgren
Lyle Lovett
Gerard Butler
Matthew McConaughey
Sean Combs
Ivana Trump
Charles Bronson
Dan Castellaneta
Nancy Cartwright
Ellen Pompeo
Henry Winkler
Anni-Frid Lyngstad
Rodney Dangerfield
Nandita Das
Ofra Haza

Shilpa Shirodkar
Josh Henderson
Esha Deol
Kimberley Walsh
Sarah Harding

ROOSTER – SAGITTARIUS

Chinese Name: JI
Rank: 10th
Hours Ruled: 5pm – 7pm
Direction: Directly West
Season: Autumn
Month: September
Western Zodiac Equivalent of Rooster: Virgo
Virgo Western Element: Earth
Eastern Zodiac Equivalent of Sagittarius: Rat
Sagittarius Western Element: Fire
Numerology: 117 = 9

Underneath all this drag I'm really a librarian, you know.
– Bette Midler

When the fine earth granules of the Rooster meet with the centaur's frisky fires, some very complementary traits are amplified and many conflicting traits create some interesting idiosyncrasies. The Rooster brings its powerful dictionary-like mind to the mix, its hyper-critical faculties that push the standards sky high and resilient spirit; the Sagittarian centaur brings its raucous spirit, raw sexuality and uninhibited nature. What is contradictory however, is that the Rooster is a colorful yet conservative creature whereas the Sagittarius is a wild intellectual, too smart to be bound by societies conventions. The Rooster, however, likes to think it fits in with the rest of the world while shining just that tiniest bit weirder; with their unusual skillset, the people of this combination will always stick out, whether they want to or not. Jay Z has said, "By the time I got to record my first album, I was 26, I didn't need pen or paper – my memory had been trained just to listen to a song, think of the words, and lay them to tape."

While it's true that Roosters like to be given preferential treatment and work extra hard to achieve it, and the Sagittarius loves to live it up when the opportunity presents itself. The criticisms they face are often just projections by those who voice them. Their success just amplifies what was already there and because they function on a plain where many people see them, it just gives these, usually resentful people access to criticize them unfairly. Lead singer of the group Evanescence Amy Lee has said, "I never really did abandon my true self. It's not like I invented this imaginary person and started to be her."

The men of this combination tend to project sexiness because of their high status, power and spirit. They know how to project high self-esteem because they recognize how important image is. When that Sagittarius side takes precedence, they will indulge in hedonistic extremes: the Rooster will work without stopping to reap the benefits of what they have achieved. Perhaps there is a lot of truth to Rooster Ray Romano's joke when he said, "My wife gets all the money I make. I just get an apple and clean clothes every morning." They also are likely to be well read as these men love to learn about history, politics and power dynamics. Success is important to them, so they will want to focus on those things that will create the framework for it. Donny Osmond has said, "If you're climbing the ladder of life, you go rung by rung, one step at a time. Sometimes you don't think you're progressing until you step back and see how high you've really gone." Rooster-Sagittarius men have always wanted to win, achieve and be better, so even if they have to work, they will be working on their entrepreneurial projects in order to achieve a bigger life. But what fuels their fire? Jay-Z has said, "The burden of poverty isn't just that you don't always have the things you need, it's the feeling of being embarrassed every day of your life, and you'd do anything to lift that burden."

The women of this combination are campy, kitsch and fun. They are actually much classier than they present, but they love to have fun and bring that fun to others too. Bette Midler has said, "I wouldn't say I invented tack, but I definitely brought it to its present high popularity." But again, it's that dichotomy of the Rooster verses Sagittarius: conservative versus reckless-hedonist. They contain both sides but at times one will take the lead. These are not the type of women who rely on others or ask permission, they get out there and make their dreams come true. No matter how big, small or unique. Singer Natasha Beddingfield has said, "I started babysitting and then I got a part-time job at a pharmacy in England. I just remember loving the feeling of going out and buying my own clothes! I'd go bargain-hunting and get secondhand vintage stuff." Remember Rooster-Sagittarians like to stick out, it is just a part of their make-up. Amy Lee has echoed Natasha Beddingfield's statement when she spoke about buying unique clothes, she said, "Urban Outfitters has become is very much how I always dressed in high school by going to garage sales and getting stuff for 50 cents. Cost a little more now, to look like crap." These ladies are equally as successful as their male counter-parts and can be even tougher. They also tend to be naturally popular. Especially when they look within and find self-acceptance first. As Jackie Stallone has said, "The bottom line is that I like myself."

Ultimately, the Rooster-Sagittarius is concerned with success, self-development and then indulging in a hedonistic lifestyle. The hedonism can sometimes cause problems as it conflicts with many of their other desires, but as long as they can strike a balance and or bring the conservative aspects along, then the life they have created can remain intact. Their work ethic, achievements and personality puts them on a pedestal and they are often adored en mass. This, of course has its pros and cons. Britney Spears has said, "I would like to be called an inspiration to people, not a role model – because I make mistakes like everybody else. When I'm offstage,

I'm just like everybody else." This combination does not let its insecurities get the better of themselves and when they start overthinking things, they let themselves indulge for a moment, get scared, then they decide to leave it on the floor while they get up and get on with it. As Donny Osmond has said, "You have to believe in yourself, otherwise you can't do it. If you don't believe in yourself, how do expect anyone else to? Because ultimately, you're the one who has to do it."

Soul Mate:	Dragon-Capricorn
Challenger:	Rabbit-Gemini
Siblings:	Rooster-Aries, Rooster-Leo
Best Friends:	Ox-Aries, Ox-Leo, Ox-Sagittarius, Snake-Aries, Snake-Leo, Snake-Sagittarius

Jackie Stallone
Bette Midler
Ray Romano
Donny Osmond
Steve Buscemi
Jay-Z
Britney Spears
Amy Lee
Natasha Bedingfield
Deanna Durbin
Ernie Hudson
Shekhar Kapur
Michael Clarke Duncan
Marc Forster
Natascha McElhone
Richard Hammond
Krysten Ritter
Josh Dallas
Diya Mirza

ROOSTER – CAPRICORN

Chinese Name: JI
Rank: 10th
Hours Ruled: 5pm – 7pm
Direction: Directly West
Season: Autumn
Month: September
Western Zodiac Equivalent of Rooster: Virgo
Virgo Western Element: Earth
Eastern Zodiac Equivalent of Capricorn: Ox
Capricorn Western Element: Earth
Numerology: 118 = 1

Its hard to be a diamond in a rhinestone world.
– Dolly Parton

When the fine earth granules of the Rooster meet with the Capricorn's tough terrain, the two soils merge to create one mega earthy monster. This is the last of the formidable double earth combinations, so a certain level of stubbornness, strength and secret-superiority is only to be expected; it is these traits that usually create great people, who have a major influence on the world at large. Whether that be within politics, philanthropy or in the arts, their influence is huge. The Rooster-Capricorn is a little power-ball of light, a sparkling star that lives to bring its humor, positivity and sparkle to everyone and everything that surrounds it. Benjamin Franklin has said, "Do not anticipate trouble, or worry about what may never happen. Keep in the sunlight." It is their goal to inspire people to live happier lives through choosing happiness over any other options; the door to that happiness usually comes from greater education about new possibilities. If they need to be the conduit to help others get there, they will. Dolly Parton has said, "If your actions create a legacy that inspires others to dream more, learn more, do more and become more, then, you are an excellent leader."

Like all Rooster signs, this combination loves to talk! The infusion of Capricorn does nothing to stop their mouth from over-flowing, in fact, it often gets them into trouble as Steve Allen noted when he said, "If my mind ever listened to what my mouth said, I'd have a lot of accounting to do." But when all else fails, this combination can always be relied upon to come in and bring some of its sparkle to the situation and brighten it up with their humor. Steve Allen has said, "Humor is a social lubricant that helps us get over some of the bad spots." Needless to say it comes as no surprise that Roosters are drawn to those who do the same for them that they do for others. Diane Keaton has said, "I find the same thing sexy in a man now as I always have: humor. I love it when they are funny. It's to die for." It's inter-esting to note that people of this combination have a reputation for being simple because they are "happy." Dolly Parton is a good example, regarding this she said, "They think I'm simple-minded because I seem to be happy. Why shouldn't I be happy? I have everything I ever wanted and more. Maybe I am simple-minded. Maybe that's the key: simple."

The men of this combination are full of smiles, laughter and wit; they are open seeming and inclusive, yet one has to earn their real friendship. They can be prickly if someone tries to get too close and they prefer to cultivate superficial friendships. Yes, they seem simple, but they are ridiculously intelligent and are not hoodwinked easily. People often wonder why they choose the friends that they choose because they do not seem like they are on the same level or as if they do not have anything in common; what they have in common is their search of the truth and authenticity. Steve Allen has said, "Beware of assuming that credentials establish intelligence." It is not easy to keep these men from the truth and if anyone tries, they may find that the

Rooster-Capricorn cockerel will find another farm to serve. Benjamin Franklin said, "Geese are but Geese tho' we may think 'em Swans; and Truth will be Truth tho' it sometimes prove mortifying and distasteful."

The women of this combination are colorful, bright and often misunderstood. They love to look and feel sexy and make it a priority; but this sometimes leads people to assume they are promiscuous. They just love to feel attractive as it makes them feel alive. Sienna Miller has said, "I'm supposed to be this complete slapper, that's my reputation." There is just something larger than life about them. Sienna Miller has also said, "I quite love sequins; I think it's the drag queen in me." Similarly, Dolly Parton has said, "It's a good thing I was born a girl, otherwise I'd be a drag queen." Choosing the light, the bright and the downright sparkling, they shine everywhere they go and people often comment that they are like a breath of fresh air. This is because of the way they perceive themselves and the way that they choose to interpret the individual world that they live in. Betty White has said, "It's your outlook on life that counts. If you take yourself lightly and don't take yourself too seriously, pretty soon you can find the humor in our everyday lives. And sometimes it can be a lifesaver." Even Princess Kate Middleton infuses her sparkling humor into everyday life, when asked about how lucky she felt about being with the future King of England, she said, "He's so lucky to be going out with me."

Ultimately, the Rooster-Capricorn is a lively, energetic and loveable combination whose sparkling spirit overshadows their business acumen and how hard they work. They make it look so effortless and "simple" but the truth is they are anything but. They know what goes into becoming successful and they do it exceptionally well. Like all Roosters, they are not scared to work every hour that exists. At the same time, they will strive to live with as much integrity as possible. Benjamin Franklin has said, "Sell not virtue to purchase wealth, nor Liberty to purchase power." Dolly Parton has said, "I always just thought if you see somebody without a smile, give 'em yours!" This sparkling specimen continues to serve until the day it drops bringing light, levity and love to all of its endeavors, because, as Betty White has so aptly put it, "Retirement is not in my vocabulary. They aren't going to get rid of me that way." This Rooster keeps crowing until its days are up!

Soul Mate:	Dragon-Sagittarius
Challenger:	Rabbit-Cancer
Siblings:	Rooster-Taurus, Rooster-Virgo
Best Friends:	Snake-Taurus, Snake-Virgo, Snake-Capricorn, Ox-Taurus, Ox-Virgo, Ox-Capricorn

Steve Allen
Dolly Parton
Kate Middleton
Betty White
Diane Keaton
Sienna Miller
Benjamin Franklin
Richard Briers
Davy Jones
Diane Sawyer
Meredith Monroe
Eddie Redmayne
Emilie de Ravin
Jennifer Ehle
Kabir Bedi
Neil Nitin Mukesh

ROOSTER – AQUARIUS

Chinese Name: JI
Rank: 10th
Hours Ruled: 5pm – 7pm
Direction: Directly West
Season: Autumn
Month: September
Western Zodiac Equivalent of Rooster: Virgo
Virgo Western Element: Earth
Eastern Zodiac Equivalent of Aquarius: Tiger
Aquarius Western Element: Air
Numerology: 119 = 2

I work really hard at trying to see the big picture and not getting stuck in ego. I believe we're all put on this planet for a purpose, and we all have a different purpose... When you connect with that love and that compassion, that's when everything unfolds.
– Ellen Degeneres

When the fine earth granules of the Rooster meet with the lofty heights of the Aquarian cyclone, two of the most eccentric signs converge to create a very interesting personality. There is much inner tension here because the Rooster, despite being a strange one, has a need to fit in, but the Aquarius has never fit in, never will and does not even know about it. But this is where it gets interesting, because the Rooster-Aquarius is aware of the fact that they do not fit in and try as they may, their spirit just will not let them conform. So they find themselves in a difficult place. The sooner they accept their eccentricities, the faster they turn them to their advantage. The more evolved Rooster-Aquarius takes this to a deeper level and finds the capacity for huge compassion, understanding and love. Ellen Degeneres has said, "I'm not an activist; I don't look for controversy. I'm not a political person, but I'm a person with compassion. I care passionately about equal rights. I care about human rights. I care about animal rights."

When these two signs unite, they are set on a complicated journey leading them to greater self-awareness. The truth is everyone is unusual, but most people are able to hide behind a mask; the Rooster-Aquarius is too strange to be able to do that. Heather Locklear has said, "I always wanted to be the pretty girl, but I thought I wasn't. When I started acting and getting pretty girl roles, I felt like I was just pretending, and nobody saw I was just this big nerd." Luckily for them and the rest of the world, the universe has blessed them with a lot of persistence, resilience and a lot of sense. They are great marketers, networkers and they know a good product when they peck one. That is why they believe in themselves and their convictions regardless of what others think and go on to create miracles. Tom Hiddleston has said, "Never stop fighting. Never stop dreaming. And don't be afraid of wearing your heart on your sleeve... I felt like my voice wasn't worth hearing, and I think everyone's voice is worth hearing."

The men of this combination are not obviously handsome as their other Rooster counterparts, but what they have is that special something that makes you want to watch them. The Rooster-Aquarius male knows first and foremost how to work hard; everything else is relegated to second priority. Speaking about the profundity yet mundaneness of life, Joseph Gordon-Levitt has said, "That's what life is: repetitive routines. It's a matter of finding the balance between deviating from those patterns and knowing when to repeat them." Whatever they attempt, they will put their all into it because, as Tom Hiddleston put it, "...work is the same. Rigor, discipline, humility, punctuality, above all: truthfulness." It is not difficult to see why they are so successful. Although many of them find it hard to switch off, they learn to do so and they soon realize how much it supports their ability to function to a higher standard and how it positively impacts their success. Former owner of Harrods Mohamed Al-Fayed said, "I sleep at night; I do not think about anything. I put everything in my bag and go to sleep. Whatever you can do to me, it does not affect me. I started my life, my own life. I did not inherit it."

The women of this combination have a super-strong need to find authenticity in all that they do, these women tend to have a very conscious development, because they are so aware of who they are compared to their peers. Especially, other Rooster peers who are all so confident in their idiosyncrasies, or at least can pretend to be pretty well. Eventually, they begin to realize the crap that society has fed them and they let their angry energy fuel their noble intentions to make a difference. Kelly Rowland has said, "As women, we have to realize what we bring to the table. What do you want to do for the world? How do you want to change it? And when you know that, you don't have to compare yourself to anybody else." Minnie Driver has said, "I'm fascinated by how much we, as women, have to subjugate and hide ourselves in order to get on in the world." They have learned how to manage themselves and know how to fight for their space in the world, nicely, and then not so nicely if need be. Ellen Degeneres has said, "Find out who you are and be that person. That's what your soul was put on this Earth to be. Find that truth, live that truth and everything else will come."

Ultimately, the Rooster-Aquarius is most commonly an activist by another name; they want to use their skills, talents and resources to serve those who are not as blessed but without a label attached to their service. They are people with big hearts and with a heightened sensitivity which they hide fearing that people will use it against them. So they serve quietly because it makes them feel good. Mohamed Al-Fayed has said, "I will continue to distribute blankets, sleeping bags, warm clothing and food on a regular basis, in the hope that my modest efforts will give some comfort to those people we are able help." When they let themselves love openly, freely and abundantly, that love comes back to them compounded. Remember, the Rooster is the traditional eccentric and the Aquarian is the altruistic eccentric; together, they are wildly imaginative individuals with a lot to offer. Ellen Degeneres has said, "Here are the values that I stand for: honesty, equality, kindness, compassion, treating people the way you want to be treated and helping those in need. To me, those are traditional values."

Soul Mate:	Dragon-Scorpio
Challenger:	Rabbit-Leo
Siblings:	Rooster-Gemini, Rooster-Libra
Best Friends:	Ox-Gemini, Ox-Libra, Ox-Aquarius, Snake-Gemini, Snake-Libra, Snake-Aquarius

Tom Hiddleston
Joseph Gordon-Levitt
Mohamed Al-Fayed
Paris Hilton
Kelly Rowland
Minnie Driver
Ellen DeGeneres
Heather Graham
Ray Winstone
Lupe Fiasco
Kathy Najimy
Robert Townsend
Vinod Mehra
Kim Novak

Yoko Ono
Lana Turner
Carmen Miranda
Matthew Lillard
Michael Wincott
Ice-T
Anita Baker
David Lynch
Bill Bixby
Tina Louise
Telly Savalas
Paul Scofield
Jackie Shroff
Tina Munim
Amrita Singh
Madhubala

ROOSTER – PISCES

Chinese Name: JI
Rank: 10th
Hours Ruled: 5pm – 7pm
Direction: Directly West
Season: Autumn
Month: September
Western Zodiac Equivalent of Rooster: Virgo
Virgo Western Element: Earth
Eastern Zodiac Equivalent of Pisces: Rabbit
Pisces Western Element: Water
Numerology: 120 = 3

I hope to break through the Top 40, not by changing what I do but by changing the way people think.
– Josh Groban

When the fine granules of the Rooster join with Pisces colorful waters, it creates a personality that desires to be seen, loved and admired but for the right reasons. It is common for these types to be working towards a professional occupation or trade whilst enjoying a creative hobby that ends up becoming a lucrative career. Rooster lends its capacity for hard work and natural talent for detailed work whilst Pisces's pure passion pushes it forward with creative integrity. The result is a highly artistic being that is motivated by highlighting injustices or neglected issues. Bryce Dallas Howard said, "Right now as an artist, what I want to do is be a part of works that are unignorable." Similarly, Javier Bardem has said, "We are so scared about talking about death that we are letting people die in silence. It is good to talk publicly." Spike Lee said, "Before, I used to think that everything was based on race. Now class matters just as much."

Disciplined, dignified and blessed with a great deal of natural talent, they tend to be quick learners and understand what is required of them. As long as they are happy with the terms, they adapt themselves with little fuss and are a pleasure to work with. Talking about *The A-Team*, Dirk Benedict said, "I enjoyed it immensely. By nature I'm terribly serious, so as an actor I tend to want to be silly." Yet, they do not confuse the reason they do anything. The main thing remains the main thing. Terence Howard said, "I work to pay the bills, not to listen to the hype." The million-dollar attribute that members of this combination share is their ability to learn their craft in detail, whether they are accountants, astronauts or actors, they are highly competent specialists who put their heart into everything that they do. Michael Caine said, "I'll always be around because I'm a skilled professional actor. Whether or not I've any talent is beside the point."

The men of this combination have a classiness and dorky authority. Rather than a seriousness, they have an earthy common sense that allows them to see the practicalities of a situation in a way that others do not always and trying to get others to understand their point of view can be difficult as they are not particularly patient, so end up coming across as condescending when what they are actually expressing is their frustration. They are often misunderstood and misconstrued. Javier Bardem said, "I truly consider myself non-sexy, which is fine for me... The only thing I can do is act, but it's not something I even feel comfortable doing." They also have an alternative view of women that is neither chauvinistic or anti-chauvinistic, just more of a commonsensical view; Dirk Benedict said, "Hamlet does not scan as Hamletta. Nor does Han Solo as Han Sally. Faceman is not the same as Facewoman. Nor does a Stardoe a Starbuck make. Men hand out cigars. Women "hand out" babies. And thus the world, for thousands of years, has gone round." Their intentions tend to be nobler than they seem, even when they present themselves like arrogant snobs.

The women of this combination are equally as classy as their male counterparts, but have to try harder to be seen for their substance. They have that typical Rooster work ethic and driven towards the more highbrow of artistic inclinations. Nina Simone said, "When I was studying...there weren't any black concert pianists. My choices were intuitive, and I had the technique to do it. People have heard my music and heard the classic in it, so I have become known as a black classical pianist." All three of the Chinese earth signs have a need to control their external environment as it provides for them a feeling of security, but the Rooster in particular likes to maintain in control of its faculties and circumstances. That is why they gravitate towards professional, sensible and conservative types who have a high level of self-command because of their self-respect. The Pisces prioritizes creative integrity so when combined with the Rooster, it creates a sign that will go against the grain in order to maintain its own self-image. Unfortunately, this sometimes comes with downsides, as the masses only really understand conformists. Speaking about alcoholism in her family, Bryce Dallas Howard said, "I've never had a sip of alcohol in my life, I wasn't interested in losing control... When I was in high school, I would never go to parties because I would be embarrassed to say no. Consequently, I had almost no social group."

Ultimately, the Rooster-Pisces has a need to feel protected so they rarely allow others to see the actual workings of their inner mind and dislike exposing any aspects of themselves without some sense of control over the whole situation. Michael Caine has said, "Be like a duck, my mother used to tell me. Remain calm on the surface and paddle like hell underneath." This does not mean that they allow themselves to get complacent or let their skills get rusty. Au contraire, they want to continue growing to be the best they can possibly be. It's the best way to inspire others to do the same and with their skillset and unique abilities, they hit heights that allow them to do just that. Josh Groban has said, "Everyone can change the world in some way, whether it's being a mentor to someone younger than you or someone that doesn't have as much experience as you. If you're passionate enough, you can do whatever you want and definitely change the world."

Soul Mate:	Dragon-Libra
Challenger:	Rabbit-Virgo
Siblings:	Rooster-Cancer, Rooster-Scorpio
Best Friends:	Ox-Cancer, Ox-Scorpio, Ox-Pisces, Snake-Cancer, Snake-Scorpio, Snake-Pisces

Bryce Dallas Howard

Javier Bardem

Michael Caine

Thomas Jane

Ryan Cartwright

Paget Brewster

John Turturro

Terrence Howard

Ryan Cartwright

Shannon Tweed

Chaz Bono

Spike Lee

Robert Sean Leonard

Timothy Spall

Majandra Delfino

Theresa Russell

Aunjanue Ellis

Kim Raver

Shahid Kapoor

Dirk Benedict

Ellen Muth
John Heard
Taylor Dooley
Elodie Yung
Jenna Boyd
Josh Groban
Barry Bostwick
David Anders
Bubba Smith
Quincy Jones

THE DOG

THE DOG

I am the independent guardian, the iconoclast, the belligerent-diva. I was born cynical, suspicious and mature of mind, I get younger as I age. My mind flowers with youthful exuberance as I realize that I was never alone and that I did not need to be so strong. Forget 20/20, I have 50/50 crystal clarity. It frustrates me that the rest of the world lags so far behind; my creativity captivates the masses as I bore of my own edgy magic. My convictions are titanium. I need not external validation for I have greater inner resources. Many come to me for validation; oh how I pity those fools! But it is my duty to create a safety net for others and as I do, the heavens create a safety net for me! All are drawn to my beauty though some fear the feral creature hiding behind my eyes. Allow my doggy-drive to inspire you to the heavens for it is in my nature to uplift. Come to me for creativity, for guidelines, for magic and watch it manifest in my paws. I am the practical dreamer.

I am the Dog.

With a universal sense of humor, witty, camp and shooting star quality that is a joy to behold, you are like a breath of fresh air. Powerfully creative forces, dogs are endowed with truly great talent. Dog women can be stunning femme fatales with diva-like reputations and the men are renowned for their genius capacity. With firm convictions and a belief in justice, you serve unselfishly for the good of mankind. The Chinese compare dog signs to the ocean: calm on the surface with unimaginable activity inside. You are essentially insecure with a noble heart that you find difficult to entrust to anyone.

Career-wise, the Dog is the ultimate all rounder. Their skill is being able to learn anything very quickly and well. On top of that, they bring their wit, clarity and spirited nature along which is an added bonus. With an audience present, they will put on the extrovert face but always need their alone time; in a work context, this allows them to work well in a team and solo. In the entertainment world, they are drawn to fashion, music and writing. Dogs have the most fertile of imaginations and need many outlets. These people are the icons, the kings and queens, seemingly in every environment. You choose it, a Dog is the icon, the king of rock 'n' roll was Elvis, king of pop was Michael Jackson, queen of pop is Madonna, king of investments is Donald Trump, queen of the charity world was Mother Teresa... Dogs do not covet such titles, but they are forthcoming. They also enjoy working in banking, housing, police enforcement, politics and within religious environments.

Compatibilities

Soul Mate: Rabbit
Challenger: Dragon
Best Friends: Tiger & Horse
Good Relations: Ox & Monkey

DOG – ARIES

Chinese Name: GOU
Rank: 11th
Hours Ruled: 7pm – 9pm
Direction: North – Northwest
Season: Autumn
Month: October
Western Zodiac Equivalent of Dog: Libra
Libra Western Element: Air
Eastern Zodiac Equivalent of Aries: Dragon
Aries Western Element: Fire
Numerology: 121 = 4

I don't think anyone knows as much about what's right for me as I do... In this world I call the shots and I think I know best.
– Mariah Carey

When the defensive Dog's whirlwind merges with the ferocious Fire of Aries, the result is a complicated personality bursting with talent and intelligence although the overriding impulse is to play and express. Compared to the other Dog combinations, this one is more openly vulnerable, openly sensitive and more susceptible to external influences, even though they always try to project an image of strength. This vulnerability is both their downfall and their biggest gift; by being open in this way, they allow for continual growth through accepting and working through adversity. Mariah Carey has said, "I'm not vain, I'm insecure."

Often times, Dog signs close down, ignore and displace blame in order to avoid dealing with matters knocking on their door, but with Aries the will is there to confront them more readily. That does not mean that the Dog tendency towards addictive behavior does not exist here, it does. Discussing his alcoholism

Gary Oldman said, "I was drinking alone, which is worse, it's often solitary and desperate... Someone once described alcoholics as egomaniacs with low self-esteem; perfect definition." The desire for a spiritual detox takes over and leads them to a rebirth of sorts usually in Dog and Dragon years, which is the Dog's opposite sign.

In most other respects, this combination is very typically *Dog*. They are loyal, have an intelligent, sarcastic wit, yet are surprisingly introverted. They have strong convictions and a powerful belief in their own intrinsic value, which often finds opposition from those less connected to their universal spirit. It is for this reason they are labeled unconventional. Gary Oldman has said, "I don't think Hollywood knows what to do with me." Likewise, Tim Curry said, "I'm not a conventional leading man at all and have no wish to be." With a powerful imagination, they receive spiritual messages through visions and dreams. Mariah Carey has said, "What I write is all from my imagination... I put myself in other women's shoes; I can feel their pain and joy." So imagination is used to highlight the truths of reality.

The men of this combination tend to have striking looks regardless of whether they are deemed attractive or not. More introverted than they seem, they prefer to keep the company of a small number of friends, one on one is ideal, though in party crowds the clown face naturally arises from the depths to enthrall the audience. Their empathic sensibility makes them good bedroom material and they seem to derive great pleasure out of giving. There is huge generosity of spirit here too. Yes, they can be selfish, prickly and precious, but more significantly, they keep perspective and know is really important. Discussing how he performs his brand of comedy, Seth Rogen said, "Reality and honesty is the most important thing. As soon as it feels like we're making a joke where there wouldn't be one, then we don't do it." There has to be integrity in things that they attempt as they feel dirty or incomplete or out of sorts without it. Vince Vaughn has said, "There's a lot of comedies lately that have been at people's expense or been kind of acidic or mean-spirited. And some folks like that... I like something that makes us all feel closer. Comedy, at its best, can be healing."

The women are independent powerhouses who have all the makings of a queen bee although they do not make use of those attributes, preferring to be lone queens. They just do not have the temperament or the energy to court followers on a day-to-day basis. They would rather reveal their excellence and be admired from a distance. They are born with a sense of their own power as a woman and know how to use it. Hayley Atwell has said, "Nude scenes can be very liberating. I feel very human. This is me, with all my little imperfections." Discussing her character Lyra in the Movie *The Golden Compass*, Dakota Blue Richards said, "I feel like I can relate to her. I like to think I'm quite brave. I stand up for myself. And I don't let other people tell me what to do. Well, unless it's my mum." She was twelve years old at the time. Being "all or nothing" types, they often go to the ends of each spectrum, some refusing to take responsibility for their lives and lazing around in with the door of creative possibilities open to them that they procrastinate walking through or they take supreme responsibility for absolutely everything. Mariah Carey said, "I decided to make my own ski-wear range after I found there were no fashion outfits for me to wear on the piste."

Ultimately, they are exceptionally accomplishment oriented and like to stay busy as it gives their mind a focus and does not slip into other destructive modes. They like to stay active, but productively active. Alan Arkin has said, "Success has to do with achieving your goals, your internal goals, and growing as a person." The way Aries's fire wraps itself around with the Dog's whirlwind more often than not creates a person who is powerfully driven. They want to succeed and achieve and be recognized for their talent, their work and their hearts. Working through each of their insecurities, they often do not let themselves stop to appreciate the fruits of their own labor, nor do they really accept a compliment; one wonders if they know how. Why don't they stop to take it all in? Strange as it seems, their own beauty freaks them out, even though it endears all else. Accept your wonderfulness! Mariah Carey has said, "I prayed very hard for this to happen and it happened. I don't even think about what I've achieved, I haven't focused on it and I wish I had, because I really want to enjoy it, and I don't know if I am enjoying it, because I am going through my life like a bulldozer. I still haven't marveled at it."

Soul Mate:	Rabbit-Virgo
Challenger:	Dragon-Libra
Siblings:	Dog-Leo, Dog-Sagittarius
Best Friends:	Tiger-Aries, Tiger-Leo, Tiger-Sagittarius, Horse-Aries, Horse-Leo, Horse-Sagittarius

Gary Oldman
Gina Carano
Cobie Smulders
Saoirse Ronan
Seth Rogen
Hayley Atwell
Jay Baruchel
Vince Vaughn
Alec Baldwin
Tim Curry
Elizabeth Mitchell
Sean Faris
Sam Huntington
Lara Flynn Boyle

Shemar Moore
Ed O'Neill
Barry Pepper
Alan Arkin
Dakota Blue Richards
Taran Killam
Chyler Leigh
Mariah Carey

DOG – TAURUS

Chinese Name: GOU
Rank: 11th
Hours Ruled: 7pm – 9pm
Direction: North – Northwest
Season: Autumn
Month: October
Western Zodiac Equivalent of Dog: Libra
Libra Western Element: Air
Eastern Zodiac Equivalent of Taurus: Snake
Taurus Western Element: Earth
Numerology: 122 = 5

I only answer to two people, myself and God.
– Cher

When the guardian Dog's cyclone hits Taurus's firm earth, it finds that the ground does not break or is even damaged by its power; in fact, its solidity allows the storm to bounce higher and higher. These two signs are exceptionally complimentary and create sparky personalities that do as they please without needing anybody's approval. Beauty, common sense and rigidity combine to create an army of one that inspires the masses to come along for the ride. Indeed, this is universally one of the most beloved combinations of all. Just take a look at the personalities born with this combined sign. With an alternative way of viewing the world, they see the details, the colors, the textures that most other people zoom past. That is why these people have so many artistic inclinations. There are many actors, singers, dancers and writers born under this combination, sometimes they do more than one, sometimes all four! writer-performer Tina Fey has said, "I like to write about women, not so much about the way they relate to men, but about the way they relate to each other." Another writer-performer, Alan Bennett has said, "I write plays about things that I can't resolve in my mind. I try to root things out." These artistic inclinations are what keep them grounded. And they really believe in what they are doing.

Consider staunch Shirley MacLaine is about her spiritual beliefs regardless of how the media have portrayed her; how fearlessly Joanna Lumley fought for the Gurkhas; how consistently Cher has always stood up for herself regardless of the "controversy" surrounding her. They always listen to their own instinct if they want to be guided best. Cher has said, "I wish that I did the things that I really believe in, because when I do, my life goes much smoother."

The men of this combination are sexy, intellectual and competitive; they have a need to be the top Dog! As Andre Agassi has said, "Being number two sucks." They are prepared to throw down the gauntlet and put themselves on the line to achieve their greatest desires. Inside most Dog men, is a teenager that sometimes acts like a grown up, but most of the time, he is as he feels, a youngster in this crazy grown up world that doesn't know what it's doing or where it's going. Maybe that is why when he released his youthful hip hop album at 40 years old, Jordan Knight of New Kids on the Block fame said, "There's this idea that when you turn 40, you automatically go to adult contemporary heaven, but I want to try and challenge that." If anyone was going to, it would be a Dog sign. It is also interesting to note that both of these men had a struggle with addiction. Letting go of their youth and everything that comes with that is never easy for this combination because they often get so much mileage because of their "cool" factor. If growing older is tough for the men, imagine what it is like for the women.

The women of this combination are very prominent in the performance arts, whatever genre or style, when there is a woman who is as gutsy as she is beautiful, as seductive as she is independent, as fearless as she is intelligent your first guess ought to be Dog. And if she is the sort who stands up for people whose voices are being drowned out with selfless gusto, your next guess ought to be Taurus. As Shirley MacLaine has said, "Don't be afraid to go out on a limb. It's where all the fruit is." The beauty aspect is one that Dog women cannot get away from. This part of the 144-combination cycle especially seems to produce women with natural beauty and they seek to preserve it as much as they can. Cher has said, "I kill myself for my body." Joanna Lumley has said, "I would do anything to keep looking the job. I think you make an extra effort if you're on show." Dog women are stereo-typed as the beauties of the Chinese cycle; for Eastern astro-logical folk *Dog* equates to *Beauty*. So when stunning Michelle Pfeiffer said, "I have days when I just feel I look like a dog..." one wonders whether she knew what she was saying? Super spiritual mother Dog Shirley MacLaine has set out what the Dog-Taurus manifesto is very well when she said, "I want women to be liberated and still be able to have a nice ass and shake it." Well rest assured, the Dog-Taurus women most definitely do! As youngsters, these adorable puppy's want nothing more than to grow up so that they can live with some influence, some power and really have some fun. As Uma Thurman has said, "I was an escapee of childhood. I always wanted to grow up." But as they reach their forties, they begin to feel like they have wasted their youth and not lived as effectively as they might have done. This is really not true and they just need to relax about this.

Ultimately, the Dog-Taurus inspires people everywhere it goes and this impact is probably much larger than it can comprehend. In their being true to who they are, they unconsciously give permission to everyone around them to do the same. And because they are so prominent, they inspire on a huge level. The issue that they face is that the Dog is a bit of a cynic, as is the

Taurean Bull; when they come together, they have a field day discussing everything that is wrong with the world, deciding which cause to take on next. Or they could just lighten up. Michelle Pfeiffer said, "Somewhere along the line I made the switch and was able to look at the bright side rather than the dark side all the time. Now I look at everything I have and think how lucky I am."

Soul Mate:	Rabbit-Leo
Challenger:	Dragon-Scorpio
Siblings:	Dog-Virgo, Dog-Capricorn
Best Friends:	Tiger-Taurus, Tiger-Virgo, Tiger-Capricorn, Horse-Taurus, Horse-Virgo, Horse-Capricorn

Arletty
Simone Simon
Bea Arthur
Shirley MacLaine
Alan Bennett
Henry Cooper (Boxer)
David Suchet
Cher
Joanna Lumley
Candice Bergen
Maureen Lipman
Michelle Pfeiffer
Andie MacDowell
Uma Thurman
Jason Lee
Tina Fey
Louis Theroux
Andre Agassi
Jordan Knight
Tionne 'T-Boz' Watkins

Pooja Bedi
Kirsten Dunst
Kelly Clarkson
Bridget Moynahan
Cory Monteith
Harry Shum Jr.
Eric West

DOG – GEMINI

Chinese Name: GOU
Rank: 11th
Hours Ruled: 7pm – 9pm
Direction: North – Northwest
Season: Autumn
Month: October
Western Zodiac Equivalent of Dog: Libra
Libra Western Element: Air
Eastern Zodiac Equivalent of Gemini: Horse
Gemini Western Element: Air
Numerology: 123 = 6

"Show me someone without an ego, and I'll show you a loser.
– Donald Trump

"I never diet. I smoke. I drink now and then. I never work out.
I work very hard, and I am worth every cent."
– Naomi Campbell

When the Dog's tornado merges with Gemini's hectic hurricane, air meets air, idealism meets humanitarianism and the search for beauty meets the need to make a statement. These two air signs have much in common, which creates a somewhat consistent character, but one that is not easy to manage. The Dog comes with deep convictions, is prepared to take risks to explore them and on some level, sees itself as an example for others to learn from; the Gemini lends its frisky sense of fun, love of social play and desire to inspire. The Dog-Gemini is not necessarily the most likeable of combinations with their highly opinionated views that often polarize people either for or against them. This is why they are supremely celebrated as well as denigrated. When asked about her looks, Supermodel Naomi Campbell stated, "I don't think I was born beautiful. I just think I was born me." Naturally beautiful, Dog-Geminis seek to preserve and augment their beauty even more so. This never-ending chase of beauty is a very Dog sign trait and it is most powerful at this part of the cycle. Along with this however, is the need for personal authenticity at all costs. They can handle not being liked (or so they claim), but what they cannot handle is not living up to their own expectations, especially regarding their standards of integrity, even if they are unattainable. Judy Garland said, "I'm a woman who wants to reach out and take 40 million people in her arms."

Dog signs in general are trendsetters, have the most fertile imaginations and also the broadest skill set. They are multi-talented people whose abilities rank almost as highly as their looks. Despite the icy surface, they can be highly insecure creatures even though they claim not to care what other people think about them. Some may say, *they protest too much*. This might also explain the mask of narcissism so many of them wear. It could also be the reason why addiction is often a problem for this combination. Naomi Campbell, Judy Garland and footballer George Best all had public struggles with addiction; it is what is believed to have taken Garlands and Best's life. George Best said, "I was born with a great gift, and sometimes with that comes a destructive streak...I was ill, and everyone could see it but me."

The men of this combination can be exceptionally alpha types, endowed with looks, money and power. Who better to illustrate the Dog-Gemini male than Donald Trump? Describing himself, he said, "Love him or hate him, Trump is a man who is certain about what he wants and sets out to get it, no holds barred. Women find his power almost as much of a turn-on as his money." These men are smart, sharp and instinctive. Their feelings offer them powerful guidance and they listen, but they just don't talk about it. The last thing that they would want is to be seen as airy-fairy; no, they are top dog; they demand to be taken seriously and perceived as in-control, powerful with a touch of the cool. And what is "cool" to them? Superstar Prince has said, "Cool means being able to hang with yourself. All you have to ask yourself is 'Is there anybody I'm afraid of? Is there anybody who if I walked into a room and saw, I'd get nervous?' If not, then you're cool."

The women of this combination tend to be quiet, intelligent and sharp. Their minds pick up on the details of a situation quickly and that activist part of them is always ready to fight for a cause. They are notorious for putting in complaints because someone did not do their job properly or did not fulfill the terms of their agreement. They get a real sense of validation when they make a difference for their community, even if that very same community shuns them. But even the gentler, softer Dog-Geminis will not be moved if they do not choose to. Even Judy Garland said, "You think you can make me sing? Do you think you can? You can get me there, sure, but can you make me sing? I sing for myself. I sing when I want to, whenever I want to, just for me. I sing for my own pleasure, whenever I want. Do you understand that?" Incidentally, when Hollywood was going to make a biopic of Judy Garland's life, it was going to star Annette Bening, who is also a Dog-Gemini.

Ultimately, they can be the most respected of people and at other times they are criticized all the way down to hell; but whatever the social weather, one thing that remains is that they will be who they are at all costs. Personal authenticity, loyalty and fairness are the most important priorities to a Dog-Gemini. As Naomi Campbell has said, "I loved watching so many of the great designers I've worked with do what they do. That's why I'm still loyal to the designers that I've known since I was 16." Pleasing people comes a distant second to staying true to what they stand for and they can be verbal ninjas when at their best. Donald

Trump has said, "When somebody challenges you, fight back. Be brutal, be tough." So despite all of their prickliness, sourpuss criticism and egocentric narcissism, why are they still so talked about and actually, so popular? Because they are troupers who have a larger than usual struggle which when they decide to take on, do so admirably. Beyond everything, it is their refusal to give up that wins them everyone's respect because it is a rare and quality trait. It doesn't entirely make sense, but as Prince has said, "A strong spirit transcends rules."

Soul Mate:	Rabbit-Cancer
Challenger:	Dragon-Sagittarius
Siblings:	Dog-Libra, Dog-Aquarius
Best Friends:	Tiger-Gemini, Tiger-Libra, Tiger-Aquarius, Horse-Gemini, Horse-Libra, Horse-Aquarius

Judy Garland
Annette Bening
Naomi Campbell
Donald Trump
Prince
George Best
Prince William Windsor
Joseph Fiennes
Jamie Kennedy
Jenny Jones
Helen Baxendale
Drew Carey
Federico García Lorca
Paulette Goddard
Christopher Lee
Joan Caulfield
Eileen Atkins
Jackie Wilson

Paul Weller
Neil Finn
Brian Cox
Lasse Hallström
Stefania Sandrelli
Keenen Ivory Wayans
Leah Remini
Izabella Scorupco
Glenn Quinn
Jane Goldman

DOG – CANCER

Chinese Name: GOU
Rank: 11th
Hours Ruled: 7pm – 9pm
Direction: North – Northwest
Season: Autumn
Month: October
Western Zodiac Equivalent of Dog: Libra
Libra Western Element: Air
Eastern Zodiac Equivalent of Cancer: Sheep
Cancer Western Element: Water
Numerology: 124 = 7

I'm my own worst critic. I could tell the critics a thing or two about my shows.
– Jennifer Saunders

When the Dog's tornado meets with the Cancer's serene stream of secrets, the Dog's fertile imagination is further fuelled by the crab's copious creative resources. They have ideas faster than they know what to do with. In addition to their shared creative capacities, these two signs are quiet, peace loving and homely. They also both like to lead, let it be their vision that is being created and let it be their rules that are being obeyed. The more evolved Dog-Cancers strive to lead by example and work towards a just world, but they start where they can make the biggest difference first. Sylvester Stallone has said, "For every guy, there is an opportunity to be a lot better than he thought he could be. We can't all be the star of the team, but we can be a star in our life. That's where you set your goal."

All Dogs are known for their powerful convictions and most are very well read, but there are those less evolved Dog signs that just want what they want and let their ego lead their life journey. Most Dog-Cancers are not this way, although this vanity is a part of their make up and the sooner they accept it, the faster it moves to a place of balance where something productive can be done with it. Mel Brooks has said, "A brushstroke of vanity is good to add into the mix, to balance your timidity. We're all blessed with a lot of timidity and a lot of worry and anxiety, and vanity is a good antidote."

Where the Cancer seeks to understand their emotions and share them openly, the Dog wants to understand them and bury them again, as the Dog finds it harder to accept certain aspects of itself. This is why so many are drawn to creative positions where they can express their feelings through their work and conceal their personalities in everyday life. It's a common manifestation of their contradictory needs. Jennifer Saunders has said, "My job gives me the attention I'd otherwise crave." Dog signs generally are very drawn to fashion, especially at this part of the cycle. This sign in particular has many fashion icons such as Pierre Cardin, Giorgio Armani and Jennifer Saunders is also known for creating the show *Absolutely Fabulous* which spoofed the world of fashion. As a side note, this show was full of Dog signs in the main cast and the guest stars, much like the camp and outrageous *Rocky Horror Show*.

The men of this combination tend to be gifted with intelligence, charisma and a competitive spirit. Mel Brooks has said, "I don't believe in this business of being behind, better to be in front." Remember that the Cancer sign perceives itself as a leader. The Dog is Yang, the Cancer is Yin so there is a complementary mix of polarities here. That could be why Kevin Bacon has said, "I'm very comfortable being married to an extremely strong, opinionated, and driven woman. But I also sit at the head of the table. I have both of those sides to me." At the same time, he had previously joked "It's getting laid when you're not famous that takes some talent." With their looks and charisma, these guys can and do have a lot of fun but they also have the sense to know when they have met someone worth holding onto and they are prepared to grow up some. Chris O'Donnell has said, "I knew when I got into this business I couldn't have it both ways: I could live the playboy lifestyle, which is not a bad thing to do, or have a traditional family life, which is how I grew up. And that was more important to me."

The women of this combination are open to universal energies, ethereal inspiration and they love to play. But at the same time, they are private creatures that need their own space. Priyanka Chopra has said, "I am a very private person. No one ever knows anything about me as I don't think it is necessary. I tell people as much as I want them to know about me." With a need to be seen, heard and valued, they also find the same trait highly vulgar if one is trying to be seen and heard without cause. They love to express their inner child and it is exceptionally healthy for them to do so; it keeps them fresh, frisky and fun. But, they are very picky about who to share this energy with. But when they do give you their affection, that characteristic Dog-Cancer loyalty will amplify their love and they become friends for life. Talking about working on a TV show, Jennifer Saunders has said, "You get crushes on people. You have to see them every day in that week. They're a fantastic person, and it could be a man or a woman."

Ultimately, the Dog-Cancer has the sort of spirit that believes in its own creative superiority, therefore does not take no for an answer if confronted by it. They have an inner knowing that what they are proposing will work and this remains even as they age so they continue to do all that inspires them. Director Mel Brooks said, "I'm still a horse that can run. I may not be able to win the Derby, but what do you do when you retire? People retire and they vegetate. They go away and they dry up." The producers of *Rocky* wanted Sylvester Stallone's script and offered him $350,000 (in 1976) if they could cast somebody else in the lead role, but Stallone refused, despite only having $106 in his bank; the film with Stallone in the lead role eventually went on to earn $226 million at the box office. The creative and competitive spirit that Sylvester Stallone and his character of Rocky embody perfectly illustrates the Dog-Cancer. Sylvester Stallone has said, "I believe there's an inner power that makes winners or losers. And the winners are the ones who really listen to the truth of their hearts."

Soul Mate: Rabbit-Gemini
Challenger: Dragon-Capricorn
Siblings: Dog-Scorpio, Dog-Pisces
Best Friends: Tiger-Cancer, Tiger-Scorpio, Tiger-Pisces,
                  Horse-Cancer, Horse-Scorpio, Horse-Pisces

Chris O'Donnell
Kevin Bacon
Jennifer Saunders
Sylvester Stallone
Danny Glover
Sydney Pollack
Mel Brooks
Priyanka Chopra
Louise Fletcher
George W. Bush
Jared Padalecki
Rain
Justin Chambers
Shawnee Smith
Sean Hayes
Mike White
Beck

Jason Orange
Bruce Campbell
Peter Tolan
Neetu Singh
Michael Flatley
Cheech Marin
Giorgio Armani
Pierre Cardin
Harry Dean Stanton
Fred Gwynne

DOG – LEO

Chinese Name: GOU
Rank: 11th
Hours Ruled: 7pm – 9pm
Direction: North – Northwest
Season: Autumn
Month: October
Western Zodiac Equivalent of Dog: Libra
Libra Western Element: Air
Eastern Zodiac Equivalent of Leo: Monkey
Leo Western Element: Fire
Numerology: 125 = 8

I'm tough, ambitious and I know exactly what I want...if that makes me a bitch – okay!
– Madonna

When the Dog's cyclone driven storm meets the Leo's firestorm, the super storm rages unapologetically. Entering their worlds with an instinctive understanding of what motivates people, they love nothing more than to toy with those whose values oppose their own by setting psychological traps to "accidentally" reveal their adversary's agenda. Their mental acuity and devilish nature makes them quite difficult to navigate. Although academically they excel, they are not made for the educational system as it stands because their desire for the freedom of the truth, exploration of innovative options and wanting to do it *their way* rubs people *the wrong way*. Anna Paquin has said, "I was honestly never a huge school person." Like most Dog signs, they are born old but as they age, they get younger, more relaxed and learn to find pleasure in the simple things. Until then, they let themselves be guided by their senses, utilize their acute minds and live in their fertile imagination. Madonna has said, "When I'm hungry, I eat. When I'm thirsty, I drink. When I feel like saying something, I say it."

With brave hearts, the Dog-Leo treads into the wilderness knowing that its is not the biggest animal in the jungle, but that is okay, because they know who they are, what their skills are and best of all, they know how to project their spirit in such a way that it will scare the life right out of the bigger, stronger types. With the fusion of Leo here, there is also more ego. Most Dog signs are vain anyway, but with Leo, this creature has an expectation that everyone assumes that they are the fairest of them all. Madonna has said, "I can be really snotty to people but that's not anything new really. I always acted like a star long before I was one."

The men of this combination tend to be quiet and spicy looking with thick auras. They exude power and sex. They are very appealing; even when you do not like them and do not want to like them, there's a part of you that does, despite their irrational outbursts and egocentric diatribes. Even though, with a fire sign added to the Dog, they do become more openly vulnerable, they do their best to prevent it from being visible so that they are perceived as confident, in control and hopefully, heroic. Cam Gignet has said, "I've played so many jobs where I'm fearless, but it's far from me. I wish I were like that in real life." So what are they like in real life? One cannot contain this much sex appeal without it stemming from a darker recess. These are naughty, nasty, dirty boys with more than few secrets. Perhaps that is why they are stereotyped as the bad boy or the rebel. Cam Gignet said, "It hasn't gotten fun for me, (playing) the good guy. Maybe because I don't know how to do it..." Also, they learn to chill out slower than their female counterparts and it takes them longer to grow "young" as they age. Chris Nolan has said, "I never considered myself a lucky person. I'm the most extraordinary pessimist. I truly am."

The women of this combination are also dominant forces to be reckoned with. The quieter they are, the easier it is to love and deal with them because their mouth causes no end of drama. Active participants in the creation of every moment of their lives, they come with a naughty, haughty sex appeal from a young age. These are not women who allow themselves to be perceived as or treated like victims; their strength is just too obvious. Perhaps that is why Madeline Stowe felt so opposed to being offered certain roles in her acting career, she said, "While it was nice working with a lot of those people, ultimately it was unsatisfying to play a victim, and I realized I couldn't do it anymore. It had to stop." They are sexually provocative and do what they can to highlight the damage that repression of the self causes. It also makes them appealing to people at the same time as garnering attention. Actress Anna Paquin has said, "I'm Anna Paquin. I'm bisexual and I give a damn." The Dog-Leo vixen would argue that her personality is naturally controversial because what others see as risqué or salacious, is all in a day's work for her. While that is true, she does have a greater need to be seen, heard and listened to, so may employ techniques to be so, especially when she is lacking in esteem. She just really likes to get her own way. Quoting from Madonna's book *Sex*, Madonna said, "A lot of people are afraid to say what they want. That's why they don't get what they want."

Ultimately, the Dog-Leo is a combination that has its head screwed on, its instinct tuned and that fertile Dog imagination working to create the next pathway that the team will take. They do not slow down and find that they like to be in the midst of the activity, ideally, leading it in some way. When they have made up their mind about the next course of action, they are like a *Dog with a bone* and do not lose sight of their vision until it is a manifested reality, despite the consequences. Anna Paquin has said, "Stubborn people get themselves in a lot of trouble, but they also get things done." They are not easy people to understand and they often do not describe themselves accurately. Just like Madonna who is famous for reinventing herself, these creatures are always in a state of artistic evolution, so how could they possibly keep up with themselves? If *they* can't, how do they expect the rest of the world to? It's not entirely possible because the Dog-Leo is always one step ahead of even itself. Superstar Madonna has said, "I am my own experiment. I am my own work of art."

Soul Mate:	Rabbit-Taurus
Challenger:	Dragon-Aquarius
Siblings:	Dog-Aries, Dog-Sagittarius
Best Friends:	Tiger-Aries, Tiger-Leo, Tiger-Sagittarius, Dog-Aries, Dog-Leo, Dog-Sagittarius

Christopher Nolan
Kevin Smith
Cam Gigandet
Anna Paquin
Madeleine Stowe
Madonna
Angela Bassett
Nikolaj Coster-Waldau
Paul Wesley
Yvonne Strahovski
Charisma Carpenter
Abbie Cornish
Elisabeth Moss
M. Night Shyamalan
Devon Aoki
Mark Salling
Anthony Anderson
Brad Renfro

Ben Chaplin
Jason Robards
Saif Ali Khan
Fred Durst

DOG – VIRGO

Chinese Name: GOU
Rank: 11th
Hours Ruled: 7pm – 9pm
Direction: North – Northwest
Season: Autumn
Month: October
Western Zodiac Equivalent of Dog: Libra
Libra Western Element: Air
Eastern Zodiac Equivalent of Virgo: Rooster
Virgo Western Element: Earth
Numerology: 126 = 9

I won't be a rock star. I will be a legend.
– Freddie Mercury

Children show me in their playful smiles the divine in everyone. This simple goodness shines straight from their hearts and only asks to be loved.
– Michael Jackson

When the Dog's tornado meets with the Virgo's fertile earth, magic happens. This is the sign of the artistic icon! In the performance world, this is one of the most prolific combinations of all. This is the combination of the born artist, one who is naturally most connected to the desires of their heart, the one who finds manifesting their dreams that much easier because they live in their fantasies so fully that there is no place for doubt. But their genius is not limited just to the arts, because of their supernatural connection to their dreams and subconscious, their capacity to love is huge, so they do, they love everyone and everything, so the spiritual rewards avalanche in their favor. They understand that love is everything and they have the

649

ability to stay in a place of love, even when the circumstances around them or even the people around them are not particularly loving. Leonard Cohen has said, "This is the most challenging activity that humans get into, which is love. You know, where we have the sense that we can't live without love. That life has very little meaning without love." Mother Teresa has said, "The poverty of being unwanted, unloved and uncared for is the greatest poverty. We must start in our own homes to remedy this kind of poverty." Even, Michael Jackson said, "Let us dream of tomorrow where we can truly love from the soul, and know love as the ultimate truth at the heart of all creation." In short, people born under this combination become icons in their field. Other examples are, River Phoenix, Sophia Loren, Claudia Schiffer, Keith Moon, Freddie Mercury and Tim Burton to name a few.

Dog-Virgos are highly tuned machines and that is the source of their immense talent. There is a reason there are so many child stars that go on to become superstars born under this combination: River Phoenix, Leann Rimes and even British pop star and Actress Billie Piper. Of course, the most famous child star in the world Michael Jackson had this to say about this topic, "I was a veteran, before I was a teenager." Everything must feel be meaningful to them. The discipline that they then apply to developing their skills is not only possible, but invigorating for them. Claudia Schiffer has said, "I will continue modeling until they don't want me anymore basically because I do love it very much." Because of the preparatory work that they have put in, they are more than ready when the opportunity presents itself, which fuels that Dog determination with added confidence. Sophia Loren has said, "Getting ahead in a difficult profession requires avid faith in yourself... Many people think they want things, but they don't really have the strength, the discipline."

The men of this combination tend to be very original, pioneering types with unusual temperament. Although they are approachable and humanitarian, they have a need to believe in themselves as these bigger beings and often live in a fantasy world. This bleeds into their real life and these guys often have mythological personas. Freddie Mercury said, "I always knew I was a star And now, the rest of the world seems to agree with me." But this is also a hugely humanitarian combination and whatever realm they find themselves working in, the will always strive to give back or use their presence to highlight injustices wherever they may be. Another gift is that they are able to simplify complicated issues down to the basics for people to understand, often through their art where they make the example of themselves making the change first. River Phoenix said, "I can't on my own change the regime in South Africa or teach the Palestinians to learn to live with the Israelis, but I can start with me."

Drama appeals to the Dog-Virgo male, but it embarrasses them when the myth is removed and they return to reality. Keith Moon has said, "The Keith Moon the public knows is a myth, even if I have created him. When I've done damage to a friend's house I come back sheepishly the next day and offer to put things right, which means I'm willing to foot the bill."

The women of this combination also have that dramatic energy which is why so many are drawn to the world of fashion in particular. There is no denying that Dog women are some of the most prominent and beautiful the world has ever seen. Not only because they are naturally gifted with chameleon oval faces and long legs, but because they know how to work with what they have to its maximum effect, despite any seeming drawbacks. Claudia Schiffer has said, "I've never hidden the fact that I used to be shy, even when I was 30. However, I might have been self-conscious on the inside, but I was never inhibited about my body." They are also compassionate, understanding and selfless.

Mother Teresa has said, "I have found the paradox, that if you love until it hurts, there can be no more hurt, only more love."

Perhaps more than any other Dog combination, the Dog-Virgo is connected to the subconscious realm so has an affinity with animals, children and nature. That is why they spend so much time in humanitarian pursuits and even spend much of their own money to shine light on these issues. They can feel the heartbeat of the world and when it throbs, they hurt too. But essentially, they believe in the inherent goodness and potential power the world as an international community can have, that is why they appeal to a universal market. They believe that they can make a change; they have a utopian ideal that they believe can be achieved, so do their bit to use their energy to support it. As long as everybody does their bit to change themselves, a domino effect will see the world transform. As Michael Jackson said, "I'm starting with the man in the mirror..."

Soul Mate:	Rabbit-Aries
Challenger:	Dragon-Pisces
Siblings:	Dog-Taurus, Dog-Capricorn
Best Friends:	Tiger-Taurus, Tiger-Virgo, Tiger-Capricorn, Horse-Taurus, Horse-Virgo, Horse-Capricorn

Mother Teresa
Sophia Loren
Claudia Schiffer
LeAnn Rimes
Michael Jackson
River Phoenix
Leonard Cohen
Tim Burton
Freddie Mercury
Keith Moon

Billie Piper
Tommy Lee Jones
Oliver Stone
Barry Gibb
Jennifer Tilly
Chris Columbus
Joan Jett
Lenny Henry
Andrea Bocelli
Shakti Kapoor
Melissa McCarthy
Tom Everett Scott
Deborah Gibson
Andy Roddick

DOG – LIBRA

Chinese Name: GOU
Rank: 11th
Hours Ruled: 7pm – 9pm
Direction: North – Northwest
Season: Autumn
Month: October
Western Zodiac Equivalent of Dog: Libra
Libra Western Element: Air
Eastern Zodiac Equivalent of Libra: Dog
Libra Western Element: Air
Numerology: 127 = 1

My songs are the one place where I won't mince my words. One on one, I have a lot of fear and inhibition. I think this is why I am so bold in my songs... My guitar has this truth serum in it, and lo! the people that wander into my canon.
– Ani Di Franco

When the Dog's tornado meets with Libra's cool breeze, they blend perfectly into one and the same storm because they are of the same brand; the Dog sign is the Chinese equivalent of the Western sign of Libra and vice versa. So this is in fact the double Dog or pure Libra combination. This amplifies all of the positive and negative traits; in this case, their humanitarian nature is pushed to an extreme and these people are often seen at protests and rallies because they believe that every voice matters and must be used to provoke change at all costs. The Dog is known to have deeply held convictions about everything, even with the infusion of Libra, these people are not indecisive or dilly-dalliers, they move with purpose, even if, in actuality, there is no purpose. They will be who they are and verbalize what they *be*. Brigitte Bardot has said, "I have the courage of my convictions...I say what I think and I think what I say."

With so much independence of mind, it comes as no surprise that they do not follow the crowd and forge pathways where they did not previously exist. This combination more than any other could be seen as the iconoclast, those who attack cherished beliefs and traditions opening the world to new perspectives.

They just find it difficult to tolerate stupidity, simplistic arguments and lazy thinking. Tim Robbins has said, "I love iconoclasts. I love individuals. I love people that are true to themselves, whatever the cost." Dog signs also have a need to be beautiful and chase beauty in its various forms. The double Dog combination would have an even greater desire for this. Viggo Mortenson has said, "Every time I see something beautiful, I not only want to return to it, but it makes me want to see other beautiful things."

The men of this combination are gifted with that Dog's sharp mind, independent spirit and the appearance of confidence: sometimes they are confident, but even when they are not, they will find something inside of themselves, even if it is pure arrogance. Rather arrogance than vulnerable or weak. Russell Peter's has said, "When I'm on stage, I'm that confident and that cocky because I have a microphone in my hand, and there's a few thousand people staring at me." Dog signs are natural fighters, the double Dog, then, can be a bit of superhero. That under-Dog spirit that refuses to accept defeat is very present here and this combination either rises to the challenge or creates a fantasy world where they are the superhero of their world. Speaking about growing up in the slums, John Woo has said, "I had to fight to survive. Whenever I got beat up, I got upset, I also ran into the theater to watch a movie. But I have a very strong character, I never surrender, I (am) never afraid, no matter how big they are, how cruel they are, they never beat me down." Like all Dog signs, the Dog-Libra is born old and gets younger as they age. Perhaps it is even more visible in this combination because there is so much Dog energy here. Tim Robbins said, "My father described me as the oldest baby he'd ever seen. I apparently was very serious and reflective."

The women of this combination are doubly dog-diva-beautiful! If the Dog is the Diva sign, imagine what the double dog is like? Their beauty comes from their spirit, from their audacity, from their intelligence. But even those not as stereotypically Dog-intelligent or as liberal, they will still come at you without much of a filter. Brigitte Bardot has said, "I am shocking, impertinent and insolent that's how it is." You may not agree with their views as they can be polarizing, even more so because of the way they provide their viewpoints; they often hit like a wrecking ball, but that's just the way they are and is actually the source of their potent sexuality. And as they age, their conviction only grows. Susan Sarandon has said, "Sexuality...is something that develops and becomes stronger and stronger the older you get..." As a result of the above, these women are usually powerful feminists, activists and change agents. They see through bullshit in a second and will not easily be dissuaded from their own viewpoint with rhetoric. Ani Di Franco has said, "My idea of feminism is self-determination, and it's very open-ended: every woman has the right to become herself, and do whatever she needs to do... Either you are a feminist or you are a sexist/misogynist. There is no box marked 'other'."

Ultimately, the Dog-Libra iconoclast lives to provoke a reaction from lesser minds, preferably to open their eyes to the injustices in the hope that they too will join the cause. They do not usually do this blindly as everything they do must be aligned with their higher ideals. This is why they do not agree to take on projects easily, because once they have, they will fully commit to them. Viggo Mortenson said, "I have a work ethic. If I say I'm going to do something, I do it." But this is the wrong combination to try and box in or put walls in front of because if this Dog cannot jump over it, or dig under it, it will bite its way right through it! There is no stopping this super-hero-double-diva-dog! The Dog Libra will be its beautiful self in all its beautiful glory so everyone will know about it too. This Dog knows who it is and that is why they are so attractive to the rest of the world. Tim Robbins has said, "I think the enemy is self-censorship. In a free society the biggest danger is that you're afraid to the point where you censor yourself."

Soul Mate:	Rabbit-Pisces
Challenger:	Dragon-Aries
Siblings:	Dog-Gemini, Dog-Aquarius
Best Friends:	Tiger-Gemini, Tiger-Libra, Tiger-Aquarius, Horse-Gemini, Horse-Libra, Horse-Aquarius

Brigitte Bardot
Susan Sarandon
Viggo Mortensen
Tim Robbins
Matt Damon
Kelly Ripa
Russell Peters
John Woo
Ne-Yo
Kevin Sorbo
Richard Carpenter
Chris Tarrant
Timothy West
Virginia Bruce
Felicity Kendal
Vinod Khanna
Amy Jo Johnson

Lacey Chabert
Kieran Culkin
Matt Dallas
Lil' Wayne
Ranbir Kapoor
Ani DiFranco

DOG – SCORPIO

Chinese Name: GOU
Rank: 11th
Hours Ruled: 7pm – 9pm
Direction: North – Northwest
Season: Autumn
Month: October
Western Zodiac Equivalent of Dog: Libra
Libra Western Element: Air
Eastern Zodiac Equivalent of Scorpio: Boar
Scorpio Western Element: Water
Numerology: 128 = 2

My agent said, 'You aren't good enough for movies.' I said,
'You're fired.'
– Sally Field

It takes a minute for me to let my guard down, but once I do
and I get to know someone, I'm very open, very trusting.
Some might say too trusting...
– Anne Hathaway

When the Dog's dry storm meets Scorpio's deep and dark waters, it's a bit of a mix and match personality. Sometime the Dog leads, with its nobility, desire to serve and eternal fight for equality, albeit, filtered through the Dog's inability to surrender its childish superficiality; at other times the Scorpio leads, with its intuitive grasp, buried emotions and seemingly selfish manifesto, peppered by anonymous acts of love. Sometimes these two signs are complimentary, at other times, they are at odds with each other, but the outcome is a sensitive and strong Dog who knows itself, its boundaries and its rights. But when, circumstances outside of their sphere of influence hold them back, they find it difficult to accept their lack of power to do anything about it. Hollywood screen icon Dorothy Dandridge said, "If I were white, I could capture the world."

Generally, Dog signs are known to be strong minded, independent and have firm convictions in their beliefs. That is still the case here, but Scorpio's water element brings a heightened sensitivity to the Dog that opens them up in a way that the Dog probably is not much pleased about making it more receptive to the needs of other people. This is why they often struggle with their need to people-please. The Dog does not respect people-pleasing behavior, so when it observes itself engaging in said manner, it offends itself. Anne Hathaway said, "There's something very addictive about people pleasing. It's a thought pattern and a habit that feels really, really good until it becomes desperate." That is why they end up developing such an acute level of self-awareness in their effort to rid themselves of undignified behavioral patterns. Sally Field has said, "I was raised to sense what someone wanted me to be and be that kind of person. It took me a long time not to judge myself through someone else's eyes."

The men of this combination tend to be savvy, loving and judge themselves by a high standard so work hard to meet and exceed their own expectations and nobody else's. Like all Dogs, they have an inbuilt bullshit meter; they cannot tolerate too much pretentious behavior, it grates on their nerves and although they might choose to be gracious in the moment, they may choose not to spend their precious time with you in the future. As Charlie Kaufman observed, "Constantly talking isn't necessarily communicating." If you can't be honest with them, why should they lavish you with their presence? It doesn't matter what your status is or how important you think you are, you are never "better" than the Dog-Scorpio. Ethan Hawke has said, "I met a lot of famous people when I was about 24. And none of them seemed very appealing. And so I didn't know why I would struggle to be that kind of person."

The women of this combination are typical Dog women with the Scorpion's deadly bite. Unfortunately, the trappings of the high life will not pass this specimen by without some indulgence. She will love follow fashion and adorn herself extravagantly if she has the means. Whether these women are conventional beauties or not, they are most definitely appealing and have that playfully feisty Dog woman deportment. Anne Hathaway has said, "I think fashion is a lot of fun. I love clothes. More than fashion or brand labels, I love design. I love the thought that people put into clothes. I love when clothes make cultural statements and I think personal style is really cool. I also freely recognize that fashion should be a hobby." Just a hobby? Most Dog women love to use fashion to make a statement and the Dog-Scorpio is no different. As previously mentioned, they step into their power when they lose the need to live up to anybody else's expectations and that is when they align with their higher self and begin to flow as one with life." Sally Field has said, "I never really address myself to any image anybody has of me. That's like fighting with ghosts." Because of their heightened sensitivity, they have a tendency to live in sort of a raw way, therefore, are sometimes easily offended; when this happens, these women do not always find it easy to take the spiritual high road and may choose to go for vengeance instead. This is not particularly wise and can lead to complicated entanglements.

Ultimately, when the Scorpio sign is combined with the Dog, the level of independence is pushed to somewhat of an extreme in that they do not really like to depend on anyone but themselves and sometimes it part of their journey to learn to do so. This also extends to how they view their relationships and what they need from their partner. Sally Field has said, "There isn't any second half of myself waiting to plug in and make me whole. It's there. I'm already whole." If their first family does not provide them with the support or affection that they need, they go out and create some sort of support system that does and if they cannot, they become the sort of person that provides it purely from within. The Dog-Scorpio chooses to live expressing whom they are, revealing what they consider to be their beautiful side or sometimes, their darker shades, whether it meets with the good opinion of others or not, they simply must be true to their soul's essence. Actually, it may be this very trait that makes them so popular. Charlie Kaufman has said, "The only honest and generous thing for me to do is to give people myself. That's all I've got as an artist, so I want to do that in an unflinching way."

Soul Mate: Rabbit-Aquarius
Challenger: Dragon-Taurus
Siblings: Dog-Cancer, Dog-Pisces
Best Friends: Tiger-Cancer, Tiger-Scorpio, Tiger-Pisces,
                Horse-Cancer, Horse-Scorpio, Horse-Pisces

Barbara Bel Geddes
Dorothy Dandridge
Sally Field
Anne Hathaway
Ethan Hawke
Charlie Kaufman
Jamie Lee Curtis
Robert Patrick
Megan Mullally
Mo Gaffney
Simon Le Bon
Nia Long
Tabu
Raveena Tandon

Tamzin Outhwaite
Craig Kelly
Warren G.
Matt Smith

DOG – SAGITTARIUS

Chinese Name: GOU
Rank: 11th
Hours Ruled: 7pm – 9pm
Direction: North – Northwest
Season: Autumn
Month: October
Western Zodiac Equivalent of Dog: Libra
Libra Western Element: Air
Eastern Zodiac Equivalent of Sagittarius: Rat
Sagittarius Western Element: Fire
Numerology: 129 = 3

Even in literature and art, no man who bothers about origi-
nality will ever be original: whereas if you simply try to tell
the truth (without caring twopence how often it has been told
before) you will, nine times out of ten, become original
without ever having noticed it.
– CS Lewis

When the Dog's tornado meets the centaur's frisky fire, limitless imagination meets rawness, raucousness and rather remarkably, routine. This creature will know how to work hard and play hard, but in its appropriate time and place. Somewhat strangely, they are organized people with a need to know what they are doing and when, because it gives them the security they need to let go and dive deep into their subconscious world where they feel most at home. This combination could be one of the biggest dreamers out of all 144, when you consider that people like C.S. Lewis, Nick Park and even Stephen Spielberg belong to this clan, the latter two creating their own production-studios where they autonomously create physical manifestations of their dreams. Maybe C.S. Lewis would have done the same thing if he were born in this generation? Regardless, the truth remains that this combination is exceptionally connected to its inner child and has an internal thrust to open others to theirs. C.S. Lewis said, "You are never too old to set another goal or to dream a new dream."

Although the Dog has a naturally pure nature, they do not like this to be known concerned that people may try to take advantage of it, so they put up a defensive wall, usually in the form of humor or a sharp tongue to deflect any potential exploiters. However, this sometimes backfires, because this same mechanism keeps them earning below their worth and these exceptionally talented people have to learn their value from their friends and loved ones. But once it penetrates, they will expect to be paid for their creative services, and paid to live well. Gianni Versace said, "Even Michelangelo got paid for doing the Sistine Chapel. To those artists who say they're doing it for the love of art, I say: Get real." There is some truth to the fact that what they do, they do for the love of, as they do not slow down once they have achieved their dreams, instead, they move on to bigger and better ones. The money tends to be a by-product, even if they don't know this at the beginning of their journey. Uri Gellar has said, "So, I am independently well-off and don't have to do anything, but I still do. I write books, lecture around the world, work with scientists and governments."

The men of this combination are typically taller than average, with full lips. They have traditional values with a taste for the new and innovative; just because they want the old-fashioned romantic affair, it does not mean they cannot go to NASA for their first date. Like all Dog signs, the Dog-Sagittarius is born old and grows younger as it ages. So the intellectual cynic slowly dies away to let the spiritual being come to life. C.S. Lewis said, "I gave in, and admitted that God was God... Miracles do not, in fact, break the laws of nature." The more they observe nature, the more they recognize universal patterns that resonate with some inner part of them. There may not be any words to describe their feelings, but somehow it makes sense to them. Uri Gellar has said, "I believe in past lives but I know nothing about mine and I don't want to know. I live in the present, taking one day at a time." Living without resistance, without attachment and allowing their minds the flexibility to go where it will is key to their success. Stephen Spielberg has said, "I don't plan my career. I don't think I'll go dark, dark, dark, then light, then dark. I react spontaneously to what falls into my arms, to what is right at the time."

The women of this combination come in the Dog women package: tall, beautiful and smart, but they are more sensitive and openly vulnerable. They are not as selfish or as narcissistic as other Dog combinations yet they have all of the talent, intelligence and creativity. Dame Judi Dench has said, "I am very undivaish." But the Dog is the sign of the Diva. This combination is perhaps the least Diva-esque of all. What they lack in audacious edge, they make up for with work ethic, professionalism and an endless amount of smart ideas. Charlene Tilton said, "My mother decided that I was Lithuania's answer to Shirley Temple, and so I ended up here. I wrote, produced and starred in shows here... You have to have a strong sense of self in this business – otherwise they're going to spit you out." One thing all Dog signs come with, indestructibly built-in is their wit. Dog signs see the world in colors the rest of the world cannot access and they give it to the world with a twisted-humorous-twang, which above all, they themselves enjoy. Regina King has said, "Sometimes I make myself laugh, but that's because I appreciate my sense of humor."

Ultimately, the Dog-Sagittarius is an open-minded, curious dreamer who does not know how to be any other way. Sometimes life and well-intentioned people step in to inform them that they are wasting their time in idle fantasy, when it is anything but idle for them. It is juicing their mind to come up with ideas that make their hearts rejoice. This combination should be allowed to dream big, because, as C.S. Lewis put it, "Aim at heaven and you will get earth thrown in. Aim at earth and you get neither." Let them play and live in their minds, let these kids sleep longer than other kids if they want to, let them determine their own parameters. They are unconventional people whose inner guidance wants to lead them to their own personal version of success. Let them be guided by their dreams so that they can do as their Dog-Sagittarius peer Stephen Spielberg does, he has said, "I dream for a living." It is their nature, it is their gift and it is their destiny.

Soul Mate:	Rabbit-Capricorn
Challenger:	Dragon-Gemini
Siblings:	Dog-Aries, Dog-Leo
Best Friends:	Tiger-Aries, Tiger-Leo, Tiger-Sagittarius, Horse-Aries, Horse-Leo, Horse-Sagittarius

C.S. Lewis
Gianni Versace
Uri Geller
Nick Park
Steven Spielberg
Judi Dench
Charlene Tilton
Regina Hall
Jean Genet
Jennifer Connelly
Tyson Beckford
Benny Andersson
Paul Winchell
Redd Foxx
Dilip Kumar

Lucian Freud

Robert Towne

Eugene Levy

Gloria Loring

Patty Duke

Sharmila Tagore

Sheree J. Wilson

Sarah Silverman

Michael Shanks

Sean Patrick Thomas

Kevin Sussman

DMX

Kara DioGuardi

Damien Rice

Elisha Cuthbert

Charlie Cox

Riz Ahmed

Keri Hilson

DOG – CAPRICORN

Chinese Name: GOU
Rank: 11th
Hours Ruled: 7pm – 9pm
Direction: North – Northwest
Season: Autumn
Month: October
Western Zodiac Equivalent of Dog: Libra
Libra Western Element: Air
Eastern Zodiac Equivalent of Capricorn: Ox
Capricorn Western Element: Earth
Numerology: 130 = 4

The coloured folks been singing it and playing it just like I'm doin' now, man, for more years than I know.... nobody paid it no mind 'til I goosed it up. I got it from them.
– Elvis Presley

When the Dog's tornado meets with the Capricorn's dense earth, imagination meets practicality, conviction meets humility and the Dog's originality meets with the Capricorn's perseverance to bring new ideas into the world that astonish and amaze. This combination has an interesting contradiction, in that they are both arrogant and humble. They need both so that they can make the impact that they want to achieve; they need to believe that they are special, but they know that everything they have has come to them from the grace of the universe. Much like the preceding combination of Dog-Sagittarius, they are dreamers, but Capricorn grounds them much more and expects to work for what it receives. That is why, this combination is known for its originality (which comes from the Dog) and its work ethic (which comes from the Capricorn). Elvis Presley said, "I was a dreamer. I read comic books, and I was the hero of the comic book. I saw movies, and I was the hero in the movie. So every dream I ever dreamed has come true a hundred times."

Essentially, these people are small-town folk who end up in big-city worlds because of their talent, drive and ambition. But that does not mean that they are ashamed of their roots. Ava Gardner said, "Although no one believes me, I have always been a country girl and still have a country girl's values." The Dog-Capricorn is also given the ability to create mental roadmaps, which show them how to go from where they are to where they want to go. Overtly, they would hate for anyone to think that they believe their success makes them better than others, while secretly, they do think that. Speaking about his numerous incarnations and reinventions, David Bowie said, "I always had a repulsive need to be something more than human." Speaking about why he changed his name, comic book creating legend Stan Lee said, "I felt someday I'd write the Great American Novel and I didn't want to use my real name on these silly little comics."

The men of this combination tend to be multitalented and usually musically gifted if David Bowie, Taye Diggs and of course the King of Rock 'n' Roll are anything to go by, as Elvis has said, "Rhythm is something you either have or don't have, but when you have it, you have it all over." Speaking about how he was hugely inspired by (a fellow Dog-Capricorn) Elvis Presley, David Bowie said, "I saw a cousin of mine when I was young. She was dancing to 'Hound Dog' and I had never seen her get up and be moved so much by anything. It really impressed me, the power of the music. I started getting records immediately after that." Dog-Capricorn men push themselves outside of their comfort zone because they know that when they are uncomfortable, they are growing. Jeremy Renner has said, "I'll take any risk there is… If I'm afraid of it I'll do it just so I'm not afraid of it anymore." They are also typical Dog signs in the sense that they need to be in alignment with their higher selves so that every action they take feels authentic to them. Even if who they are or what they choose to do may be controversial or ahead of its time. David Bowie also said, "I had no problem with people knowing I was bisexual. But I had no inclination to hold any banners or be a representative of any group of people."

The women of this combination have been bequeathed with the Dog's sharp tongue, spicy personality and deep conviction in their beliefs. They know that in order to be effective, they have to believe in themselves first; the more they do so, the more powerful their impact upon the world. Kate Bosworth has said, "You have to have confidence. You can't be someone who's so insecure that she's a basket case." Yes, they project confidence… and then some. Maggie Smith has said, "It's true I don't tolerate fools but then they don't tolerate me, so I am spiky. Maybe that's why I'm quite good at playing spiky elderly ladies." These are ladies one does not want to get on the wrong side of. They have the ability to freeze you out with a glare and if they start on you with words, tears are not unusual. Ava Gardner said, "When I lose my temper, honey, you can't find it any place." They give it out because they can take it, in fact, they are under no illusions and are often their own biggest critic. With a good level of self-awareness, they strive to overcome their weaknesses and stay focused on their strengths. Speaking about her critics, Mary J. Blige has said, "I don't think there's anything they can say about me that I haven't said about myself already."

Ultimately, the Dog-Capricorn is furnished with a greater level of talent than most, but it is what they choose to do with it, how they choose to view their world and how positive a self-perception they can maintain. There are many rags-to-riches stories from within this combination. They do what they love and they do it exceptionally well. Yes, they have that mental road map that can get them to success quickly, but whether they choose to go there or not, the pleasure of creative exploration is what gets their juices flowing. Mary J. Blige has said, "It's up to us to choose, whether we win or lose and I choose to win." It all starts with self-awareness. When the Do-Capricorn feels that something is not right, something feels off with the circumstances in their lives or that they are not being authentic, they must take action or they will begin to go down destructive routes. The sooner they take action, the sooner their lives will flourish. Elvis Presley said, "Truth is like the sun. You can shut it out for a time, but it ain't goin' away."

Soul Mate: Rabbit-Sagittarius
Challenger: Dragon-Cancer
Siblings: Dog-Taurus, Dog-Virgo
Best Friends: Tiger-Taurus, Tiger-Virgo, Tiger-Capricorn,
                   Horse-Taurus, Horse-Virgo, Horse-Capricorn

Elvis Presley
David Bowie
Stan Lee
Jeremy Renner
Ava Gardner
Maggie Smith
Kate Bosworth
Mary J. Blige
Taye Diggs
Regina King
Alison Brie
Kristin Kreuk
Maddie Hasson
Clancy Brown
Shawn Wayans
Kid Rock
Marianne Faithfull

Al Capone
Paula Deen
Imran Khan (Actor)

DOG – AQUARIUS

Chinese Name: GOU
Rank: 11th
Hours Ruled: 7pm – 9pm
Direction: North – Northwest
Season: Autumn
Month: October
Western Zodiac Equivalent of Dog: Libra
Libra Western Element: Air
Eastern Zodiac Equivalent of Aquarius: Tiger
Aquarius Western Element: Air
Numerology: 131 = 5

The kids that are different and out there and expressive and are bold with those choices, those are the people that grow up to be people we all want to hang out with, that become celebrities or become really successful in what they do because they believe in who they are.
– Adam Lambert

When the Dog's tornado meets with the lofty heights of Aquarius's clouds, two different air sign merge to create a mini concentration of thunder. In Eastern astrology, the Dog sign is known for its passionate convictions, sharp wit and physical beauty. In Western astrology, the sign of Aquarius is known for its wisdom and inquisitive nature. Together, this combination creates a sort of activist type who likes to lead by the presentation of his example. They can be inspirational to the masses, although, many have a need to be in control that which they may not like to be revealed. By observing politics, powerful people and the methods employed, they become highly skilled at handling people and situations, covertly directing the events as they choose and still coming out smelling of roses. Usually, their intentions are noble so any seemingly manipulative behavior is usually undertaken for honorable purposes. Both of these signs are hugely original and independent so the universe kind of broke the mold when the Dog-Aquarius was introduced. Adam Lambert said, "There's not a blueprint for me to follow."

Dog-Aquarian's personal beauty, external and intrinsic, is evident to all and nobody knows their worth more than they do. Many have illustrious careers in fashion, in films, as writers, singers and dancers. Not only do they bring a unique, sometimes offbeat or unconventional perspective, they also bring bucket loads of personality and of course, their physical beauty. Franco Zefferelli said, "I have always believed that opera is a planet where the muses work together, join hands and celebrate all the arts." They take traditional approaches and give them a unique twist. Adam Lambert has said, "I started rejecting the proper way to sing and I started singing." They are not lazy when it comes to their artistic intentions and don't want their audience to be either. They believe everything should have a point and layer their pieces of work to add a little magic for those who really care. Art for art's sake is a bit pointless. Making a difference and creating meaning is what matters. Natassja Kinski said, "I still want to fulfill the desire I have to do things that are beautiful and meaningful."

The men of this combination tend to be ordinary with extraordinary natural talent. They don't think much of their looks and it takes them time to realize how attractive they actually are. When these guys obsess about their work, the 10,000 hour rule of practice towards becoming an expert becomes irrelevant: either they are naturally talented that they don't need to practice or they practice every moment they have because they love it so much. Simon Pegg said, "Being a geek is all about being honest about what you enjoy and not being afraid to demonstrate that affection. It means never having to play it cool about how much you like something. It's basically a license to proudly emote on a somewhat childish level rather than behave like a supposed adult." With most double air signs, a certain level of activism is only to be expected and the Dog-Aquarius is no different. They have many number of causes that are close to their hearts but they cannot commit to all of them. More often than not, they will use their art to highlight what is most important. Adam Lambert said, "I definitely have my opinions that I'm very vocal about and I'm not afraid to put them out there... I'm trying to be a singer, not a civil rights leader."

The women of this combination tend to be slim, lean and feminine in looks. That activism streak tends to be more pronounced in the female of the Dog-Aquarius species and they seem perfectly rational, open and sometimes malleable, at first sight. Most of the time they are open and rational, until one disagrees with one of their deeply held beliefs, then they can turn onto a rock of opposition. Malleable, they are not. They know who they are, they know what they stand for and they do not care about the repercussions of them expressing who they are. Kelly Lynch has said, "I don't care what people's myths are about me." With Aquarius in the mix, unconventionality is a given so many of these ladies do not follow established feminine roles. This is not to be a trailblazer by any means, they are just following what comes naturally. Linda Blair has said, "If I had children, I would be very selfish. I wouldn't be out doing things. But by not having kids, it makes me freer to travel the world and talk about things I feel are important." This combination is likely to suffer from personal insecurity because the Aquarius lends the Dog a heightened self-awareness, which, is both a gift and a curse as it can lead to heightened self-critique occasionally causing blocks. In extreme cases, this can lead to eating disorders and other addictive behavior.

Ultimately, the Dog-Aquarius is usually a small being with a huge spirit. They have a competitive winners mindset which gets them into situations and has them fighting their way through to the end. Losing is an impossibility, winning is inevitable. On top of this they come with a quietly loving disposition that seeks to understand before all else. Linda Blair has said, "Compassion and sharing: that's the true journey of the human spirit." It's not just people that they care about. The environment, animals and even just making the world a more beautiful place, the Dog-Aquarius has an opinion about how to improve things for the better. The more they lead by example, the more people listen to their novel views and recognize them for the innovative activists they inadvertently become. Adam Lambert has said, "I want to upset people, I want to make people think, I want to keep people interested... At least I can say that I'm honest."

Soul Mate:	Rabbit-Scorpio
Challenger:	Dragon-Leo
Siblings:	Dog-Gemini, Dog-Libra
Best Friends:	Tiger-Gemini, Tiger-Libra, Tiger-Aquarius, Horse-Gemini, Horse-Libra, Horse-Aquarius

Adam Lambert
China Kantner
Gary Barlow
Simon Pegg
Lawrence Taylor
Kelly Lynch
Cris Collinsworth
Linda Blair
Gregory Hines
Bob Uecker
Alan Bates
Florence Henderson

George Segal
Chuck Yeager
Franco Zeffirelli
Brendan Behan
Keefe Brasselle
James Dickey
Carol Channing
Norman Mailer
Anne Jeffreys
Helen Gurley Brown
Kathryn Grayson
Dick Martin
D.W. Griffith

DOG – PISCES

Chinese Name: GOU
Rank: 11th
Hours Ruled: 7pm – 9pm
Direction: North – Northwest
Season: Autumn
Month: October
Western Zodiac Equivalent of Dog: Libra
Libra Western Element: Air
Eastern Zodiac Equivalent of Pisces: Rabbit
Pisces Western Element: Water
Numerology: 132 = 6

Reality is something you rise above.
– Liza Minelli

When the Dog's tornado joins with Pisces's creative streams, it compliments and amplifies many of the traditional Dog traits as perceived in the Chinese astrological cycle. It is said that people born in Dog years are born old (and cynical) and they grow younger as they age. Sharon Stone said, "I was, like, forty at birth. When I wasn't even a year old, I spoke, I was potty trained, I walked and talked. Then I started school and drove everybody crazy because they realized I had popped out as an adult. I had adult questions and wanted adult answers." Many performers who found a lot of success while still in their youth such as Liza Minnelli, Thora Birch, Jessica Biel, Dakota Fanning and Justin Bieber belong to this club. Bursting with talent beyond their years and a liking for fantasy, they are drawn to the creative realm like moths to a flame. And as they age, the women especially, learn to relax, not take themselves too seriously and physically become even more radiant.

Aside from their precocious nature, disarming beauty and

clever wit, they are also highly professional creatures that pride themselves on a job well done. Alan Rickman has said, "I do take my work seriously and the way to do that is not to take yourself too seriously." Sharon Stone said, "Being professional in what I do is very important to me. Flakes don't make it to the top, pros do." Liza Minelli has said, "I'm always looking at the next thing...it's very hard to be unhappy when you're curious and grateful. You're busy. You don't have time to be unhappy. My biggest talent is I know who is more talented than I am. I find them and I go to them, and I learn."

As a young Actor, Michael Rapaport had the good fortune to work with some of the best Actors in the business. Despite being intimidated, he left "the fan at home. I come to work as a professional. I think if you go into something looking at people as better than you, if you give people too much respect, I don't think it benefits you or them." Dog signs believe in their own worth and the more they do so, the further they go.

Learning and growing is a very powerful motivation for them. They understand their internal mechanism and instinctively know how to nurture it. Even if they ask friends for advice, they tend to know what will or will not work for them. Holly Hunter has said, "To me, being creative is a very fragile thing, the environment in which one can create is a very particular one, and somehow I've always felt the need to be very protective of that."

In their youth, the men of this combination are often highly sought after, knowing how to present a "Cool" image on the surface concealing the myriad of insecurities that lie within. They also cannot help but be who they are in an uninterrupted way, this is why many of them become so successful so young. Justin Bieber has said, "I'm crazy, I'm nuts. Just the way my brain works. I'm not normal. I think differently. My mind is always racing." Introverted, discerning and somewhat severe looking; one wonders what goes through their mind, what their limits are, as cynical mutts, they are always guarding the entrance to their hearts with their sharp wit and acute observational humor. Michael Rapaport said, "It takes a genius to play a fool" discussing his early pigeonhole when he started his performing career. Men born in Dog years generally need to be careful that this trait to internalize, fearing open expression, not lead to addictive behavior; that goes double for this combination. Take the bull by the horns, avoid closing in on yourself and express how you're feeling.

The women, are forces to be reckoned with. Strong, talented and classically beautiful, they know how to get their way and have an arsenal of weaponry if their first request is unsuccessful. Sharon Stone has said, "Any man in Hollywood will meet me if I want that. No, make that any man anywhere." Intelligent, coy and flirtatious, there is something rather old school about them. Rachel Weisz said, "I don't feel very modern at all." The combination of these two signs blend exceptionally well for women as they are gifted with a feisty yet feminine attitude that serves them well. They say and do what others will not out of a powerful desire for expression and need to be who they are. Sharon Stone has said, "If you have a vagina and an attitude in this town, then that's a lethal combination... We Barbie dolls are not supposed to behave the way I do." A few years later in her career, she said, "I'm more honest, more true, more vulnerable because I used to think that I was supposed to be fearless. Now I know that it's okay to be afraid as long as you show up."

Ultimately, the Dog-Pisces is one of those combinations that is remembered. Although they are quiet, they have a strong aura and their presence can be felt. When they feel an injustice is taking place, their Dog nature springs into action and you realize that the bite is just as bad as the bark! The defining nature of the Dog-Pisces however, can be found in their spiritual connection.

Rue McClanahan said, "Compassion is the foundation of everything positive, everything good. If you carry the power of compassion to the marketplace and the dinner table, you can make your life really count." They arrive with enough talent to last a few lifetimes and enough beauty to melt every heart; when they develop their self-belief and own themselves, nothing can stand in their way. Queen Latifah has said, "I had to tune out what the hell everybody else had to say about who I was. When I was able to do that, I felt free... Dreams become reality when we put our minds to it."

Soul Mate:	Rabbit-Libra
Challenger:	Dragon-Virgo
Siblings:	Dog-Cancer, Dog-Scorpio
Best Friends:	Tiger-Cancer, Tiger-Scorpio, Tiger-Pisces,
	Horse-Cancer, Horse-Scorpio, Horse-Pisces

Dakota Fanning
Rachel Weisz
Alan Rickman
Jessica Biel
Thora Birch
Justin Bieber
Julie Bowen
Sharon Stone
Holly Hunter
Queen Latifah
Miranda Richardson
Frank Welker
Michael Rapaport
Anthony Daniels
Patricia Heaton
Linda Fiorentino
Adam Pally

Samm Levine
Jack Coleman
Liza Minnelli
Rue McClanahan
Katherine von Drachenberg
Joan Hackett
Martin Kove
Kate Maberly
Mark Moses
Tyne Daly
Brenda Blethyn
Rik Mayall
Greg Germann

THE BOAR

THE BOAR

I am the capitalist, nature's raw sensualist, the baby of the astrological cycle. I am the completion of the cycle and the beginning, so within me is both the spiritual wisdom of my former maturity and the enthusiasm of this frisky fresh being. I am the sophisticating country child working to leave my humble beginnings behind. My past conditioning affects me with its heavy haze. Sometimes, I know not where I am or where I stand but am committed to figuring it out. Time is an enigma for I live partly in the past, partly in the present whilst tipping a trotter into the future for a peek. I live not for myself, but for my tribe. No role is beyond me, regardless of my gender, for my love comes without boundaries. This causes me much heartache and I learn to love with more discernment, leaving my self-sacrifice and martyr complex behind, I step into this sophisticated, compassionate and highly successful creature that everybody adores.

I am the Boar.

Happy-go-lucky and overtly sexual, you are positive and fun to be around. One of the most sensual signs, you love beauty in all its forms. You aren't massively demanding and accept the cards you've been dealt. You have the capacity to endure all kinds of hardships admirably with a smile on your face. But this can take its toll and you are prone to emotional outbursts that seem to come from nowhere, ill health and paranoia. Peaceful and sensitive, you can come across as passive or shy, but that goes away when you display your highly developed creative abilities.

Career-wise, the Boar is a creature that puts its family first, so it will do any job to ensure that its family is well taken care of, mollycoddled even. Often, they create wealth through businesses that they will pass on to their children aware that their offspring might not have the same skills or ability as they do. Usually, this is because they have spoiled their children rotten and forgot to encourage them to learn the family business. Aside from this, they enjoy developing their skills to a high level, but even then sometimes are overlooked for edgier signs. When the Boar stops self-sacrificing and fights for airspace their peers cower in fright! The most prominent Boars are those that know when to turn off their "niceness" and come with a plan. Look at Simon Cowell, Alan Sugar and Arnold Schwarzenegger. Dance, directing and drama appeal to them in the performance world. Otherwise, they like interior design, property, social work and the alternative healing world.

Compatibilities

Soul Mate:	Tiger
Challenger:	Snake
Best Friends:	Sheep & Rabbit
Good Relations:	Rat & Dog

BOAR – ARIES

Chinese Name: ZHU
Rank: 12th
Hours Ruled: 9pm – 11am
Direction: North – Northwest
Season: Autumn
Month: November
Western Zodiac Equivalent of Boar: Scorpio
Scorpio Western Element: Water
Eastern Zodiac Equivalent of Aries: Dragon
Aries Western Element: Fire
Numerology: 133 = 7

The confidence I now have is rooted in the discovery that who
I am is okay.
– Dudley Moore

When Aries's raging fire meets the Boar's gentle yet formidable waters, the blend is an interesting one; complimentary yet tension filled. Aries's forceful nature encourages the Boar to ignore its consuming doubts and just get on with things making them exceptionally productive. There also tends to be a noted instance in every Boar-Aries's life where they learn to manage their internal critic.

Another similarity that both Aries and the Boar have in common is their capacity for hard graft. They just keep going ignoring their pressing desires until the collaborative goal has been reached. David Tennant has said, "I do thrive on hard work." They do not like to let people down and often are more than ready to self-sacrifice. This however can sometimes back fire as their sacrifices are not always seen or appreciated which can sometimes lead them to victim town. James Woods has said, "My biggest, probably most irrational complaint has been that I've had to work harder for what I've gotten. I've seen other people with nepotism or wealth or cheesy good looks on their side who've had it easy, whereas I felt that I had to 'over-prove' myself." Not that their complaints are not valid, their energy could be better utilized looking ahead rather than backwards at what "should" have been.

Although they may seem like their sex appeal is obvious and natural, often times they have had blocks in this area that they have had to consciously work through and come to a place of balance with. When they understand that their own sex appeal is emanates from who they are and not some artificial construct, they feel released. Dudley Moore said, "The ability to enjoy your sex life is central. I don't give a shit about anything else. My obsession is total. What else is there to live for?" Maybe that's why Ewan McGregor has said, "It's a great feeling of power to be naked in front of people."

Aries brings much to this union, but there are some non-negotiable matters that the Boar sign refuses to compromise on; the main thing being the family focus. As the Boar is one of the most family oriented and domestic signs, it derives the most pleasure being in service to their loved ones. Ewan McGregor said, "I was with a friend of mine recently who was dying and while he was lying there with his family around his bed, I just knew that was it, that was the best you can hope for in life – to have your family and the people who love you around you at the end."

The men of this combination tend to have a metro-sexual magnetism that appeals to everyone. After having done the film, Velvet Goldmine, Ewan McGregor said, "I got fond of wearing nail polish and eye make-up. I used to wear it quite a lot." Whether it comes from their looks, their cheeky charm or their clever wit, their sex appeal is undeniable. Even the most "butch" seeming man is a sensitive soul. Sean Bean has said, "A common misperception of me is...that I am a tough, rough northerner, which I suppose I am really. But I'm pretty mild-mannered most of the time." They strive for integrity in all of their actions so that they can teach by example for their children, their friends and all who might be lucky enough to have an open window into their little world. Nicholas Brendon said, "I want to do good work, but more than that, I want to stay a good human being. That's more important than any character I play." In truth, the Boar male is a bit of a universal father figure to the world although he would not presume to advertise this, he'd rather father from a distance and not let his children even know.

The women of this combination are quite similar to their male counterparts in that they project the Aries strength with a gentleness. Whether in the guise of the cultured, sophisticated lady such as Emma Thompson or the so-called "rebel" like Shannen Doherty, their individual power is as visible as their vulnerability. This perfectly illustrates Aries merging with Boar. Emma Thompson said, "When I was at Cambridge, I shaved my head and wore baggy clothes. What I did was to desexualise myself. It was partly to do with the feminism of that time: militant and grungy... I mind having to look pretty, that's what I mind, because it is so much more of an effort." They may feel like they ought to care more about the superficialities that social pressures dictate but they just feel so inane and "fake" to them. Amanda Righetti said, "Guys blow my looks up more than I ever would. I guess I have issues with myself. I don't think I'm as pretty as everybody thinks." Even when they do involve themselves with glitz and glamour, that inner voice constantly reminds them to keep their head out of the clouds, their feet on the ground and don't think too much of themselves.

Managing excessive energy is never easy for this combination, male or female as there tends to be a strange complex at play. The tougher they present, the higher the emotional intensity fuelling their rise to one extreme followed by a descent to the other of the superiority/inferiority scale. Shannen Doherty has said, "I still get nervous on dates. I'll be sitting at dinner with a guy and I have to excuse myself and go to the bathroom because I can't breathe." Similarly, Dudley Moore said, "I certainly did feel inferior. Because of class. Because of strength. Because of height..." the reason is irrelevant; this feeling causes vibrational resistance. Every Boar sign is a survivor; their struggles and compassionate understanding gives them a perception unlike any other which they draw upon to live lives of service and artistic merit. Despite everything, they strive to maintain a healthy spirit that keeps them grooving to a beat all of their own. Ewan McGregor has said, "I fight cynicism. It's too easy... It's much harder to be positive and see the wonder of everything."

Soul Mate:	Tiger-Virgo
Challenger:	Snake-Libra
Siblings:	Boar-Leo, Boar-Sagittarius
Best Friends:	Rabbit-Aries, Rabbit-Leo, Rabbit-Sagittarius, Sheep-Aries, Sheep-Leo, Sheep-Sagittarius

Peter Billingsley
Ewan McGregor
Sean Bean
Jamie Chung
David Tennant
Emma Thompson
Nathan Fillion
Amanda Righetti
Matthew Modine
James Woods
Matt Lanter
Catherine Keener

Shannen Doherty
Alice Braga
Diora Baird
Clint Howard
Krista Allen
John Ratzenberger
Miranda Kerr
David Hyde Pierce
Julian Glover
Nicholas Brendon
Dudley Moore
Method Man
Mark Consuelos
Elton John
David Letterman

BOAR – TAURUS

Chinese Name: ZHU
Rank: 12th
Hours Ruled: 9pm – 11am
Direction: North – Northwest
Season: Autumn
Month: November
Western Zodiac Equivalent of Boar: Scorpio
Scorpio Western Element: Water
Eastern Zodiac Equivalent of Taurus: Snake
Taurus Western Element: Earth
Numerology: 134 = 8

In necessary things, unity; in doubtful things, liberty; in all things, charity.
– Anne Baxter

When the Boar's gentle waters wash over Taurus's tough terrain, the water nurtures the soil with love and the soil happily accepts everything the water offers. Taurus equates to Snake which is the Boar's opposite sign so in effect, there is some astrological opposition inherent within this combination, which is not a bad thing as it makes for a much more interesting personality with a somewhat contradictory nature, possibly more insecure with the two sides tugging from within wanting to go in separate directions. When this personality learns how to manage these opposing parts of themselves, they can be exceptionally powerful in all aspects of their lives because they have a greater understanding of their own psychology and know how deal with inner conflict. Maybe this heightened awareness is what led Anne Baxter to say, "See into life, don't just look at it."

Like all Boar combinations, Boar-Taureans are creative, sensitive and family oriented, but their sensitive nerves do not always allow them to put themselves on the line, for fear of criticism, embarrassment and failure but the bull charges in first and worries about the mess later. So what happens is the Bull creates chaos and the Boar has a panic attack about it afterwards. As time goes on, the Boar does learn to rein in the Bull when it needs to. Anne Baxter has said, "It's best to have failure happen early in life. It wakes up the Phoenix bird in you so you rise from the ashes." And once they learn to manage this wild side of themselves, there is no stopping them and they often arise to heights nobody would have expected. Once they have paid their dues and earned their position, mistakes begin to take on a different meaning altogether. Fred Astaire has said, "The higher up you go, the more mistakes you are allowed. Right at the top, if you make enough of them, it's considered to be your style."

The men of this combination tend to be domestically oriented and usually put their loved ones first. Their career is important to them of course but the family more so; if they can merge their family life with their professional life, they will. This is not always wise, but the more time they spend with their family, the more alive they feel so whether it is wise or not becomes irrelevant; remember, the Boar is a sensually led creature and will do whatever brings it the most pleasure. Often times that means bringing pleasure to those that they love most. Aaron Spelling said, "I love my wife, she deserves anything and everything."

Being sensually-led has its downsides too though as Iggy Pop illustrated at the beginning of a gig when he said, "Look, you're here to see me, and I can't go on until my dealer is here, and he's waiting to be paid, so give me some money so I can fix up, and then you'll get your show." Being so emotional allows them the opportunity to analyze their own functioning, which develops their objectivity, not that they always use it, but they have it. Ben Elton has said, "I'm easy to work with, not a pushover, but I respond to criticism and find it inspiring." More than anything, they are sensitive, loving people who are constantly managing their emotional volatility and self-esteem. So do not get angry if they have a screaming fit, they will be more angry at themselves than anyone else; just show compassion and understanding and they will love you forever.

The women of this combination are grounded, softhearted and brave. They will stand up for themselves in an unobtrusive way so that it doesn't seem confrontational but they do not like to tolerate bigotry or sexism. With certain influences, when they feel they have no choice but to be openly confrontational, they might leave the scene in anger, only to lock themselves in a room and cry in fear of what they have just done. Once again, they have to manage their overflowing emotions. Sofia Coppola has said, "I don't like being told what to do." Nobody does, but when the wild Boar and the wild Taurus bull are given orders, especially orders that go against their value system, rebellion is only to be expected. The problem that a lot Boar women have is that they look much tougher on the surface than they actually are, yet they are aware of the perception people have of them and they do not want to let them down or lose their esteem.

Ultimately, this self-sacrificial creature, the Boar-Taurus works tirelessly to keep its family happy and living in as high a standard as they can. Wherever possible they will choose occupations where their keen perception and eye for aesthetics can be used. Aaron Spelling has said, "Right now I'm doing four shows at a time, trying to read four outlines every week, four scripts every week, and watching four rough cuts; it's a lot of good work. It's fun to do it, but it does wear you out." There is a noted tendency to dwell over the past and wishing that they could go back and redo things. Iggy Pop said, "I find it hard to focus looking forward. So I look backward." This is a complete waste of time and energy, and that is why it is better for them to keep active and busy so that they can use their introspective super powers more productively. Ben Elton has said, "We've all got to look at ourselves, start with yourself, that's all you can do. I believe that we can act responsibly as a group, it's just that there are vested interests telling us not to bother." When they open to the loving nurturance of the universe, they realize that they do not have to worry about getting it wrong or making mistakes or letting people down, instead they can just *be*, knowing that love will always be there for them; when this truly registers within the Boar-Taurus, they ease themselves into a life of full of joy.

Soul Mate:	Tiger-Leo
Challenger:	Snake-Scorpio
Siblings:	Boar-Virgo, Boar-Capricorn
Best Friends:	Rabbit-Taurus, Rabbit-Virgo, Rabbit-Capricorn, Sheep-Taurus, Sheep-Virgo, Sheep-Capricorn

Fred Astaire
Maureen O'Sullivan
Anne Baxter
Aaron Spelling
Richard Jenkins
Iggy Pop
Paul Gross
Randy Travis
Ben Elton
Sofia Coppola
Eric Mabius
Henry Cavill
Adrianne Palicki
Holly Valance
Gabourey Sidibe
Natalie Cassidy

BOAR – GEMINI

Chinese Name: ZHU
Rank: 12th

Chinese Name: ZHU
Rank: 12th
Hours Ruled: 9pm – 11am
Direction: North – Northwest
Season: Autumn
Month: November
Western Zodiac Equivalent of Boar: Scorpio
Scorpio Western Element: Water
Eastern Zodiac Equivalent of Gemini: Horse
Gemini Western Element: Air
Numerology: 135 = 9

I sometimes feel that I'm impersonating the dark unconscious of the whole human race. I know this sounds sick, but I love it.
– Vincent Price

Attractive, intelligent and creative, the Boar's strength meets the agility of the Gemini. They tend to be athletic and quick mentally which lends their skill-set to many occupations, especially where diplomacy and staying ahead of the game is required. That being said, they may dislike the pressure that comes with such occupations, preferring to express themselves creatively instead. When the Boar meets the twins, we get a personality that is extremely creatively gifted, has a huge need of variety in every respect with a somewhat pessimistic perspective on life. The negative experiences they have seem to penetrate every part of their being and they don't forget hurts easily. Highly sensitive and trusting, these experiences can have lasting consequences tinting their vision towards the morose. Many of the inhabitants of this combination seem to focus on the downside, even publically. The iconic British singer Morrissey is quoted as saying, "Britain's a terribly negative place. And it hammers people down and it pulls you back and it prevents you." Similarly, actor Hugh Laurie, is quoted as saying, "I waste time thinking of what I should have said or done, I can't bear going through the same dance of despair" ...but they often do.

There tends to be deep-seated insecurity that is imbedded in these types that they learn to live with, as no amount of success alleviates the feeling of not being enough. As Hugh Laurie said, "I have a Black Belt in Guilt." Taken further, they can get absorbed in self-bullying almost as a pastime. Needless to say this is not healthy and is something that requires some attention. Whether they realize it or not, this is a very physical combination and exercise may benefit them in more ways than just the obvious. For many it can be akin to a spiritual experience. When Boar-Geminis spend time outside, especially near water, they are somehow lightened. Their mood lifts and everything feels better to them. When they exercise outdoors, the effects are doubly productive. As Vincent Price said, "A man who limits his interests limits his life."

At the very core of this combination is the desire for new experiences. Paul Bettany said, "I just get bored if I don't do different things." They feel compelled to make sacrifices believing they will be cosmically rewarded. Secretly, they think this suffering is the key to their creativity and will not be talked out of their somber modes. But there is so much more to these cute and sexy creatures besides their melancholic veneer. They actually love life, it's just when they are not in the midst of it, which they cannot be all the time, they come face to face with their mortality and they choose to dwell on it. That is when they think and talk themselves into depressive modes. It is always wise for them to be involved in activities and around children that remind them of the good in the world.

The men of this combination have quite a sardonic front. Witty and sharp their observations are always on point and clever. Highly sexual, despite what they say in the press, they cultivate sexiness even in their later years that keep the admirers rolling in. Their vulnerability is more obvious then other signs, but their concern is not with appearances as much as it is with the truths of the world. Unlike their neighbor the Dog, they are not interested in causing direct change, but want their ideas to permeate the consciousness of all who they come into contact with, to get them to think in a more open way. Tupac Shakur said, "I'm not saying I'm gonna change the world, but I guarantee that I will spark the brain that will change the world."

The women of this combination tend to be highly feminine, conventionally attractive with big soft hearts. Their love can be suffocating for lovers and children. The Boar's self-sacrificial trait rears its head here and the women of this combination can inadvertently become subservient and subsequently neglected because of the way they put themselves second, thus making themselves vulnerable to being mistreated. Yet they will put up with this mistreatment until they reach eruption point. Lisa "Lefteye" Lopes burnt down her mansion in an angry rage at her partner who had been unfaithful. "There's a thin line between genius and insanity and I always get labelled as the crazy one."

Ultimately, they retain their youthful naivety and there tends to be an air of innocence about them, even in their elder years. That is why they are such popular performers. Many are iconic: Tupac Shakur, Lisa "Lefteye" Lopes, Idina Menzel, Morrissey, Mark Wahlberg, Vincent Price and Hugh Laurie to name a few. With their humble yet ruthlessly honest voices, they just want to communicate their personal truth. Mark Wahlberg said, "Imitators don't last and I'd like to last" about his career in Hollywood; and Hugh Laurie has said, "Celebrity is absolutely preposterous" about his own career in Hollywood. Oftentimes they are misunderstood because their honesty is of a brand many do not subscribe to and some may even find vulgar. Morrissey said, "Don't talk to me about me about people who are 'nice' 'cause I have spent my whole life in ruins because of people who are nice.'" But it is their truth, warts and all, which is not easy to tell, yet they are often publically reprimanded for it. These beautiful yet vulnerable creatures, they spend their lives dealing with demons of their own creation and express their feelings in countless creative ways striving always to be ruthlessly truthful for the betterment of society. Is it any wonder so many of them choose to get lost in the fantasy rather than deal with their gloomy version of reality. Tupac Shakur put it best, "Reality is wrong. Dreams are for Real."

Soul Mate:	Tiger-Cancer
Challenger:	Snake-Sagittarius
Siblings:	Boar-Libra, Boar-Aquarius
Best Friends:	Rabbit-Gemini, Rabbit-Libra, Rabbit-Aquarius, Sheep-Gemini, Sheep-Libra, Sheep-Aquarius

Clint Boon
Rupert Everett
Hugh Laurie
Paul Bettany
Lisa "Lefteye" Lopes
Robert Maxwell
Morrissey
Idina Menzel
Noah Wyle
Bob Mortimer
Vincent Price
Mark Wahlberg
Billie Myers

Salman Rushdie
Bif Naked
Paulina Rubio
Tupac Shakur
Dennis Roussos
Jennifer Ellison
Steve Strange
Ronnie Wood
Lee Ryan
Mark Selby

BOAR – CANCER

Chinese Name: ZHU
Rank: 12th
Hours Ruled: 9pm – 11am
Direction: North – Northwest
Season: Autumn
Month: November
Western Zodiac Equivalent of Boar: Scorpio
Scorpio Western Element: Water
Eastern Zodiac Equivalent of Cancer: Sheep
Cancer Western Element: Water
Numerology: 136 = 1

Today, more than ever before, life must be characterized by a sense of Universal responsibility, not only nation to nation and human to human, but also human to other forms of life.
– Dalai Lama

When the Boar's still waters meet with Cancer's serene stream of secrets, two similar signs come together to create a personality that usually has a massive impact in the general world. It is a double water combination so the two rivers converge and rush forth towards the big blue ocean, creating a powerful creature that thinks like the everyman, but leads without needing to seem dominant. Although, they do not like to share information about their own personal lives particularly, this combination feels an overwhelming responsibility to bring truth to the world from the shadows and highlight hypocrisy, but as the Boar is a self-sacrificial creature, it often ends up putting itself on the line inadvertently. Wiki-Leaks Journalist Julian Assange, Whistleblower Edward Snowden and the Dalai Lama, have all been exiled, extradited or placed within asylum for services to mankind. In fact, both Julian Assange and the Dalai Lama won the Sydney

Peace Medal, two of only four people ever awarded the prize (2014). The Dalai Lama has said, "I consider myself as a free spokesman for the people."

Quietly, they go about their lives and occasionally, they come across a cause that resonates with their core. Even though they carefully consider the potential drawbacks and personal risks to taking a set action and even when they decide it is too precarious, they go ahead and do it anyway. Recognizing that the established rules were put in place by a minority of people who benefit from the majority falling into line, they simply ignore established rules. In their unconventional way, they push the boundaries of the existing status quo and accidentally contribute towards shaping the new world order. Edward Snowden said, "Because, remember, I didn't want to change society. I wanted to give society a chance to determine if it should change itself." The world order is slowly shifting and the Boar-Cancer is there to lessen the power of those in charge to force the doors open. The Dalai Lama said, "I always believe the rule by king or official leader is outdated. Now we must catch up with the modern world."

The men of this combination tend to be taller than average and are also quite distinctive looking, almost clumsy yet almost regal. They have an ability to shut out everything but that which is immediately important, a mental function that sometimes kicks in when the fight or flight mechanism is activated, but it seems like they can go for weeks in this mode, neglecting all else until they reach their goal...but then they have to deal with the consequences of neglecting the other areas of their life. In a somewhat extreme example, speaking about the furor caused over WikiLeaks, Julian Assange said, "When it comes to the point where you occasionally look forward to being in prison on the basis that you might be able to spend a day reading a book, the realization dawns that perhaps the situation has become a little more stressful than you would like." Usually acting from their good intentions, it frustrates them that these are not always taken into consideration. Larry David has said, "I'm surprised sometimes at how some of my actions are misinterpreted." They are not givers in the conventional sense, their service, their work is what they give. They want to put their resources into their life purpose rather than into what they may consider to be frivolous. The Dalai Lama has said, "Our prime purpose in this life is to help others. And if you can't help them, at least don't hurt them."

The women of this combination strive to maintain their common sense, remain grounded and remember where they came from. That does not mean that they are not naughty every now and then, they can be. Generally though, these women want to *keep it real*. Speaking about her image in the hip hop world, Missy Elliott said, "I didn't want to be a genius! That ain't cool." With all of the water that is present here, they are likely to be exceptionally creative, original and inventive but they know the difference between fantasy and real life, which is why they know how to get results. Super Nanny Jo Frost has said, "I've been looking for the yellow brick road and I can't find it." At the end of the day, they care about people and want to make a difference in their lives, even if that means doing whatever it takes to "make it." Missy Elliott has said, "I'm blessed to be living this dream of writing and singing, but that's not the real dream I had. The real dream was to make enough money to take care of all the pain and suffering that my mother has been through."

Ultimately, the Boar-Cancer is one of those rare gems programmed to keep going until the road ends altogether. They put others first, but not in the conventional sense, usually in a grander, bigger picture sort of way. What they are known for is their heart, idealism and a simple yet profound perspective. The Dalai Lama has said, "I have always had this view about the modern education system: we pay attention to brain development, but the development of warm-heartedness we take for granted." With that idealistic bent, they are constant self-improvers, even a tad vain, but they usually have enough self-awareness to remember what remains consistently important in their lives. Albert Brooks has said, "Be generous and you can be the best person who ever lived." All they strive to do is to be true to what inspires their hearts; but sometimes this rubs others the wrong way, they are stubborn enough to refuse to go away until their goal is reached and can and have played David to a number of Goliaths in their time. What is the secret to their personal power? The Dalai Lama has said, "With realization of one's own potential and self-confidence in one's ability, one can build a better world."

Soul Mate:	Tiger-Gemini
Challenger:	Snake-Capricorn
Siblings:	Boar-Scorpio, Boar-Pisces
Best Friends:	Rabbit-Cancer, Rabbit-Scorpio, Rabbit-Pisces,
	Sheep-Cancer, Sheep-Scorpio, Sheep-Pisces

Donald Sutherland
Diahann Carroll
The Dalai Lama
Albert Brooks
Larry David
Missy 'Misdemeanor' Elliott
Jo Frost
Lorrie Morgan
Bob Dole
Robert Downey Sr.
Cheryl Cole
Brian May
Don Henley

Carlos Santana
Jason Lewis
Sandra Oh
Corey Feldman
Monica Potter
Aileen Quinn
Laila Rouass
Gregory Smith
Sharni Vinson
Marco Dapper
Michelle Branch
Vincent D'Onofrio
Robert Knepper
Richie Sambora
Kevin Nash
Billy Campbell
Pauline Quirke
Peter Weller
Kim Darby
O.J. Simpson
Jimmie Walker
Camilla Parker-Bowles
Judge Joe Brown
Dale Robertson
Rehman
Tun Tun
Julian Assange
Edward Snowden

BOAR – LEO

Chinese Name: ZHU
Rank: 12th
Hours Ruled: 9pm – 11am
Direction: North – Northwest
Season: Autumn
Month: November
Western Zodiac Equivalent of Boar: Scorpio
Scorpio Western Element: Water
Eastern Zodiac Equivalent of Leo: Monkey
Leo Western Element: Fire
Numerology: 137 = 2

Winning narrowly didn't make me feel good; I wanted my dominance to be clear.
– Arnold Schwartzenegger

When the Boar's still waters meet with the Leo's firestorm, the resulting creature is gifted with the Boar's happy-go-lucky charm, sweet nature and business acumen along with the lion's presence, persistence and power. This combination seems to know how to filter its unbridled passion through its common sense and they tend to make productive decisions on the whole. At the same time, all Boar signs are highly emotional beings and have a reputation for taking on too much, holding their tongue in order to avoid hurting someone's feelings and then erupting when it all gets too much; this wild-boar-lion is no different to that stereotype. But generally speaking, when they are not too emotionally invested or are in balanced state of mind, they have a systematic and sensible approach to life that leads them to all kinds of honors. Arnold Schwarzenegger has said, "I know that if you leave dishes in the sink, they get sticky and hard to wash the next day."

With a huge appetite for all that life has to offer, they tend to go off in search of adventure younger than most. They also learn that they cannot be too open as there are people who will take advantage, so they either close up some, or they become overtly vocal about their boundaries; both mechanisms work to provide them with a certain level of security that they crave. It does not however, entirely alleviate their concerns that people are not being fair to them or maybe mistreating them. So they work harder to develop their own self-worth and seek spiritual remedies for their overactive imaginations. Andrew Garfield has said, "I think too much. Being in my body is much more satisfying than being in my head." Whatever method works best for them, they should pursue as it is important for them to be "successful" and their overthinking is often a hindrance. Arnold Schwarzenegger has said, "When you are not confident of your decision-making process, it will slow you down. Overthinking is why people can't sleep at night: it cripples you."

The men of this combination tend to be disciplined, determined, and with the combined sex appeal of the wild pig and the wild lion, this is one sexy wild creature. What they really want is a good, sweet, innocent partner, because actually, they are good, sweet, innocent boys who know how to curb their testosterone driven urges. Chris Hemsworth has said, "Work all paled into the background as soon as I had a baby." When receiving the AFI Lifetime Achievement award, Alfred Hitchcock said, "I beg permission to mention by name only four people who have given me the most affection, appreciation, and encouragement, and constant collaboration. The first of the four is a film editor, the second is a scriptwriter, the third is the mother of my daughter Pat and the fourth is as fine a cook as ever performed miracles in a domestic kitchen. And their names are Alma Reville." Alma Reville is also a Boar-Leo. These men want to be better tomorrow than they were today and every millimeter of progress is important to them so they live and work on the edge of their capacities as it forces them to grow, closing down any other option! Arnold Schwarzenegger has said, "To test yourself and grow, you have to operate without a safety net. Forget Plan B. If there is no Plan B, then Plan A has to work."

The women of this combination are typically charming in that warm Boar-woman way, but they also possess the lion's dramatic razzmatazz. Commonly known for their wit and humor, they know how to put on a show and tend to be very welcome guests wherever they go. Sometimes though, people expect them to be "on" all of the time, which is an unfair expectation that they learn to deal with in time. Speaking about her reputation as a *funny-girl*, Mila Kunis has said, "I think the second you think that you're funny is when you stop being funny." Lucille Ball has said, "I'm not funny. What I am is brave." Even Christine Taylor has said, "My family's always been really funny. I feel like comedy's hard. I feel like it's so important." With their warmth, intelligence and compassionate nature, they forge out into the world ready for adventure which they most definitely find. Many are also deeply touched by the injustices they see and often choose to rectify them in some way. These ladies are forever young at heart and do not let their age define how they perceive themselves, they alone will decide that and the world adjusts. This Boar-lioness is in charge of her world, but not entirely in charge of her emotions, for they are as wildly active as she is. In any case, wherever she will go, her elegant presence adds glamour, laughter and heart.

Ultimately, the Boar-Leo is a sensitive, sociable, slogger who is not afraid of doing his fair share of the work in order to pass the finish line. In fact, they don't just want to pass it; they want to obliterate it! But they also recognize the role spirituality and healthy self-esteem plays in achieving that success. Lucille Ball has said, "I have an everyday religion that works for me. Love yourself first, and everything else falls into line." They know that that the image of what they want must first be segmented in their minds eye before it manifests in the physical world. Arnold Schwarzenegger has said, "If I can see it and believe it, then I can achieve it." This is a somewhat unconventional sign and although from the outside, they look like they are hugely popular and adored by the millions, they themselves often feel like an outsider and often feel lonely, even when the whole world wants them to come to their party. It is a condition that keeps them striving for more, keeps them growing towards the successful beast they inevitably become and also allows them the space to be who they really are without interruption. Kevin Spacey has said, "I'm used to people thinking I'm nuts. And you know what? I kind of love it."

Soul Mate: Tiger-Taurus
Challenger: Snake-Aquarius
Siblings: Boar-Aries, Boar-Sagittarius
Best Friends: Rabbit-Aries, Rabbit-Leo, Rabbit-Sagittarius,
                 Sheep-Aries, Sheep-Leo, Sheep-Sagittarius

Chris Hemsworth
Andrew Garfield
Arnold Schwarzenegger
Kevin Spacey
Alfred Hitchcock
Mila Kunis
Lucille Ball
Christine Taylor
Ashley Johnson
Richard Armitage
Richard Griffiths
Justin Theroux

Marcia Gay Harden
John C. McGinley
David Walliams
Tom Green
Estelle Getty
Sanjay Dutt

BOAR – VIRGO

Chinese Name: ZHU
Rank: 12th
Hours Ruled: 9pm – 11am
Direction: North – Northwest
Season: Autumn
Month: November
Western Zodiac Equivalent of Boar: Scorpio
Scorpio Western Element: Water
Eastern Zodiac Equivalent of Virgo: Rooster
Virgo Western Element: Earth
Numerology: 138 = 3

I have a permanent address in the people's republic of paranoia.
– Stephen King

When the Boar's still waters meet with the virgin's fertile earth, the simple, cheerful and adorable wild pig gets dressed up and civilized by the fussy and overbearing Virgo. The country bumpkin meets the city dweller here resulting in a personality that is traditional but is open to the unconventional, accepting of people's flaws yet critical of them anyway, is not a fan of change, yet continues to break boundaries down not just for themselves, but for others too throughout their life. There is also an active imagination here; all Virgos worry, they need to, it's in their constitution and sometimes this causes chronic illnesses. With the Boar's creative water energy, these worries are often amplified to turn into fully-fledged fantasies that are often tinged with a touch of paranoia. Perhaps that is why there are so many prominent writers of this combination, writers who tend towards the somewhat pessimistic, or macabre side of life. Stephen King has said, "Never let the facts get in the way of a good story."

Although they may have diverse spiritual beliefs, the Boar-Virgo has an interesting relationship with God or the universal powers that be. Firstly, they are hugely drawn to the subject and are interested not just in their own persuasion, but that of others and the reasons behind their decision. Jada Pinkett Smith said, "I love religion and have contemplated going back to school to get a world religion degree." Even though they cannot be sure that there is a "God" they often believe but don't or don't believe but do. It's an intriguing trait. Amy Winehouse said, "I believe in fate and I believe that things happen for a reason but I don't think that there's a high power, necessarily. I believe in karma very much though." To illustrate this interesting behavior further, Stephen King described, "You simply make an agreement to believe in God because it will make your life easier and richer to believe than not to believe. So I choose to believe."

The men of this combination have a cuteness of looks, a sweetness of presence and as one digs a little deeper, a sourness is also revealed. As previously mentioned, they tend towards pessimism and it can sometimes color their entire perspective. William Golding said, "Man produces evil as a bee produces honey." Occasionally, they scare themselves with the evils they believe lurk outside so they create safer worlds to inhabit. That Virgo side of them also makes them persnickety and critical. But sometimes it serves them well in their chosen careers that are usually creative, color focused and based around property. Nate Berkus managed to combine all three in his career as an interior designer, he has said, "I didn't know this was going to be my calling, I just knew I was sensitive to surroundings." They do have a knack for creating spaces and environments that are calming to the nerves. Perhaps because they need it more than anyone. Martin Freeman has said, "If I could get bands to come and play in my house, I'd like that. I've never been to a festival. I'm a creature of habit, mashed-potato comfort, I like rugs. Our sofa's squishy. Maybe too squishy – it's hard to get up sometimes." However, paranoia seems to be common for people belonging to this combination. When they focus on what is going right rather than what is going wrong, they attract more of it into their lives. Stephen King continues to be so prolific in his writing, because he believes, "Talent is cheaper than table salt. What separates the talented individual from the successful one is a lot of hard work." There is also a hedonistic, reckless side to this guy typified by Boar-Virgo men like James Hunt and Lance Armstrong.

The women of this combination present an innocent yet tough front and that is exactly what they are like! They are tougher than they realize and more naïve than they would like to acknowledge. They have simple desires and do not like to be confronted by any boundaries. If they do, traditional or otherwise, they will break through them in order to alleviate the emotional blockage they feel building within them. This Boar-woman needs to feel free. Jada Pinkett-Smith has said, "It's kind of a catch-22: Strength in women isn't appreciated, and vulnerability in women isn't appreciated. It's like, 'What the hell do you do?' What you do is you don't allow anyone to dictate who you are." Aware of what society expects of them, but also very connected to their actual needs, they eventually decide to let the heart have its way; that is when their difficulties subside and the ease begins. Stella McCartney said, "I have been struggling furiously all my life to be independent." Releasing, letting go and genuinely trusting in that higher power is all they need to do in order for their desires to come rushing towards them. Amy Winehouse said, "The minute I even start to think about what I'm doing I just lose it. I have to just shut my eyes and flow."

Ultimately, the Boar-Virgo combination is one that often loses itself in its daydreams, sometimes positively and sometimes negatively. With a mind that chatters incessantly, it is no surprise that they often worry themselves senseless. Lesser-evolved Boar-Virgos allow their fantasies rule to such an extent that they take huge gambles to ensure their outer image reflects the fantastic, grandiose inner image that they have dreamed up. Lance Armstrong has said, "Two things scare me: the first is getting hurt, but that's not as scary as the second which is losing." Not as easy going as they initially seem, they also have a prickly side, which surfaces inconsistently. But the Boar-Virgo flourishes when in the presence of loving energy, whoever it is coming from, it gives them the feeling of safety which they need. It is also good for them to be around animals and plants. Jada Pinkett-Smith said, "I learned that surrounding myself with people who are able to help me is like being surrounded by tangible godliness." They are loving people with a lot to contribute but they need to realize this first before they can make that contribution.

Soul Mate: Tiger-Aries
Challenger: Snake-Pisces
Siblings: Boar-Taurus, Boar-Capricorn
Best Friends: Rabbit-Taurus, Rabbit-Virgo, Rabbit-
                 Capricorn, Sheep-Taurus, Sheep-Virgo,
                 Sheep-Capricorn

William Golding
Stephen King
Jada Pinkett Smith
David Arquette
Stella McCartney
Amy Winehouse
Martin Freeman
Nate Berkus
Luke Wilson

Richard Attenborough
Hank Williams
Sam Neill
Anne Archer
Russ Abbot
Rebecca De Mornay
Carla Gugino
Lance Armstrong
Maggie Grace
Joseph Mazzello
Pippa Middleton
James Hunt
Lance Armstrong

BOAR – LIBRA

Chinese Name: ZHU
Rank: 12th
Hours Ruled: 9pm – 11am
Direction: North – Northwest
Season: Autumn
Month: November
Western Zodiac Equivalent of Boar: Scorpio
Scorpio Western Element: Water
Eastern Zodiac Equivalent of Libra: Dog
Libra Western Element: Air
Numerology: 139 = 4

Success rarely changes anyone. Rather it gives them the power to be what they always were.
– Simon Cowell

When the Boar's still waters meet Libra's cool breeze, the surface of the pond gets cold even though there is more temperate water seeping through to the top through many tiny holes. They are hard and soft and squishy and sharp. The Boar's business mind comes to the fore here and there are many prominent business people born under this combination. Creative energy is always present with the Boar and when Libra is added to the mix also, it adds even greater depth. These people have a business-like approach to everything without necessarily being particularly professional, yet, they put in the hours and become very good at their chosen craft. Speaking on this topic, Snoop Doggy Dog has said, "If it's flipping hamburgers at McDonald's, be the best hamburger flipper in the world. Whatever it is you do you have to master your craft."

With a simple perspective on life, they listen to their own gut instincts about everything. They also have an ability to articulate their instinct also in very plain, clear language that people can understand. That is why it creates people like Simon Cowell who have made careers out of sharing their opinions. He has said, "No, what I am doing is kind by telling people who are useless 'Do something that you're good at'. So I would only feel guilt if I misled somebody who was terrible... I have become famous for being rude. I'm the honest one." Their honesty is a very valued commodity, even if it comes in the prickly package that they are. In actuality, they are not so hard or harsh at all, they just know how to play it for effect. Charlton Heston has said, "A lot of men in positions of authority are difficult people, because they're right, and they know they're right." Even Snoop Doggy Dog has said, "I tell the truth. And I know what I'm talking about. That's why I'm a threat."

When the water element mixes with the air sign, it creates eternally youthful characteristics and these people find ways to let their inner child live on the surface for much of their adult life. They are also connected to ethereal energies deeply and as a result, can experience high and low moods for no reason, seemingly for no reason. But what is happening is they are tuning into to energies that have existed in previous years by previous spirits. Simon Cowell has said, "I get very dark moods for no reason. Nothing in particular brings it on. You can be having the best time of your life and yet you're utterly and totally miserable." It is important for them to remain focused in a positive way otherwise they can find themselves slipping into a mournful state. Jesse Eisenberg has said, "If things seem to be going good, I'm worried that it's going to end; if things are bad, then I'm worried that it's going to be permanent. It's not a very comfortable attitude to have all the time."

The men of this combination tend to be given a level of credit that many people feel they do not deserve but because they develop a high level of self-worth, they attract all sorts of universal blessings that others envy. Despite these gifts, they are still fallible human beings with Boar sensibilities. Charlton Heston has said, "I am seen as a forbidding authority figure. I only wish I were as indomitable as everyone thinks." Whether it is humility or insecurity, the point remains that these men ride the fine line between narcissism and low self-esteem. Either way, they usually return to the knowledge that their individual skillset is powerfully unique and that there is much they can achieve, personally and professionally that will inspire generations to come. Pavarotti said, "If you see me once, you cannot confuse me with another." The main reason for this is that amazing work ethic. They have it and they expect their associates to have it also. Simon Cowell has said, "I have little patience for anybody who isn't prepared to put in 15-hour days."

The women of this combination also have the talent, business acumen and desire to be seen. But first and foremost, they have a much more amenable image. Julie Andrews has said, "Sometimes I'm so sweet even I can't stand it." Julie Andrews, Danni Minogue and pop star Tiffany leveraged their innocence to establish their careers but found it difficult to lose the label as they matured because, they all still retained a youthful, innocent air and likely will for the rest of their lives. But of course, Boar-Libra women are multifaceted beings and tire of being perceived in a single dimension. Some go to extreme lengths to expand it Speaking about posing for Playboy, Tiffany said, "I became aware that the world still views me as the 15-year-old performer I once was, I view my appearance in Playboy as the first step in presenting myself to the world as I am." Similarly, Danni Minogue also posed for *Playboy* magazine. She said, "Since I've been in *Playboy* myself in Australia, I love it, and I think it's really empowering and positive towards women, which is not a view that many women hold." Despite their attempts otherwise, these ladies continue to leave a *sweet* aftertaste.

Ultimately, the Boar-Libra is a tenderhearted, soft-natured, beast with a bite. With a competitive streak, they play to win and do not take no for an answer. They tend to live dramatic lives, especially early on where they might lose all of their money, or all of their assets and it looks like they have to start again from scratch. This is just the universe testing their mettle. As soon as they get back up and attack, the universe rewards them with all sorts of material and spiritual benefits so the Boar-Libra knows first hand that action backed by a powerful desire always leads to success. That's why there are so many inspiring business people of this combination. Simon Cowell has said, "No matter how bad things are, if you've got the guts and the determination, you can fulfill your dream."

Soul Mate:	Tiger-Pisces
Challenger:	Snake-Aries
Siblings:	Boar-Gemini, Boar-Aquarius
Best Friends:	Rabbit-Gemini, Rabbit-Libra, Rabbit-Aquarius, Sheep-Gemini, Sheep-Libra, Sheep-Aquarius

Simon Cowell
Luciano Pavarotti
Meat Loaf
Julie Andrews
Jesse Eisenberg
Sacha Baron Cohen
Snoop Dogg
Tiffany
Dannii Minogue
Sam Raimi
Ashok Kumar
Dev Anand
Johnny Mathis

Mary Kay Place
Jon Snow
Ann Widdecombe
'Weird Al' Yankovic
Sarah Ferguson
CeCe Winans
Youssou N'Dour
Jenna Elfman
MC Lyte

BOAR – SCORPIO

Chinese Name: ZHU
Rank: 12th
Hours Ruled: 9pm – 11am
Direction: North – Northwest
Season: Autumn
Month: November
Western Zodiac Equivalent of Boar: Scorpio
Scorpio Western Element: Water
Eastern Zodiac Equivalent of Scorpio: Boar
Scorpio Western Element: Water
Numerology: 140 = 5

Happiness has a bum rap. People say it shouldn't be your goal in life. Oh, yes it should
– Richard Dreyfuss

The still waters of the Boar and the Scorpio are exactly the same color and consistency because they are from the same family. The Boar equates to Scorpio and vice versa so in effect we have the pure Boar or the double Scorpio combination here. This is one combination that is soft and subtle yet can be forcefully forthright and unafraid of controversy. With an incredible depth of feeling, heightened empathy and humane orientation, they go about life with the intention to live the fullest life they can without imposing on anyone else. The Boar likes to be appreciated but does not necessarily require excessive adulation, in fact deep down any such desires are probably looked down upon as some sort of weakness. Doing a job well is more important than anything else. Bryan Adams has said, "I always knew I'd be in music in some sort of capacity. I didn't know if I'd be successful at it, but I knew I'd be doing something in it. Maybe get a job in a record store. Maybe even play in a band. I never got into this to be a star."

The Yin energy that comes with this combination is exceptionally potent. The sensitivity, creativity and passivity are unusual in that one can feel their existence, its potential power and invisible force. The Pure Boar is sweet; the Double Scorpio is more than a little sour; their sting is capable of causing a little anarchy so watch your step. But Scorpio is both the Scorpion and the Royal Golden Eagle. This duality is very present in this combination. They can be the majestic, spiritually evolved leaders who seem to understand everybody's problems and are willing to lend a helping hand to anyone in need. But that does not mean that they are opening the door to be taken advantage of. In 2009, Hilary Clinton was asked by a student what her husband thought about Chinese economic policy by a student. Her response was, "Wait. You want me to tell you what my husband thinks? My husband is not the Secretary of State – I am. So you ask my opinion, I will tell you my opinion. I'm not going to be channeling my husband!"

Like most Boar signs, this combination has a loud internal critic that questions their every move making them second-guess every decision sometimes prevents them from really enjoying the present moment. Kevin Kline has said, "I've never felt completely satisfied with what I've done. I tend to see things too critically. I'm trying to get over that." This experience does not last long as the Boar's buoyant spirit cannot be repressed for long and eventually they see self-created fairy tales for what they are.

The men of this combination are often blessed with pretty looks with a great deal of natural talent. This is male is relatively malleable and heads in too many directions. Theater appeals, as does music. But the men of this combination are also drawn to the medicine or social services. They like to get involved on the grass roots to make a change because they have the understanding to be able to influence people out of negative mental patterns. Whatever they choose to do, they will do it with single-minded focus. Discussing his acting career, Harry Lloyd has said, "You've got to be confident. You can't think: 'Well, I'll just keep my carpentry course up my sleeve.' No. You romantically believe that, whatever happens, I'll do it for a living." As the Pure Boar combination, the typical Boar traits are amplified here. They become even more self-sacrificial and prefer to rely solely on themselves without asking others for help unless it is a last resort. They always struggle with this one even when they know that a one-man-band will never be as effective as a team of people. Bryan Adams said, "I never took a grant or borrowed a penny from anybody. It was partially because I didn't really know how to do that, but secondly, my pride never would have allowed me to. In the beginning it was about doing it the right way, on the merits of the music."

The women of this combination are soft on the surface with a quiet strength that is sensed more than seen. They tend to be glamorous with big hearty smiles and many prefer the short hair sophisticated look. They are very vocal about the development of women's rights, esteem and liberties. Bestselling author Cheryl Richardson's books: the Unmistakable Touch of Grace and The Art of Extreme Self Care have touched the lives of women internationally. Hilary Clinton has said, "When women are excluded from the political process, they become even more vulnerable to abuse. ...It is no longer acceptable to discuss women's rights as separate from human rights. These abuses have continued because, for too long, the history of women has been a history of silence." Many Boar Scorpio women are interested in politics. Winona Ryder has said, "My godfather Timothy Leary coined the phrase 'question authority,' it is one of my favorites. To question our government is the most important thing people can do..."

Ultimately, the Boar-Scorpio is powerfully connected to its spirituality. Richard Dreyfuss has said, "I really think that living is the process of going from complete certainty to complete ignorance" echoing a popular definition of enlightenment which is a *process of unlearning*. Winona Ryder has said, "I still practice Buddhism to a certain extent and I believe in karma." With simple desires and a simple aim to be better tomorrow than they were today, they slowly evolve to a place where their actions begin to look complicated or "weird." Michael Winner has said, "I don't want to live in a tolerant society. I want to live in a very intolerant society." Stepping outside of the box is never without resistance; ironically, it is this very resistance that provides the contrast that pushes them higher and higher up the spiritual scale.

Soul Mate:	Tiger-Aquarius
Challenger:	Snake-Taurus
Siblings:	Boar-Cancer, Boar-Pisces
Best Friends:	Rabbit-Cancer, Rabbit-Scorpio, Rabbit-Pisces, Sheep-Cancer, Sheep-Scorpio, Sheep-Pisces

Kevin Kline
Joe Mantegna
Bryan Adams
Winona Ryder
Hilary Clinton
Richard Dreyfuss
Minnie Riperton
Dolph Lundgren
Cheryl Richardson
Michael Winner
Hoagy Carmichael
Sean Young
Allison Janney
Meenakshi Sheshadri

Leslie Grossman
Joe Thomas
Harry Lloyd
Marie Antoinette
Alain Delon

BOAR – SAGITTARIUS

Chinese Name: ZHU
Rank: 12th

Rank: 12th

Hours Ruled: 9pm – 11am
Direction: North – Northwest
Season: Autumn
Month: November
Western Zodiac Equivalent of Boar: Scorpio
Scorpio Western Element: Water
Eastern Zodiac Equivalent of Sagittarius: Rat
Sagittarius Western Element: Fire
Numerology: 141 = 6

It is discouraging how many people are shocked by honesty and how few by deceit.
– Noel Coward

When the Boar's still waters meet with the centaur's frisky fire, the Boar's simple, honest approach is amplified by Sagittarius's uninhibited thrust, adding a great dollop of playful energy to everything they touch. Both the Boar and Sagittarius are known for their sex appeal, but where they differ is that the Boar is a domestic sign and Sagittarius is an eternal nomad, so it is likely that the people of this combination will experience both at different points in their life, and not necessarily in a conventional order; they may settle down in their youth and then travel, explore and play around later on. With Sagittarius here, the Boar is challenged to push beyond its comfort borders even though it really doesn't want to go, this Boar wants to be content within its pen, but Sagittarius refuses to let it, so they push themselves out while fully expecting that they will fail, embarrass themselves and all hell will break loose upon them. Jonah Hill has said, "I assume everything I do in life is gonna be a failure, and then if it turns up roses, then I'm psyched." Deep down, Boar-Sagittarians are not really so negative. Emily Mortimer said, "I'm always sort of anticipating life being difficult, but on a basic level, that's sort of on the surface, on a basic level, I'm optimistic in the sense that I think it's all going to be alright in the end."

It is interesting to note just how many unconventional writers who are known for their wit belong to this combination. The Boar brings the warmth, consideration and creative desire and the Centaur adds a heavy dose of its intellect, detachment and edgy spark. These artists are well aware of their gifts and they also know exactly how to maneuver themselves for effect. Playwright Noel Coward said, "Wit ought to be a glorious treat like caviar; never spread it about like marmalade." Responding to a critic, David Mamet said, "Of course I'm alienating the public! That's what they pay me for." Boar-Sagittarius artists are so uninhibited that they have an ability to let their subconscious take the lead, whether that be in writing or directing, they have an instinct that takes over, almost using their body as an instrument for source to come through and leave powerfully beautiful pieces of work. Along with the Boar-Sagittarian humorous twist. Woody Allen has said, "I'm astounded by people who want to 'know' the universe when it's hard enough to find your way around Chinatown."

The men of this combination have soft features and an approachable energy, like an everyman. Their sexuality is in their spirit, not always in the way that they look. They do not project themselves in a way that places them on a higher level than anyone else so are generally easy to work with and easy to like. Speaking about his thirst for artistic success and inability to settle for a typical middle-class existence, Noel Coward said, "I'll go through life either first class or third, but never in second." They also have a decent level of emotional intelligence because of their self-honesty, in fact, much more than just decent, but it reveals itself sporadically, so pay attention when they verbally splurge, if not for the profundity, then at least for the entertainment value. David Mamet said, "I've always been more comfortable sinking while clutching a good theory than swimming with an ugly fact." Finding ways to turn a perceived weakness into a strength is also something they excel at, but they have to remind themselves and develop a habit of positive thinking and positive vibrating, even if they cannot always be positive in words. Woody Allen has said, "The talent for being happy is appreciating and liking what you have, instead of what you don't have."

The women of this combination know how to utilize the combined energy of these two signs. With that hourglass shape, sultry lips and domestic housewife look, they are conventionally appealing. Speaking about her sexy image Gloria Grahame said, "It wasn't the way I looked at a man, it was the thought behind it." Though they move slowly and backtrack sometimes, they also have moments when they charge ahead without a break. The more they forge ahead, the greater their self-confidence stabilizes. Emily Mortimer has said, "But I now know that I have a reserve of courage to draw upon when I really need it. There's nothing that I'm too scared to have a go at." Incurable romantics, they have the capacity to love every single one of their lovers they have ever had without the ferocity of that love lessening. Speaking about sustaining a long-term relationship, Christina Applegate has said, "I think another problem people have is they are always searching for that high, and they don't realize they can get that same high with that same person again."

Ultimately, when they learn to manage their inner critic and focus on all of the things that are going right in their life, they have an ability to manifest the most magical things into their experience. They are big kids at heart and it is the source of their creativity, unique perspective and connection to their subconscious world; it is also the reason they have such enthusiasm for everything that comes to them. Sometimes, they struggle to let that sardonic, sarcastic, weary-eyed exterior down because they feel people take them more seriously because of it. But actually, they are more like excitable ten-year-olds, as Jonah Hill illustrates here speaking about all of the opportunities he has been lucky enough to experience, he has said, "All this stuff is so mind-blowing to me that I get to do in my life. Throwing the first pitch out at the White Sox game on a random Wednesday? Like who am I? How did I get this life? I'm glad I'm not jaded, and little kids are the least jaded people in the entire world, so it's fun to be around people that still find wonder in how cool things are."

Soul Mate:	Tiger-Capricorn
Challenger:	Snake-Gemini
Siblings:	Boar-Aries, Boar-Leo
Best Friends:	Rabbit-Aries, Rabbit-Leo, Rabbit-Sagittarius, Sheep-Aries, Sheep-Leo, Sheep-Sagittarius

Noel Coward
Phil Donahue
Woody Allen
David Mamet
Jonah Hill
Christina Applegate
Gloria Grahame
Emily Mortimer
Lorraine Kelly
Eamonn Holmes
Lee J. Cobb
Broderick Crawford
Ted Knight
Harold Gould
Lee Remick

Dharmendra
Dwight Schultz
Teri Garr
Ben Cross
Gregg Allman
Judd Nelson
Maxwell Caulfield
Jimmy Shergill

BOAR – CAPRICORN

Chinese Name: ZHU
Rank: 12th
Hours Ruled: 9pm – 11am
Direction: North – Northwest
Season: Autumn
Month: November
Western Zodiac Equivalent of Boar: Scorpio
Scorpio Western Element: Water
Eastern Zodiac Equivalent of Capricorn: Ox
Capricorn Western Element: Earth
Numerology: 142 = 7

You just have to get rid of fear and confront the world. Look at yourself in the mirror and say to yourself, 'I love you and nothing will destroy you and you're not going to fall.'
– Ricky Martin

When the Boar's still water meets with the Capricorn's dense earth, the water moistens the earth, the water seeping deeper into the ground fertilizing it rather than flowing away. The Boar lends its heart, passion and creativity here whereas the Capricorn brings its work ethic, exacting nature and calculator, in case somebody forgets the impact of the financial costs. Where the Boar can be naïve, the Capricorn is thrifty; where the Capricorn can be heartless, the Boar is compassionate; in many ways these two signs complement for each other's weaknesses very well. There is also a powerful need for spiritual wholeness that they spend much of their time seeking until they realize that wholeness always existed within them. Ricky Martin has said, "The part that I like the most from Buddha's teachings and from His Holiness, The Dalai Lama (Boar-Cancer) is that the most powerful weapon is to not attack, to be able to have self-control."

Although, the Boar is a very likeable, simple, honest and upright type, it's self-aware enough to know that there are parasites out there that like the taste of pork, so they come with a somewhat defensive stance to protect their own interests. The Capricorn makes this creature even more prickly, harder and not as open as many other Boar signs. Nigella Lawson has said, "I'm not someone who's endlessly patient and wonderful." The more they access their inner resources, the stronger they become; they begin to see through the pretenses that pervade all areas of conventional life and quietly reject those that no longer serve their interests. This is when they learn how to start living in the present, moment to moment, taking simple pleasure pleasures. Tracy Ullman has said, "I've never looked ahead very much in my life. I've never had any grand plan from the outset. I had no burning ambition to do what I do."

The men of this combination are pretty, pretty and even more pretty! The Ricky Martin's, Jared Leto's and Val Kilmer's of the world are Boar-Capricorns. They are blessed that their looks last into their mature years as long as they make a conscious effort to give their health the appropriate attention. Jared Leto has said, "I'm pretty healthy so I think that helps a lot. I've been that way for a long time – 20 solid years of eating vegetarian/vegan and taking care of myself. That probably helps the preservation process." They definitely seem to have the secret to eternal youth so it worth considering what Ricky Martin had to say about staying youthfully handsome, he said, "When you take things too seriously, you get old. You have to be silly. Whenever people say, 'Hey, man, are you ever going to grow up?' That's when you know you're doing things right." Whatever they choose to do, they bring their whole self to the project and take it personally. There is that side to them that complains, picks at the details and will likely disagree with those in charge if they feel something can be improved, but it is because they want everything to be of the highest standard possible. Despite their awkward manner, this usually translates and they find popularity in professional and personal contexts. Humphrey Bogart said, "I've been around a long time. Maybe the people like me."

The women of this combination have substance, intelligence and the determination to have it all. If one is looking for the All-Woman, here she is! Tracy Ullman has said, "There's nothing I won't attempt." This is very true. These ladies have a grounded, domestic energy with the skills to do anything any man could do. They do not let gender roles define them, nor do they make a big fuss about it, they just get on with it. They are expected to undertake the role of a wife, mother, sister, daughter and every other female role along with having a full-time job and taking an equal share of the work in every other regard in general life. Dido has said, "I like being a strong, independent woman, and to be honest, I was never afraid to be on my own." Perhaps the reason for this is when she is in a relationship, the Boar-Capricorn lady takes on way more than her fair share of the workload and this she does, self-sacrificially and usually, without complaint, until she has had enough. That is when she erupts and the wild nature of the Boar surfaces. She can be scary when she is mad and then she will cry, upset at herself for losing control. When she learns that just because she loves someone, it does not mean she has to do everything for them or be everything to them. Her beautiful little Boar-Capricorn-ness is more than enough just as she is.

Ultimately, the Boar-Capricorn is a down-to-earth sort with a powerful connection to their personal form of spirituality. They are sensitive, without letting their senses take them to modes of self-wallowing, thanks to the Capricorn side of them. Ted Danson has said, "If you actively do something, it will stop making you feel like a victim and you'll start feeling like part of the solution, which is just a huge benefit to your body and your psyche." Also, they are practical without becoming robots about it and bringing an aesthetic perspective to everything, thanks to the Boar side of them. Dido has said, "I always want to bring emotion across in a straightforward way. I don't want to get histrionic when I'm singing. For me that's just not interesting; it goes too far down one road." Together, these two signs balance each other well to create a personality that is real, grounded, sweet, loving and all things to all people...even though they do not need to be.

Soul Mate: Tiger-Sagittarius
Challenger: Snake-Cancer
Siblings: Boar-Taurus, Boar-Virgo
Best Friends: Rabbit-Taurus, Rabbit-Virgo, Rabbit-
               Capricorn, Sheep-Taurus, Sheep-Virgo,
               Sheep-Capricorn

Nigella Lawson
Tracey Ullman
Dido
Val Kilmer
Jared Leto
Ricky Martin
Humphrey Bogart
Ted Danson
Gurinder Chadha
Amanda Peet
Patricia Clarkson
Daniel Sunjata
Anil Kapoor
Michael Stipe
Sarah Beeny

BOAR – AQUARIUS

Chinese Name: ZHU
Rank: 12th
Hours Ruled: 9pm – 11am
Direction: North – Northwest
Season: Autumn
Month: November
Western Zodiac Equivalent of Boar: Scorpio
Scorpio Western Element: Water
Eastern Zodiac Equivalent of Aquarius: Tiger
Aquarius Western Element: Air
Numerology: 143 = 8

I'll let the racket do the talking.
– John McEnroe

When the Boar's still waters meet with the lofty clouds of
Aquarius, the Boar's gentle heart is met by Aquarius's detached
bemusement; the self-sacrificial giver joins the eternal idealist to
create a personality that wants to inspire others to live big and
make themselves proud. Even if sometimes, their attempts feel
more forced than infectious, their efforts are always appreciated
and they get to experience a popularity that they probably don't
even realize they have. It isn't important, for them, it is all about
inspiring other people and the best way to do that is to be the best
version of themselves that they can be. With the Boar's high pain
threshold, they enjoy activities that push them beyond their
current limits so anything that is physically, emotionally and
mentally tough appeals, activities such as bodybuilding,
gymnastics and of course, dance. Legendary ballet dancer,
Mikhail Baryshnikov said, "I do not try to dance better than
anyone else. I only try to dance better than myself."

If the Boar thinks too much, it finds reasons not to leave the house, so adding Aquarius here helps a lot to, not bring perspective as much as divert the perspective to stranger pastures. As the resident weirdo of the Western cycle, Aquarius is anything but conventional, so it focuses the docile Boar's attention towards otherworldly concerns, neo-spirituality and the general unknown. Aquarius also urges the Boar side of the personality to develop its self-awareness and think about the bigger picture, which the Boar does through artistic means. Jackson Pollock has said, "Painting is self-discovery. Every good artist paints what he is." When the soft, sweet charm of the Boar energy meets Aquarius's distant nonchalance, its collaborative effect is that of a powerful sex appeal. But it is not something that they cultivate. Mikhail Baryshnikov said, "Oh, that's nonsense. Sex symbol? A cup of tea will do it. Sex is overrated. Absolutely. Forget about it. A good golf game, a nice conversation with friends, will do better." This is an uninhibited personality that doesn't entirely realize how attractive it is, but it does know how to get what it wants; the Boar-Aquarius knows that having whatever its heart desires is its birth right. But they are under no illusions themselves. That which is real is important, the fantasy is just for fun. Alice Cooper has said, "I may not be the typical middle-aged Joe, but I'm closer to normal than you think."

The men of this combination are above all, sensually led, like most Boar signs; they want to experience all the flavors of the world and they want to have done it by yesterday. Aquarius adds a decent dose of originality and the need to be different or stand out in some way. Michael Hutchence said, "I've never tried to emulate anyone. I've never idolised people, I prefer instead to get off on attitudes." With the noble Aquarius energy here, they also take a huge amount of responsibility to ensure that they live up to their personal moral code. Alice Cooper has said, "I have never made fun of religion. Religion is something I don't even want to mess with, because I am really afraid of the clouds opening up and my being struck by lightning." Collaboratively, these two signs create a combination that secretly sees itself as a little bit special, a little better, but of course, that does not mesh with the Boar-Aquarius's notion that everybody is equal, fairness and justice for all. But they cannot help but feel that way, so they do only in the privacy of their own world. And they work exceptionally hard at whatever occupation they decide upon in order to feel worthy of that "special" distinction. Mikhail Baryshnikov said, "No one is born a dancer. You have to want it more than anything."

The women of this combination are coy, warm and inviting. They also have that Boar woman sultry, sexy housewife look that says, I can be your secretary, wife and mistress all in one. But they would absolutely disdain such a description because they are too intelligent and too feminist to be defined thus. Their looks are important to them, especially since they have had to grow into them. Speaking about her school years, Denise Richards said, "Yeah, some kids called me fish lips because I had these really full lips. Now I'm sure all those same girls are getting collagen injections, so I'm having the last laugh." The way people react to them does affect them, hard as they may try to put up a wall, the Boar-Aquarius woman is highly sensitive and has a side of her that really wants to please people. Barbara Hershey has said, "I am not afraid of aging, but more afraid of people's reactions to my aging." The biggest reason though, that they are afraid of losing their looks is because it is their biggest weapon against the opposite sex. It is their favorite tool to use. Farrah Fawcett has said, "God gave women intuition and femininity. Used properly, the combination easily jumbles the brain of any man I've ever met."

Ultimately, the Boar-Aquarius is an idealistic character with the best of intentions. They have the capacity to be strong in many different levels of life, physically, mentally and emotionally, which is something they have a natural aptitude for but develop over time. John McEnroe has said, "I think it's the mark of a great player to be confident in tough situations." They also have that deep connection to all things spiritual. Many Boar-Aquarians find that they have clairvoyant gifts and the ability to predict future events. Boiled down to its basics, they believe that what they do comes back to them, so they spend their lives giving and loving and sharing their artistic gifts. The more they are able to sustain that energy of compassion, their lives shine like beacons and they have a clarity most other combinations do not, without necessarily being particularly psychologically-read, they have a great understanding of the human-spiritual condition. Speaking about karma, Farrah Fawcett has said, "When you do bad things, bad things happen to you...everything has positive and negative consequences."

Soul Mate:	Tiger-Scorpio
Challenger:	Snake-Leo
Siblings:	Boar-Gemini, Boar-Libra
Best Friends:	Rabbit-Gemini, Rabbit-Libra, Rabbit-Aquarius, Sheep-Gemini, Sheep-Libra, Sheep-Aquarius

Michael Hutchence
Alice Cooper
Mikhail Baryshnikov
Jackson Pollock
John McEnroe
Farrah Fawcett
Barbara Hershey
Denise Richards
Renée O'Connor
Rob Thomas

Gabriel Macht
Dara O'Briain
Mark Owen
Tom Wilkinson
Christopher Guest
Rick James
Benny Hill
Michael C. Hall
Damian Lewis
Amanda Holden
Sara Evans
Jonathan Banks
Randhir Kapoor
Sonny Bono
Ronald Reagan
Merle Oberon

BOAR – PISCES

Chinese Name: ZHU
Rank: 12th
Hours Ruled: 9pm – 11am
Direction: North – Northwest
Season: Autumn
Month: November
Western Zodiac Equivalent of Boar: Scorpio
Scorpio Western Element: Water
Eastern Zodiac Equivalent of Pisces: Rabbit
Pisces Western Element: Water
Numerology: 144 = 9

Don't be afraid to fail.
– Jon Hamm

When the Boar's still waters meeting Pisces creative stream, this collision exaggerates the yin aspect of the personality. This is the very last double water combination and the very last combination in the 144 cycle. It is both the vulnerable baby and the one closest to its non-physical source as it has so recently emerged. This gives the Boar-Pisces access to spiritual knowledge intuitive understanding and a well-developed sense of justice, but perhaps not in a conventional sense. However, this baby needs to learn a lot to survive so is exceptionally open to all influences, which causes many issues. They protect themselves by presenting personalities with a sharp edge. However, this leads them to be perceived as tough or mean, even unnecessarily egotistical when this could not be further from the truth. Emily Blunt has said, "I'd love to be exciting and say that I was the rebel at school, but sadly I wasn't." Even Johnny Knoxville has said, "People think by challenging me they're going to show they're tough. But I'm not tough."

Instinctive, intuitive and emotionally raw, this combination is an excellent one for the acting profession. They are often exceptionally talented but do not always know it. Peter Saarsgard has said, "Frequently, other people know what I can do more than I do." Sometimes, Boar-Pisces' just do not understand the value of their own talent. Emily Blunt has said, "It was just crazy. It just sort of fell into my lap. It's an awful story for people who've struggled and waited. It's a horrible thing to hear. It was just incredibly fortunate. And now I can't believe I was so casual about it, because I really wouldn't want to do anything else."

Being natural observers, they make excellent performers, writers or anything that requires a detailed understanding of the human condition. Luc Besson said, "I do what I do because I want to do it, because I want to explore, go looking for things." Similarly, Emily Blunt said, "I stammered all the time, so I would just watch. I'm fascinated by human behavior." They also do well in social work settings because they powerfully believe in the good of humanity. Peter Saarsgard said, "I don't believe there are bad people. Just people who do bad things."

Handling their self-esteem and protecting themselves creates a certain tension that requires constant mental management. Glenn Close has said, "I am extremely shy. I am not happy in crowds of people." Developing a strong faith in universal protection and knowing that they are always safe is a great step towards letting go of the unnecessary mental activity. This then leads to a more healthy self-esteem and opens the gates to making use of their amazing creative gifts. Their personal challenge is to learn how to do this as early as possible.

Becoming comfortable with being uncomfortable is also important. Creator of Spanx, Sara Blakely has said, "You've got to embrace what you don't know."

The men of this combination have an approachable quality, like a boy next-door appeal whilst also being a little bit cool. They are the sort of guys that can make you laugh and attract many crushes for their casual disregard for conventions. Johnny Knoxville said, "I just love that spirit that makes people do things that they probably shouldn't." Discussing why he thought he wasn't a bigger star, Aidan Quinn said, "A lot of it is my fault, because it doesn't interest me. And I break the rules all the time." There is also a noted nomad tendency with this group. Aidan Quinn also said, "I think my being such a nomad let me into acting. I was always having to create a new image whenever we moved...I'm happiest when I'm tromping through the woods." Similarly, on discussing how he gets away from the rigmarole of the performance industry, Edward James Olmos said, "I would drive to Joshua Tree and spend the night there in my sleeping bag. The desert – it's spiritual...sleeping outside is what's wonderful. It's so darkly clear, and there's no light from the city so the stars are very impressive."

The women of this combination present like they are tough in order to hide their vulnerability which is very much tied to their femininity, so much so, that some accidentally end up hiding their femininity, but their vulnerability is still usually obvious. Glenn Close has said, "It is very difficult for girls. They're told to look one way, but to act another way." Their openness, vulnerability, femininity, emotions, zest, tanginess, creates the sort of girl that other girls love to talk to and that guys feel comfortable with. However, the door needs to be closed to any influence attempting to change or improve the Boar-Pisces. They are great as they are; they just need to see it for themselves. Changeable and reactive, they respond in the moment to whatever stimulus surrounds them rather than allowing themselves the luxury of time to construct a more conscious controlled comeback. This is why they often seem inconsistent, unpredictable and fickle. Emily Blunt has said, "I was confused about what I wanted to do or who I was; I didn't really feel I had an identity growing up."

Like a sponge they absorb the immediate prevalent energies or live up to expectations by re-molding themselves. When they create a new face, it is a real thrill for them. Donna Murphy has said, "I love any kind of transformation. I want to look in the mirror and not see Donna looking back at me."

Ultimately, when they decide to put themselves first and realize that their own instinct knows the best way forwards for them, they open up a two way communication with their higher source. This is when their self-esteem skyrockets. Jon Hamm said, "Now there's 100,000 people ahead of you in line." But for whatever reason, it didn't faze me. I just kept plugging away, and putting one foot in front of the other, and showing up...I certainly go after what I want. But I just have detached amusement about a lot of it." This baby contains the wisdom of the universe and as it realizes, magic manifests.

Soul Mate:	Tiger-Libra
Challenger:	Snake-Virgo
Siblings:	Boar-Cancer, Boar-Scorpio
Best Friends:	Rabbit-Cancer, Rabbit-Scorpio, Rabbit-Pisces, Sheep-Cancer, Sheep-Scorpio, Sheep-Pisces

Emily Blunt
Donna Murphy
Kate Mara
Sara Blakely
Jon Hamm
Luc Besson
Peter Sarsgaard
Sean Astin
Alan Tudyk
Mélanie Laurent
Aidan Quinn

Aziz Ansari
Glenn Close
Johnny Knoxville
Kyle MacLachlan
Annabeth Gish
Rob Reiner
Talia Balsam
Cara Buono
Edward James Olmos
Matthew Vaughn
Rafe Spall
Carrie Underwood
Tamara Tunie
Natasha Alam
Judd Hirsch
Tasha Smith
Tom Arnold
Irene Cara

Bibliography

Quotes for each combination are taken from:
www.IMDB.com
Brainyquote.com &
www.wikiquote.com

Statistical information for each combination taken from Theodora Lau's *Handbook of Chinese Astrology*. Sovereign Press. 1987.

Dodona Books offers a broad spectrum of divination systems to suit all, including Astrology, Tarot, Runes, Ogham, Palmistry, Dream Interpretation, Scrying, Dowsing, I Ching, Numerology, Angels and Faeries, Tasseomancy and Introspection.